DARTMOOR
BOUNDARY MARKERS

AND OTHER MARKERS ON AND AROUND THE MOOR

DARTMOOR BOUNDARY MARKERS

AND OTHER MARKERS ON AND AROUND THE MOOR

DAVE BREWER

HALSGROVE

First published in Great Britain in 2002

Copyright © 2002 Kath Brewer

Drawings and photographs by Dave Brewer

British Library Cataloguing-in-Publication Data
A CIP record for this title is available from the British Library

ISBN 1 84114 172 0

HALSGROVE
PUBLISHING, MEDIA AND DISTRIBUTION

Halsgrove House
Lower Moor Way
Tiverton, Devon EX16 6SS
Tel: 01884 243242
Fax: 01884 243325
email sales@halsgrove.com
website www.halsgrove.com

Printed in Great Britain by HSW Print, Rhondda

ACKNOWLEDGEMENTS

I wish to thank all those who have contributed in some measure to the additional information now embodied in this new edition covering boundaries and boundary stones on Dartmoor, and especially Mike Brown for sending me information he came across during his own researches at the West Devon Record Office when he knew I was unable to make the journey to Plymouth myself, and for the correspondence between us to try to sort out the Buckland in the Moor boundary. Thanks also to Peter Ratzer for his help with the Throwleigh Bounds, and R. (Dick) Wills and Stephen Woods who were unstinting in sharing their vast knowledge on the parishes of Ilsington and Widecombe respectively with me, and also to Stephen for copies of relevant drawings from the Boundary Remark, Report and Sketch Books.

My thanks must also be extended to the following people for their interest and help: the late C.T. (Bud) Ambrose, Mrs S. Boustead, the late John V. Somers Cocks, Tom Endacott, Ted Fitch, Dr H. Fox, E.J. Friend, Dr T.A.P. Greeves, Charles Hankin, the late Dot Hills, R.J. Joy, Miss E.M. Knowling, Mrs M. Lawrence, Lawrie Manton, the late E.N. Masson Phillips, P. Rendell, the late John Robins, H. Robinson, the late Lady Sylvia Sayer, Mrs Scott, J.S.V. Simpson, Mrs Sparkes, Elisabeth Stanbrook, Les Sutton, Maureen and Robin Vane, H.W. Whitley and Mrs F. Wilkinson.

Thanks are due to the Ashburton Museum, Devon and West Devon Record Offices, Torquay Reference Library and the West Country Studies Library for their help on many occasions, the Dartmoor National Park Authority for allowing me access to maps recording the boundary changes in 1987, and the Ordnance Survey offices in Southampton for answering my various queries as thoroughly as they could.

Last, and not least, my sincere thanks to Kath, my wife, for all her support and help, particularly during recent years when Beating the Bounds of a number of Parishes has been beyond my capability and I have had to rely on her reports.

Dave Brewer (May 1995)

During the last couple of years of Dave's life, he was not up to putting all his notes on the boundaries and boundary stones in order, and in hindsight, I should have endeavoured to do this for him then. I am afraid when he died in 1998 I could not face this task, but I am now very pleased that I have finally done so, and I hope the context and layout is as he would have wished. I take full responsibility for any errors and omissions.

Kath Brewer (November 2001)

CONTENTS

INTRODUCTION

I am indebted to several correspondents and friends for their encouraging comments on the First Edition of *A Field Guide to the Boundary Markers on and Around Dartmoor* (Devon Books, 1986). No sooner was it in print than I was aware of the considerable amount of further material that I had already accumulated, to which I have been adding additional information ever since, both from documentary sources and that resulting from more recent fieldwork, enabling a considerably expanded Second Edition to be prepared and a few unfortunate errors in the First Edition to be corrected. Now the whole of the Forest of Dartmoor boundary is taken in chronological order, point by point, and in more depth than heretofore, and here I must admit that I have had to amend a couple of statements. Once again extracts from the Ordnance Survey Boundary Remark and Boundary Report Books appear, but now with the addition of drawings reproducing sketches from their Boundary Sketch Books.

Almost all the Boundary Stones mentioned in this book, if not within what is generally considered to be Dartmoor proper, are at least within the bounds of the Dartmoor National Park. To me all the granite country east of the Tamar ought to be considered as a region as a whole, but in their wisdom the Boundary Commission, after five years of consideration of the best course to take, have opted for excluding the active Lee Moor china clay complex, but to include part of Shaugh Moor within the park. The new boundary line was announced in April 1994, and besides this more major change there are others, where the boundary line now follows the A38 and A30. On the southern side farmland to the south of the A38 will be excluded from the Park, whilst further west the whole of South Brent and Bittaford are included in it. On the northern side, whilst the A30 will define parts of the boundary, that area between the Okehampton bypass and the town itself will remain within the Dartmoor National Park. Other types of boundary are not static – changes are not rapid but are continually taking place. The Forest of Dartmoor boundary has changed considerably over the centuries, and there are many parishes too that have changed their bounds, either on the one hand encroaching into what was originally the Forest, i.e. Lydford Parish, or, on the other, the older parishes giving up a part of their land to enable the foundation of completely new civil parishes to take place, usually based around the focal point of a village, as has happened at Ivybridge in 1894, at Horrabridge in 1950, and more recently at Sticklepath, Lydford and Dartmoor Forest in 1987.

The first real boundaries on Dartmoor were those of the Late Bronze Age peoples, who carefully divided up much of the moor by means of what are called reaves, that is to say low banks of stone perhaps 6ft wide or more and about 2ft in height, now generally covered with turf or heather. They were not walls as we know them today, but merely lines of demarcation, some of which were to be used much later to define the bounds of parishes and or manors. It was only during the last century that some attention was paid to them when there was a divergence of opinion as to their purpose, and only during the past couple of decades has their full significance become apparent. Antiquaries of the nineteenth century were divided, some of the opinion that these stone banks represented early 'trackways', others that they were indeed boundary markers, an opinion strongly held by William Crossing, and now accepted as their true purpose.

Reaves may be classified into certain categories: watershed reaves, that is those running along high ground between two river valleys, often terminating in a cairn of an earlier period, contour reaves, those following a contour around the moor at around 1000ft level, and those constituting parallel reave systems. These latter systems comprise parallel reaves running from the lower moorland, or land now enclosed as fields, up to a point where they dramatically stop at right angles to a terminal contour reave, thus giving high moor grazing and enclosures at lower levels for stock and cultivation, probably with hurdles erected on the top of the reave banks to contain the animals.

Those reaves mentioned in passing by Crossing were generally of the watershed type, some of which run for several miles in length, and examples of which are those between the valleys of the Walkham and the Meavy on Walkhampton Common, between the Meavy and the Plym valleys up to the Eylesbarrow cairns, the Rook reave up to Penn Beacon between the Plym and the Yealm, that going up to Three Barrows cairns between the Erme and the Avon, and that which runs up between the Avon and the Mardle to the summit of Pupers Hill before dropping down to the latter river. But it was the work done by Elizabeth Gawne and John Somers Cocks (T.D.A. 1968) that first brought a detailed examination of the parallel reave system on the south-eastern side of the moor to our notice and revived and extended our knowledge of their extent, starting the exposure of an organised division of huge areas of land hitherto unsuspected as being attributable to the Late Bronze Age, more details of which have been brought to our notice in the more recently published works of Andrew Fleming and Jeremy Butler. Whereas the watershed reaves had firmly separated one valley from the next, the parallel reave systems were aligned on such an axis that they all pointed to the highest parts of the moor, ignoring any intervening valleys, even the Dart Gorge in the case of the Dartmeet/Venford system, and ending at terminal reaves somewhere near the height of the later Forest boundary. Some earlier stone rows and other funereal remains were respected by the reaves, others ignored and crossed by them, with many of the fields or 'strips' formed by the parallel systems containing individual or small groups of hut circles. The two systems investigated by Gawne and Somers Cocks were the Holne/Dartmeet and Rippon Tor/Dunstone Down ones, by far the largest, the former aligned along a south-west to north-east axis, and the latter south-east to north-west. Later other less extensive systems similarly pointing to the high moor were found by Andrew Fleming and John Collis, though the north moor has far fewer and smaller ones, the north-western sector the fewest of all.

It is thought that the high moor was probably communal ground, as was the Forest to the Commoners in later times, and that the parallel system or systems radiated down and around the lower slopes to, and into, what are now enclosed fields, many of these retaining their alignment due to the fact that they have been utilised as foundations for the later field walls. But how far into the enclosed land did they extend? Fleming speculates that the Rippon Tor system might have extended as far to the south-east as Ashburton and the A38. Were the several differently aligned 'systems' around the central high moor the work of a group of chieftains from the local tribes who had a common purpose, or of a single paramount chief with considerable organisational ability, using heights and prominent objects to direct the line of the reaves, as did the Romans when building their roads? The huge Rippon Tor/Dunstone system appears to have had a terminal reave from Dunstone Down, contouring around the eastern side of Hameldon and extending to the south as far as Buckland in the Moor, northwards to Blackhill in Manaton parish, and embracing Ashburton and much of Widecombe parishes, with parallel reaves clearly defined over Halsanger Common to Top Tor, etc.

It is a curious coincidence, but one of the earliest detailed written descriptions of a boundary associated with Dartmoor covers, or embraces, much of the same area, being of Saxon origin, and thought to date from the early eleventh century by the type of script used. The original document, the charter itself, now lost, possibly dates from as early as the mid-eighth century, when this part of the west had become a settled part of Wessex. The document is known as the Peadington landscore, and was found in documents deposited in the Royal Albert Memorial Museum, Exeter, in the nineteenth century, having formerly been in the archives of St Peter's, the mother church of Exeter. It enumerates the bounds of land granted to the Bishop of Crediton, and later bishops of Exeter, by the King, and possibly formerly attached to the coastal manor of Paignton, also held by the See. The 'landscore' would have been inserted into the charter; other similar landscores are held in the British Museum. This massive episcopal estate covered either the whole or large parts of the later parishes of Ashburton, Buckland in the Moor, Widecombe, Manaton, Ilsington, Bickington and Woodland, following the bounds of manors.

As settlement of the far west spread ever further west in the eighth to tenth centuries, other Royal grants were made relating to the South Hams, stretching from between the River Erme and the Avon. The Om Homme charter dates from 846, and the Hiwisce or Sorley charter from 962, this latter, interestingly enough, having been discovered in the possession of the Petre family papers, the forebears of Lord Petre having bought part of the lands formerly belonging to Buckfast Abbey, before the Dissolution, whose land bordered on the area described in the charter.

Whilst much of the land described in these two charters is outside the sphere of our interest, there is a large sector of the bounds of the Om Homme charter that was once thought to extend to the boundary of the Forest of Dartmoor by Rose Troupe (T.D.A. 1929), but now thought to encompass a much smaller area of the South Hams.

Following the eighth/eleventh-century Peadington boundary, we next have copies of the first known perambulation of the bounds of the Royal Forest of Dartmoor in 1240, together with later perambulations and surveys of this forest, when the objects used to define the bounds were either, with one notable exception, all totally natural phenomena such as rivers and tors, or Bronze Age remains in the form of cairns and to a lesser extent reaves. It was only much later, principally from the seventeenth century, that 'set' boundstones were erected to define parish and manorial boundaries; they too often utilised streams and tors and other prominent rock formations. The set boundstones may be anything from a very rough, unmarked, piece of stone erected at a specific place, to a carefully dressed slab of stone inscribed with either the initials of the relevant parish or manor, or those of the landlord, etc. The Ordnance Survey walkers maps of the scale of 1:25 000 are those most suitable for exploring the moor, but even these mark only the boundary of the Forest of Dartmoor and the boundaries of the various parishes. Thus, whilst almost all parish boundstones on present boundaries are marked as current at the time of writing, only a relatively small number of other boundstones, whether they be manorial or of some other origin, appear on maps of that scale, and where they do so only because they lie either on the Forest and or a parish boundary. However in compiling this book reference has been made to the larger six-inch-to-the-mile and 1:10 000 scale maps which show the positions of many, though not all by any means, additional 'Stones', which can be either boundstones or those set up for some other reason entirely, such as guide stones, etc. The boundstones so marked are invariably inscribed, and may be either natural rocks or set stones.

Perhaps a few words about the formation of the Ordnance Survey and the valuable work that they do may not be out of place here. Its origins date from 1790 when it was known as the Trigonometrical Survey. It soon became associated with our country's defence due to the continual conflicts with France and her allies, from that time until the end of the Napoleonic Wars in 1815, the Board of Ordnance being formed in 1791. Maps of the scale of one-inch-to-the-mile were first prepared for the Home Counties but following their publication Devon and Cornwall were then selected to be pioneer counties in the west in 1800, from which date eight maps of the same scale were prepared of the County of Devon and published in 1809.

The Board of Ordnance was used as a training school for Royal Engineers, officers and men being trained as draftsmen since part of their duties was the surveying of terrain and the preparation of plan drawings. Hence the Royal Engineers' connection with the sketches made in later Ordnance Survey Boundary Report and Boundary Remark Books which are preserved at the Ordnance Survey headquarters in Southampton, each entry being signed by a Sergeant or Corporal of that unit. With the passing of the Ordnance Survey Act of 1841 new surveys were made, and it is from this period 1841 to 1893 that the original documents at Southampton date. Some of them were lost during the Second World War bombings but surprisingly most survived, but were not sorted and indexed until relatively recently, classified into three categories: Boundary Remark Books, Boundary Sketch Books and Boundary Report Books. In 1858 Standard Scales were set at six-inch-to-the-mile for commons and waste, and 25-inch-to-the-mile for cultivated areas. The Boundary Remark Books contain information received from meresmen concerned with a particular parish boundary or boundstone, and in these books sketches were made to show the agreed line, drawn by a member of the Royal Engineers, and initialled by him, together with confirming signatures of meresmen from all parishes concerned, these men having been elected by their respective parish councils to preserve and maintain their rights. The Boundary Sketch Books also contained less elaborate drawings of a particular point of interest, especially where there was some specific feature relating to it, perhaps the inscription on a boundstone, or its relative position to some other prominent object such as a cairn etc.

Boundary Reports were made in cases of dispute, and this could occur more frequently on a place such as the open moors of Dartmoor, resulting in the setting up of many boundstones on the unenclosed commons. Naturally the Ordnance Survey maps of Devon, and the data marked upon them have seen many revisions over the years since the first maps of 1809; one of the more recent necessary changes was that of imperial measure to metric, and the consequent change in the measurements shown on contour lines, still often converted back to feet for a better comprehension of one's height! The first maps showed no contours at all, just shading increasing in intensity the higher the ground. Later 'Levellings' up to the year 1921 were made using a Datum Line based on Liverpool, but due to cumulative errors this was abandoned in that year in favour of a Datum Line taken at Newlyn South Pier, as the result of a number of readings taken between the years 1915 and 1921. The Ordnance Survey's original six-inch-to-the-mile scale maps were first produced in the 1880s, the modern equivalent being their 1:10 000 scale, and show bench marks used in their surveys, in the case of Dartmoor dating from 1849 to 1950, the earliest dating from the initial Geodetic Levelling Line from Bristol to Tavistock. These bench marks were inscribed upon all sorts of sites so long as they were considered to be permanent objects, earth bound rocks, milestones, buildings, gateposts and walls, and even setts of the Haytor Granite Tramway. In the original survey only one boundary stone was so used, this on the outskirts of Okehampton, but it was unfortunately destroyed before 1950. Other bench marks found on boundstones must therefore date from the 1880s to 1950. Their use to the Ordnance Survey came to an end when they were replaced by a network of upwards of 6000 triangulation points which, though started in the 1930s, was not completed until 1960 due to the intervention of the Second World War. Now these too have been largely superseded by the introduction of Global Position System using a satellite, but certain of the trig points on high ground continue to be useful for other purposes, including those on Yes Tor, Ryder's Hill, etc.

The inscribed Boundary Markers recorded in this work can be divided into three categories:

1. Those shown on the standard 1:25 000 scale maps on Parish boundaries.
2. Those shown on their old six-inch-to-the-mile scale and the metric equivalent 1:10 000 scale, where they are simply marked 'Stone'.
3. Inscribed non-parochial stones unrecorded by them.

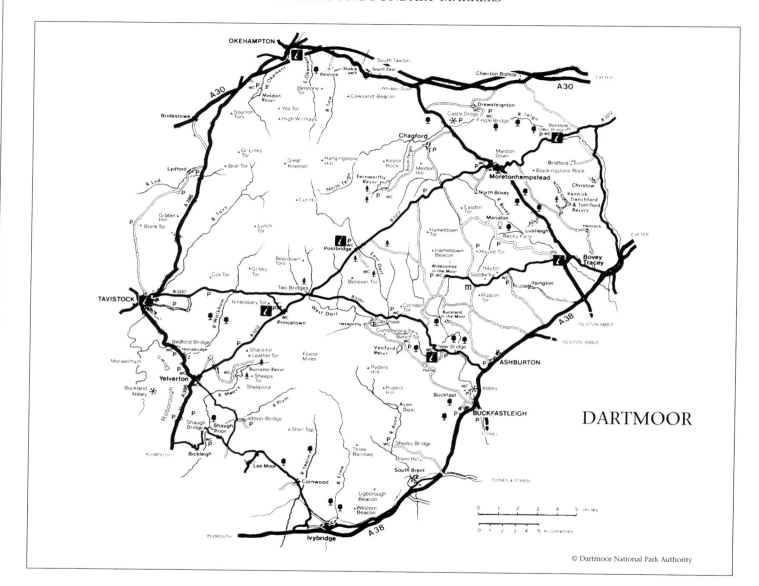

DARTMOOR

© Dartmoor National Park Authority

1

THE BOUNDS OF THE FOREST OF DARTMOOR

In medieval times the word 'forest' was used to define land reserved as a Royal hunting ground, which need not necessarily be a wooded area, and was subject to Forest Law, where deer and certain other species of wild animal were protected from all but the king. In Devon, William the Conqueror declared the Forests of Dartmoor and Exmoor to be such areas, but at Domesday in 1086, when surveys were made of all manors and estates together with their owners at the time when Edward the Confessor was 'alive and dead', no mention was made of either forest. Nor at the time of the survey when William not only held those properties formerly belonging to Edward, but had also 'acquired' many others from Saxon lords, giving hundreds to his knights and barons in appreciation of the services they had rendered to him during the conquest.

Amongst those held by William was Lydford, the Domesday Book simply saying 'The King has a Boroughe, Lideford. King Edward held it in demesne'. No mention is made of any pasturage being attached to this Royal Manor either, though later the Forest of Dartmoor is recorded as being attached to Lydford. On Exmoor there is a single Domesday reference to 'three Foresters' holding a ½ hide of land at Withypool on the day that King Edward was alive and dead, showing that these Royal Forests were of Saxon origin. A study of the pasturages that were attached to other Dartmoor Royal manors at Domesday shows several to

have then been much larger than they became later, with South Tawton, an 'in demesne' Royal manor, having a huge pasturage of an estimated '4 leagues x 4 leagues', around 23 000 acres at that time, today only approximately 1500 acres. Was this then representing the Royal Forest?

By the Charter of Liberties (1101), Henry the First declared that 'The Forests by the Common Consent of my Barons, I retain in my hands, as my father held them', but in the following century through the reigns of Henry the Second and Richard, much additional land was reserved for the King's pleasure, causing resentment amongst his barons which led to King John making a promise to disafforest all the lands of Devon and Cornwall 'up to the metes of the ancient regardes of Dertemore and Exmore, as these regardes were in the time of King Henry the First' on 18 May 1204. All of Devon, outside of the bounds of the said Forests of Dartmoor and Exmoor, was to be given its freedom from the harsh Forest Law on payment of a 'fine' of 5000 marks, but in 1209 some landowners were fined for attempting to stop the Chief Forester, Hugh de Neville, from holding an inspection or 'regard' of the Forests of Devon, that is perambulating the boundaries between the King's Forests and their lands, at a time when the precise extent and bounds of these Royal Forests were still uncertain and in dispute. The Chief Forester may well have held another perambulation in 1213, for in the following year fines are recorded as being paid, the Court of Justice-Seat only being held every three years.

The disafforestation of the whole of Devon and Cornwall, excluding Dartmoor and Exmoor, was confirmed by Henry the Third in 1217, but it was not until 1240 that the Forest of Dartmoor and the ancient Borough of Lydford, 'our Manor of Lydford, with the castle of the same place, and all its appurtenances, together with the Forest of Dartmoor', having been granted by Henry to his brother, Richard, Earl of Cornwall, in 1239, was first ordered to be perambulated to determine its precise bounds.

In that year Richard had been in dispute with four knights who had land adjoining the Forest, Sir William de Pruz, Sir William Hamlyn, Sir Robert de Hellion and Sir Henry de Merton. Following a plea for a perambulation to be made, Henry issued a writ directing the Sheriff of Devon to summon a jury of twelve knights to make this perambulation, who were under oath to send their findings to the King 'wherever we may be, clearly and distinctly, and under thy Seal and the Seals of the four knights aforesaid'. This was dated 13 June 1240.

Thus on 24 July 1240, the twelve knights appointed for the purpose, together with the Sheriff, and the four protesting knights, with their retinues, started their perambulation, though by this time the 'Forest' of Dartmoor had strictly become a 'chase', that is to say was not in the King's ownership, but continued to be so called, as it still is to this day. On 1 April 1300, six justices were appointed to report on the boundaries of all the Royal Forests in the Kingdom, one being appointed to each of six regions, the South West

covering Devon, Somerset and Dorset having Justice Gilbert de Knovill, Sheriff of Devon in 1299. He reported 'Concerning the perambulation of the forests to be made in the County of Devon nothing has been done, because the Forest of Dertemore is in the demesne of the Earl of Cornwall by the gift and grant of the Lord King Henry, father of the King now, and the venison belongs not to the King, nor has any encroachment been made by any King or his officers, as is made clear to us by the jurors'. (30 Edward the First.)

In 1300 the 'Forest of Dartmoor', then correctly described as 'The Chase of Dartmoor with appurtenances', reverted to the Crown on the death of Edmund Plantagenet who died without issue, and in 1337 was given to the Prince Edward of Woodstock, better known as the Black Prince, by Edward the Third, when the title 'Duke of Cornwall' was created and bestowed upon him. Henceforth this newly created title passed traditionally to the eldest son of the reigning monarch, and still does so, the 'Forest' only reverting to the Crown when the reigning monarch has no male issue.

The original document detailing the course followed in the perambulation in 1240 no longer exists, but several copies do, only differing in so far as spelling variations occur here and there, as it was copied by the scribe. The text as given by the author Samuel Rowe in *A Perambulation of the Forest of Dartmoor* published in 1848 is:

ad hogam de Cossdonne et inde linealiter usque ad parvam hogam que vocatur parva Hundetorre, et inde linealiter usque ad Thurlestone, et inde linealiter usque ad Wotesbrokelakesfote que cadit in Tyng, et inde lin-

ealiter usque ad Heigheston et inde linealiter usque ad Langestone et inde linealiter usque per mediam turbariam de Alberysheved et sic in longum Wallebroke et inde linealiter usque ad Furnum Regis et inde linealiter usque ad Wallebrokeshede et sic in longum Wallebroke usque cadit in Dertam, et sic per Dertam usque ad aliam Dertam, et sic per aliam Dertam ascendendo usque Okebrokysfote, et sic ascendendo Okebroke usque ad la Dryworke, et ita ascendendo usque ad la Dryfeld ford, et sic inde linealiter usque ad Battyshull et inde linealiter usque ad caput de Wester Wellabroke et sic per Wester Wellabroke usque cadit in Avenam, et inde linealiter usque ad Ester Whyteburghe et inde linealiter usque ad la Redelake que cadit in Erme, et inde linealiter usque ad Grymsgrove et inde linealiter usque ad Elysburghe et sic linealiter usque at crucem Sywardi et inde usque ad Ysfother et sic per aliam Ysfother et inde per mediam Mystor usque ad Mewyburghe et inde usque ad Lullingesfote et inde usque ad Rakernesbrokysfote, et sic ad caput ejusdem aque et deinde usque ad la Westsolle et inde linealiter usque ad Ernestorre et inde linealiter usque ad vadum proximum in orientali parte capelle Sancti Michaelis de Halgestoke et inde linealiter usque ad predictum hogam de Cossdonne in orientali parte.

Of the other records available to us of the 1240 perambulation, perhaps the most interesting is the ancient map now held in the West Devon Record Office, Exeter. This, once thought to be contemporary with the perambulation, was the subject of an article by that well known nineteenth-century antiquary, C. Spence Bate. It shows not only the Forest of Dartmoor, stylised in the form of a circle, with all the boundary points in their correct sequence around the perimeter (Fig 1) but also many features on the southern part of the moor in the parishes of Harford, Ugborough and Brent. Now thought to be possibly, or partly, sixteenth century in origin, due to the detail given to that southern portion of the moor, it was possibly prepared for, or adapted for, use to define the sixteenth-century bounds and rights associated with Brent Moor, the Manor of Brent being owned by Buckfast Abbey until its dissolution in 1539. In the Preface to Carrington's *Dartmoor Poem*, W. Burt (p.xiv) says that in 1556–57 another perambulation was directed: '*De metis et bundis inter Forestam de Dartmore, et moram vocatum Brentmore eidem Forestae adjacentem*' – could this relate to the map? Not only are the bounds of the Forest, as of 1240 but with some different spellings, written on the reverse side of the map, together with the names of the twelve knights, but there are other additions in the same hand. Spence Bate gives us a very good description of the map which was drawn onto two sheepskins sewn together, as follows:

Within the circle which marks the precincts of the Royal Forest the map is painted yellow. All beyond is coloured green, except the rivers, which are white, longitudinally striped with blue. Some of the roads are black and white, and others are red and yellow. The churches are all of a reddish brown tint, the outline being definitely drawn in black. The points of the compass are shown in yellow letters in a large pink or salmon coloured circle; and a tablet on the corner is painted yellow, with a white border, adorned with black spots – ornamented on the top with a central scroll, supporting a human face; and in the same position at the bottom is a similar scroll, but no head. At each end there is a less ornate scroll. The index on the tablet is written in the old English square letter, while the reference letters are in Roman type. All the names upon the map besides are in the Old English character, excepting one word, and that is on the River Tavy. This corresponds in style to that of the writing used in the perambulation, which is on the back of the map... the names are mostly on labels of painted scrolls. Some few are written without labels, but these are chiefly the names of churches.

Spence Bate then suggests that the part of the map relating to the Forest was more carefully executed than the rest, but does not comment on the fact that whilst the wording relating to the Forest is viewed looking at the map west to east, the inscriptions relating to the rest of the map are viewed at an angle of 90° to this.

In 1608, in the fifth year of the reign of King James the First, a further survey of lands, manors, forests and chases 'and other proffits' belonging to the Duchy of Cornwall took place, the bounds of the Forest of Dartmoor taking precedence, being the first estate to be perambulated. There were twenty-five jurors appointed to carry out the task of redefining the bounds, which were presented to a Survey Court at Okehampton on 16 August 1609, when they said they 'do fynde partlie by the coppies of auncient recordes partlie upon the evidence of other persons and partly upon their owne knowledge but especiallie as the boundes have been and are used and accustomed to be'. In their report we find further variations of spelling and new names appearing for what were thought to be some of the old original points of reference, and also some new additional place

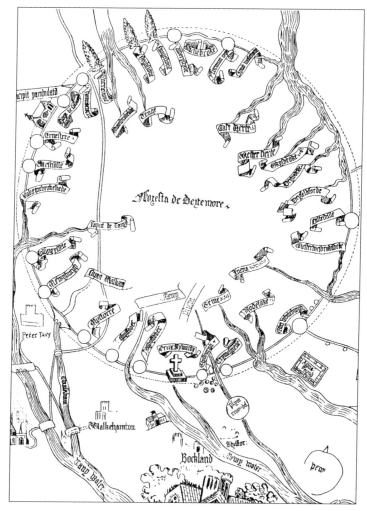

Fig. 1 Sixteenth-century Map depicting the Bounds of Dartmoor Forest

names. There were, too, estimates of distances between two points of reference on a couple of occasions, though they were very rough, a feature completely lacking in the original 1240 survey.

Once again the perambulators made their journey in a clockwise direction, as was the normal custom, thus:

Beginning at a high hill lying in the north quarter of the said fforest called at this day Cosdon, al's Cosson and in the old records written Hoga de Costdonne and from thence lineallie eastward by estimacon one mile or more unto little houndtorr wch. in the said records is called (hoga de parva houndetorr) and from thence lineallie to a place named in the said records Thurleston, now as they suppose called Waterdontorr being about three-quarters of a myle from Houndtorr aforesaid, and from thence near a myle to Wotesbrooklake foot wch. falleth into Teyne and wch. lake they thinke to be the same wch. is now called Whoodelake, at wch. place they accompt the North Quarter to end; and from thence nere one mile to Hingeston, al's Highstone, in the east quarter lyinge near ffernworthie hedges, and from thence lineallie nere one mile to Yeston, al's Geston, now com'onlie called Hethstone, and from thence lineallie through a fennye place now called Turfhill, but named in the old records per mediam de Albersheved to a place called Kinge's Oven and in the said record namely Furnum Regis and from thence to Wallebrookeheade and so alonge by Wallebrooke until it falleth into easter Dart, and so downwards by the said easter Dart to another Dart called wester Dart and from thence ascendinge by the said wester Dart unto Wobrookefoote when the east quarter endeth; and thence linyallie ascendinge to Drylake, al's Drywoorke, and from thence ascendinge by Drylake unto Crefeild fford or Dryefeild ford and from thence to Knattleburroughe, wch. they take to be the same that is called in the old records Gnatteshill, and so from thence descending linyallie to Wester Wellbrooke headd and so by the same Wester Wellebrooke until it falleth into Owne, al's Aven, and from thence linyallie to Easter Whitaburrowe and from thence linyallie to Redlake foote whir it falleth into Erme, and from thence linyallie ascendinge unto Arme headd; wch. they take to be a place named in the same records Grimsgrove; and from thence to Plimheadd, where the South quarter endeth; and from thence linyallie to Elisboroughe and from thence linyallie to Seward's Cross and from thence linyallie to little Hisworthie and so from thence linyallie to another Hisworthie and so from thence linyallie through the midst of Mistorr moore to a rocke called Mistorpann, and from thence linyallie to Dedlakeheadd wch. they thinke to be the next bound which is called in the old records Meuborough, and from thence linyallie northwardes to Luntesborowe wch. they think to be the same that is called in the records Lullingesete, and from thence linyallie to Wester Redlake between wch. said two bounds the wester quarter endeth; and from thence northward to Rattlebrooke foote and soe from thence to the headd of the same Rattlebrooke, and so from thence linyallie unto Steinegatorr and from thence linyallie to Langaford, al's Sandyford, and so from thence linyallie to the ford wch lyeth in the east syde of the chapple of Halstocke and so from thence linyallie unto the said hill called Cosdon, al's Cosson, wher they did begin.

As will be seen, this perambulation also tells us where the bounds of the four quarters of the Forest, divided thus for the purpose of the drifts, rounding up stray animals within the Forest, touched upon the Commons of Devonshire, the Forest having been thus divided since 1404, prior to which time there were but three 'quarters', North, East and West.

The North Quarter extended from the foot of Wester Redlake, where it joins the infant Tavy, thence going to Spriddle Combe, Horse Hole south of West Dart Head, to Teign Head and down the Teign to Whoodlake Foot. Animals impounded from this section were taken to Creber Pound. The Eastern section went from Hugh or Whood Lake, back to Horse Hole and thence to Dart Hole and down the West Dart to O Brook foot. The South Quarter retraces the East Quarter from O Brook foot back up the West Dart to Cholake foot, and then up that stream to its head, on to Strane head and Plym head. The West Quarter used the relevant parts of the foregoing bounds, impounded animals from these three quarters being held at Dunnabridge. Latterly an enclosure at Merrivale Bridge has been used to hold the ponies gathered at the animal drifts that still take place. Erme Pound was, it seems, once used as an intermediate stop for strays, otherwise destined for Dunnabridge to save them the longer journey, a fine of 3d, twice the then rate was levied, later increased to 1/-. If not paid the animals were then taken to Dunnabridge regardless.

The 1240 and 1608 perambulations show that natural or Bronze Age features were used to define the Forest bounds, only Siward's Cross, standing in 1240 marking an earlier bound or used as a waymarker, was of post-Bronze Age construction, and perhaps Furnum Regis (King's Oven), though there has been debate and some doubt about this.

A few notes relating to the bounds quoted in the 1240 and 1609 documents and information from other sources will show how in many parts Commoners of various parishes surrounding the Forest have over the centuries made encroachments upon the ancient bounds to a greater or lesser extent, and how differences of opinion as to the true bounds of the Forest persisted into the nineteenth century. Another Court of Survey of the Manor of Lydford and Forest bounds took place in 1786. In this survey some specific points of reference mentioned in the earlier perambulations are omitted, no mention being made of any between Hound Tor and Whodelake foot where it falls into the Teign, leaving its interpretation in some doubt, perhaps intentionally! In addition to this later survey we have other references to the Forest bounds either as a whole or in part. The evidence given at the Tithe cases of 1699, when the then vicar of Lydford, David Birchincha, claimed tithes from two moormen living within the Forest, and in 1702 when another vicar, Thomas Bernaford, claimed tithes from all thirty-five tenement holders, also named various points that they considered to be on the Forest boundary, and it will be instructive to make our own perambulation considering each point of reference in turn, from the time of the 1240 perambulation to the present day. Thus:

ad hogam de Cossdonne et inde linealiter usque ad parva hogam que vocatur parva Hundetorre (1240); a high hill lying in the north quarter of

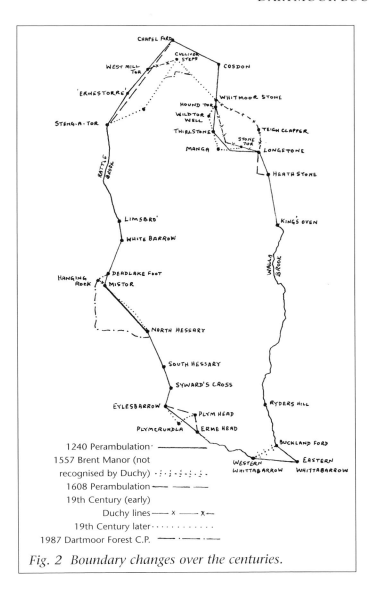

1240 Perambulation ⸺
1557 Brent Manor (not
  recognised by Duchy) ·⸱·⸳·⸱·⸳·
1608 Perambulation ⸺ ⸺
19th Century (early)
  Duchy lines ⸺ x ⸺ x ⸺
19th Century later ··········
1987 Dartmoor Forest C.P. ⸻ ⸺ ⸻

Fig. 2 Boundary changes over the centuries.

the said fforest called at this day Cosdon, al's Cosson, and in the old records written Hoga de Costdonne and from thence lineallie eastward by estimation one mile or more unto little houndetorr wch. in the said records is called Hogna de parva houndetorr (1609).

After the passing of almost 400 years between 1240 and 1608 it is not surprising that the jurors of 1608 had some difficulty in some cases, in identifying or interpreting the boundary intended in 1240, the names of many points of reference having through the course of time become changed, either to something resembling the old name or to something entirely different. However there is no doubt about their starting point which was the summit of Cosdon. Crossing comments on the fact that when hills are mentioned in perambulations, it is the summit that is intended and that in such cases the whole of the hill or tor would be within the bounds concerned. But even so, he speculates as to whether the early perambulators might not have mistaken Whit or White Hill as an outlier of Cosdon, and that they thus may have begun near the head of the Smallbrook. It is not likely, but it must be accepted that the changes in the boundary line here, putting the whole of Cosdon Hill within the parish of South Tawton, may have come about through encroachment by the Commoners of that parish as others have done elsewhere, particularly in this north-eastern sector, though South Tawton itself was once a large Royal 'in demesne' manor.

The original name 'parva Hundetorre' also made for confusion. From Cosdon nineteenth-century students of the Forest bounds, and the Duchy, attempted to follow the instructions of the 1609 perambulation and go 'lineally eastward one mile or more' to Shilstone Tor, but this was clearly an error of direction on the part of the jurors and of judgment on the part of the nineteenth-century students. Acknowledging that this was so, the distance quoted if taken west of south brings us to what we now know simply as Hound Tor, other early records giving variations such as Little Hound Tor, Hounderet, etc. The original 1809 Ordnance Survey map of a scale of one-inch-to-the-mile also called it Houndtor as we do today, but at that time it was commonly known as Round Tor; a sketch in their Boundary Remark Book of 1881 shows this together with a correction, substituting the letter 'H' for the 'R', with a note to the effect that there was a 'Pile of Stones' on the summit at that point where the bounds changed direction.

In spite of the 'parva Hundetorre' of 1240 being acknowledged as referring to Houndtor itself, the name 'Little Hound Tor' yet persists, and is still marked on the

Hound Tor.

Ordnance Survey maps by a curious circumstance, for there never was, in truth, any such tor though the Duchy took their Forest bounds to this supposed point quite erroneously in the nineteen century. The point so named is on the south side of Whit Hill and this resurrection of the name 'Little Houndtor' came about through a man by the name of Simon Moore who was in 1834 renting the North Quarter of the Forest. Realising that by erecting a false 'tor' on a slight shelf of native rock that he could considerably extend his grazing rights, at a time when the true Forest bounds were still in some doubt, he employed a James Underhill of Gidleigh to draw stone to the required spot where he built a cairn, the evidence of Underhill at a later enquiry (1842) stating that he took stone to 'a place on White Hill now called Littel Round Tor ... and they were pulled up to a round pile'. The Ordnance Survey sketch depicting Round or Hound Tor also showed a boundary point known as the Whit or White Moor Stone, a Bronze Age monolith, of which more anon, which at that time was attempted to be linked with the name 'Thurlestone', nearby, and which Underhill denied. More confusion and uncertainty!

Little Hound Tor with Cosdon in the background.

et inde linealiter usque ad Thurlestone (1240); and from thence lineallie to a place named in the said records Thurleston, now as they suppose called Waterdontorr being about three-quarters of a myle from Houndtorr aforesaid (1609).

Though the distance between Hound Tor and Watern Tor is far in excess of three-quarters of a mile, there is no doubt about what the 1240 perambulators intended. A 'thirled' stone is one that has been pierced and such is the appearance of two such rock formations at the northern end of Watern Tor when viewed from a certain angle. (Fig 3.) This point is still on the Forest bounds and that of Gidleigh parish.

Variants of the name appear including 'Thueurlestone', 'Waterdown Tor', 'Walter Torr', etc., these last two being applied by John Clement, priour or moorman of the East Quarter of the Forest, in his evidence at the Tithe Enquiries at Lydford in 1699 and 1702. However, the Duchy, until early in the nineteenth century, continued to claim a line from Whit Moor Stone to the confluence of the North Teign and the Wallabrook, of which more anon.

As time went on, intermediate points of reference creep in, and in 1702 John Clement mentions 'Willtorrwill', Wild Tor Well, as one such.

et inde linealiter usque Wotesbrokelakefote que cadit in Tyng (1240); and from thence near a myle to Wotesbrookelakefoot wch. falleth into Teynge and wch. they thinke to be the same wch. is now called Whoodelake (1609).

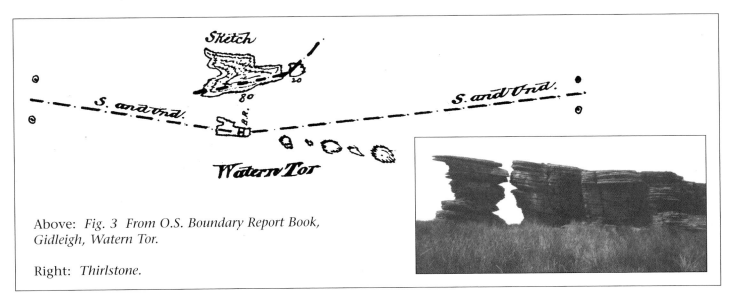

Above: *Fig. 3 From O.S. Boundary Report Book, Gidleigh, Watern Tor.*

Right: *Thirlstone.*

The 1608 jurors only 'thought' that the Whoodelake was one and the same as the Wotesbrokelake, and even as late as the 1809 map prepared by the Ordnance Survey no such name appeared on it. The Duchy held to the view that it was the Wallabrook that was intended, since it too fell into the North Teign, drawing their boundary accordingly to 'Ting Clapper' as given in the evidence of Anthony Torr. However John Clement in 1699 had given the point as 'Woodlake which falls into North Ting', and enlarged upon that in 1702, describing it as 'to Hugh Thorn, from thence to Hugh Lake, falling into the River of Ting at a place called Blackstone', an incursion into the original line by Gidleigh at Hawthorn Clitter, but giving the stream the name by which we still know it today.

The modern boundary between the Duchy and Gidleigh was agreed on 25 March 1843 at Moretonhampstead when the Tithe maps were being prepared, this Lydford/Gidleigh boundary one of the last to be settled. It was not until this settlement that Hawthorn Clitter and Manga Rock, earlier known as the Manger Stone, officially became boundary points though the Gidleigh Commoners had claimed them to be on their boundary as early as 1639 when a parish map, 'A Map of Gidley Common taken in a Perambulation Rogation Week 1639', was produced showing what they then considered to be their bounds. Today the Forest/Gidleigh boundary from the Thirlstone goes first to the highest group of clitter inside the Teignhead newtake wall where there is a rough 'cairn' of stone, of which more under Parishes, thence going to Manga Rock directly on the southern side of the Hugh Lake. However a little below this line at approximately SX 6220 8615 there is a natural stone, earthfast and not within clitter, about 7ft long and somewhat resembling Manga in shape which bears the letters 'GP' on its eastern vertical face, and yet another lettered simply 'G' on the lower edge of some clitter about 75 yards nearer Manga.

In 1843 the agreed line had gone from Manga Rock directly to Stone Tor, the top of which is inscribed 'GP', but this was later changed to the present one, the Ordnance Survey Boundary Remark Book of 1881 showing a sketch of both the former and later boundary lines. From Manga the later route still current, deviates on the crest of Langridge, where a rock is inscribed 'GP', by several degrees to pass through the Teignhead newtake wall to Two Stones at Crownhall Bottom, the more easterly of which is also inscribed 'GP'.

et inde linealiter usque ad Heigheston (1240); and from thence nere one myle to Hingeston, al's Highstone, in the east quarter lyinge near ffernworthie hedges (1609).

This Bronze Age menhir stands over 10ft in height, well qualified to be called the highstone, and is now known as the Longstone, and situated on Shovel Down near Batworthy, part of a comprehensive range of Bronze Age funereal remains. In the evidence of John Clement in 1699 he called it the 'Fewstone' and 'then around Farmer Lightfoot's estate', and in 1702 as 'Hughstone'. At the latter date Clement described himself as a 'yeoman living in the village of Fernworthy', which on a later survey of 1786 was described as having 'several tenements'. In the opinion of John Somers Cocks the word 'Fewstone' might well have been an error of transcription for 'Hewstone', and that other references to the stone,

Longstone.

Heath Stone.

spelling it 'Hengheston' and 'Hengston are also mistranscriptions, the letter 'u' having been converted into an 'n', and that they were intended to be spelt 'Heugheston' and 'Heugston' – he cites the fact that other stones of this name are known including one at Natsworthy (Widecombe), recorded in 1566. By 1786 the Highstone had come to be known as the Longstone. It now bears the letters 'DC' (Duchy of Cornwall), 'GP' (Gidleigh Parish) and a rather crude 'C' (Chagford) on three of its four sides. It is said that there used to be the single letter 'G' for Gidleigh but this was removed when the bounds at this point were still in dispute in the early nineteenth century.

Prior to the Tithe Commissioners' settlement the Duchy maintained that the Longstone was approached by way of Teign Clapper and Batworthy Corner, or Battery Corner.

et inde linealiter usque ad Langestone (Yessetone) (1240); and from thence lineallie nere one mile to Yeston, al's Geston, now commonly called Hethstone (1609).

Does it not seem strange that in one instance the 1240 perambulators used the term 'Highstone' for a menhir 10ft in height, and then in the same breath, so to speak, appear to use the word 'Langestone', or Longstone, where no proper menhir appears to exist. The term 'Langestone' however does not appear in any other account of this point on the Forest bounds, except those known to have been transcribed from the copies of the 1240 document, including the sixteenth-century map where it appears both on the face of the map itself and in the description of the bounds on the reverse side.

Later records seem to favour alternatives which led to the use of the word 'Hethstone' locally. Perhaps William French of Widecombe's evidence in 1702 is revealing when he described it as 'Lowton Borough Heath's Stone', thus placing it near the Lowton Brook, a small tributary of the South Teign right bank, rising just outside the Fernworthy enclosures, and also John Clement's evidence 'and then round Farmer Lightfoot's estate to Halfstone'.

The present 'Heath Stone' on our current Ordnance Survey maps is a large orthostat forming part of an old enclosure just to the east of the old Fernworthy Hedges, and not standing on its own as might be expected. Nevertheless it is just in the right place to fit in with other factors, including the next point of reference, and were the modern trees around Fernworthy not there, could be seen right across the South Teign valley, being a chunky 4ft 6in in height. Crossing was of the opinion that it was a menhir but that there was no certainty, (see *Guide* page 65 where he considers 'Hurston' to derive from 'Hare' or 'Hoar' stone, a Saxon term used to denote Boundary Markers), and in 1609 the jurors then placed it 'nere one mile' from the Longstone on Shovel Down, the distance between the Longstone and today's Heath Stone being something over the mile. But other measurements made by them are also only very approximate. The Heath Stone was the only object to appear on the whole of Dartmoor on Moll's 1813 map of Devon, no doubt due to its proximity to the Exeter/Truro track nearby, and *Britannia Depicta* or the Ogilby Improved map of 1736 by Owen, one of the old strip type, shows a tall stone to the right of the track as the traveller goes westward between Tawton Gate and Stats Bridge. Col Mudge's map of 1809 also

still showed this route over the moor long after the turnpike road had been built, showing it hugging the old Fernworthy enclosures at Lowton, later passing to the north of the cairn on Water Hill before bending south to Stat's Bridge. The Heath Stone now bears a modern biblical inscription made by Sydney Potter, Reservoir Superintendent, in 1979.

> et inde linealiter usque per mediam turbariem de Alberysheved et sic in longum Wallebroke (1240); and from thence lineallie through a fen-nye place now called Turfhill, but named in the old records per mediam de Alberesheved (1609).

The words 'turbariem' and 'turfhill' obviously refer to peat and turf ties situated at the head of the Metherall Brook. The reference to the Wallebroke in the earlier record is completely omitted from the report of the 1608 jurors and is now thought to have been a scribe's error when making a copy from the original, but cannot be checked since the original is now lost. The same phrase recurs later giving some substance to this theory but in spite of this the Duchy and the O.S. still try to perpetuate the name 'Wallebrook' in the area of Hurston Ridge by calling one of the sources of the Bovey the 'North Walla Brook'. Elsewhere it is known as Bovey Combe Head or Hurston Water. Turfhill was called 'Black Fen' by John Clement in 1702 and, in the same year, Anthony Torr gives 'Bovey Combe Head' and John Gascoigne of Widecombe 'Jutsone'.

The Torrs of Wreyland continued to have trouble with the Duchy over the bounds of the Forest in that part of the moor, and in 1870–71 action was taken by the Duchy resulting in a court case being brought by them which they subsequently had to drop. Cecil Torr recalls this incident in *Small Talk at Wreyland* since Hurston was a part of their estates adjacent to the disputed land. In 1870 the Duchy had granted a lease to a Bristol man of some 280 acres of land then unenclosed, within what they considered to be the Forest, and enclosing was started, but the Commoners of Chagford held that the land in question was in fact within their parish, whereupon the Duchy claimed that both the Ordnance Survey and Tithe maps were in error 'and all the inhabitants were wrong, although they had beaten the bounds since they were young, just where their elders used to beat them'. It seemed said Torr, 'that nobody outside the Duchy offices knew where the boundaries were, and referred to the 1240 perambulation, which did not prove their case'. The outcome was that the farmers pulled down the 'fences' that had been erected and made the Duchy try to prove its case, which they then dropped.

et inde linealiter usque ad Furnum Regis (1240);
to a place called Kinge's Oven and in the said record namely Furnum Regis (1609).

King's Oven.

Here again there is some doubt as to what was originally intended by the 1240 perambulators, though the boundary line is now taken to the cairn on the summit of Water Hill. The term 'King's Oven' was once taken to signify a Royal smelting house, used in the early days of tinning before the introduction of the water wheel, when it was necessary to make two smeltings, the first producing only an impure 'black tin', and the second smelting having to take place at a site appointed by the King. (Hansford Worth in *Dartmoor* describes King's Oven as 'a place appointed for the 2nd smelting at the hiring of the king' (p. 274), but on p. 277 says 'the 2nd smelting could only be made at an authorised market town', i.e. a stannary town). For many years the site of this particular smelting house was believed to be north-east of the Warren House Inn on the Moretonhampstead/Two Bridges road, within an old enclosure in which there was once a building. Many are the accounts of the nineteenth-century and earlier writers of Dartmoor, and their thoughts about this site. Some remarked upon the cairn on the top of Water Hill either because they could find no other suitable object to apply the name to, or for some quite fanciful reason, but they were scoffed at by others who held to the opinion that the site still marked 'King's Oven' by the Ordnance Survey was the one intended by the 1240 perambulators. Now considered opinion leans to the conclusion that it was the cairn that was intended, and that the early perambulators of 1240 had noted the entrance passage on the eastern side of the cairn, a unique feature so far as Dartmoor is concerned, but typical of a 'passage tomb'. This theory was again put forward in recent years, and makes sense in that the cairn is just the sort of landmark they used. As long ago as 1882 the Ordnance Survey showed the cairn as 'Burrow' (termed King's Oven by some). J. Lloyd Page, writing in 1895 in *An Exploration of Dartmoor* was perhaps the nearest of the older writers to this way of thinking when he said that the cairn was what was intended and that it was 'no smelting house of the old men' and 'nothing more than a ruined Kistvaen'. William Crossing, on the other hand, was quite scathing of this reasoning, saying that 'It is rather amusing to find the summit of this hill described by a writer under the impression that he was giving the reader an account of King's Oven', and he also has less than complimentary remarks about the Rev. Bray on the same subject. Another reference to King's Oven is made by E.L. Chambers (*Arthur of Britain*, 1927). He describes a fund-raising tour of England taking place in about the year 1100AD, at which time nine Canons of Laon were shown, when in 'Denavexeria', the chair and oven of 'that King Arthur famed in the fable of the Britannii'. All rather fanciful!

> et inde linealiter usque ad Wallebrokeshede et sic in longum Wallebroke usque cadit in Dertam (1240); and from thence to Wallebrooke heade and so alonge by Wallebrooke until it fall into easter Dart (1609).

Here we have our second reference to 'et sic in longum Wallebroke', this time in its proper sequence. From Wallabrook Head there are no problems for some distance, the route of the Forest boundary going from the Wallabrook into the East Dart, thence down that river to Dartmeet and up the West Dart as far as O Brook Foot.

> et sic ascendendo Okebroke usque ad la Dryworke et ita ascendendo usque ad la Dryfeld

ford (1240); and from thence linyallie ascendinge to Drylake, al's Dryworke, and from thence ascendinge by Drylake unto Crefeild fford or Dryfeild ford (1609).

The 'Drylake' in question is Yonder Drylake, the higher of the two gullies so named, and certainly not dry, for a stream runs down through it, albeit partially underground under the ancient tinners' waste, and here on the bounds of the Forest and the parish of Holne. Variants of place names occur once again introducing 'Sandyford' for Dryfeild ford, on the Sandy Way, a track coming up from Michelcombe, and 'Drylake Head'.

> et sic inde linealiter usque ad Battyshull (1240); and from thence to Knattleburrowe, wch. they take to be the same that is called in the old records Gnatteshill (1609).

Ryder's Hill. (Trig. point and Petre's Boundstone)

In 1609 this point was given as 'Notting borough' by Quentin Brown of Holne and 'Natting Borough' by Daniel Honnawill in 1702. Today we know it as Ryder's Hill, upon the summit of which is a Buckfastleigh boundstone known as 'Petre's Boundstone'. Until a few years ago there was also a fragment of a far older boundstone belonging to Holne called 'Petre on the Mount', this fragment bearing the letter 'H', but in 1986 this finally disappeared. (For subsequent developments see Holne Parish bounds.)

Eastern Whittabarrow (Children from South Brent shaped the top in the 1930s).

> et inde linealiter usque ad caput de Wester Wellabroke et sic per Wester Wellabroke usque cadit in Avenam (1240); and so from thence descending linyallie to Wester Wellbrooke headd and so by the same Wester Wellebrooke until it fall into Owne, al's Aven (1609).

This part of the Forest boundary has never been in dispute. Again we have variations of spelling for Avon, including Auena, Avena, Avona, Owen and Aun. Evidence given by Daniel Honnawill in 1702 also cites Huntingdon Cross, of which more under Buckfast, as does Burt in 1826. The 1786 Survey of Lydford, etc., also records Huntingdon Foot as did Anthony Torr.

> et inde linealiter usque ad Ester Whyteburghe (1240); and from thence linyallie to Easter Whitaburrow (1609).

Rowe quotes his copy of the 1240 perambulation as reading 'Ester Whyteburghe' but Risdon gives 'Easter' followed by a nonsensical 'Wellbroke' and who may well have got his Easter from a description of the 1240 bounds written on the reverse side of the 'Platte de Dertemore' map, in a different hand to that of the actual map, where it appears as 'Yester'.

But is Rowe right in his reading of the first word as written in his copy of the 1240 perambulation, for the Platte de Dertemore map, if correctly copied from the original, now missing, could be interpreted as reading (see Fig 1) 'ulter' an abbreviation of 'ulteriorem', a word spelt out in full in reference to Western Whittabarrow in an old Buckfast Abbey document defining the bounds of Brent Manor, which they held from very early times. 'Ulteriorem' or 'ulterior' is defined by *Chambers Dictionary* as 'on the further side; beyond; in the future; remoter, beyond what is seen or avowed: (L. ulterior – comp. of Ulter – that is beyond or on the other side.'

As has already been said, the Forest bounds are not in dispute as far as Wester Wellabrook Foot, but proceeding from that point what would we consider to be 'ulter Whittabarrow'? Eastern or western? Eastern would not, of course, have had its relatively recent wall around its summit, but would still have been clearly visible on the skyline, whilst western would be further west and out of sight over the horizon, and more fits the description 'ulter' or remote and 'beyond'. The Buckfast Abbey description of Brent Moor bounds, part of Brent Manor, approaches 'ulterioram Whitaboroughe' from the opposite direction, i.e. from Three Barrows, where the interpretation could be said to be Eastern Whittabarrow, were the name not already fixed to describe Western Whittabarrow as such. So where are we, other than confused and in doubt? A case can certainly be made out for either of them, the Brent bounds going from 'ulter' Whitabarrow 'versus orientam' to Buckland Ford on the River Avon. It is only natural that the Duchy should claim that the Forest extends to Eastern Whittabarrow, as this would encompass more land within the Forest, and maintained this assertion in the 1609 and 1786 surveys, as they do to this day, but are they justified in light of the above?

> ad la Redelake que cadit in Erme (1240); and from thence liniallie to Redlake foote whir it falleth into Erme (1609).

Here we see no mention of Western Whittabarrow, and all other remarks recorded during the period to 1702 omit it too, excepting, that is, the sixteenth-century survey of Brent Moor. The present line from Wester Wellabrook Foot via Buckland Ford to Western Whittabarrow is now marked by a boundstone and the remains of the cross set on Western Whittabarrow. The remains of Petre's Cross (see Brent Moor) on the top of Western Whittabarrow is a reminder of the purchase of Brent Moor by Sir William Petre after the dissolution of Buckfast Abbey. The Duchy have

never accepted that the Forest bounds went to Western Whittabarrow – the boundstone known as Little Petre has now been erected on the present line as it comes up Pipers Beam at SX 6545 6560 – it is uninscribed.

> et inde linealiter usque ad Grymsgrove (1240); and from thence liniallie ascendinge unto Arme headd, wch. they take to be a place named in the same records Grimsgrove (1609).

There is a fair certainty that Grimsgrove and the head of the Erme are one and the same; Erme Head (Fig 4) being pronounced 'Arme Head' by the moormen, as the boulder there testifies. It is inscribed with the legend 'A/Head' at SX 6206 6727; Spence Bate, in the nineteenth century, tries to equate Grimsgrove with Grim's Grave, a Bronze Age cairn circle and cist on Langcombe Hill. On Dartmoor the word 'Grim' also occurs, of course, in the name 'Grimspound', a walled Bronze Age settlement under the northern end of Hameldon, and Crossing expresses the opinion

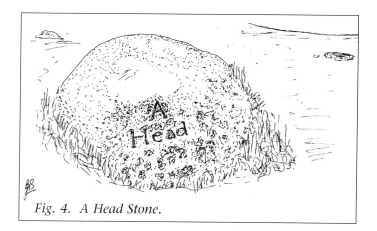

Fig. 4. A Head Stone.

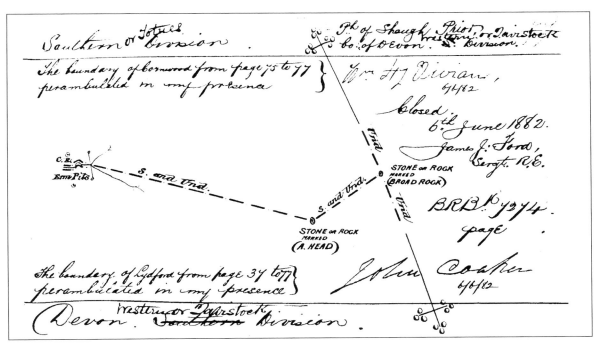

Fig. 5. From O.S. Boundary Report Book, Erme Head.

that the word 'Grim' derived from the Anglo-Saxon 'Grima', the evil or unknown one. About 300 miles away from Dartmoor, in north-west Norfolk, the name crops up again in 'Grime's Graves', there applied to what were once thought to be a number of burial mounds, but which, in Victorian times, were found to be the waste from an extensive Neolithic flint mine, having no less than 366 former shafts of up to 40ft in depth in the underlying chalk, where the best and hardest flints were to be found.

In recent years one of the shafts has been cleared of debris and is open to the public. The leaflet says:

The name Grime's Graves was given to this place probably by Anglo-Saxons who clearly felt that such a fantastic landscape could only have been created by God, and a powerful God at that, for 'Grim' is another name for 'Woden', chief of the Anglo-Saxon Gods. But they did not think it was a burial place, for 'Graves' means holes or hollows.

So are graves and groves synonymous, and all hollows? Erme Head is certainly a hollow and yet we have the Grim's Grave cist!

> et inde linealiter usque ad Elysburghe (1240); and from thence to Plymheadd, where the south quarter endeth; and from thence linyallie to Elisboroughe (1609).

Here we appear to have no difficulties. The earliest mention of an intermediate point between Erme Head and Eylesbarrow is that given in the document describing the bounds of lands granted by Amicia, Countess of Devon, in 1278 for the formation of Buckland Abbey, which included the Manor of Walkhampton, and where a place is named as 'Plymcrundla'. This is now thought to be on a right bank entrant into the Plym, the Crane Lake, and in Crossing's opinion to have a connection with either a

Eylesbarrow.

spring or well. This same point of reference is again referred to on the sixteenth-century map defining the Forest bounds where it is spelt 'Plym crowndel' and given the same status as other Forest boundary points, i.e. shown within a circle.

Today's 'Eylesbarrow' has formerly been spelt in many ways, including Elesburghe, Gyllesburgh, Ailsborough, etc. and it was not until the mid-nineteenth century that the question of whether the Forest bounds went up to Plym Head or Plym Steps was finally settled. Today the line from Erme Head first goes to Broad Rock (see Blachford Manor) and then on to Plym Ford, roughly opposite Crane Lake and on to Eylesbarrow. Evidence given in 1702, however, names several points allegedly between Erme Head and the Plym, including Woodlake Head (Wollake), Foxtorr Head (head of Fox Tor Stream), Stevon Head (Strane Head?), Reddicliff Head and Harborlake Head (Hartor Brook Head?), all by Anthony Torr!

> et inde linealiter ad Crucem Sywardi (1240); and from thence linyallie to Seaward's Crosse (1609).

There is no doubt here as the cross (Fig. 6) still stands just where it did all those years ago, but the line of the bounds was strengthened during the last century by three intermediate plain boundstones. The magnificent cross stands at over 7ft in height with arms that have not been foreshortened and yet still seem to be too narrow in proportion to the bulk of the shaft, so that it has a very individual character. On the Forest/Walkhampton parish bounds, this also is mentioned in the grant to Buckland Abbey. The cross has the word 'Syward', or possibly 'Siward' on its eastern side between the arms, and on the western side is a small incised cross

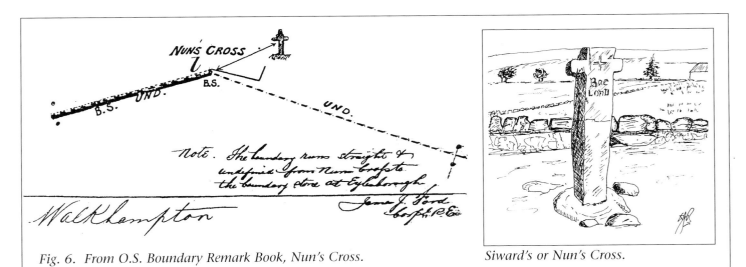

Fig. 6. From O.S. Boundary Remark Book, Nun's Cross.   *Siward's or Nun's Cross.*

between the arms and below this the inscription 'Boc/LonD' in Saxon-type lettering. If this 'Boclond' refers to land granted by charter, the Charter of 1086, that is Bookland, the derivation of the many 'Bucklands' in Devon and elsewhere, and to Buckland Abbey, the inscription must of necessity be of a later date than 1240. It is quite possible that the cross was originally erected as a 'waymarker' between the abbeys of Buckfast, first founded circa 760 but refounded as a Benedictine abbey in 1018, and Tavistock, founded in 960, and adopted as a boundary marker at a later date.

As to 'Syward' it is known that this was the name of an eleventh-century Earl of Northumberland who was a witness to the signing of the charter founding Exeter Cathedral in 1050, and who was Lord of the Manor of Tavei during the reign of King Edward the Confessor, but it seems that there is doubt that he owned land as

far into the moor as the cross. Siwards are also recorded at Cholwich Town, Lee Moor, from at least the thirteenth century, but once again there is no evidence that they were associated with Siward's Cross.

W.G. Hoskins describes Cholwich Town as a fine example of an ancient farmstead, but it is now sadly isolated by china clay works. He quotes a charter which is in the British Museum relating to Cornwood and Cholwich Town, an 'Anntient deed for Cholleswich granted by Guy de Bryttavilla, Lord of the Manor of Cornwood unto Erdyke Syward with the common ther', the document being ascribed to the period 1200-1230. The then bounds are quoted but extend nowhere near Siward's Cross. The cross also appears on the sixteenth-century map, there shown as standing upon a plinth as is the only other cross shown, but this is only a symbolic, stylised representation in both cases. However not only is it depicted on the face of the map as one of the boundary points of the Forest, in its correct position, but there is also a comment on the reverse side written in the same hand as the 'Perambulation' of 1240 thus:

> hit is to be noatid that on the one syde of the crosse abouesaid their is graven in the stone Crux Siwardi, and on the oth. side is graven Roolande.

The interpretation of the inscription on the cross is now accepted as being simply 'Syward' or 'Siward' and 'Boc/lonD'. The cross was damaged in the mid-nineteenth century so that the shaft is now held together by two iron straps, having been repaired in 1847 at the instigation of Sir Ralph Lopes, Lord of the Manor of Walkhampton, on the bounds of which manor the cross stands. It is not until 1699, and the evidence of Quintin Brown of Hole (Holne) that we see the introduction of the name 'Nannecross', later to become transmuted into the present 'Nun's Cross'.

> et inde usque ad Ysfother et sic per aliam Ysfother (1240); and from thence linyallie to little Hisworthie and so from thence linyallie to another Hisworthie (1609).

There is no difficulty here in the line of the bounds, probably originally following the reaves north of South Hessary and south of North Hessary tors. Older spellings include Heghysfoder, Ghysfoder, Efforther, Esforthere, Ysfothere, Yfforchere, Hyffother, etc. It was not until the evidence of the moormen in 1699 and 1702 that we see the 'Hissary' version introduced.

et inde per mediam Mystor (1240); and so from thence linyallie through the midst of Mistorre moore to a rock called Mistor Pann (1609).

There is no doubt at all that the perambulators of both 1240 and 1608 intended the boundary to go directly from North Hessary Tor to Great Mis Tor, as it does now. In 1608 the line was taken to a specific point on the tor called Mistor Pan, a rock basin on the eastern edge of the most easterly of the several rock piles forming the tor. The outer lip of this rock basin was, unfortunately, broken away by vandals many years ago. However the line taken from the eighteenth century appears to have deviated from this straight line according to evidence given in 1702, but by 1867 the direct line had been re-established and several plain boundstones erected by the Duchy to define the line, this time not to Mis Tor Pan but to the centre of that same eastern pile of rock, where an iron bar was set into it bearing the letters 'WB' and 'FB' (see

Mistor Pan.

Walkhampton Parish). Both the change of direction from the erroneous one was used before 1867 and the precise point at which the iron bar had been set are recorded in the Ordnance Survey Boundary Remark Book dated 2 September 1881 (see Fig 49, p157).

Although the agreement between the Duchy and the Lord of the Manor of Walkhampton, Sir Massey Lopes, in regard to the Forest/Walkhampton bounds between the rivers Walkham and Plym, was not signed until 1867, they both agreed the eighteenth/nineteenth-century boundary from North Hessary to the Rundle Stone was erroneous some time before that date, and in 1852 we see the Duchy leasing the sliver of land between the two boundaries, the original and present direct one from North Hessary to Mistor. The Duchy were thus merely reclaiming the land they had 'lost' due to the erroneous line being used from about 1700 to the mid-nineteenth century.

The evidence given at the 1702 Tithe case by both Andrew Badcock and Anthony Torr mention intermediate points of reference which they said were on the bounds, Rundlestone and Fice's Well, which Torr calls 'Fitzwell', but this latter was never on the boundary of the Forest. And what precisely was referred to as 'Rundlestone', the tor of that name or another feature called 'The Rundle Stone'? The tor gains its name from the fact that rock basins formed on the top of the tor in the long distant past, have, through the ages, been displaced by natural weathering of the rock. Formerly called 'Roundels', they have slipped down the eastern side of the tor. The 'Rundle Stone' was, however, something quite different, and in all probability the cause of the eighteenth-century deviation eastwards into the true Forest boundary. Until about 1880 this object was to be seen on the southern side of the road just to the west of the Princetown slip-road on the Tavistock/Two Bridges road. There may be earlier references to this object but the author's first is that of, if not 1702 evidence, then Ogilby's maps of Devon, where the route from Exeter to Truro shows a menhir-like stone to the north of the pre-turnpike track, and having the annotation 'A Great Stone called Roundle'. Next we turn to Mrs Bray's *The Borders of Tamar and Tavy*, a collection of notes and letters written by the Rev. Bray in 1802, which says that in walking from North Hessary Tor 'we fell into the road again at Rundle Stone, on which, on the south side, is the letter 'R', in alto releivö, a set boundstone. John Lloyd Page writing in *Exploration of Dartmoor* in 1889 also says 'what the Rundlestone may have been I know not, nor could ever ascertain', with a note below saying 'A tall stone stands by a gate in the wall near the turning to Princetown. It is inscribed with a raised 'R'. This may be the Rundlestone but no-one in the neighbourhood could tell me what it signified'.

Yet another, more thorough description is made by William Crossing in his *Guide* thus:

> This was a granite pillar which stood on the Forest boundary line. It is not named as a bondmark in any of the surveys, but was, however, recognised as such in 1702. It was formerly to be seen on the south side of the way opposite to the modern boundary stone, which we shall observe on the left. This bears the names of the parishes that here meet each other – Lydford and Walkhampton – and on passing it we again enter the Forest. The Rundle Stone was broken up several years ago, when a wall was being built

nearby. It is much to be regretted that an ancient landmark should have been wantonly destroyed. About 1881 I took measurements of the Rundle Stone. It stood 7ft above the stones in which it was set, and was 4ft in girth. Near the top was the letter R, cut in relief. It is marked on the map dated 1702 as a 'Great Stone called Roundle'.

Whilst the early Exeter/Truro track may not have followed exactly the same line and route as the later Tavistock Trust road, built in 1772 to 1776, it seems strange that the 'menhir' was on the north side of the old track and the inscribed stone on the southern side

of the Trust road. By Act of Parliament the Tavistock Trust was formed in the year 1762, and by that act they were obliged not only to erect suitable milestones at one mile intervals along their roads, but also to erect boundstones wherever their roads crossed parish bounds, and here we come to the obtusely angled faces of what Crossing calls the 'modern' boundstone on the north side of the road inscribed 'Walk/hamp/ton' to the west and 'Lid/ford' to the east, directly opposite the spot where the Rundlestone used to stand.

It is clearly shown by the sitings of similarly shaped boundstones that these were not erected by a parish

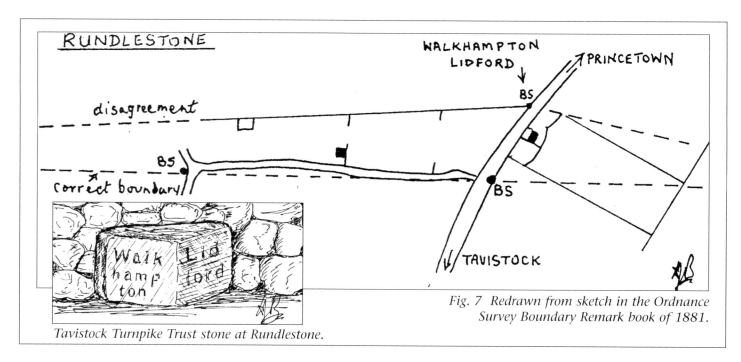

Tavistock Turnpike Trust stone at Rundlestone.

Fig. 7 Redrawn from sketch in the Ordnance Survey Boundary Remark book of 1881.

but by the Tavistock Turnpike Trust, and the author suggests that it was the Rundle Stone being sited where it was, about 150 yards inside the true Forest boundary, that caused the Trust to put the boundstone where they did. In the 1881 sketch in the Ordnance Survey Boundary Remark Book the Trust boundstone is shown, but not the Rundle Stone, which might suggest that it was no longer there, or unrecognised for what it was. Subsequently the Prison Authorities also took the same line from North Hessary Tor, presumably when they considerably extended their bounds by 1000 acres in 1867, additional to the original 390 acres lease.

R. Hansford Worth doubted whether the raised letter on the Rundle Stone was an 'R', but with at least three independent sightings it does not seem to be in question. Not only did he think that Crossing had made a mistake, but he also tried to say that the letter was in all likelihood a raised 'A' for Ashburton. This argument is flawed, however, as in pre-turnpike days, the route of the important link between the two stannary towns of Tavistock and Ashburton left the Exeter line at Merrivale to cross the Merrivale Bronze Age funereal sanctuary to round North Hessary Tor from the west by joining part of the equally ancient Plymouth/Exeter track. That the 'Walkhampton/Lidford' boundstone was sited where it was as a result of the position of the Rundle Stone is also supported by the fact that this line would put all the farms and cottages on the Rundlestone/Mistor track within Walkhampton parish, erroneous though it was, for to do otherwise would place part of them within the Forest and part within Walkhampton, which does not make sense.

At the Presentment of the Jury who made the 1608 perambulation at Okehampton in 1609 they also made the point that 'all the waste groundes, moores and commons wch. have bene heretofore claymed by the ancestors of Gamaliel Slanninge Esquire and scituate lyinge in the west parte of the bounds afore said, that is to saye, from Elisboroughe unto Seward's Crosse from thence to little Hisworthie, from thence to great Hisworthie and from thence to Mistorpan and from thence extendinge towardes to auncient cornditches, are parcell of the Duchie of Cornwall; without wch. auncyent cornditches, that is to say towards the forest, the auncestors of the said Gamaliel Slanninge have caused to be erected certayne howses and have enclosed some parcells of the said wast grounds and that he or his tenants do now use and occupie the same to his or their own use, the whole contayninge by estimacion ten thowsand acres as it is specyfied in the exemplificacion of a judgmt, geven against Nicholas Slanninge Esquire ancester of the said Gamaliel for the same wastes and moores in the sixth yere of the raigne of Queen Elizabeth.' A massive encroachment restored to the Duchy, but that is not to say that the Forest bounds extended to the cornditches.

> usque ad Mewyburghe et inde usque ad Lullingesfote (1240); and from thence linyallie to Deadlakeheadd wch. they thinke to be the next bound wch. is called in the old records Meuborough and from thence linyallie northwards to Luntesborowe wch. they think is called in the records Lullingesete (1609).

Mewyburghe is thought to be what we now know as White Barrow, the Forest bounds going from Mistor across Greena Ball to the river Walkham, and then

Top left: *Limsborough cairn.*

Top right: *Stengator.*

Left: *Chapel Ford.*

across the river to Deadlake Foot, and up that stream as the perambulators indicate to its head and White Barrow (marked a Pile of Stones by O.S. in 1881), thence to Limsborough cairn near Lynch Tor. However, in the nineteenth century, the Duchy once again claimed a line taking in more of the commons, going north westwards from Mistor, rather than north, to Hanging Rock on the Walkham, SX 556 777.

et inde ad Rakernbrokysfote et sic ad caput ejusdem ague et diende usque ad la Westsolle (1240); and from thence linyallie to Wester Redlake … thence northwards to Rattlebrooke foote and so from thence to the headd of the same Rattle-brooke, and soe from thence linyallie unto Steinegtor (1609).

The 1240 perambulators made no mention of following the Wester Redlake as do the later jurors of 1608, but the course of the Forest bounds continue to follow that same later line, and ascend the Rattlebrook from foot to head. Part of this now separates the newly created Civil Parish of Lydford from Dartmoor Forest C.P. as from April 1987. After 1609 'la Westsolle' does not recur, but variants of the later name are used including 'Stengator' as is used today, 'Steing-a-torr', 'Stinkatorr', 'Stenaker tor' and W. Burt in 1826 introduces 'Sourton Tor' as another alternative.

et inde linealiter usque Ernestorre et inde linealiter usque ad vadum proximum in orientali parte capelle Sancti Michaelis de Halgestoke (1240); and from thence linyallie to Langaford, al's Sandyford, and so from thence linyallie to the ford wch. lyeth in the east syde of the chapple of Halstocke (1609).

So whilst the 1240 perambulation went from height to height, to 'Ernestorre', the 1609 perambulators ignored this, marking their route via Sandy Ford, each then giving no intermediate points until they reached Chapel Ford, to the east of Halstock, recorded in a survey of the bounds of Okehampton Chase in 1532 as 'Netelham Stappys', which document also listing High Willes (Hight Wyll), Mill Tor (West Mil Tor) and Rowtor. This early survey was carried out at the instigation of the Marquis of Exeter, a Courtenay having interests in the bounds of the chase.

'Ernestorre' is thought to be High Willes, overlooking the valley of the West Ockment; W.G. Hoskins, in his *Making of the English Landscape*, gives other instances of 'Ern' or 'Arn' for Eagle including Arncliffe, in Yorkshire and Earnwood, Eagles wood, in Shropshire.

The ford 'lying east of the chapel of St Michael', Chapel Ford, is mentioned in all three major Duchy surveys, but Rowe in his perambulation takes us to Cullever Steps which was, it has been suggested, not on the Forest bounds until the nineteenth century, perhaps due to pressures from the Commoners of Okehampton. Some of the stepping stones at Chapel Ford bear drill holes where there was once a rude bridge made from a single tree trunk. Of the chapel nothing can now be seen but until 1536 it had belonged to Tavistock Abbey. The Licence of Alienation of that date reads 'Be it known that we, for 6 shillings and 8 pence (*recorded elsewhere as 6s 5d but more likely to have been 6s 8d, i.e. ½ Mark*) have given to Richard Andrews and Nicholas Temple those messuage lands in Halstock within the parish of Okehampton, formerly belonging to the Monastery of Tavistocke, now dissolved'.

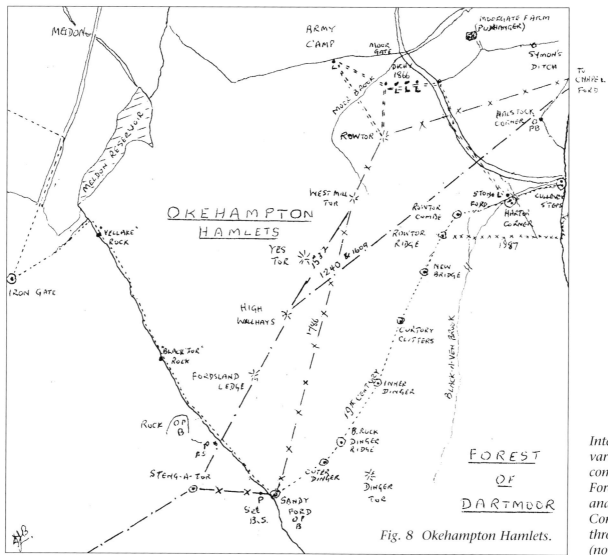

Fig. 8 Okehampton Hamlets.

Interpretations of the various boundaries common to the Forest of Dartmoor and Okehampton Common (Hamlets) through the centuries (not to scale).

Whilst Yes Tor and High Willhays are now well outside the present Forest bounds, boundstones still remain on the moor, unmarked by the Ordnance Survey, which clearly show that in the eyes of the Duchy much land within the parish of Okehampton Hamlets was theirs. One such boundstone is just outside the enclosures of Okehampton Camp, west of Anthony's Stile, simply lettered 'L' for Lydford at SX 587 925. It is obvious that the stone is of nineteenth-century erection however as it shows the marks of feather and tare. To the east of this stone there are three more, on the east side of the Moor Brook, similarly inscribed, together with a fourth one, uninscribed, on the same line, taking the boundary to the corner of the Moorgate Farm enclosures. Yet another is to be found at Stone Ford on the Black-a-Ven above Cullever Steps, and there is another plain stone just outside the most southerly field of Higher Halstock known as Kelly's Field.

et inde linealiter usque ad perdictum hogam de Cossdonne in orientali parte (1240); and so from thence linyallie unto the said hill called Cosdon, al's Cosson, where they did begin (1609).

All the perambulations of 1240, 1608 and 1786 took a line directly from Chapel Ford to Cosdon, strengthening the opinion that Cullever Steps only became a point on the Forest bounds at some time during the nineteenth century. It has been suggested that Irishman's Wall, directly east of Cullever Steps, might have been followed over the Belstone range to Cosdon, but the accepted line during the nineteenth century was a more southerly one to the south of Higher Tor, crossing the river Taw at the higher end of the Taw plain, thence going up near the Smallbrook to the Whit Moor Stone, which the Duchy acknowledged as being on their boundary with the letters 'DC' inscribed upon it. The old six-inch Ordnance Survey map also shows a 'Boundary Rock' near the head of, and on the left bank of, the Smallbrook at SX 6185 8975 just off the present line, but this is uninscribed. On 1 April 1987, when Dartmoor Forest Civil Parish was formed, one of the two boundary changes affected this part of the Forest bounds insofar as East Ockment Farm (Hartor Farm) was transferred to Okehampton Hamlets.

Thus we complete our examination of the bounds of the Forest of Dartmoor, to show how they have changed over the centuries. Some other points of interest will arise when dealing with individual parishes bordering on the Forest and other classes of boundstone. It is of interest to note that the Dartmoor Estate of the Duchy of Cornwall, as defined in their 1983 *Future Management of the Dartmoor Estate* publication, comprises not only the Forest of Dartmoor as we know it, but also that they still lay claim to much of the Commons of Devonshire, especially those lying on the north moor where their boundary encompasses the whole of Bridestowe and Sourton Common, and from the east side of Meldon reservoir takes a line to the south of Okehampton Army Camp along the line of 'L' stones previously mentioned, embracing the whole of Cosdon Hill and the Commons of Throwleigh and Gidleigh.

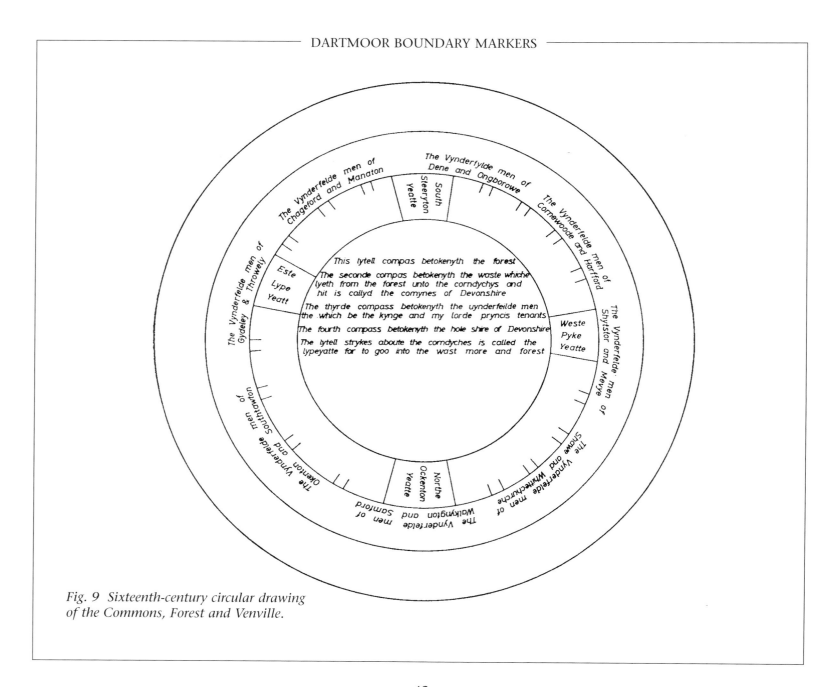

Fig. 9 Sixteenth-century circular drawing of the Commons, Forest and Venville.

42

2
MANORIAL AND PARISH
BOUNDARY MARKERS

MANORIAL BOUNDARY MARKERS

Most of the manors of the in-country parishes around Dartmoor date from Saxon and Norman times, many being recorded in the Exon Domesday Book. In the county of Devon and elsewhere they were grouped into Hundreds for the purpose of administration and the meting out of justice. The boundaries of these manors may, in part, coincide with those of either the Forest of Dartmoor, a parish, or both, and where they do so any boundstones erected by them are marked on the Ordnance Survey's 1:25 000 scale maps in accordance with their policy. There are, however, many manorial boundstones that are not sited on either the Forest or a Parish boundary and these are simply marked 'Stone' on the Ordnance Survey old six-inch-to-the-mile and 1:10 000 scale maps, this term being used to include other inscribed stones that have no relevance to boundaries, such as guide stones.

PARISH BOUNDS AND MARKERS

R. Hansford Worth records the finding of a very simplistic sketch drawn at the foot of a document dating from the reign of Henry VIII circa 1541 to show the King's Council how the lands of Devon were then divided, entitled 'Instructions for my Lorde Prynce to the Kyng's most Honorable Counsell concerning my said Lord Prince Forrest of Dartmore in the Countys of Devonshire and in the moores and wasts of the same belongyn'. This drawing basically consisted of four concentric circles, the Forest of Dartmoor being within the centre circle, surrounded by the Commons of Devonshire, that is the waste or uncultivated land outside the Forest, described in the document as 'the waste which lieth from the Forest to the Cornditches'. The second circle represented the cornditches, a physical boundary, the Commons of Devonshire lying entirely within the bounds of the twenty-two parishes bordering the Forest. The outer boundary of the enclosed land belonging to these parishes is represented by the third circle, the fourth circle embracing the whole of Devon. The third circle is described as 'betokeneth the Vyndefeilde men the which be the Kings and my Lord Prince his tenants'. Outside this line were the outer moors and parishes that are still within what we now term 'Dartmoor'. The purpose of this sketch may have been to examine the claims of pastoral rights in the Forest formerly belonging to the Abbot of Buckfast Abbey, who had the Manors of South Holne, Buckfast and Brent in his possession until 1539. The document makes it plain that when the annual drifts were made, that is the rounding up of all cattle and ponies of a particular quarter of the Forest, the Duchy drove all animals found both within the

Forest bounds and up to the cornditches, notwithstanding the boundaries and boundstones of the 'in venville' parishes.

The twenty-two parishes whose boundaries touch upon the Forest at some point are as follows, starting at the most northerly point and going in a clockwise direction: Belstone; South Tawton; Throwleigh; Gidleigh; Chagford; North Bovey; Manaton; Widecombe; Holne; Buckfastleigh; Dean Prior; Brent;

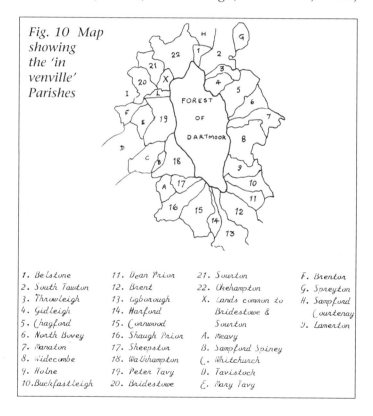

Fig. 10 Map showing the 'in venville' Parishes

1. Belstone	11. Dean Prior	21. Sourton	F. Brentor
2. South Tawton	12. Brent	22. Okehampton	G. Spreyton
3. Throwleigh	13. Ugborough	X. Lands common to	H. Sampford
4. Gidleigh	14. Harford	Bridestowe &	Courtenay
5. Chagford	15. Cornwood	Sourton	J. Lamerton
6. North Bovey	16. Shaugh Prior	A. Meavy	
7. Manaton	17. Sheepstor	B. Sampford Spiney	
8. Widecombe	18. Walkhampton	C. Whitchurch	
9. Holne	19. Peter Tavy	D. Tavistock	
10. Buckfastleigh	20. Bridestowe	E. Mary Tavy	

Ugborough; Harford; Cornwood; Shaugh Prior; Sheepstor; Walkhampton; Peter Tavy; Bridestowe with Sourton; Okehampton, and also that part of Lydford lying outside the Forest, the whole of the Forest being within that parish until 1 April 1987.

In addition to the above 'in venville' parishes, certain other parishes or ancient vills also enjoyed the same privileges, being designated as 'lying within the purlieus of the Forest'. These include Meavy (in part), Sampford Spiney, Whitchurch, Twyste and Cudlipptown in Tavistock, Mary Tavy, Brentor and Spreyton. W. Burt, in his introduction to Carrington's *Dartmoor* poem (first edition 1826), also records Sampford Courtenay, Lamerton and Taverton Tithing in Tavistock. There may have been others.

Neither Bridestowe nor Sourton parishes in themselves touch upon the Forest bounds, but there we have the unique situation where Bridestowe and Sourton Common, land held jointly by these two parishes, does so and thus made them eligible to benefit from venville rights in former times.

Most of these parishes, and others outside that area but still with extensive wastes, set up boundstones at appropriate points to define their boundaries, not only between them and their neighbours but also along their part of the Forest where appropriate. The majority of these are to be found marked with the initial letter or letters of the parish concerned, some adding the letter 'P' for parish or 'B' for bounds. Most are well-set-up posts of granite, some rougher than others, but natural features, tors and smaller rock formations, were also used, a number being similarly inscribed. Some of these latter have been omitted from the Ordnance Survey 1:25 000 scale maps but one has to be careful, for there are several so marked, both the natural rocks and set stones, that are no longer on the accepted boundary line and are thus intentionally omitted. Just one or two parishes continued to be satisfied with the old way of doing things, using natural unmarked features as did the Forest, including the parish of Widecombe. Others such as Chagford, whilst erecting or using some boundstones, were content to leave them unmarked in some cases.

BELSTONE

From Cullever Steps the pre-1987 Lydford–Belstone boundary line went first to the north-east corner of East Ockment or Hartor Farm enclosures, where there is a not very conspicious Belstone 'B.B.' boundstone, with feather and tare and thus nineteenth-century origin. The line then goes to a point on the Belstone ridge under the south side of Higher Tor, where there are two Belstone boundstones side by side, a small one inscribed 'BB/P' and a later and taller one inscribed 'BB' only. We now drop down to the River Taw where South Tawton has boundstones lettered 'ST' on both the left and right banks, asserting that the Belstone/South Tawton boundary line continues downstream with South Tawton claiming the river, which was in dispute for many years. A little downstream on the left bank, sited on a small 'tump' there is a relatively modern boundstone erected in 1968 bearing the letters 'BB', indicating that Belstone lays no claim to the river, the boundary line being the left bank. At the base of this stone are the initials 'PC', thought to be the initials of the stonemason. In times past the dispute had been over which parish had the right to remove gravel from the river.

Fig. 11 Belstone boundary stones

Belstone: BB 2000AD. SX 6213 9331

On 3 June 1993 the Belstone Commoners beat their bounds in a clockwise direction and, arriving at the spot in question not only up-ended and bumped a youngster in the traditional manner, but also ceremoniously claimed other rights no longer theirs, by firing a gun to claim game rights, which might be acceptable to South Tawton, but also the right to cast rods for catching fish, which the boundstones certainly indicate was no longer the case.

The Belstone bounds below the village are now defined by the river downstream to near Sticklepath. However, did they always do so, for near the left bank of what the Ordnance Survey calls the Ivy Tor Water, but which Hemery calls the Lady Brook, deriving from a corruption of 'Lud-a-Brook' as recorded in a Court Roll of 1383, there is at SX 626 926 a set boundstone which is inscribed with the letters 'BB' as per Belstone. These are somewhat elongated and appear to be of

Belstone: BB above left bank of Lady Brook (O.S. Ivy Tor Water). SX 626 926.

some age. The stone is approximately 2ft 6in in height, and it may be relevant that it is sited at a point that is barely off a straight line drawn between the original Forest bounds of Chapel Ford and the summit of Cosdon.

On 1 June 2000, the Bounds of Belstone were beaten, but this time there were no fishing or firing of guns, due no doubt to the inclement weather on the moors, but quite a number of miles were walked in sunshine when 'off' the actual moor. The first stop was to see a new boundary stone which had been erected near the footbridge on the River Taw below the village. It was inscribed 'BB' with 2000AD below. The River Taw was followed to the boundary stones near the Ford, over the hill near Higher Tor to Cullever Steps, down the East Ockment to Fatherford, through fields and along roads to Skaigh Wood and along Belstone Cleave back to the start. About 12 miles.

SOUTH TAWTON – SOUTH ZEAL

South Tawton beat their bounds on a Whit Monday, and it is recorded that in 1929 no less than thirty-five fires were then observed blazing on and around Cosdon, swaling in May, a practice that is no longer allowed to take place so late in the year when many birds are nesting.

Many years ago when crossing the bridge over the River Taw in Sticklepath, the initials on the boundary stone had been painted by the South Tawton parishioners on a Beating of the Bounds. One of the 'C' stones for this bridge is actually built into the fabric of Primula House.

Left: *South Tawton/Sampford Courtenay on Sticklepath Bridge.*

Below: *South Tawton with Throwleigh boundstone nearby. SX 6405 9005.*

'Old South Tauton Boundstone', showing original small 'T' for Tawton. SX 678 895.

On 27 August 2001, the Summer Bank Holiday, part of the bounds were beaten. Starting at South Zeal, the party followed a lane, crossed the old A38, and around the top of Ramsley Hill on a track to the Throwleigh Road which was followed to the Blackaton Brook, and up to Shilley Pool, around the top of the mire to the two boundary stones below Raybarrow Pool both of which had the 'ST' painted; across the mire to the Whitmoor Stone, their initials not being painted as it is a scheduled monument now and also one of the members tried to say it was not on their boundary which does not appear to be true. Next the Smallbrook was crossed and the group went around Metherall Hill to another boundary stone which was painted, and then to Taw Marsh for lunch, with races and tugs of war taking place, some of the latter across the river, so consequently many participants were either pulled in by the opposing team or jumped in! Either the Taw or the track to Belstone was followed to below Belstone, with a variation either still along the Taw or over the side of Cosdon and down one of the tracks to return to South Zeal.

On the north side of Cosdon, which is virtually all within South Tawton, we find boundstones erected in 1885 as a result of a fracas between the South Zeal villagers and the Duchy of Cornwall, the latter regarding the Commons there to be their property. The villagers of South Zeal had already started to enclose common land on the north-eastern side of Cosdon as far south as the valley of the Blackaton Brook, and had taken in a considerable amount of land before the Duchy became aware of their activities, who then sent their bailiff and men to demolish those walls already erected. This action caused other locals to support their neighbours with both harsh words and crude weapons, with such force that the Duchy's men were obliged to retire. Later the men who had started the enclosing realised their rather tenuous position, and agreed to pay the Duchy a nominal rent for the land that they had started to enclose, thus satisfying both parties, the Duchy asserting what they considered to be their rights, and the locals having an assured legal right to enclose the land known as 'Balaclava'. Three boundstones were erected to mark the extent of this agreement, Crossing stating that the posts mark both the boundary of 'certain mineral rights, and also that between what was anciently known as the Manor of Zeal Teony, and the land over which the Duchy claims jurisdiction'. Crossing further states 'a writ of 1221 directs that Roger de Teony shall have the same liberties in Dartmoor which his father had'.

South Tawton/South Zeal.
SZ/1 near the corner of
Skaigh Warren.
SZ/2 at Foxes Holt.

The more northerly of these three boundstones is set on a relatively modern reave or bank just to the west of Skaigh Warren enclosures at SX 633 933, and is inscribed 'DC 1' to the north and 'SZ 1' to the south, being approximately 5ft 6in in height. The second is a full 7ft in height and situated at Foxes Holt, SX 641 925, where we actually disturbed a fox on one visit there, but which Crossing calls 'Rabbits Holt'. This stone is inscribed 'DC 2' and 'SZ 2', and is marked on the old Ordnance Survey six inch maps as 'Stone Post'. According to Crossing, the third example was sited 'near the enclosures to the south east' but now appears to have disappeared.

THROWLEIGH

Between the mid-nineteenth century and the earlier part of the twentieth century the practice of regularly 'Beating the Bounds' of the parish, that is physically walking the bounds usually in Rogation Week and at seven-year intervals, seems to have fallen by the wayside somewhat, and Throwleigh, in the north-east sector of the Moor, was no exception. Their commons extended to the Forest at some points on their western boundary, and with bounds in common with the parishes of South Tawton to the north and Gidleigh to the south.

When it came to renewing the ancient custom after a lapse of a considerable period of time certain difficulties seem to have been encountered, and the whole business gives us a good insight into the general pattern of change. Throwleigh had neglected their moorland bounds for so long that on 2 May 1923 a 'Beating the Bounds' Committee, consisting of Messrs O. Aggett, A. Dicker, J. Dunning, J. Endacott, Thomas

Hill jnr, Major G.C.B. Musgrave, J. Powlesland and E. Wonnacott, was set up to rectify the situation. The Committee decided that 'the stones on the boundary be marked with the letters 'T.P.' (Throwleigh Parish) and that a 'sum not to exceed £1 be allowed for expenses in marking and errecting (sic) Boundary Stones' agreeing to meet at Shilstone Tor on Friday, 18 May at 9a.m. They were keen to get on with the job! At a Parish Meeting held in the Parish School the then rector, the Reverend George Lincoln Gambier Lowe, rector between 1895 and 1933, presided and produced a copy of an old document dated 1786 describing the bounds of Throwleigh Commons, stating that they 'had not been beaten for 100 or 200 years', that the original document could not be found, and that there was no record of who had been the last person to have its safe keeping. Obviously in 1923 they were unaware of earlier, perhaps infrequent, beatings of the bounds in the nineteenth century, but the Throwleigh Churchwardens' Account Book, begun in 1835, records expenses incurred in 'Prembling the Commons', including 15 gallons of cider at 15/-, 'Pd for fetching Henry Aggett for goin to Dartmore when the Commons was prembling 2/-', 'ditto for Philip Endacott', etc.

Whilst there may be no particular significance in the date, 1786 was the year in which the Duchy of Cornwall had had a survey made of the 'Rights, Customs and Boundaries of the Manor of Lidford and Forest of Dartmoor', but the boundary points of reference presented on this occasion were far more sketchy than those given at the original 1240 and later 1608 perambulations. For literally centuries the Duchy appear to have taken little interest in Dartmoor and the precise bounds of the Forest, but by the 1780s leases were being granted on a grand scale to 'gentlemen farmers' for the enclosing of vast areas of former open, unenclosed moorland, thus creating large newtakes which were to be a source of additional revenue to them.

The records of the Parish Meetings of 1923 include three descriptions of Throwleigh's Commons boundary, as described in the copy of the 1786 document, a 1923 description no doubt compiled by the committee on their survey and the record of a later Beating of the Bounds, each of which differs in some detail, together with parts of the six-inch Ordnance Survey maps of the area concerned annotated to show the alleged positions of the boundary stones and rocks and the route followed at the Beating. The preamble to the actual record of the bounds of 1786 states that 'The several depositions of James Crocker aged eighty-eight years and Jeffery Endacott aged eighty both of the Parish of Throwleigh on oath this 10th day of July 1786, before me, John Luxmore Esquire of His Majesty's Justices of the Peace in and for the said County – and first the said Jeffery Endacott who says that upwards of sixty years ago the bounds of the Parish Commons of Throwleigh aforesaid, was viewed by William Northmoore Esquire, the Lord of the Manor of Throwleigh aforesaid and a great number of Parishioners'. In 1786, for the north-eastern section of the Forest, they merely recorded 'Beginning at a Hill lying on the North Quarter of the said Forest called Cawson Hill and from thence to Hound-torr from thence to Whodelake foot where it falls into the Teigne', no mention being made of the Thirlstone on Watern Tor, as had been the case in the earlier perambulations. This was perhaps due to their own uncertainty of the correct line to take at a time when there was a difference of opinion of what had been intended by the 1240 reference to 'Wotesbrokelakesfote', which in 1608 became 'Whoodelake' and which the Duchy maintained was the Wallabrook, not today's Hugh Lake, both of which fall into the North Teign.

The bounds were viewed from Mill Court 'to a post near Paine's Bridge water' now called the Blackaton Brook but formerly also known as the Lovebrook, and it was from Paine's Bridge that the 1923 Beating began. The original post here was destroyed in October 1962 by men from the Water Board when they were laying a new main to the village but by the 1970 Beating it had been replaced. The bridge itself is recorded as having had the letters 'TP' inscribed upon it in 1923, but this could not be found – it is possible the inscribed stone was in the parapet which may have been rebuilt.

Throwleigh Parish: Paine's Bridge. SX 6580 9155.

We take the points of reference in sequence, going in an anti-clockwise direction:

Up by the water called Paine's Bridge water, and up by the water to the South side of Rayburrow Pool (1786); from Mill Court to a Stone Bridge called Pain's Bridge, marked with the letters TP (Throwleigh Parish) and up by the water to a post marked TP the South side of Rayburrow Pool (1923 description); at Rayburrow Pool the first boundary Stone was found (1923 Beating).

There are now two boundary stones on the south side of Raybarrow Pool, the more easterly bearing a large 'ST' of South Tawton, and which for many years was almost fallen, but has been re-erected, and a few yards to the west of this the Throwleigh 'TP' one at SX 6405 9005. Both bear the marks of the feather and tare. The latter is not shown on the earlier Ordnance Survey maps.

Raybarrow Pool. SX 6405 9005.

from thence to a post called Weekmon's Stone (1786); from thence to a post called Weekmon's Stone marked TP north-east of Round Tor or Hound Tor (1923 description); from thence to Weekmon's Stone via an old South Tauton Boundary Stone (1923 Beating).

The relative positions of Weekmon's Stone and Hound Tor, and the reference to 'an old South Tauton Boundary Stone' determine that it is, in fact, what we now know as the Whit or White Moor Stone that we are directed to. It is situated at SX 638 895, and bears both the original small letter 'T' for Tawton and the later, larger 'ST' below, making clear that it is South Tawton that is intended, not Throwleigh, some of whose earlier marking had also been the single letter 'T'. The Whit or White Moor Stone is a monolith standing some 6ft in height and approx 3ft in width, of which R. Hansford Worth says:

> This stone forms the boundary of the parishes of Lydford, South Tawton and Throwleigh, which raises the unfortunate question whether, in its present position, it has not always been a bound stone; if so it may possibly have been stolen from the stone circle which lies 520ft away to the NNW. On the other hand, the presence of that circle is favourable to the contrary view, that the stone is in its origin prehistoric, and has been adopted as a boundary by a later race.

Either way, in 1882 the Ordnance Survey Boundary Report Book and the Boundary Remark Book both showed that it was then unmarked by Throwleigh, but bore the 'DC' of the Duchy of Cornwall (Lydford) at the the top of its southern face, and two 'T's, one on the narrow eastern edge and another high on the northern face, for South Tawton. Depositions made at the Boundary Dispute between Gidleigh and its adjoining parishes in 1842 include at least two references to this stone, one when a Mr Drake said that shortly before that date he had inscribed the letters 'DC' on 'Whitestone'. One must assume that

Throwleigh's 'TP', also on the southern face, may only date from the 1923 re-marking of their boundary. The sketch in the Ordnance Survey Boundary Report Book shows the uncertainty of the times, even as late as 1882, for it names this stone 'Thurlestone or Whitmoor Stone', at a time when the Duchy were still claiming that the Forest Bounds went from Hound Tor to the confluence of the Wallabrook and the North Teign, endeavouring to incorporate a 'Thurlestone' in

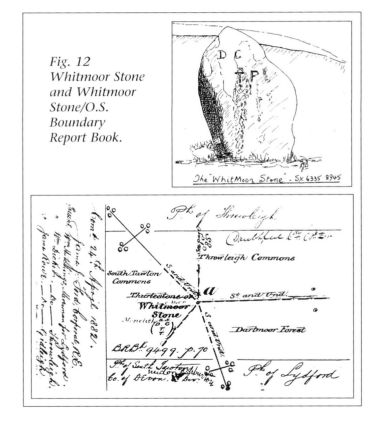

Fig. 12
Whitmoor Stone and Whitmoor Stone/O.S. Boundary Report Book.

that line to fit in with the description of the bounds as given in the 1240 and 1608 perambulations.

The 'Thurlestone' or 'Thirlstone' is, of course, part of Watern Tor now on the Forest/Gidleigh boundary and it was, perhaps, for this reason that James Rowe of Gidleigh was present as meresman for Gidleigh at this 'Doubtful' and disputed boundary point, representing their interests. In his evidence concerning Gidleigh's bounds at the 1842 dispute, James Underhill, 'yeoman, aged thirty-three, who had lived all his life in Gidleigh', working for Simon Moore, renter of one of the Quarters of the Forest, stated that he 'knows Thurston commonly called Water Tor which is between Hewthorne and Weltor Well' and that regarding the Whitemoor Stone said 'I have never heard it called Thurlestone'. Today no one uses the term 'Weekmon's Stone'! The Ordnance Survey Boundary Report Book shows a sketch and records that William Dicker was meresman for Throwleigh, no doubt a forebear of A. Dicker of 1923, and William Hutchings as meresman for Lydford and the Duchy. South Tawton was not represented, presumably because their bounds were not in dispute.

> from thence to Round Tor (1786); from thence to Round Tor, the Tor being marked 'TP' facing East (1923 description); from thence to Round Tor or Hound Tor where the boundary mark was seen on the Tor itself (1923 Beating).

The Ordnance Survey Boundary Remark Book dated 1882 shows amendments, including the alteration of Round Tor to Hound Tor, together with the notation 'Pile of Stones' on top of the tor where the boundary line changed direction. The Throwleigh 'TP' is on the

'T/P' stone south of Hound Tor. SX 6285 8890.

vertical face of the north-eastern side of the tor, facing towards the Whit Moor Stone, grid reference SX 6290 8903.

> from thence to Will Tor (1786); from thence to Will Tor or Wild Tor, the tor being marked 'TP' facing east (1923 description); from thence to Wild Tor or Will tor (passing a low stone with the letter 'T' on it about 100 yards from Round Tor), the boundary mark being found on a rock near the Tor on the north side (1923 Beating).

Will Tor, Well Tor, or as it is now known, Wild Tor, has never been on the Forest boundary, but within the Forest, i.e. the Parish of Lydford, and from Hound Tor, Throwleigh is definitely making an encroachment into the Forest, no matter which of the various boundaries claimed by the Duchy between 1240 and 1482 is considered. In both the 1240 and 1608 perambulations they went from Hound Tor to the 'Thurlestone or Thirlstone or Watern Tor', and all later claims were also well to the south and east of Wild Tor, whether or not to what is now called Hugh Lake on the confluence of the Wallabrook and North Teign. However the Prouz family owned the adjoining Manor of Gidleigh by the thirteenth century, and by the marriage of Alice, last of the Gidleigh Prouzes, she brought to her husband, Sir Robert Moeles, both the manors of Gidleigh and Throwleigh, together with Aveton Giffard and Brixton in the South Hams. She was married a second time to Sir John d'Aumarle, Daumarle or Damarell, who is mentioned in a four-teenth-century document relating to Dartmoor, where he is said to have 'made encroachments in the Forest'. Was this Throwleigh or Gidleigh Manor, and is there some relevance to the encroachment at Wild Tor?

Throwleigh 'TP' is inscribed upon a vertical north-eastern face of one of the many rock formations

comprising this tor to the north-east of the main masses. The 'low stone with the letter "T" on it' 100 yards south of Hound Tor is a natural rock set on its edge, the narrow eastern side now marked not just 'T' but 'T/P', the latter letter probably added in 1923. Grid reference SX 6285 8890.

> from thence to the middle of Willtor Clitter' (1786); from thence to a stone marked 'TP' in the middle of Will Tor Clitter' (1923 description); from thence the party moved down to Willtor Clitter where there is a stone high up on the clitter facing east bearing the Parish Boundary Mark' (1923 Beating).

This stone is another natural one more or less upright, having 'TP' as stated on its eastern side, and still within the Forest/Lydford boundary line. It is barely 50 yards from our next point of reference at SX 6265

Throwleigh 'TP' on Wild Tor. SX 623 876.

Above: *Higher Throwleigh B.S. in Wild Tor Clitter. SX 625 875.*

Right: *Lower of the two Throwleigh B.S's in Wild Tor Clitter SX 626 876.*

8760, and probably only dates from 1923 for at the 1991 beating of the bounds another, lower one and inscribed only 'T' was found.

> from thence to Willtor Well (1786); from thence to Willtor Well near and under Willtor Clitter (1923 description).

At the beating of the bounds in 1923 Wild Tor Well was not mentioned by name but this is hardly surprising if a stone in the clitter is only 50 yards away, and the cart mentioned as bringing them their lunch suggests that they were, in fact, at the well. After lunch they had a pony race to the top of Headon and back! Nor is there any mention of a boundstone at Wild Tor Well which is rather surprising; there is a fine one, known to some since the mid-nineteenth century at least. This is a trigged up natural block approximately 3ft square and several inches thick, inscribed with the letters 'TP' facing north and 'G' facing south, both sets of letters on the flat top surface of the rock. It is at this point that the bounds of the commons of Gidleigh and Throwleigh meet those of the Forest, though the rock is not shown on the Ordnance Survey maps. 'Willtorrwill' was claimed to be on the Forest bounds by John Clement, yeoman of Fernworthy, in 1702 and Gidleigh claimed it to be on their bounds at least from 1639, when it was shown on a parish map of that date. At the time of the Gidleigh disputed bounds in 1842, concerning the parishes of Lidford, Gidley and Throwleigh, 'Welltorwell' was known to some and Philip Endacott recorded that 'there is a stone there in the cluster of rocks, T and G on it. I have seen it there' – but no mention of the letter 'P' which may have been added later.

from thence back by a Bank to the top of Haydon (1786); from thence back NNE by a low Bank to a stone post marked 'TP' on the the top of Haydon (1923 description); the party moved on to the Boundary Stone on Haydon (1923 Beating).

The 'bank' or 'low Bank' is that of an old leat channel going round Haydon.

This is the first 'set' boundstone that we have encountered since the one at Raybarrow Pool, as opposed to boundary rocks, and which was erected on Hadon or Headon, the High Down, in the early years of the nineteenth century as the result of an agreement between the Duchy of Cornwall and the 'Active Person in Parochial Affairs of Gidley', James Rowe, but not sanctioned by the parish. It was one of three boundstones erected on an arbitrary line between Hound Tor and the Longstone on Shovel Down in 1813 (Duchy Records of 13 May 1808 records the then Duchy claim that the bounds of the Forest were 'abutting upon Hey Down'); at the Gidleigh boundary dispute enquiry it was stated that 'two (were) lineally from the corner of Crawford's wall towards Houndtor, one some distance from the other – I made marks 'DC' on one side and 'G' on the other – I have seen the stones lately. They are in the same places but not standing'. The positions of these three stones are pencilled in on contemporary maps dated 1841.

The Headon example must have been re-erected by Throwleigh when they utilised it as one of their boundstones. The 'DC' is now on its north-west side, and the 'G' for Gidleigh on the south-east side. Throwleigh's 'TP' is inscribed below the 'DC' –

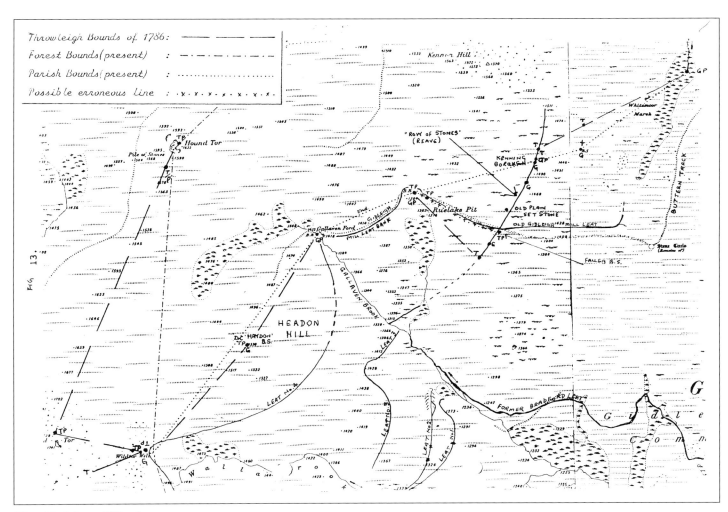

Fig. 13 Map of Headon area.

position SX 6302 8800 – but they make no reference to the fact that they were using a stone originally erected by another party, nor did they do so at 'Weekmon's Stone'. It is not shown on the Ordnance Survey maps but is very near to the present parish bounds.

Fig. 14 Wild Tor Well and Headon Hill boundstones.

from thence down the middle of Haydon to a heap of stones and through the Ford (1786); from thence continuing in a direct line down the middle of Haydon to and through the Ford, Gartaven Ford, (the heap of stones between the top of Haydon and Gartaven Ford having disappeared since 1786) (1923 description); from thence to Gartaven Ford (1923 Beating).

Though the 1786 record only says 'the Ford', Gartaven Ford must have been intended, but a seventeenth-century Beating of the Bounds of Gidley, made by either Bartholomew Gidley (d. late 1650s) or his nephew of the same name, states that at that time the horsemen 'rid round the Hier Garliven Ford Being more firmer Ground' and that the footmen 'went down by the row of Stones on Headon to Lower Garlyven Ford'. This latter is opposite the foot of Rue Lake. 'Headon is covered with heather and as we moved off from the boundstone on the summit we put up two brace of red grouse, and clouds of heather pollen' (July 1989). The 'row of stones' on Headon, however, was not apparent, but the hill has been a source of peat for the parishioners and there are many depressions where they have cut ties or removed vags, the Buttern track leading up to the hill via Gartaven Ford. However we take a direct line from the boundstone to the ford as directed, without seeing any sign of the 'heap of stones' – the cairn marked on current O.S. maps seems to be out of place to be what they were referring to. At Gartaven Ford there is a Gidleigh boundary rock inscribed with 'GP' on the right bank of the stream, the Gallaven Brook, or as Hemery prefers to call it the Headon River. The rock is at SX 635 886 but does not bear any marking by Throwleigh.

from thence by a Bank (1786); from thence to a stone near a Bank marked 'TP' (1923 description); from thence by a low mound to a Boundary Stone on the right' (1923 Beating).

At the Gidleigh boundary enquiry of 1842, it was there stated that 'As to the Boundaries (of Gidleigh) against Throwleigh there is little difference between the lines first claimed by Gidley and that by Throwleigh. The only variation is as to the line taken *between* certain points.

The measurements between the relevant points given in the alternative surveys that took place in 1842 are much the same, measured in Land Yards. The modern boundary between the Gartaven Ford and Rue Lake is a straight line drawn between them, but just below Gartaven Ford there is the take-off point of a leat from the left bank leading to Rue Lake and beyond, and it is the retaining bank of this leat that is here referred to, the Buttern/Headon track using the same line above the leat channel. This is part of the old Gidleigh Mill Leat. It is somewhat surprising that the Rue Lake workings, through which it passes, are not mentioned by name. At the western side of these workings, where the track crosses them, there is another Gidleigh Boundary Rock – SX 639 887 – lying against a bank with the south east side inscribed 'GP'. Though perhaps 3ft high, only about a few inches of the reverse side is free of vegetation and clear of the ground, but on this section, almost level with the bank, Throwleigh inscribed their 'TP'. This is correctly placed 'on the right' of the leat channel as approached from Gartaven, another instance of Throwleigh utilising another parish's stone without acknowledging the fact.

Throwleigh 'TP' stone east of Ruelake.

over a plain by a row of stones over Kennon (1786); from thence along a Bank over a plain by a row of stones to an old stone post at the foot of the stone row marked with the letter 'T' (Throwleigh) (1923 description); and on to a very old Boundary Stone standing up bearing the mark 'T' (Throwleigh) at the bottom of the row of stones going over Kennon Hill (1923 Beating).

According to the annotated six inch map connected with the 1923 Beating the Bounds, the 1923 perambulators took the modern direct line between the Gidleigh/Throwleigh Boundary Rock at Rue Lake and the eastern side of Kennon Hill, in a north-easterly direction, and marked this map 'Row of Stones' where none exists, marking the 'T' stone on this line too. If however we go eastwards from Rue Lake following the Buttern track across the plain, alongside which is the leat bank, we pass another 'TP' boundary rock, about 2ft in height, which they do *not* mention, at SX 640 887.

Continuing along the track we come to the 'row of stones', the Kennon Reave, here with many stones quite prominent both below and above the point at which we have intersected it. Just to the south of where the track crosses it there is a post-like stone, approximately 6ft long, lying recumbent, but one which has obviously once stood upright, bearing the letters 'TP' at the top. At first it was thought that this must be the 'T' stone, stated to be upright in 1923, but

Fig. 15 'T' stone at foot of 'stone row'/the fallen 'TP' stone.

it is not at the bottom of the 'row of stones', and proceeding south-west to the end of the prominent stones we find an orthostat set within the row, about 4ft in height, which does bear the letter 'T' on its western side. This is the 'very old' boundary stone at SX 641 885. Looking further to the south-west we can trace the reave to Rue Lake Pit, where there is a break, thence continuing from the right bank of the workings, where it is more typically a reave, a low mound with just a few more prominent rocks protruding, largely heather covered, extending as far as the Gallaven Brook.

'Rue' Lake should be spelt 'Rewe' Lake – we find this term applied to other similar reaves which have been used as later boundary demarcation lines such as that to the north and south of Three Barrows (Le Rowe Rewe) on the Ugborough/Brent parish bounds, and south of Pupers Hill (Ruherewe) on the Dean Prior/Buckfast parish bounds. In fact in 1842 Philip Endacott records 'I know Rew Lake, I know the Row of Stones at Rew Lake Pit. It divides Gidley from Throwley. This Row of Stones lies for half a mile. It divides the parishes all the way. It is a Bond mark between the two commons. Homeby the row of stones there was a Post with 'T' on it.' It is not a post as such but as already stated an orthostat, visible for some distance.

We now make our way up the row of stones, retracing our steps to the fallen 'TP' stone, and in doing so come across another marked stone in the 'row', this inscribed 'G' for Gidleigh on its eastern side, about 60 yards below the 'TP' one.

But what of this 'TP' stone, for no mention is made of it in any of the records, nor the other 'TP' one east of

Rue Lake? Were these inscribed in 1923 when they could not find the originals? The 6ft long stone is at SX 642 886. All other markings on stones associated with the stones in the 'row' relate to either Gidleigh or Throwleigh but no stone bears the initials of both parishes – in the event the 6ft stone was too heavy to lift to see the underside as it lay! From this stone we follow the reave upwards north of east and in about 150 yards observe another set stone just to the left (west) of the reave, a far older natural one, unmarked but quite possibly a Bronze Age marker?

> to a stone with a letter 'G' cut (1786); from thence over Kennon by the row of stones to a stone near the top with the letter 'G' cut (1923 description); from thence up over the Hill by the row of stones to a heap of stones having one marked with the letter 'G' (1923 Beating).

We continue up the reave from the point where we have examined the old plain set stone and soon find another in the 'row', here more fragmentary, bearing the required letter 'G', but it is not in a 'heap' and thus not the one we are looking for. It is an additional one at SX 643 888. A further 100 yards or so beyond this inscribed stone we come to the 'heap of stones' referred to, known as Kenning Borough, at SX 644 889, spelt by some 'Kanning'. Amongst these stones there are now not one but two inscribed ones, a 'G' stone facing west and a 'GP' one facing east. Hemery (*High Dartmoor*) comments that 'once upon a time it was a little stone cairn, but in recent years it has been pushed over in the spirit of interference so prevalent today; concealed in the ruin are two marked stones'. They are far from concealed now, plainly on view. The 'GP' example has very individually shaped letters and

suggests that this too is of some age. The letter 'P' could have been added later.

> from the end of a row of stones to a place near Kennon Mires (1786); from thence to a flat stone marked 'TP' in a low place near Kennon Mires (1923 description); from there bearing off half right to an old land mark Boundary Stone having the letter 'G' on one side and a cross on another side '†', from thence to the Mire where there is a stone marked with the Parish mark, this stone lying flat with the ground between two mounds (1923 Beating).

One might think that the 1786 instruction intended one to go to the mire from the aforementioned 'G' stone at Kenning Borough, but if we go north from Kenning Borough we are still following the reave, though it is very fragmentary. About 65 yards north of Kenning Borough there is a small boulder inscribed with the letter 'T' both on its southern and northern sides, possibly indicating a sharp change of direction from north to east. 'From the end of a row of stones to a place near Kennon mires' suggests that the next stone would be on the low ground near the mire, where we unsuccessfully endeavoured to find it, but much later in 1994 another 'T' stone was found but on much higher ground at SX 648 891 on a rounded but flattish piece of ground from where the mire was visible.

It is clear from the two 1923 references that they indicate different lines. The earlier Bounds Committee survey obviously went from Kenning Borough directly to the mire and, on failing to find any marked stone, duly inscribed one with the letters

Throwleigh 'T' stone above Whitmoor Marsh. SX. 648 891.

Rock marked 'T' 65 yards above Kenning Borough. SX 644 889.

'TP' – this still has to be rediscovered. However at the Beating of the Bounds they went from Kenning Borough to a nineteenth-century 6ft tall boundstone at SX 6465 8895, bearing feather and tare marks, hardly an old landmark in relative terms. It is shown on the earlier O.S. six inch map and on the Blue and Green 1:10 000 series but is omitted from the current Outdoor Leisure one, thus possibly not on the present line. It bears a 'G' on its south-eastern side and a 14in cross on the adjacent north-east side. From this point they dropped down to the 'TP' stone which they had marked earlier in the year, we presume, though the six inch map on which they are supposed to have marked the route they followed appears to contradict this.

The instructions at the 1923 Beating of the Bounds is revealing for it tells us to bear off half right. Now if they had approached Kenning Borough via the reave this is exactly what they would have to do, but had

they taken the course of the present boundary line between Rue Lake and the standing boundstone, as the annotated map suggests, they would have had to continue straight on! So what exactly did they do?

Kennon Mire is a very tricky place to explore except in times of drought but in July 1989 after weeks without rain, it was possible to walk almost dryshod to its centre and the clump of trees there from the right bank. Here we found the Gidleigh 'Broad Stone', 6ft in length and 2ft across, lying recumbent with the inscription 'GP' on the upper surface. We could find no trace of the Throwleigh stone, though the author was assured by Tom Endacott, late of Clannaborough Farm, that 'the stone lost in the marsh was marked 'TP' (not the same as Gidleigh)' – so it must be there somewhere. It may well be that the 'G/Cross' set boundstone was erected about the time that the Tithe map was defining the boundaries of all parishes – it is known that one

Aish [Ash] Green Gate. SX662 898.

about 300 people attending. Beginning at Paine's Bridge, according to custom also, they first erected a small boundstone below the bridge on the left bank to replace the one placed there in 1970 which had been missing for a number of years, inscribed with the usual 'TP'. The party being so numerous, it soon spread out up to Raybarrow Pool and beyond, this vanguard element largely following the present boundary of the parish up to the Whit Moor Stone and Hound Tor, thence down to Wild Tor Well. However another group, led by a stonemason, followed the older 'traditional' route from Hound Tor to Wild Tor, and thence to Wild Tor Well, where they all had lunch provided by the parish, drawn there by tractors along the Buttern Track. The stonemason re-cut the inscriptions on all the Throwleigh stones including the incised cross on the tall

deposition in 1842 stated, when they were in conflict with Gidleigh, that the bounds in this area were: 'east to marked stone on Kenning, north-east to stone, south-east to stone, north-east to Whitemoor head'.

> and down the north side of the water to Endsworthy Corner from thence by Endsworthy Hedge to where the water turns down Ash Green (1786); and down the north side of the water to Endsworthy Corner where a stone marked 'TP' is in the right bank of the stream, from thence by Endsworthy Hedge to where the water turns down Ash Green (1923 description).

This slab of stone is at SX 662 898.

On August Bank Holiday Monday, 26 August 1991, on a beautiful summer's day, the Throwleigh Commoners beat their bounds at the customary 7-year interval with

Chiselling the letters 'TP' on the Throwleigh/Gidleigh stone at Wild Tor Well. SX 6275 8765

boundstone on the east side of Kennon Hill, and also all their stones in Kennon Reave, the 'T' stone at the foot of the reave, the fallen boundstone adjacent to the Buttern track and the most northerly stone bearing two 'T's. At the fallen boundstone three children and a lady were gently 'bumped' but nowhere else was this old practice performed.

The Throwleigh 'T' stone between the top of the reave and Kennon Mire had not then been found, but two others not found by us in 1989 were recorded, one at the foot of Wild Tor Clitter just a few yards above the trigged up slab, and a second stone on the left bank of the Forder Brook at Ensworthy, i.e. the north side as specified in the 1786 and 1923 perambulations, almost opposite the other example on the right bank, where the bounds follow the wall.

The stone or B. Rock at Wild Tor Clitter or Well, situated between another in the clitter higher up, and the slab below it, was inscribed with the single letter 'T' and may well be the earliest marker here, predating the inscribed slab which, in the 1850s, Philip Endacott described as bearing not just a letter 'T' but also the letter 'G'. The rock inscribed with 'TP' higher up the clitter may well be a 1923 replacement stone when the older 'T' stone could not be found. Granted, the 1786 reference says 'the middle of Willtor Clitter', but there is no mention of a marked stone there and the date 1786 reference to Willtor Well may well be referring to this stone since it is near the lower edge of the clitter.

It was nice to see the old custom of re-cutting the letters on their boundstones maintained, also to hear that some of the older generation know Wild Tor as 'Willtor' still.

GIDLEIGH

Gidleigh Common, as has been implied in our examination of the bounds of Throwleigh, has a boundary in common with that of Throwleigh from Wild Tor Well to Ensworthy and beyond, other sides being in common with the parishes of Chagford to the east and Lydford (the Forest of Dartmoor) to the south and west, the Commoners of Gidleigh being in dispute with the Duchy over various boundaries claimed by them until the 1842–43 settlement. The cause was the aforementioned uncertainty of what was intended by the old perambulators when they gave the bounds as going to Wotesbrokelakesfote, and which the 1608 jurors said they 'thinke to be the same wch. is now called Whoodlake', and which the Duchy interpreted as being the Wallabrook. The next point of reference in 1240 was the 'Heigheston', now called the Longstone, on Shovel Down, where the Forest bounds

Gidleigh: Teigncombe Gate, marked 'GP' SX 6670 8730.

meet those of both Gidleigh and Chagford. As time went on other intermediate points of reference crept in, a Gidleigh map of 1639 naming a number of these.

An early perambulation of Gidleigh's Commons, an undated copy of which is in the D.R.O., made by one of the Bartholomew Gidleys circa 1630/90 describes the boundary as follows:

The Parishioners meet at Gidley town between seven or eight o'clock in the morning. The Parke Gate being set open The Horse and Footmen went in and down the North Park And the Footmen went up by the South Park to Tinkcombe Stile.

From thence down the Lane to the South Park where they meet the Horsemen as they come thro the Higher Ford in the Park to the above Gate From thence they went up the Lane together till they came to a large long Stone in the Lane facing Brimstone Down which the day before the fewing was cleared out by one Streafen Hatherly a Labourer Mr Batholomew Gidley employed and at the Vewing the Commons one Boy or two creaped under this large Stone as a Bond mark of Gidley Commons. (*This stone is still there, an orthostat at the junction of Teigncombe Lane, the Mariners' Way and the Batworthy Road.*) From thence to Tinkcombe Gate against the Moore, From thence to Cow Bridge from thence to a Boun Stone with a large letter G for Gidley Commons (*the Longstone on Shovel Down*). From thence to Stone Tor from thence to Stone Tor Lake from thence to Lower Manger Ford threw North Ting. From thence up

Headon [*in context this must refer to Hew Down*] to Watern Tor where was a ram roasted by Eliz Discombe, From thence to Wilters Well, the Horsemen *rid* round to *Hier* Garliven Ford Being more firmer Ground The Footmen went down by the row of Stones on Headon to Lower Garlyven Ford, From thence my father told (me to go) direcly (sic) to the north-east and cross over the Head of Forder Brook and keep as close down by Forder Broke as possible as that Brook parts Gidley and Throwly Parishes as Fare down as Gidley Parish contains.

As we have established when examining the old Throwleigh/Gidleigh bounds, this more or less follows the present line except that part going eastwards from Rue Lake to the foot of the 'row of Stones' over Kennon Hill, part of Kennon reave, as is amply proved not only by the earlier references to it but also by the succession of stones inscribed either with 'G' or 'T', no less than seven in all. Many of these old boundary markers, boundary rocks and set boundstones may date from the seventeenth century, and Gidleigh Common is particularly well endowed with them. At the time of the Tithe Commutation in 1842 it was said that:

these Boundaries it seems were formerly identified by well known Tors and granate (sic) Bond Stones, having distinguishing letters indented on them and were undisturbed and undisputed till about the year 1808 when a grant was made by the Duchy of a considerable Tract of unenclosed Land in Lidford to a Mr Crawford and Col Fleming who inclosed *all they could* and it appears also inclosed at the same time a portion which is situate in Gidleigh.

In 1791 a Petition had been put before the House of Commons seeking authority to enclose large parts of central Dartmoor, and all this took place at a time when the Duchy were granting leases to enclose huge new newtakes within the Forest to enlarge farms or create new ones, in this case Teignhead Farm on the North Teign, begun in 1808. As has previously been stated, it was the Duchy's continued insistence that their chosen boundary between Hound Tor and the Longstone on Shovel Down was the correct one that led to the Gidleigh/Lydford/Chagford/Throwleigh bounds being the last to be settled in 1843. The Teignhead Farm lease involved the enclosure of some 1551 acres which extended far beyond the line of the Forest accepted by the Commoners of Gidleigh, to the order of 700 to 800 acres it is said. Crawford and Fleming employed a William Rogers to supervise the erection of a wall around this land when Commoners in general were beginning to feel under pressure, and it was Rogers' later about-face, giving evidence in favour of the Commoners, and divulging the shenanigans that had taken place, at the 1842 enquiry of the Tithe Commissioners, that was largely responsible for the Duchy finally backing down. Rogers' original wall had so incensed the Gidleigh people that at the next beating of their bounds they cast this down, but later Rogers was instructed to build another one which is what we see today, not on the same line as the first one but still encroaching well into Gidleigh Common, though by this time the Duchy had amended their claim as to the Forest boundary, taking it then from Hound Tor over Headon Hill to Stone Tor and the Longstone.

In his evidence Rogers stated that:

in building the (original) wall when we came to Stone Tor Hill we found an upright Stone marked 'G'. It was a very old stone. We built up the wall against the Stone. I found two flat stones on part of Langworthy ridge inside our enclosure, about 30 or 40 land yards, one of them marked 'G', upright Stones placed in the ground. I had them taken up and built into a wall for foundation stones. Manger Stone was inside our enclosure about 50 or 60 land yards. At Manger Stone I found an upright Rock marked 'G'. I obliterated the 'G' to lead Gidley people astray. Mr Crawford ordered me to obliterate the mark. I knocked out the letter with a pick. I was annoyed with the Gidley people for knocking down the wall. The Gidley people threatened several times to pull down the new wall but they did not do so.

What a carry on! Other marked stones of the same period simply marked 'G' and presumably dating from the seventeenth–eighteenth century remain on other parts of Gidleigh Common, at Hawthorn Clitter and Wild Tor Well for instance, and on the Kennon Hill reave where there are three examples. That at Wild Tor Well was known in 1842 to Philip Endacott and mentioned in his evidence in the Tithe Commutation (see Throwleigh), as were two marked stones in Hawthorn Clitter, one marked 'G', the other 'GP', on a direct line between the turning point in the bounds and Manga Rock, and only about 50–75 yards apart. And, of course, those in the 'row of Stones' on Kennon were known to both Throwleigh and Gidleigh. The stone in Stone Tor Hill wall was still marked on the 1906 Ordnance Survey six inch map, though it has long since disappeared.

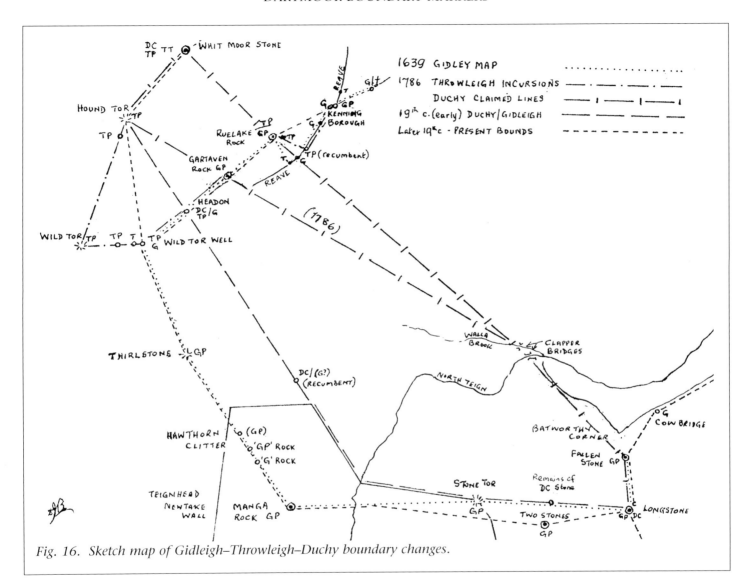

Fig. 16. Sketch map of Gidleigh–Throwleigh–Duchy boundary changes.

In 1804 a Thomas Grey had produced a map for the Duchy on the advice of the Reverend James Holman Mason, vicar of Widecombe between 1815 and 1860, and who in 1816 was appointed one of the Deputy Riders and Master Forester of Dartmoor on the death of Edward Bray. In 1842 it was stated that:

In May 1813 there was a meeting and viewing of the disputed bounds which began at Water Down Tor, with Mr Mason and Mr Shillabeer, the Duchy Surveyor, taking the lead. Parson Mason read Bounds as running from that Tor to Manger Ford on Woodlake Foot. Then I shook for fear the wall should be thrown down as a straight line would cut through our wall. I said 'To be sure you are not going to pull down Mr Crawford's wall.' He was silent a little while then he answered 'we will go whatever way you bring us'. They then went to Manger Ford round the wall. There was a little further confusion on Stone Tor Hill. Later he (Mr Rogers) met Mr Mason by appointment at Two Bridges, who said he was authorised by the Duchy to try to get Mr Rogers to come to an arrangement with Gidley about the bounds and to put up new bound marks to be paid equally by the Duchy of Cornwall and Gidleigh. I agreed to do this. With Rowe of Gidley (no other Gidley people would agree) he put down the first stone in a direct line between Stone Tor and Longstone say from 20 to 30 perches Gidleigh side of Two Stones at Crownhall Bottom. Two more stones in a direct line from the corner of our wall near Manger Stone Ford towards Houndtor and cut 'DC' on Longstone. He then reported back to

Mr Mason and other Duchy officials. Mr Shillabeer asked me if I had embossed the letters. On replying 'no' and asking what difference it made, he said 'it would look more ancient'.

All three stones were inscribed 'DC' and 'G' on opposing sides – we have already referred to that on Headon Hill – the first to be erected being the one near Crownhall Bottom, an 1841 map (D.R.O.) having the pencilled note 'placed by Rogers'. In 1842 all three stones were reported as being fallen with one broken. The broken one was the example near Crownhall Bottom between Stone Tor and Longstone, and the butt of the shaft is still in situ, with pieces of the rest lying nearby at SX 656 857 about 400 yards from Two Stones. One of the smaller fragments appears to bear a man-made curved line, part of either the letter 'C' or 'D'.

The second stone was situated about 300 yards west of north from the north-west corner of the newtake wall at SX 638 867, also marked on the 1841 map. This is still there, lying recumbent with its 'DC' inscribed face uppermost. That nearest Hound Tor was the one on Haydon Hill (see Throwleigh). If this was fallen in 1842, in all likelihood it was when the stone was re-used by Throwleigh that it was re-erected. Regarding the Longstone, also marked 'DC' at this time, it was said that 'there was a G on it before, a very old letter' – there is no sign of this today.

The cost of erecting the three Duchy/Gidleigh stones and marking the Longstone amounted to the sum of £2.17.0. The invoice for this work was worded as follows:

1813	The Parish of Gidley and the Duchy of Cornwall to John Rowe overseer of the Parish of Gidley. Dr:	
Oct		
12	To 4 Horses drawing Stone Posts to put between the Commons	
13	of Gidley and the Forest of Dartmoor as a boundary lineally between Hound Torr an Woodelake Foot and from thence to Longstone at 3 Shillings	0.12.0
	To 10 men putting in the posts and providing them	2. 0.0
	Engraving the letters DC - G on four posts	0. 5.0
		£2.17.0

Half of the sum of Two Pounds seventeen Shillings Received from the Parish of Gidley this by me *(torn and illegible)*

On 20 August 1842 James Jerwood, Barrister at Law of Southernhay, was appointed Assistant Tithe Commissioner to look into the disputed boundaries relating to Gidleigh and its adjoining parishes of Lydford (the Forest), Chagford and Throwleigh, meeting 'interested parties' at the White Hart Hotel, Moretonhampstead, at various dates in September to November in that same year.

The Duchy were now claiming that the Forest bounds went from the Whit Moor Stone, no doubt due to the fact that it was sometimes called 'Thurlestone'

erroneously, this name being perpetuated by the Ordnance Survey as late as the 1880s, through to Rue Lake Pit and to Wallabrook Foot, thence up to a stone on Shovel Down [the fallen stone associated with the Four Fold Circle] (see Fig. 18) 'Near Battery Corner [Batworthy Corner].' A Mr Tucker said that about seventeen years prior to 1842 'when I went with the Commoners it was the first time I ever heard of Lidford claiming that [Rue Lake Pit] as the boundary'. Another quote says that 'The old presentments of the perambulators of Dartmoor Forest of which there are several in Books containing descriptions and Histories of Devon describe the Boundaries in favour of those set up by Gidley.'

In 1847 Arthur Whipham of Gidleigh Park agreed to convey to His Royal Highness, the Duke of Cornwall, the manorial rights and the freehold of that part of Gidleigh Commons that had been claimed by the Duchy before the Tithe agreement, the part lying westward of a line running from the Longstone, in a straight line to 'Stones on Shovel Down, and from thence to Teign-over Clapper, where what they call the Willis Brook falls into the Teign, and from there in a straight line to Roolake Pool or Pit,' thus giving the Duchy ownership of land claimed before the settlement.

SHOVEL DOWN AND BATWORTHY CORNER

This entry in the Ordnance Survey Boundary report Book dated 14th July 1882 (see Fig. 17, p68) depicts a sketch of the above area showing the line that the Duchy formerly maintained was the boundary of the Forest from Wallabrook foot and Teign Clapper to Batworthy Corner and thence to the Longstone. Here this is shown deleted, together with the then approved bounds.

An enlargement of the Four Fold Circle clearly shows that the fallen stone marked 'GP' by Gidleigh was not the turning point of the boundary, but that it was the centre of the circles.

The Tithe map of 1843 showed an additional stone near Batworthy Corner, where there is another slight change of direction.

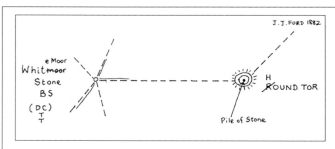

AS DRAWN IN O/S BOUNDARY REMARK BOOK 1882

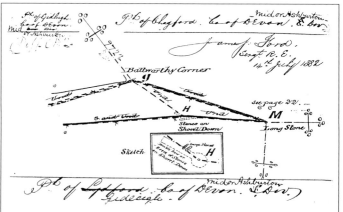

Fig. 17 O.S. Boundary Report Book, Batworthy Corner.

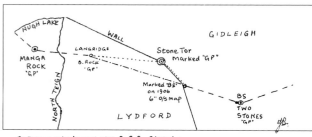

OLD LINE SHOWN ON 1881 B.R.B. Sketch: ....
RE-ALLIGNMENT SHOWN ON SAME : —.—.—.—.—

Although inscribed 'GP' on the top, Stone Tor is no longer on the Forest/Gidleigh bounds. The Ordnance Survey Boundary Remark Book of 1881 shows both the older route to Stone Tor and thence to the Longstone, and the present deviation from Longridge through Stone Tor Hill newtake wall together with the now missing boundstone.

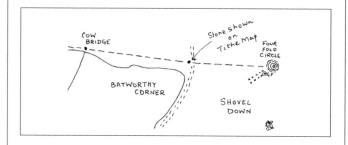

Fig. 18 Whitmoor–Round Tor–Gidleigh stones at Stone Tor and Batworthy.

Regarding the fallen stone associated with the Four Fold Circle and double stone row on Shovel Down, the Ordnance Survey Boundary Report Book of 1882 shows the turning point of the Gidleigh–Chagford bounds as not being the inscibed large stone but the centre of the Four Fold Circle itself, an enlargement emphasising this (Fig. 18). Cow Bridge is at SX 6617 8648, having a small letter 'G' on its top surface.

A septennial Beating of the Bounds of Gidleigh Commons took place on 27 August 1990, led by Mr Jordan of Moortown Farm on horseback, with a few other riders and approaching a hundred on foot. It was formerly recorded that the stones were re-cut, but various people cleaned the inscriptions on all of them with a wire brush.

Starting at Teigncombe Gate, or Northern Gate as it was sometimes known, where the boundary used to be defined as being in the middle of the gateway, but is now on the western verge of the road; along to Cow Bridge where the youngest member of the party, a

Cow Bridge, marked with 'G' only. SX 6617 8648.

Fallen Menhir in the Four Fold Circle, marked 'GP' SX 659 860.

Two Stones in Crownhall Bottom, one marked 'GP' SX 6525 8545.

Stone Tor. SX 649 856.

three-year old, was bumped seven times upon it; next to the fallen menhir in the Four Fold Circle; Longstone where a cash prize was given to the first boy who had climbed on top of it; Crownhall Bottom; a deviation of the correct route to Stone Tor; down and through the gateway; across Stone Tor Brook before reaching the present boundary line on Longridge. When the newtake was constructed, 'G' stones were found and destroyed, but later an earthfast stone was inscribed 'GP', which was of course cleaned.

Mr Jordan following the ancient custom of going through the Thirlstone. Note 'GP' marked to right of horse's tail. Gidleigh Beating the Bounds 27.8.1990.

At Hewthorn or Hawthorn Clitter, Mr Jordan was familiar with a natural stone marked 'G' but not with another marked 'GP' only about 75 yards away. The horse and riders jumped the wall at the north-west corner of the newtake, whilst the footsloggers went over the stile nearby. No effort was made to look for a boundstone in the rough cairn where the boundary line changes direction slightly. Is there a fallen one there somewhere? One was marked on maps of the 1960s.

At Watern Tor Mr Jordan led his horse through the aperture, 'GP' being incised on the east side. Wild Tor Well is the traditional stopping place for lunch and games, the tractors having arrived with provisions. The stop-over lasted about two hours, with various races held, but not the pony races up to Headon Hill and back as happened many years ago.

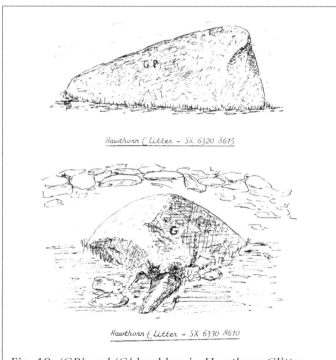

Hawthorn Clitter - SX 6320 8615

Hawthorn Clitter - SX 6330 8610

Fig. 19 'GP' and 'G' boulders in Hawthorn Clitter.

Headon was the next boundary stone visited; then along to Gartaven Ford; Rue Lake where most were unaware of the 'TP' at the top of the opposite side of their stone. The direction taken was rather too far south and consequently one of the 'G' stones in the reave was found before Kenning Borough was reached where the stone marked 'GP' was cleaned but not the one with 'G' on it.

In the 1933 T.D.A. Mrs Eckett Fielden refers to Gidleigh Commons where, she says, 'some of the boundaries being stone crosses'. There are no true crosses on Gidleigh's bounds but our next port of call was the nineteenth-century set stone bearing a 'G' and an inscribed cross on adjacent faces and so down the steep eastern side of Kennon to Whitemoor Mire. One or two members of the group did try to reach the boundary stone in the mire, but were unable to get to it. The Forder Brook was then followed downstream

Top left: *Gidleigh stone being cleaned with a wire brush, 27.8.1990. 'TP' for Throwleigh is on the small piece above ground at the rear where the boy is sitting. SX 6390 8878.*

Above: *Above stone showing Throwleigh's 'TP'. Photo taken 27.8.1990.*

Top right: *Kenning Borough showing Gidleigh's 'G'. SX 644 889.*

Fig. 20 Gidleigh B.S. with Cross on Kennon Hill.

to Ensworthy Corner and the last Gidleigh stone in the right bank of the stream found and cleaned and only a yard or two from the Throwleigh one also on the right bank, thus completing the Beating.

Further details of many of these boundstones are mentioned in both the Forest of Dartmoor and Throwleigh Bounds.

The boundary between Gidleigh and Chagford was adjudged to be from the centre of Teigncombe Gate to the centre of Cow Bridge, a trigged up orthostat just outside the Batworthy enclosures, thence to the stone associated with the Four Fold Circle on Shovel Down and on to the Longstone.

A Thomas Irish, Surveyor, of Buckfastleigh, was engaged to measure and map several parishes for the purpose of Tithe Commutation in partnership with Arthur Parker, and stated that:

The uninclosed Common belonging to the Parish including the part in dispute contain altogether between 2400 and 2500 acres statute measure. We have also measured the length of the Boundary of the Parish of Gidley as pointed out to us by the landowner from Teigncombe Gate to Ainsworthy Corner and found the same as follows:

	Stat Measure, Yards
Teigncombe Gate to Cow Bridge	192
Cowbridge to Stones on Shovel Down	88
Stones on Shovel Down to Longstone	72
Longstone to Crownhall Bottom	156
Crownhall Bottom to Stone Tor	56
Stone Tor to Langridge	135
Langridge to Manger Stone	117
Manger Stone to Hawthorne	117
Hawthorne to Water Down Tor	144
Water Down Tor to Well Tor Well	168
Well Tor Well to Garlaven Ford	245
Garlaven Ford to Rewlake Pool	91
Reulake Pool to Stone on Kenning	116
Stone on Kenning to Whitmoor Marsh head	140
White Moor Marsh head to Ainsworthy Corner	<u>280</u>
	<u>2117 yards</u>

or 9 furlongs and 137 yards statute measure which, according to the Cornish measure of 18ft to the yard, makes about 8 furlongs 200 yards.

These are land yards again, of approx 5$\frac{1}{2}$ ordinary yards, or a rod, pole or perch. Other similar measurements are also recorded, and the bounds confirmed by James Jerwood on 25 March 1843.

CHAGFORD

Chagford beat their moorland bounds on 7 September 1986, commencing at Jurston where the vicar said prayers before the group moved off. Green Combe was followed to the junction of roads at the top, where the first unmarked boundary stone was seen. It was suggested that these should be marked, but this had not been completed by the time of the Beating in 1993. The Moretonhampstead to Postbridge road was followed to Bennett's Cross, where virtually opposite on their boundary with North Bovey at SX 889817 is a boundary stone which was set up by the Turnpike Trust as was the practice when crossing the junction of two parishes. The inscription is carefully but shallowly inscribed and difficult to read unless the sun is just in the right place, low in the sky. Both parish names are set out in full reading downwards with a zig-zag line between them (see Fig 21). After lunch at/by the Warren House Inn, the group climbed to King's Oven cairn, walked across Hurston Ridge to Fernworthy

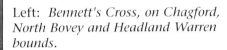

Above: *The Puggie Stone, on Chagford's Bounds.*

Left: *Bennett's Cross, on Chagford, North Bovey and Headland Warren bounds.*

Below: *Stone placed near the top of Green Combe on the junction of Chagford and North Bovey's Boundary. May 1994. SX 696 833.*

Chagford: Following the correct boundary across Fernworthy Reservoir. Chagford Beating their Bounds, September 1986.

Reservoir where a few people were taken across by boat on the correct boundary which has been inundated by the reservoir, the rest of the party walking around below the dam, on to Longstone which is inscribed with a 'C', Roundy Pound where drinks were supplied, along an old lane to the Puckie Stone and on to Chagford Bridge, tea being provided in Chagford for the participants.

Apart from the 'C' for Chagford on the Longstone on Shovel Down and the Turnpike one opposite Bennett's Cross at SX 880 817, Chagford's moorland boundary stones were uninscribed. However, at their Beating of the Bounds on 29 August 1993, a new dressed stone had been erected, possibly jointly with North Bovey Parish, near the head of Green Combe, with the letters 'C' and 'NB' engraved on it. Chagford also beat their moorland bounds in 2000.

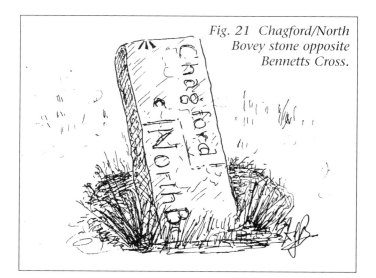

Fig. 21 Chagford/North Bovey stone opposite Bennetts Cross.

NORTH BOVEY

There are a number of North Bovey boundstones on their boundary with Manaton which zig-zag over Easdon Down, then over Hookney Down near King Tor where, apart from the set stones, there is an earth-fast boulder near one of the old anti-aircraft poles with a single letter 'B' engraved on it. Down to Grim's Lake and two standing and one possibly fallen boundstones to Firth Bridge. On the track leading to Headland Warren is an orthostat forming part of an old wall on one's left as one approaches the farm, this also has a 'B' on it. Up and over Challacombe Down to the north edge of Soussons Wood which is followed to the

North Bovey boundary stone at SX 7094 8124.

North Bovey: Recumbent stone at SX 7120 8135 marked 'B' for North Bovey.

Spitchwick stone on the West Webburn. The next stone is up on Hameldon where the Duke of Somerset Natsworthy Manor stones are followed from Two Barrows to Single Barrow, Broad Barrow, Hameldon Cross, Grey Wethers, Blue Jug, and Pit Stone, via Jay's Grave to the stone marked 'WID/M/ILS' near Hemsworthy Gate. More Duke of Somerset stones, this time in Ilsington Manor, to the Duke Stone, Long Pool, the Horse Shoe Stone, a stone marked 'I/M', up to Hole Stone and Prince of Wales, along to the Three Parish Stone 'M/I/B', down to the north-west corner of Yarner Wood and then to the 1980 Lustleigh wooden post which is on the Manaton bounds and the last marked stone on Trendlebere Down marked 'M/L' (Manaton/Lustleigh). The route is then down to the Becka Brook which is followd to its junction with the River Bovey, this then followed to Clapper Bridge.

Wallabrook and along the Brook to the road near the Warren House Inn. The road is followed, passing Bennett's Cross and the turnpike Chagford/North Bovey boundstone on the other side of the road, and along to the stone near the head of Green Combe. The tracks and lanes to the north of the road are followed, crossing it and returning to North Bovey via Bughead Cross.

On beating their bounds on 21 June 2000 a fallen boundstone near King Tor was re-erected.

MANATON

Manaton apparently has boundary stones on its bounds but the majority are only inscribed with the initials of the other parishes on their joint boundaries. They follow the same boundary as North Bovey to the Wallabrook, but then turn downstream to the Spitchwick stone with plaques showing the initials for Widecombe, Lydford Forest and Spitchwick, followed by the Cator stones on Cator Common to the second

Manaton: Lower Terrace on Manaton/Lustleigh boundary. SX 7685 7970.

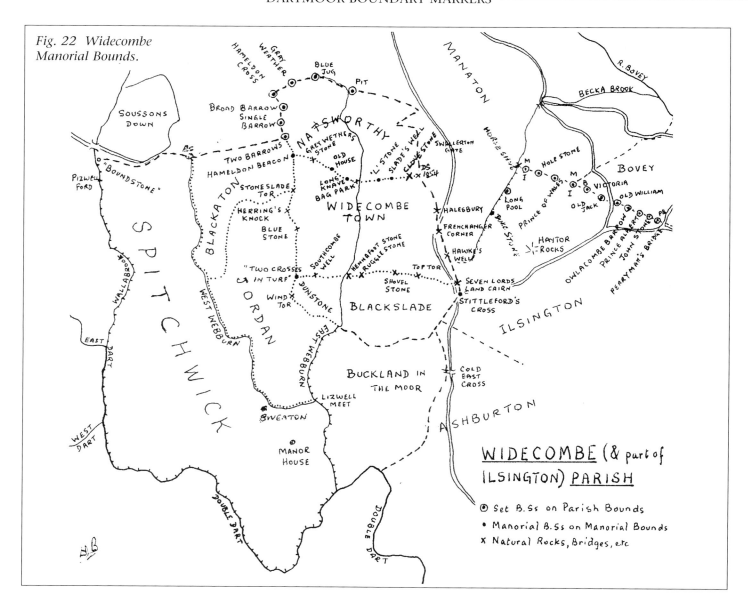

Fig. 22 Widecombe Manorial Bounds.

WIDECOMBE (& part of ILSINGTON) PARISH

⊙ Set B.Ss on Parish Bounds
• Manorial B.Ss on Manorial Bounds
× Natural Rocks, Bridges, etc

PARISH OF WIDECOMBE IN THE MOOR

Within the large parish of Widecombe, which covers some 11 000 acres, there are now six manors, Spitchwick being by far the largest, the others being Jordan once known as Dewdon, Blackaton or Blagdon Pipard, Natsworthy, Dunstone cum Blackslade and Widecombe Town, all being recorded in the Domesday Book with the exception of Widecombe Town which was formed later, as was the parish itself, the six Widecombe manors and that of Buckland in the Moor forming a detached part of Haytor Hundred. In the Domesday Book Dewdon was listed as a moorland addition to the coastal manor of Cockington, and Scobitor as one of 15 properties formerly belonging to thanes which were added to Bovey, that is Bovey Tracey.

Spitchwick Manor

At the time of Domesday, Spitchwick was spelt Spice wite (the Exchequer version) and Espice wita (Exon version). Later we find Spykwyt, Spichewyke and Spychewike. In 1207 Thomas de Spichwik is recorded. In 1896 the Court Leet of this manor listed the representatives of the farms within the manor attending and who were on the jury, viz: Great Cator, West Shallowford, Sherwell, Corndon, Christianhayes, Lower Cator, Middle Cator, Lake, Leigh Tor, Lower Uppacott, Middle Sherwell, Grendon, Tridycott, Uphill, Sherwill and Sweaton.

Spitchwick Manor has a western boundary line of no less than six miles from its most northern point between Pizwell Ford and Runnage Bridge on the Wallabrook/Forest bounds, where a granite gatepost was erected at the time of the 1973 beating of the

Above left: *Spitchwick Manor: B.S. above Blackaton Bridge. 16.11.95. SX 6882 7875*

Above right: *'Arthur's Stone', facing south, on the Wallabrook. 16.11.95. SX 6715 7720*

bounds of Spitchwick Manor, the only Widecombe Manor to maintain the old tradition, doing so every ten years or so, latterly in 1973, 1983 and October 1995. The stone is sited on the left bank of the Wallabrook where an old reave runs down to the river bank, which marks the important junction of Spitchwick in Widecombe Parish, Lydford across the river and Manaton. The name given to it is Arthur's Stone, which relates to the hind of Spitchwick, Arthur Routley, who erected it in 1973. It remained uninscribed until the 1995 beating, when circular plaques of bronze, about 4ins in diameter, were attached to it lettered in relief and reading vertically, 'LYD' facing west, 'WID' facing east and on the south-facing side SPITCHWICK MANOR encircling the initials 'SJVS' – the initials of the Lord of the Manor of Spitchwick, Stephen John Valentine Simpson.

On the same 1995 perambulation another new bound-stone was erected, being another broken gatepost from near Grendon, damaged by the Americans during the Second World War. This was set up at SX 6885 7885, with a Spitchwick Manor bronze plaque similar to that mentioned above, to make clear a doubtful boundary point with Blackaton Manor.

Cator Manor

The reave on which Arthur's Stone is situated runs eastwards from this, forming the boundary of Cator Common and Widecombe Parish. On this reave are two Cator boundstones, rough pieces of moorstone clearly inscribed with the letters 'CB', and a third is on the same line just to the east of the Widecombe Church Way path from Pizwell. One of the two on the reave has been used by the Ordnance Survey as a reference point and still has the brass head and incised arrow. A fourth is not on the parish bounds and thus not on the Ordnance maps – this is on the edge of Soussons Wood near the cairn circle (see Fig. 23). This latter has also formerly been used as a boundary marker when it was known as Ringastones.

Another 'CB' was found in 1988 at 6765 7795, report-ed to Kath Brewer in September 2000 – see *Dartmoor Magazine*, Spring and Summer 2001.

Like so many other Dartmoor settlements, the origins of Cator go back several centuries. In the thirteenth

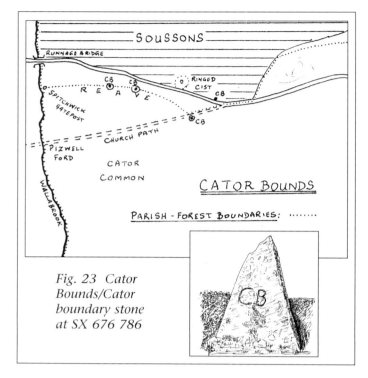

Fig. 23 Cator Bounds/Cator boundary stone at SX 676 786

century a Thomas de Spicwyk is recorded as having granted the gift of some of his lands as a marriage settlement. The document reads:

I Thomas de Spicwyk have granted and con-firmed to Gilbert son of Leno de Cadetrew and his heirs 2 ferlings of land in Chadetrew which Michael my father gave to Leno his father with An. his daughter and my sister in free marriage with these bounds namely: from Wedebourne as to the lands of William de Dawedunn (another variation of Dewdon, at that time owning one

Above: *Cator Manor: 'Piked Stone',
SX. 685 760*

Left: *Another 'Piked Stone' re-erected
on Cator Green. SX 680 767*

Above: *Cator boundstone
on Cator Common. SX 6718
7873*

Right: *Another Cator boundstone on Cator Common,
showing the O.S. bench mark.
SX 6730 7872*

of the Lower Cator farms); extending as far as the corner of the meadow Churtais and in line as far as the Pikestann above the back of the hill at Holeshafde; and in line to the lands of Warin son of Joel extending as far as the Fennie Ford; and in the watercourse of Walebroke as far as the Horebrygge Ford; and in line as far as Didelake hafde and in line to the Pichedestann on Chokeard and in line to the Clampitte and beside the corndych of the land of William Giffard extending as far as the Wedeburne.

The first mentioned 'Pikedstone' stands prominently on the moor about 15 yards westward of the gateway

to Lower Cator Farm on the Bellever road at SX 685 760. The boundary then crosses the northern end of Corndon Down, where on the crest, there are two set stones apparently on the line leading down to Fenny Ford on the Wallabrook, an ancient crossing place between the old Babeny and Riddon enclosures, and where the holed stone from the former 'wood and stone' gate is still built into the wall. From Fenny Ford we proceed upstream to Horebrygge Ford at SX 674 767, another usage of the term 'hore' to signify a boundary, thence eastwards up the 'Deadlake' to Chokeard or Cokers Hill to Cator Green where the second 'piked' stone was erected a few years ago on what is thought to have been its original site – SX 680 767 –

after having been used as a gatepost at Middle Cator for several centuries, seven hundred years according to Hermon French (T.D.A. 1963). The site of Clampit is unknown but is possibly near Middle Cator. This boundary does not follow the course of reaves over Corndon, but crosses some.

Widecombe Town Manor

Widecombe Town Manor had an area of some 1575 acres with, in the late nineteenth century, 706 acres of this on the open moor or common, and the then manor house at Bag Park, anciently sited at North Hall. At Domesday it included Scobitor, mentioned in Domesday as 'Scobetor in la More'. A perambulation of the bounds of Widecombe Town Manor in the nineteenth century are entered in the Court Rolls as:

From Seven Lords Land to Hawk's Well, and from thence to Frenchanger Corner, thence to Halesbury, thence through Hedge Newtake along a reave and across the wall between Hedge Newtake and Bonehill Common to Clove Stone Rock, otherwise Saddle Clove Rock, from thence to Slade's Well, from Slade's Well to L. Corner, from thence to Pit Park's Bridge, from thence to a broad rock in Bag Parks, from thence to Long Knave Stone on Hameldon, from thence to Old House on Hameldon, from thence to Grey Wether's Stone, from thence to Hameldon Beacon, from thence to Stoneslade Tor, from thence to Herring's Knock, from thence to a Blue Stone at the corner of Kingshead, from thence to Two Crosses (these cut into the turf), from Two Crosses to Southcombe Well, from thence including Southcombe Estate, to Hennafoot Stone to the north part of

Rugglestone Rock, from thence to Shovelstone Rock, from thence to the north point of Top Tor and from thence to Seven Lords Lands.

'Herrings Knock' will be more familiar to walkers as 'Aaron's Knock', the name applied to this stone by Crossing in his *Guide*. There he says little about it but in another of his works, *Folk Rhymes of Devon*, he tells us about a couplet that was said to have been repeated each time the bounds of both the Manors of Widecombe Town and the adjoining Jordan were beaten:

Aaron's Knock
Made this chock

Crossing says this is a reference to the gash or cleft, said in folklore to have been made by Aaron's staff in the top of the natural stone in question. It is situated about 20 yards to the west of Kingshead Tor on the southern slope of Hameldon at SX 7985 7815. Speculating as to the origin of the name, Crossing refers to the possibility of it being derivated from 'Heron's Cnoc', the hill of the herons. Here we are getting closer to the version of the name entered in the Court Rolls of Widecombe Town Manor, 'Herring's Knock', and one can well see how, through the passage of time, one word can be transmuted into something of similar sound but having a completely different meaning. The old

Fig. 24 Aaron's, or Herring's, Knock.

The Blue Stone, SX 7075 7760.

English 'knoc' also means 'wether' or sheep, and as we shall see, 'Herring's Knock' continues to be recorded as the name applied to this boundary marker. Thus how can Crossing substantiate his jingle?

The Blue Stone is only a few yards from the west corner of the Kingshead Farm enclosures at SX 7075 7760. It is a rough boulder of coarse red granite with intrusions of tourmaline giving it a greyish blue appearance. At 'Two Crosses in Turf', SX 7080 7622, there is now a plain granite boundstone, on the crest of the down above Southcombe Lane. Of which more anon.

A report in a local newspaper described the Beating of the Bounds of Widecombe Town Manor that took place on 21 June 1934, where it is recorded that the Manor was then held by Alexander Radcliffe. It said:

The custom of beating the Bounds is a strenuous undertaking conducted every five years, the route lying over the highest ground in Widecombe and covering a course of about 16 miles. A portion of the property at one time in the hands of the Somerset family, and a number of the stones which form the boundary are marked with the initial 'S' and the year 1854.

TWO ROUTES

Commoners and others assembled in force in the morning and split into two parties. One took a route through Ruggleston out over Widecombe Hill, Hedgebarton Reeve to Clove Stone Rock, over Chinkwell, past Slades Well and Ell Corner down to Bagpark. The second party passed through Southcoombe to Two Crosses, Herring's Knock, to Hamildon Beacon, which is 1760 feet above the sea, on to Old House, Long Knave, Broadstow, Pitts Bridge, and back to Bagpark. Here the two parties merged, and adjoined to the Old Inn for a convivial lunch, where the felicitations of the beaters were extended to Mr and Mrs Radcliffe.

The reference to stones marked 'S' is only partly accurate, for they all bear the letters 'DS' of the Duke of Somerset, and refer to the bounds of Natsworthy Manor, in part conterminous with those of Widecombe Town. It is interesting to note that this account also gives the name 'Herring's Knock' in preference to Crossing's 'Aaron's Knock'. From 'Two Crosses' the boundary of Widecombe Town Manor adjoins that of Dunstone with Blackslade as far as Seven Lords Land cairn. The Hennafoot Stone is near Venton Bridge but in private land, and access to the Rugglestone is only possible from the east through the bog, a good place for plants. Rugglestone Rock is in reality a small tor, the top of the northern section of which used to be a logan stone which is said to have been 'logable' with the aid of the church key, but is now firmly set. The logan stone was computed to weight 110 tons by the Rev. J.H. Mason, vicar between the years 1816 and 1860. The Shovel Stone is directly up hill from the Rugglestone, at a point just east of the south-east corner of the Southway enclosures. Standing on top of this small outcrop, it is possible to see the next boundary point, the northern tip of Top Tor.

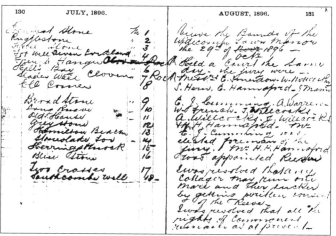

Fig. 25 Hannaford Diary, Widecombe Town Bounds, October 1806.

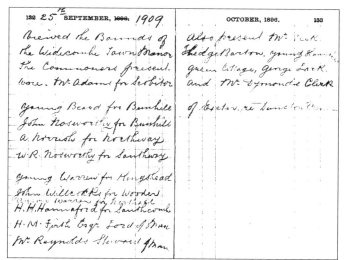

Fig. 26 Hannaford Diary, Widecombe Town Bounds, September 1909.

A page from the Diary of Herbert Henry Hannaford of Southcombe (Fig. 25) recording the Beating of the Bounds of Widecombe Town Manor on 29 October 1896 reads:

No.1 Henfoot Stone: No.2 Rugglestone: No.3 Shovel Stone: No.4 Fox Well, on the 1841 Tithe map 'Ox Well' (more generally known as Hawks Well – Ox and Fox being vernacular pronunciations), with Seven Lord land added as an afterthought – an intermediate point, Top Tor is not mentioned: No.5 French Hanger – Cloven Rock inserted erroneously, and deleted: No.6 Hill's Bay:* No.7 Slades Well – Cloven Rock added after No.6 in correct sequence: No.8 Ell Corner: No.9 Broad Stone: No.10 Long Knave: No.11 Old House: No.12 Grey Stone: No.13 Hamilton Beacon: No.14 Stoneslade Tor: No.15 Herrings Knock (not Aarons Knock as recorded by Crossing): No.16 Blue Stone: No.17 Two Crosses: No.18 Southcombe Well.

(*No.6 'Hill's Bay' – Halesbury – Harefoot? See Ilsington 1566 Bounds.)

Another page from the Diary of Herbert Henry Hannaford (Fig. 26) recording those present at the Beating of the Bounds of Widecombe Town Manor on 25 September, 1909 reads:

Viewed the Bounds of the Widecombe Town Manor. The commoners present were Mr Adams for Scobitor, Young Beard for Bunhill, John Nosworthy for Bunhill, A. Norish for Northway, W.R. Nosworthy for Southway, Young Warren for Kingshead, John Willcocks for Wooder,

Aaron Warren for Northall, H.H. Hannaford for Southcombe, H.M. Firth Esq. Lord of Manor, Mr Reynolds Steward of the Manor. Also present Mr Peck, Hedge Barton; Young Hannaford, Green Cottage; George Lark and Mr Dymonds, Clerk of Exeter, re Dunston Manor.

Natsworthy Manor

In the western side of Widecombe, the Widecombe Town manorial boundary abuts on to that of Natsworthy Manor, formerly spelt Notsworthy and Noteswrde (Domesday). In the seventeenth century it belonged to the Fords of Bagtor, who also had property at Ashburton and Chagford, but which was disposed of by them in 1684 as a marriage settlement on one of their daughters. In 1817 Natsworthy was bought by George Templer of Stover (Dymond), but by 1829 he was in financial trouble and had to sell it to the 11th Duke of Somerset, Edward Adolphus Seymour, together with the Haytor tramway and quarries which he had leased from the Duke, Seymour then owning the manors of Ilsington and Natsworthy. During 1853–54 the Duke marked the bounds of both these manors.

The Natsworthy Manor bound extends eastwards from where it crosses the Hedge Barton newtake wall, here contiguous with that of Widecombe Town Manor, the first marker is not mentioned in the records but is a natural rock ten yards west of the wall. It is one of two or possibly three in this immediate area, the second being Clove Stone or Saddle Clove Rock at SX 7315 7833, mentioned in nineteenth-century records, this having split along a natural fault horizontally, of which the upper part has fallen in an inverted position. The top of the lower earthfast section is inscribed DS/1854. Ordnance Survey six inch maps show 'Stones' in the plural, and this probably applies to these two stones only, but on my copy there appears to be another small dot making a triangle. No other inscribed stone could be found. We go westward next over the col under Chinkwell Tor to Slade's Well, a natural spring at SX 7283 7840, and a site of another of the Duke's own shaped and inscribed boundstones.

On again westwards downhill now to the wall enclosing a copse to the 'L Stone' or 'Ell Stone', another of the Duke's stones, inscribed 'L Corner' at SX 725 784, the field in which the trees are planted being called Ell Field. The boundary of both Natsworthy and Widecombe Town Manors now crosses the Natsworthy road to Pittpark where the bridge over the East Webburn is adjudged to be on the bounds, thence to 'a broad rock in Bag Park'. This is actually just outside the Bag Park enclosures at SX 7187 7850, more or less at ground level and approximately 9ft by 6ft, inscribed DS/1854 on its top surface. We now have a very steep climb to Long Knave at SX 7175 7860, a rough set stone simply inscribed 'DS' on its eastern side. Climbing yet again we reach the inscribed Duke's stone 'Old House' at SX 7145 7865, sited within the ring of a ruined cairn, referred to in 1566 records as 'Vome Borough', 'Vomeburrow' in 1659, within the mound of which there are the remains of a shepherd's shelter.

Changing direction slightly, we now proceed north of west to the Grey Wethers Stone, formerly 'Greystone' – 'to the Grey Stone' was a term used in Saxon charters and said to be a generic term for a stone of importance used as a boundary mark. The Hameldon 'Grey

Natsworthy Manor: Near the Clove Stone. OS 7318 7835

Clove Stone. SX 7315 7833

Right: *Fig. 27 Map showing Clove Stone and two possible other B.S.s.*

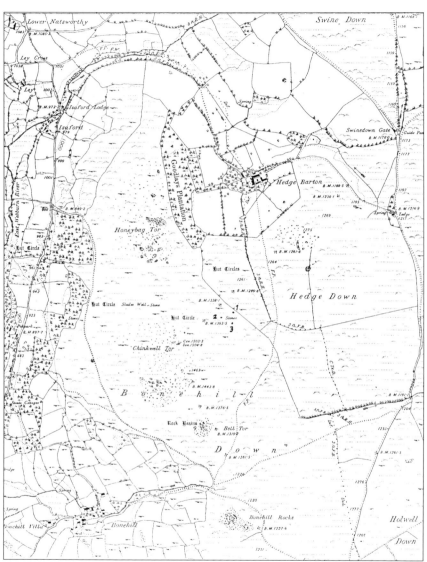

Grey Wethers Stone, formerly The Grey Stone. SX 7130 7855

Gray Weather. SX 7070 8030   *Pit. SX 7210 8017*

Wethers Stone' is situated at SX 7177 7890, a large natural boulder inscribed 'DS/1854' on its east-facing side, near Coal Mires.   Next we come to Hameldon Beacon where there is yet another of the Duke's stones, inscribed 'Hamilton Beacon', at the junction of the bounds of Natsworthy, Widecombe Town and Blackaton, formerly 'Fire Beacon' in 1566 and 'Fire Barrow' in 1659.

We now bear north along the ridge of Hameldon to 'Two Burrows', followed by 'Single Burrow' and 'Broad Burrow', all cairns on which the Duke erected his named stones, and all on the Widecombe Parish Boundary. Proceeding along the track, we find the mutilated remains of Hameldon Cross

*Hameldon Cross.
SX 7040 8010*

at SX 7040 8010, possibly one of the original markers of Natsworthy which the Duke marked 'HC/DS/1854' on its east-facing side.   North-east now to the head of East Webburn where there are two more of the Duke's stones, 'Gray Weather' at SX 7070 8030 and 'Blue Jug' at SX 7085 8038. Following the stream downwards, we veer from it as we reach the valley floor and proceed to 'Pit', the last of the boundstones on this part of the bounds at SX 7210 8017 beside the Natsworthy Road.

Dunstone
Dunstone is one of the smaller Widecombe Manors, to which the estate of Blackslade is attached, and has been as far back as records go – the remains of the old Blackslade longhouse on the open moor are still identifiable just west of Blackslade Ford. The bounds of the combined estates are as those of Jordan or Dewdon and Widecombe Town to the west and south, and as that of the Manor of Ilsington (and parish) to the east. The Dunstone entry in Domesday reads:

Ralf (de Pomeraie) has a manor called Dunestanetuna which Edwin held in the time of

King Edward and it paid geld for 1 virgate. This 1 plough can till. Roger holds it of Ralf. On it Ro(ger) has 3 villeins and 4 bordars who have ½ plough, also 5 beasts, 3 sheep, 3 acres of meadow and 30 acres of pasture. Worth 7 shillings and 6 pence a year, when he received it 30 pence. Along with this manor Ralf has a manor called Blackslade (Exon Domesday, spelt 'Blackeslach' in Exchequer version) which Edwit (Exchequer version 'Edwin') held in the time of King Edward and it paid geld for 1 virgate. This 1 plough can till. On it are 2 villeins and 3 bordars, also 2 acres of meadow. Worth 3 shillings a year.

Dunstone Manor: Two Crosses. SX 7075 7640

It is thought that the name 'Dunstone' might be derived from the large boulder on the green opposite the entrance to the Manor House, where the Manorial Courts were once held and the manorial rents paid, the stone having several small depressions in its upper surface which were filled with vinegar in time of pestilence so that monies placed therein would be cleansed and so, hopefully, contain the spread of the disease. The cross nearby was replaced only in recent years at the instigation of Miss M. Hamlyn, the family having been associated with Dunstone since the 1600s. The natural boundary markers on Dunstone's bounds are shown on the sketch map (Fig. 22).

'Two Crosses in Turf', already mentioned in respect of Widecombe Town Manor, is also on the bounds of Dunstone, and it was Robert Dymond who bought the property in 1869, who had proposed to erect either a double-headed cross or two separate crosses on that spot. Unfortunately neither plan came to pass, so that all we have today is the plain granite post.

At an interim meeting of Commoners held at Blackslade on 26 September 1903, 'The Reeve promised to have two Bondstones ready to place in the two crosses' (a Minute of the Court held at Blackslade on 30 September 1907 records that 'About 22 April 1907 the Reeve (Thomas Hern) and Mr John Mann, duly placed two Bondstones – one at Two Crosses and one between that and Wind Tor in accordance with the instructions of the Court of 1902').

Other natural points are Southcombe Well and those of the Manor of Widecombe Town as far as the Seven Lords Land cairn. A 'set' boundstone is sited near Hemsworthy

Gate, known today as Stittleford's Cross, formerly record-ed as Stentiford's Cross, both in the Ilsington Manorial records and on the Tithe map and Ordnance Survey old six inch editions. It is tucked into the corner of the wall on the Rippon Tor side of the road at SX 7420 7605, a stone of some 3ft in height and built into the base of the wall. It has the letters 'RM' inscribed upon it, above which there is a small inscribed cross.

In 1895 Richard Mallock read a paper which also bears repeating, with Dartmoor connections, including:

I remember my late brother saying that Jordan or Deandon in the parish of Widecombe-in-the-Moor had been attached to Cockington since before the Conquest. Our earliest Court Rolls, too, of nearly 500 years ago (July 20th 1437) contain records of the Dewdon Courts as well as of the Cockington Courts, and they continued to contain them down to the beginning of this century, when my grandfather (Rev. Roger) held courts there. Mr Dymond at once agreed that this Widecombe Manor was the hitherto unrecognised Deptone [the ancient 13–14th century hamlet now called 'Hut Holes' at SX703 757] of Domesday, and was strengthened in this belief by the occurrence of the common moorland names of French, Widecombe and Caunter at Dewdon Courts, and also by the fact that Clement Ellis, Clerk, is mentioned as attending a Dewdon Court in 1599, at which time it was known that the Rev. Clement Ellis was vicar of Widecombe. Why Cockington should have had this appendage on Dartmoor I cannot tell. I myself have thought it would suit my family arrangements to have a

Corner stones of the east wing of Cockington Court, Torquay

(Rawlin Mallock 1st 1648 – 91)

Stittleford or Stentiford Cross – SX 7420 7605

Fig. 28 'RM' 1673 at Cockington (top).
Fig. 29 'RM' on Stittleford's Cross.

farm on Dartmoor as an appendage to my farm here, and I have consequently held one there for 14 or 15 years. Since I took that farm I have come across letters and accounts of a predecessor of mine, Rawlyn Mallock, from which I learn that 140 or 150 years ago he occupied the farm on Dartmoor adjoining the one now in my possession.

Thus we learn that Dymond was probably the first person to realise that 'Dewdon', 'Depdona' and all the other variants of the old name referred to Jordan, and that besides owning the Manor of Dunstone from about 1748, the Mallock family also acquired another farm adjoining, in all likelihood, that of Blackslade. The boundary of Dunstone touched upon the eastern side of Wind Tor and there is in common with that of Jordan or Depdone. On the rock there are the initials 'M' and 'R' which may or may not have some relative significance. In the 1962 T.D.A. Mrs Linehan records no less than 23 variants of spelling of Depdone and Jordan.

The author was fortunate, some years ago now, to obtain a booklet published in January 1822 by Robert Dymond on *The Manor of Cockington*, who opens the text with the following:

Whilst recently turning over some ancient and very dusty documents relating to the numerous Devonshire manors once held by the Cary family, the writer lighted upon one which may be regarded as of local interest, seeing that it contains curious particulars of a manor now being rapidly absorbed by the growth of Torquay.

He quotes from various documents of the Cockington Manor Courts, and the following is an example of an entry dated 1 October 41 Elizabeth (1599) referring to 'Deoden':

To this Court came William French and John Bynney in the name of the whole tithing and, being sworn, present that William Bynney, William Widecombe and Peter Knolles remained outside the assize of the lady the Queen, the same are distrained [i.e. they had not taken the oath of allegiance]. And that the rents due to this day for common fines were 8d, and for census rent 6d, which is delivered to the Bailiff of Cockington'.

This booklet described in minute detail the types of cases that were capable of being brought before the Court Leet and Court Baron, together with all the duties that those bodies were required to perform, and which would have similarly applied to Jordan, there called Depdona, Deaudon or Deodon. One of the duties of the Jury of the Court Leet was stated to be to ascertain 'whether any encroachment be made by any neighbouring Lord upon the Lands of this Lordship, or by one tenant on another, or any ancient marks or Boundstones be removed.

In May and June 2000, Widecombe beat their bounds, starting at Newbridge, and on the third and final section on 10 June, joined the Spitchwick beaters at Ephraims Pinch, following the Wallabrook, West and Double Darts back to Newbridge. The participants all received a commemorative mug depicting the beaters and also Uncle Tom Cobley – a superb keepsake.

ILSINGTON

Ilsington is not one of the Parishes touching the Forest but, as the Duke of Somerset held both Natsworthy and Ilsington Manors, and his boundary stones continue from one to the other, it seemed sensible to have them described together here.

The Manor of Ilsington is within Teignbridge Hundred and dates from Saxon times. At Domesday, the Exeter version states that:

Radulf Paganus has a Manor called Ilestintona, which Merlesuen held on the day on which King Edward was alive and dead, and it rendered geld for two hides. These can be ploughed by twelve ploughs. Of these Radulf has in demesne half a hide and one plough, and the villeins have a hide and half and seven ploughs. There Radulf has twenty two villeins, and six bordars, and seven serfs and five live stock, and forty sheep and twenty three goats.

The Exchequer version says that:

Radulf himself holds Lestintone. In the time of King Edward it paid geld for two hides. There is land for twelve ploughs. In demesne is one plough, and seven serfs, and twenty-two villeins, and six bordars, with seven ploughs. There is one acre of meadow and two hundred and ten acres of wood. Pasture two leugas and eight furlongs in length and breadth. It is worth nine pounds.

In the thirteenth century Philip de Bello Monte, or Philip de Beaumont, who is believed to have died in the crusades of 1228–33, held 'Ilstinthon' from the Honour of Plympton. In Torquay Museum there is a 5ft x 2ft slab of Dartmoor granite with an incised outline of a cross, found in use as a footbridge over the Aller Vale Brook at Cadewell on the outskirts of Torquay. It is known to have been removed from Ilsington between the years 1884–94 and may have been removed from the nave of Ilsington Church during the restoration which took place at that time, and probably marked the burial of Philip's widow.

In 1566 Ilsington was one of the estates belonging to Lord Dynham, and a comprehensive survey says that there were then 'Lords of this Manor Mr Arundell and Mr Compton of the one half, and Mr George Fourd of the other half', and that 'Ther belongeth to this manor the wast called Idetordowne, whereupon certen Tenaunts Customary of this manor have Comen of Pasture, that is to wete, Hugh Dyggen, William Prouce, Anstyce Wyger, Isabell Brewsy, and Agnes Orchard, as belonginge to their Customary Tenements. William Dyggen free tenant of this Manor hath a comen of pasture upon the seid wast, and so hath no more of the free Tenaunts of this Manor.' Hugh Dyggen held three ferlings of land consisting of 130 acres at Smallcombe, and 'divers parcels of land lying together about the landscore next Idetordowne containing in all 60 acres'. Agnes Orchard held various parcels including 'Les Shotes lying in common about the bounds called Les Landscores', etc., references to the remains of the common field system.

The 'Waste' or Commons of Ilsington were described as extending from:

Prowces mede ende goinge Sowthward by a wale or an old dyche towardes Crondell unto the landes of George Fourde, esquier [the Fords of Bagtor], called Crostlondes, and from thence by the wale to the Sowth syde of Bynchen ball [Pinchaford Ball] turnynge over in the myddes of Smalamore into the West towardes Lether torre [Saddle Tor] almost, and from thence turnenge Northe goinge to a Rever being a bonde betweene the Manor of Ilstington and Omsworthye [Emsworthy, the 'rever' rising from a spring in the later mine workings] and from thence Northwardes to a Stone lyenge in Colmore [Haresfoot?] and thence going North to a Browke called Halwyll browke, and so downewardes by the seid Browke beneth Gretton Bridge [until the nineteenth century the Becka Brook was called the Holwell Brook], unto a greate stone standinge in the seid water called the Horse showe, being a bond betweene the Manor of Ilstyngton and the Manor of Manaton, and from thence Estwardes towardes the syde of Greate Torre unto a stone called the Horse showe [something seems amiss here – turning east from the Holwell/Becka Brook, the reference to Greate Torre must refer to Grea Tor, now called Smallacombe Rocks, and perhaps the repetition of 'Horse Showe' a mistake for 'Hole Rock'], and from thence Estwardes to a wale being a bond betwene the Manor Of Ilstington and the Manor of Bovy Tracy [a Bronze Age reave], and so from thence Estwardes by the North syde of Blaka ball [surely we should be on the south side of Black Hill] and from thence Estwardes to Owlacombe Borowe, and from thence Estwardes to the lane ende ledinge up from a Tenement of the Lords of this Manor called Myddell Cott.

The big question is, where did they place the head of the Holwell Brook? Crossing in his *Guide* takes this to be the water from the spring between Emsworthy Farm and the western edge of Ilsington parish, but the 1566 Survey does not name this stream and takes us further north before mention is made of it. If the stone in 'Colmore' is indeed Haresfoot, where there is a plain bondstone at SX 7390 7685, then the stream rising in Bonehill Mire which crosses the Hemsworthy Gate–Swallerton Gate road, may well be what they took to be its source – there is an inscribed stone where the road crosses the stream, in the south-west quadrant, which reads 'BI 1688' at SX 7392 7795. Donn's 1765 map shows the Hundred boundary passing very near to this point, so are the stone and stream perhaps on an old Manorial boundary, possibly of the sub manor of Holwell? Below this the stream falls into Snotters Bottom, so I am reliably informed, truly a wondrous name!

Bagtor Manor is the second manor recorded in the 1566 document, and was also recorded in Domesday as Bagethora. The Honour of Plympton in 1241 states it was held by William de Baggetorre, in 1285 by Thomas de Baggetorr and in 1346 by Geoffrey de Bagetor. The manor house is tucked away well below the small tor that gives it its name, and ruins of the old Bagtor Barton remain, with the present seventeenth-century house nearby. It was the home of the Ford family by the sixteenth century and the birthplace of the Elizabethan dramatist John Ford, born in 1586, who was baptised in Ilsington Church. A gravestone set into the floor of the church near the font bears the inscription: In Memory of Elizabeth Ford, died 1628, wife of Thomas Ford of Bagtor.

When the boundary marking that part of Haytor Down on which the Manor of Ilsington had rights of common and that part on which Bagtor Manor had similar rights was first fixed is not known to the author, but by the early part of the nineteenth century at least some of the boundary points recorded in the Minute Book of the

Courts Leet of Ilsington and Bagtor Manors were marked, inscribed with the respective letters 'I' and 'B', possibly dating from the seventeenth–eighteenth century, and some of which, marked on Boundary Rocks appear not to have been recorded in those records, but found by the author. All examples of the incised letter 'I' of no matter what date are of the same style, that is to say they all have serifs at top and bottom and the shaft of the letter is also crossed thus: 'I'. Some of these, on set boundstones, pillars some 4ft in height, are known to have been erected as the result of a survey in 1835, to strengthen the line of the bounds, but the curious thing is that though they were erected at about that time, and are the most conspicious markers, they are largely ignored in the manorial records and yet are the only boundary markers shown on the Ordnance Survey maps of the six-inch-to-the-mile scale and marked as 'Stone'. Perhaps the manorial records are but copies of much earlier documents – they are certainly not mentioned in the list of Boundstones on Haytor Down viewed by the Commoners on 9 October 1879, except for a couple of pencilled in additions, nor on the 1884 map of the bounds drawn by John Chudleigh of Newton Abbot in that year. Some of these 1835 boundary posts were surplus to requirements and were erected elsewhere other than on the Ilsington–Bagtor manorial boundary, which will be mentioned later.

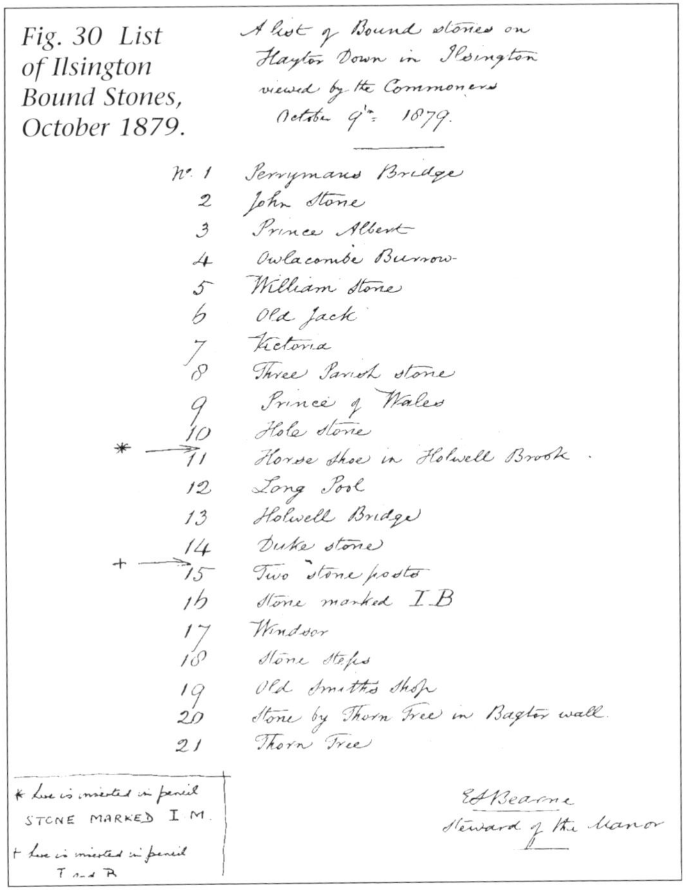

By 1853, when another perambulation took place, the 11th Duke of Somerset, who also held Natsworthy Manor in Widecombe Parish, was the Lord of the Manor of Ilsington. As the result of this survey of the bounds a number of additional boundstones were erected, or replacements made, a proper set stone substituted for a natural rock. These boundstones were generally of the same type, of 'tombstone' pattern, about 3ft in height,

Fig. 30 List of Ilsington Bound Stones, October 1879.

A list of Bound stones on Haytor Down in Ilsington viewed by the Commoners October 9th: 1879.

Nº 1 Perrymans Bridge
2 John Stone
3 Prince Albert
4 Owlacombe Burrow
5 William Stone
6 Old Jack
7 Victoria
8 Three Parish Stone
9 Prince of Wales
10 Hole Stone
11 Horse Shoe in Holwell Brook
12 Long Pool
13 Holwell Bridge
14 Duke Stone
15 Two stone posts
16 Stone marked I.B
17 Windsor
18 Stone steps
19 Old Smiths Shop
20 Stone by Thorn Tree in Bagtor wall
21 Thorn Tree

✻ Line is inserted in pencil
STONE MARKED I M.

✝ line is inserted in pencil
T and R

E.A.Bearne
Steward of the Manor

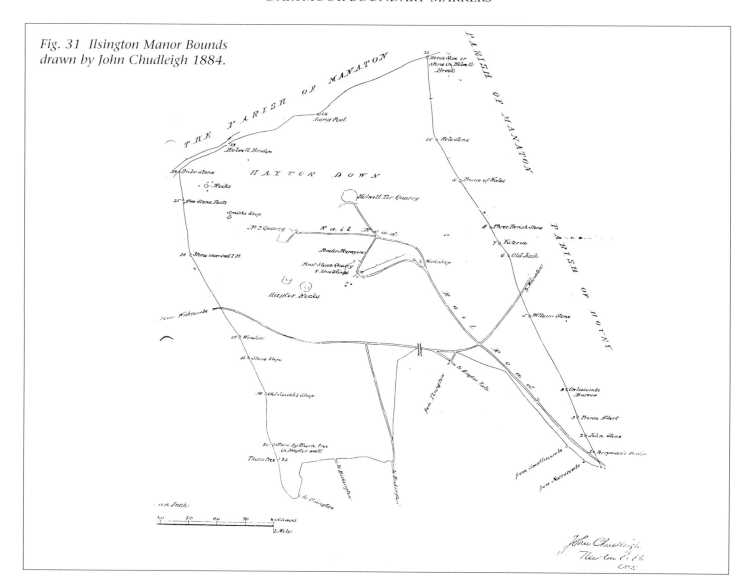

*Fig. 31 Ilsington Manor Bounds
drawn by John Chudleigh 1884.*

and with a rounded top, having the name of the stone inscribed on the face and 'DS/1853' on the reverse side. As he had had Hameldon Cross inscribed, he also had an inscription made on the odd old parish stone. The stones of this period were the last to be erected, and at the Court Leet held at Campion's Rock Hotel in October 1884, as recorded in the *Western Times*, 'The Chairman remarked on the use of these courts and the perambulations of the boundaries in preserving the common rights of the tenants from encroachments, which at one time were seriously threatened by the owners of the neighbouring manors. He also mentioned the fact that the boundary stones fixed in 1853 having now had an undisputed existence for over thirty years the rights to the common were now unassailable.'

We now make our own survey starting from the top end of Green Lane, taking each Boundary Marker in order, and as numbered on the accompanying maps (Figs. 32 and 33):

1 Perryman's Bridge, SX 7805 7740, on Ilsington/ Bovey Tracey parish bounds.

A small set stone having the inscription 'PB' on its eastern face. At the 1835 survey a Mr Hellier, representing Bovey, contested the position of this stone, being of the opinion that Islington were taking their bounds too far east. On the bend of the road between the cattle grid on the Bovey/Widecombe road and the top of Green Lane, part of the course of the Haytor Tramway was cut away to improve the bend. Here there used to be a clapper bridge taking the granite sets of the tramway over a leat. This leat was cut in 1834 from the Becka Brook, then known as the Holwell Tor Water, to Owlacombe Mine via the northern slopes of Black Hill. This boundstone is recorded by the name in 1835, 1853, 1879 and 1884, and at this period in time when the bridge was built, i.e. the 1830s, it is known that 'Perryman's' or 'Perriman's' were stonemasons tendering for bridges.

2 John Stone, SX 7795 7750, on the Ilsington/ Bovey Tracey parish bounds.

This is a natural, but set, boulder of slate stone – the area hereabouts is on the edge of the granite mass. The east face has the remains of an inscription which the Ordnance Survey Boundary Remark Book of 1882 states to be the letters 'JS', one below the other. However with the sun shining across

Fig. 32.

its face, other marks suggest that the name was once inscribed in full 'John/Stone'. Listed on all nineteenth century records.

3 Prince Albert, SX 7785 7755, on Ilsington/Bovey Tracey parish bounds.

This is one of the Duke of Somerset's 1853 stones inscribed 'Prince Albert' on its face and 'DS/1853' on the reverse side. At the 1853 perambulation, proceeding from the John Stone, they went 'from thence to a stone not named but which the Steward directed to be called Prince Albert; a new stone to be erected with the name and date thereon'. The original natural stone is still beside the Duke's 1853 boundstone. On 1879 and 1884 map.

4 Owlacombe Burrow, SX 7765 7765. On Ilsington/ Bovey Tracey parish bounds.

The 1835 mention, 'Owlicombe Burrow', must refer to either the outcrop itself or a natural stone on it, but it is not, in fact, a barrow as such though from some angles has the appearance of one. It is thought to be the 'Ruwa beorh' or rough barrow of the eleventh-century Saxon Peadington Landscore, defining the bounds of a huge ecclesiastical estate. In 1853 another of the Duke of Somerset's stones was erected, inscribed 'Owlaco/mbe/Burrow', with 'DS/1853' on reverse side. Also present on 1879 list, 1884 map and O.S. as 'BS'.

5 William Stone, SX 7710 7790, on Ilsington/Bovey Tracey parish bounds.

A rough, upright, set stone, it was recorded in 1835 when it must have had no inscription upon it, but in 1853 inscribed by the Duke of Somerset. But what was the inscription, for the Ordnance Survey call it 'Old William'. Now visible on the stone is the inscription 'Wm/Stone' on the face and '1853' on the reverse side, both near the top of the stone as we now see it. It is the only stone marked by the Duke not to have his 'DS' on it, so has the stone been fore-shortened at

some time since 1853, removing the word 'Old' and the 'DS'? It could possibly have been another boundary marker referred to in the Peadington Landscore as the 'Writelan stan', the inscribed or pointed stone. On all documents referred to and on Ordnance Survey maps marked 'BS'.

6 Old Jack, SX 7687 7810, on Ilsington/Bovey Tracey parish bounds.

Recorded in 1835, this must be a reference to a natural stone. In 1853 it says that this 'had been removed, but was ordered to be renewed'. There is now another Duke of Somerset stone there, inscribed in the usual fashion. On 1879 list and 1884 map, O.S. mark as 'BS'.

7 Victoria, SX 7660 7828, on Ilsington/Bovey Tracey parish bounds.

There was no stone here in 1835 and in 1853 a new stone was 'ordered to be erected and named Victoria', another Duke of Somerset stone with its inscription in an arc at the top, 'DS/1853' as usual on the reverse side. It is sited near some mining pits. On later records and marked as 'BS' by Ordnance Survey.

8 The Three Parish Stone, SX 7635 7827, at the meeting point of the parish bounds of Ilsington, Manaton and Bovey Tracey.

This is a shortish three-sided set boundstone bearing the relevant letters on the appropriate side, 'I', 'M' and

'B', in 1835 recorded as being 'where the Manor of Ilsington abuts on Bovey and Manaton Manors'. It is suggested that this site could also be where the Peadingtun Landscore 'Writelan stan' once stood, situated in and near the end of a reave. On all records, on Ordnance Survey as 'BS'.

9 Prince of Wales, SX 7600 7840, on Ilsington/Manaton parish bounds.

No stone was recorded here in 1835. In 1853 it was recorded that the distance between Three Parish Stone and the next one being 'considerable', it was agreed to have a new one half-way called Prince of Wales, another of the Duke of Somerset's type, now somewhat drunkenly leaning to one side. On all later records and marked 'BS' by Ordnance Survey.

10 Hole Stone, SX 7565 7850, on Ilsington/Manaton parish bounds.

Overlooking the Becka (Holwell Brook) valley, there is a natural outcrop now defined by the Ordnance Survey as Hole Rock and may be the point referred to in 1835 as Hole Stone, and quite possibly in 1853 also, but westward of the main rock pile there is a set boundstone (feather and tare), bearing the letters 'HS' on its eastern side, the letter 'S' being 'lazy', i.e. sloping similar to another in the area at Long Pool and erected circa 1853. Beside this boundstone is an unfinished millstone which has in its upper surface a small circular cavity from which the whole outcrop

may have got its name. Recorded in 1879 and 1884 and on Ordnanace Survey maps as 'BS'.

11 Un-named set Boundstone, SX 7550 7860, on Ilsington/Manaton parish bounds.

This boundstone bears the marks of feather and tare and has the letter 'M' on its north side and a crossed letter 'Ŧ' on the south side. It is one of the 'spare' Ilsington/Bagtor manorial stones cut in 1835, but is not referred to in either the 1835 or 1853 surveys or on the original list of boundstones of 1879, but has been added later in pencil on this latter as 'Stone marked 'ŦM'. It does not appear on the 1884 map but is recorded by the Ordnance Survey as 'BS'.

12 Horse Shoe Stone, SX 7525 7815, on the Ilsington/Manaton parish bounds.

Recorded in the 1566 Survey as a 'great stone standinge in the seid water (of Halwyll browke) called the Horse showe, beinge a bond betweene the manor of Ilstyngton and the Manor of Manaton'. This section of the Becka Brook, as it is now known, below Greator Bridge is one mass of huge boulders – one assumes that this ancient marker was just another, but prominent, boulder and in 1967, at the Beating of the Parish Bounds, they were unable to identify it, and presumed that it had been washed away in the severe floods of 4 August 1938. In 1879 it is referred to as 'Horse shoe in Holwell Brook' and on the 1884 maps as 'Horse Shoe or Stone in Holwell Brook'. The Ordnance Survey still shows it on their maps as 'BS', but it should, if still there, be more properly described as a boundary rock, or 'B. Rock'. (When beating the bounds in 1994, a boulder on the right bank of the brook appeared to have the shape of a horse-shoe on it. Could it be the 'missing' boundary rock?) From this point, up to which time we have been travelling in a steady north of west direction, we turn to follow the Holwell/Becka Brook upstream to:

13 Long Pool, SX 7492 7812, on the Ilsington /Manaton parish bounds.

At the 1853 perambulation of the bounds it was 'thought advisable to have a stone erected with the name Long Pool and date engraved thereon'. In the event a small set stone was erected, not of the usual Duke of Somerset type, inscribed 'LP/DS/DS', 'Ss' lazy and no date, the inscription being on the east face. It is on the right bank of the Becka. But why the repetition of the letters 'DS'? Recorded in 1879 and 1884 and marked 'BS' by the Ordnance Survey.

14 Holwell Bridge, SX 7465 7765, formerly over the Becka Brook below the ruins of Holwell Cottage.

It is not strictly a boundary stone or rock but is mentioned as a boundary point in1835, 1853, in the list of Boundary Stones of 1879 and is marked on the 1884 map. The right bank abutment is still fairly complete, but the rest of this old clapper has collapsed into the water. *Not marked* by the Ordnance Survey.

15 Gateway stop'd up which led to Holwell Farm, SX 7455 7730.

This is the 1835 reference to this boundary point. The gateway was in the old wall above the left bank of the brook and in 1853 it was agreed to erect a new stone to be called the Duke Stone.

16 The Duke Stone, SX 7460 7730, on the Ilsington /Manaton parish bounds.

As stated in No.15 it was agreed to set up this stone in 1853 'to the Memory of the present Lord-of-the Manor, the Most Noble Edward Adolphus the Duke of Somerset K.G.' This is now missing, believed washed away in the 1938 floods, but was sited on the right bank of the brook directly opposite the old gateway. The stone was one of those stated to have had its inscription repainted – 'several new stones were fixed in 1853 by order of the Duke, and these have their distinctive names – Old Jack, Victoria, Prince of Wales, Duke Stone, Prince Albert, etc. deeply cut into them, which are freshly painted at each perambulation to keep them conspicious' (*Western Times,* October 1884). A thorough search downstream from the point where it once stood has failed to reveal its resting place. It was recorded on the 1879 list of boundstones and on the 1884 map. It used to appear on the Ordnance Survey maps, and named even on the Blue Series 1:25 000 scale but all reference to it is now omitted.

On the death of F.H. (Harry) Starkey in 1989 money was raised for some sort of memorial. On the Dartmoor Preservation Association asking the author for suggestions, and as Harry lived in Ilsington, it seemed a good idea to have a new Duke Stone erected.

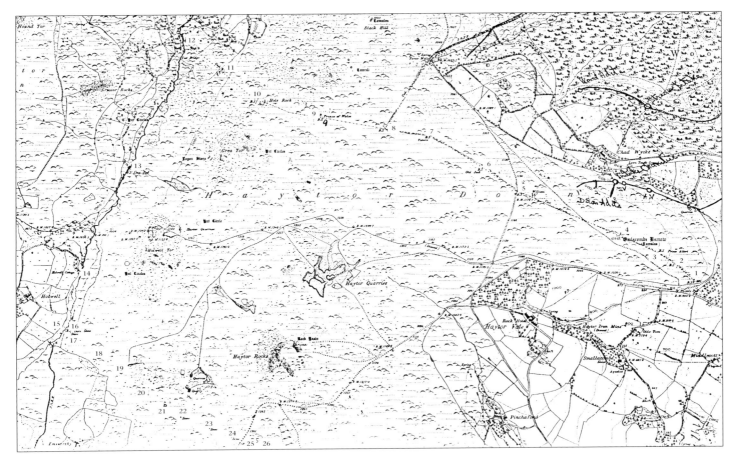

Fig. 32 Map of Haytor Down marking BSs.

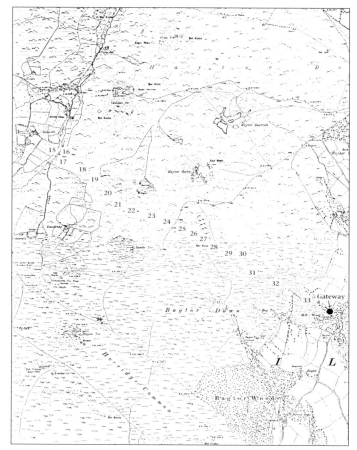

Fig. 33 Map of Haytor/Bagtor Downs marking BSs.

The stone was cut by the National Park Authority and erected on 11 May 1993 some yards away from the brook, the reverse side incorporating the letters 'F.H.S.' and which were re-cut by the Dartmoor National Park in 1998. Up to this point on the brook we have been on the bounds of Ilsington and Manaton Manors and Parishes. However the site of the Duke Stone was also where the bounds common to the Manors of Ilsington and Bagtor met, as are 17 to 33 below, dividing Haytor Down between them. We now turn south-east to:

17 Un-named Boundstone, SX 7464 7720.

This is one of the 1835 square-cut boundstones bearing the letters 'I' (on the north side) and 'B' (on the south side). About 4ft in height, as are most of the stones erected at this time, it fails to be recorded in any subsequent list of boundary markers, except this could be the one referred to in pencil after the entry of the Duke Stone on the 1879 Manorial list. It is, however, on the Ordnance Survey six inch and 1:10 000 scales marked as 'Stone'.

18 Two Stone Posts, SX 7475 7705.

In 1835 this point of reference was called 'A bar-stone post' but all later references are to 'Two Stone Posts'. The posts are at the entrance to a small Bronze Age enclosure that is associated with a reave system on the lower west slopes of Emsworthy Rocks above the mire. The more easterly of the pair has a small inscribed crossed letter 'I' on its northern side and a much larger letter 'B' on the southern side. Recorded in the manorial records referred to, but not shown on the Ordnance Survey six inch or 1:10 000 maps.

19 Boundary Rock, SX 7495 7695.

In the clitter under the south-west side of Emsworthy Rocks, this inscribed stone appears to be unrecorded elsewhere – the perambulators of 1835 must have been unaware of its existence. Has letter 'Ⅎ' on east side and 'B' on west side.

20 Boundary Rock, SX 7505 7690.

The same comments apply to this Boundary Rock as No.19, but this is more a boulder, with a rounded top, having the letter 'B' exposed on its west side; the letter 'Ⅎ' is hidden under vegetation but was observed by peeling back the overlay.

21 Irish, SX 7510 7685.

This is another Boundary Rock similarly marked to Nos 19 and 20 which was christened 'Irish' in 1835, and recorded as 'ⅎB Boundmark' in 1853 and 'Stone marked 'ⅎB' in 1879 and 1884. Nos 18 to 21 are about equally spaced out, whereas Nos 19 and 20 take some finding, No.21 stands out on the horizon between the upper end of Emsworthy Rocks and Saddle Tor when viewed from lower down the valley. Has a rounded top and is inscribed similarly to No.20. All three, Nos 19–21 must pre-date 1835. Not recorded by the Ordnance Survey.

22 Un-named set Boundstone, SX 7520 7682.

This is another of those cut in 1835. In 1835 it was decided to set up three of them 'in a straight line one to the other' between 'Irish' and the next old boundary marker south of the Bovey/Widecombe road. Only recorded by the Ordnance Survey as 'Stone'.

23 Un-named set Boundstone, SX 7530 7675.

This, the second of the three stones set up in 1835, bears the marks of feather and tare. It is sited on a north-east/south-west reave, inscribed with the usual 'Ⅎ' and 'B', again only recorded by the Ordnance Survey.

24 Un-named set Boundstone, SX 7540 7667.

The third 1835 stone, a short distance north of the Bovey/Widecombe road, inscribed 'Ⅎ' and 'B' as usual, and only recorded by the O.S.. We cross the Bovey/Widecombe road between Haytor and Saddle Tor to:

25 Black Rock or Windsor, SX 7557 7655.

'Black Rock' in 1835, and 'Windsor' at later dates, this is an earthfast rock that only breaks the surface of the turf by a few inches, and is now largely covered by vegetation, unmarked so far as anyone can see.

26 Dry Bridge, SX 7565 7647.

Referred to as Dry Bridge in 1835, in 1853 it becomes 'Stone Steps' or 'Dry Bridge' and later 'Stone Steps'. The point referred to is somewhat obscure, for in this immediate area there are certainly no bridge or stone steps. All that can be observed is a low reave bank near the southern end of which there is a slab of granite which might be said to resemble a stone from a small clapper, but it is in a direct line between Black Rock or Windsor and our next point of reference. It is unmarked, and on the next 1884 map is shown to be slightly nearer Black Rock than the next point, Blacksmith's Shop or the Old Smith's Shop.

27 Blacksmith's Shop, SX7575 7638,

'Blacksmith's Shop' in 1835, all later references to this point use the term 'Old Smith's Shop'. It is a considerable outcrop of rock almost at the head of the northern arm of the Sig above its right bank. It consists of two main masses, joined by a short row of set stones of Bronze or Iron Age, associated with reaves. The more northerly of the two masses has a few stones placed at the base, and here many years ago some charcoal was found which presumably gave rise to the name given to it. On the top of the more southerly outcrop are the letters 'Ⅎ' and 'B' incised. It is not recorded by the Ordnance Survey.

28 Boundary Rock, SX 7580 7635,

From the Old Smith's Shop we drop down to the Sig passing a hut circle to our right and what is thought might be a chambered tomb on our left. We cross the infant stream by a ford where even this small flow of water is divided into two channels, between which there is a piece of native rock, part covered by vegetation but exposing the letter 'B' – this marker is not recorded elsewhere. The letter 'Ⅎ' may well be inscribed, but under the heather etc.

29 'Ⅎ' and 'B' Set Stone, SX 7600 7630.

Maintaining our general south-easterly direction, we discover a leat channel associated with Bagtor Tin Mine, and observe that where this is crossed by a track to Bagtor there is a rather overgrown clapper bridge of six imposts. We continue up the leat towards the mine workings and see, within the leat channel, a setstone which bears the usual 'Ⅎ' to the east and 'B' to the west. It appears to be part of a sluice, and once again is unrecorded elsewhere. It seems that the leat used to take water from a shaft back to the Sig, where it would have drained into a reservoir. The area has been worked for tin for some considerable time, but this leat is probably of mid-nineteenth-century origin.

30 Set Boundstone, SX 7610 7615.

This is another of those set up in 1835 but unrecorded in the manorial records. This we find by continuing up the leat until we reach a shallow gert, beside which the stone is set, lettered 'Ⅎ' and 'B' in the usual fashion, and only remarked upon by the Ordnance Survey.

31 Set Boundstone, SX 7620 7610.

Yet another of the 1835 set boundstones, as No.30, this is situated near a large slab of granite lying on the side of a tinners' gully, but it is not our next point of reference for all that. Once again the set stone is only recorded by the Ordnance Survey.

32 Stone near Thorn Tree in Bagtor Wall, SX 7630 7600.

The 1835 Records direct us, from the Blacksmith's Shop, 'and thence in a straight line to a stone by a thorn tree near Bagtor Wall', and then follow 'the boundary of the old enclosures allowing a deer's leap on the Bagtor side to the Crownley Works'; in 1853 'to a Thorn Tree at Crownley Works'. The stone is a slab lying on the bank of the cornditch wall inscribed 'B' and 'I' on its upper surface, near a larger than average tree, but not a thorn tree.

33 Set Boundstone, SX 7668 7590.

This is the last of the stones erected in 1835 and is sited in tinners' waste near the head of the stroll giving access to the commons from Bagtor and Bagtor Mill, an ancient droveway. The stone is, once again, only recorded by the Ordnance Survey.

This completes the western boundary of Ilsington Manor and the eastern boundary of Bagtor Manor, but we still have to examine the western one of Bagtor. From 'the old stop'd up Gateway' on the Becka/Holwell Brook, No.15, the perambulators of 1835 and 1853 had examined this section by passing through the enclosed land belonging to Emsworthy Farm to:

34 Hawk's Well, SX 7405 7646, now on the Ilsington/Widecombe/ Manaton parish bounds.

This stone is another of the 1835 ones lettered 'I' and 'B'

and set just outside the wall above Hawk's Well, and is shown on the Ordnance Survey maps as 'BS' [in the vernacular recorded as 'Ox' and 'Fox' Well].

In 1853 they then went on to Hare's Foot, where 'the bound mark had been removed'. In 1821 the Commoners had presented that 'the Bond Mark known by the name Hare's Foot, which had lately been demolished, be renewed by placing another stone as a Bond Mark by the same name' – this must be the rough, plain stone at SX 739 768, approximately 3ft tall and freestanding, just inside the enclosure wall on the north side of the stream. There had obviously been a disagreement between Ilsington and Manaton, with the former trying to re-establish the old 1566 line to the Holwell Brook where it is crossed by the Hemsworthy Gate/ Swallerton Gate road. There at SX 7392 7795, on the west side of the road, is a natural boulder inscribed 'BI' 1688', the old boundary thence following the stream down to Greator Bridge and the former Horseshoe Stone.

35 Set Boundstone, SX 7410 7630.

South of Hawk's Well stone, and following the wall, we find yet another of the 1835 Ilsington/Bagtor manorial stones built into it, about half way between it and Seven Lords Land cairn – it has feather and tare marks. Unrecorded by both Manors and O.S.

We proceed to Hemsworthy Gate and Stittleford's Cross, where the Bagtor Bounds then follow the wall under the north side of Rippon Tor.

36 Boundary Rock, SX 7490 7565.

No marked stones were found in the wall to the north of Rippon Tor, but there is still at least one Boundary Rock inscribed with the letter 'B'. It is a rough stone naturally set to the north side of this wall. Between the end of the stone and the wall there is barely a space of six inches, and thus it must have been so inscribed before the wall was built, i.e. on the line of the ancient reave. Others may have existed and been used in the wall but no other inscriptions could be found. This boundary rock does not appear to be mentioned elsewhere.

This completes our examination of the Ilsington/ Bagtor manorial bounds but there are just two more stones to comment upon. One is another of the spare stones cut in 1835, but is inscribed with the crossed letter 'I' only. It is built into the northern wall of Holwell Lawn facing Greator Rocks at SX 744 784, and about 6ft tall. According to Mr Whitley of Holwell Farm, little work has been done on this wall since 1902, when Lord Justice Eve did extensive repair work to it, but of course the uncompleted bondstone may have been there long before that.

Another example has been found as far away as Red Post on the Newton Abbot—Totnes Road, in a stable yard, lettered 'I/B'.

Old as Bagtor Manor is, there is a gatepost on one of the ancient droveways (but now on private land at

SX 7673 7585) up to the commons from Bagtor which is a bit of a mystery. It has markings down the edge of one side in the manner of the Oghamic alphabet, and yet does not appear to be of that Irish origin.

At a Beating of the Bounds in 1853, permission to follow the ancient line of Ilsington's bounds south-eastwards from the 'A/1793' stone was refused by Squire Woodley of Halsanger, on the grounds that he had lately 'enclosed Rippon Tor for his freehold ground'.

Bagtor Ogham (?) Stone. On Private Land.

Between October 1967 and May 1969 the whole of Ilsington's parish bounds were beaten in four sectors for the first time in one hundred and fourteen years. They had not been beaten 'in recorded time', unless it was done in 1785 when £5. 7. 2d was paid by the Churchwardens, John Widger and Peter Mann, for 'twise vuing ye Bounds of ye parish'.

The first section to be beaten on 14 October 1967 started at Green Lane End along the line of the older parish boundstones and those dated 1853 to the Becka Brook, which they followed upstream, finishing this section at Hemsworthy Gate.

The second part took place on 11 May 1968 from Hemsworthy Gate, where Dick Wills was ceremoniously 'bumped' for photographers, but not on a boundstone. Stittleford's Cross was observed, then Grey Goose Nest, before crossing the road at Newhouse by the 'A/1793' Ashburton stone, over Halsanger and Horridge Commons to Mountsland, finishing this section at the foot of Rora Down.

The third part took place on 12 October starting at Ramshorn, where the Ilsington Commoners were accompanied by a representative of the adjoining parish of Bickington. They encountered the same trouble as the author in endeavouring to find the Ramshorn boundstones in the thick covering of bracken, only finding two of the three, including that near Rora Gate. Most of the remainder of the bounds are over enclosed land or lanes, but Dick Wills, the leader and recorder of the bounds, pointed out that they entered a field known as Bridgeland belonging to Coombe Farm 'which must have once been within the Manor of Ilsington for it carries common rights not on Ramshorn, as one would expect, but on Haytor Down'. This section via Telegraph Hill, Chipley, Seale Hayne and Gaverick Copse ended at Yellever Corner on the Exeter Cross to Stover Road.

The final section, on 3 May 1969, again started at Green Lane where the participants were called to order by a hunting horn, accompanied by television cameramen, and due to the lack of boundstones on this last section, they 'trudged through the bracken and heather a hundred yards or so in the direction of the Manaton road, to the Old Jack boundary stone where ten-year-old John Donaldson was bumped. Turning our backs on the moor, we made our way down Green Lane'. The route went through Brimley to Langaller, on to the main road on Bovey Straights along which is

Erected on Ilsington/Newton Abbot boundary. SX 8315 7520.

the boundary as far as Drum Bridges, where the party crossed the road by way of the central island much to the puzzlement of onlookers. The large scale O.S. map of 1938 shows the junction before the dual carriageway was constructed, and there were then two 'Guide Posts' at the junction, one on the north and another on the south side, and through which the boundary passed. With a flourish of the horn the mammoth perambulation was finally concluded.

In recent years the boundary has been changed slightly here, formerly going from north to south quadrants into Pitts Plantation, but now crossing the north to east quadrants, where a Newton Abbot boundary stone, inscribed 'NA/ILS' was erected a few years ago.

In 1994 the bounds were again beaten, at roughly monthly intervals, the first three sections being in an anti-clockwise direction, with the fourth section being clockwise, as in 1968.

Ilsington: 'IPC/100' Celebrating the Centenary of the foundation of Parish Councils. SX 804 733 752

The foundation of Parish Councils dates from 1894, 1994 seeing the celebration of the Centenary of this event. On Dartmoor, the parish of Peter Tavy celebration took the form of beating their bounds, in spite of having beaten them only a couple of years earlier. Ilsington went one better by not only beating their very extensive boundary in four stages, but also erecting a new boundstone to celebrate this event, calling it the Centenary Stone. The stone itself was donated by Dick Wills of Narracombe Farm, a longstanding member of the Parish Council, which bears the inscription 'IPC' and the figure '100'. It was erected on 3 December 1994 beside the old A38 at SX 804 733 near the Welcome Stranger public house on the bounds of Ilsington and Bickington Parishes. The letters and figures are within a recessed panel.

BUCKLAND-IN-THE-MOOR

Buckland-in-the-Moor is another manor of early origins, dating from Saxon times. The name perhaps derives from the fact that it is included within the bounds of lands ecclesiastically held under the Bishop of Crediton in, and possibly before, the eleventh century. In 1066 it was held by the Saxons Alric and Ailsi but at Domesday a Nicholas Arbalisterius was in

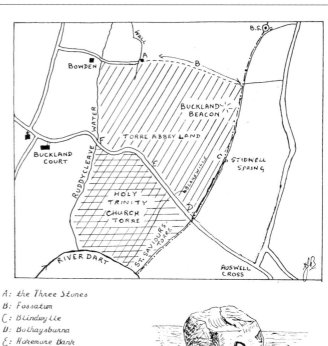

A: the Three Stones
B: Fossatum
C: Blindwylle
D: Bothaysburna
E: Hakemore Bank
F: Colreforde

Right: Longstone (1543 and 1704)
(Crooked Stone (1613)
Bond Stone (1837)

SX 7378 7498

Fig. 34 *Sketch of Torre Abbey grant to Buckland. The Longstone (inset).*

possession, and held by a soldier, Roger, who took his name from the manor, Roger de Bokelonde. The de Bokelondes gave generously to the Canons of Torre Abbey, Torquay, a Premonstratensian Order, founded by William Briwere in 1196, and to the parish church at Torre, charters, undated but from the period 1200 to 1250, being extant.

Charter No.80 records a gift in perpetual arms for his own soul and that of Alice, his wife, of Woodland, glebe and open moorland defined as extending from 'Colreforda' on the Buckland road up the Millbrook or Ruddycleave Water, to a point just below Bowden Farm, thence to 'Three Rocks' at 'Mahimorhilhead', these rocks still being in place just outside the moor, or Lidgate, now called Ripman's Gate, at the end of Bowden's lane giving access to the open moor, thence via a 'Fossatum' or sunken way up to the crest of the hill and down the southern side, bordering Welstor Common to a Blind Well, Stidwell Spring, and thence south again to 'Bolshayburna', and then west along the Ashburton–Buckland road to the starting point, this completely encircling Buckland Beacon, and giving the Canons of Torre rights of grazing, etc. Other gifts to Torre included one to the Abbey church, dedicated to the Holy Trinity where the Millbrook or Ruddycleave Water was again the western boundary down to the Dart, the eastern bounds being from Hokemore Bank and down the Blakewille Stream, rising from a spring of that name just north of the Ashburton–Buckland road. Yet another smaller gift was to the Parish Church of Torre, St Saviour's, this extending from the Blakeswille Stream eastwards as far as the Manor/Parish bounds where the Buckland estates adjoined those of the Bishop of Exeter, as Lord of the Manor of Ashburton, and still on the parish boundary line.

Other gifts were also made to the Canons of Torre, Charter No.76 offering Scobetorre 'in perpetual arms' by a later Roger de Bokelonde, land which his grandfather, William, gave to the Canons with his body, giving grazing rights throughout his land at Buckland and 'husbote and hailbote' in his woods at Hokemore, binding himself to a penalty of $1/2$ Mark (6/8d) if the rights were infringed. Scobitor was then two small holdings of a ferling each, and this gift refers to one only – the two old houses are now joined together as a single dwelling and within the parish of Widecombe. Charter No.79 confirms that a ferling of land at Scobitor was given to the Canons by one Girard de Spineto, which William bequested to them 'with his body'.

Charter No.77 records another gift from William de Bokelonde of the whole of 'Radyclyve', Ruddycleave, circa 1200, which on the dissolution of the Abbey in 1539 became the property of the parish of Buckland, the ford over the Ruddycleave Water being called 'Judelisforde'.

In 1578 the Manor of Buckland-in-the-Moor was sold by Thomas Carewe to Ralph Woodley of Halsanger, who then sold it to the Bastards of Kitley in 1614, which family we have to thank for a fine series of perambulations describing their bounds between that date and 1837, erecting a series of boundstones on a number of former cairns or barrows in that year on the Buckland/Ashburton boundary lines. These were erected by Edmund Pollexfen Bastard, who died in the following year, which were inscribed 'EPB/1837' on one face and the initials for Ashburton and Buckland on the east and west-facing sides. Amongst these there is one stranger, a stone post inscribed 'PW/1837' on its east-facing side. This pertains to Philip Woodley which family, whilst selling Buckland Manor to the Bastards in 1614, retained the neighbouring Manor of Halsanger, holding this from 1585 until 1925. Prior to 1547 Halshanger had formed part of the lands of the Chantry Chapel of St Lawrence, Ashburton, at which date it was suppressed and their former lands bought by local men. The 'PW' boundstone mentioned above is shown on the modern O.S. maps as it is on a parish boundary, but another only appears on larger scale maps since it is only on a manorial boundary at SX 7435 7380.

Of this post-Dissolution period the West Devon Record Office holds documents recording presentements and surveys for the years 1593, in which year Ralph Woodley died, 1613, 1683, 1698, 1709, 1771 and 1837, all defining the eastern boundary line of Buckland, in the case of 1837 also including those of the whole manor. The south/north line stretches from the river Dart at Lover's Leap to Blackslade Ford, and beyond, giving a variety of names to some points through the passage of time, though the line remained much the same. References to Boroughs or Burrows as late as 1837 are repetitions of former records before they were robbed to form walls and had the 1837 Bastard boundstones placed upon them in some instances, the building of the Welstor wall dating from the mid-eighteenth century.

We compare the various references to this boundary line, from the River Dart, going northwards, bearing in mind that the 1837 Survey went clockwise, whereas the others went anti-clockwise:

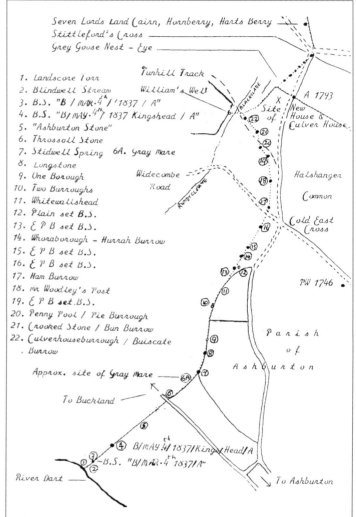

Fig. 35 *Sketch showing Buckland boundary stones.*

1 Landscore Torr, 'the foot of' (1613).

Left bank of the Dart at SX 7165 7220, was recorded as 'Lownstone or Long Score Tor' in 1593, becoming Launceston Torr in 1709 and Launson Torr Rock in 1837. On this particular point we have a far earlier reference, the thirteenth-century one in Torre Abbey Charter No.80 defining the bounds of the gift of land by de Bokelonde to St Saviour's Church, Torre 'the stream above Landscore... divides the boundaries of the Lord Bishop from those of Bokelonde', the Bishop of Exeter holding Ashburton Manor. The summit is now called Lover's Leap.

2 Blyndwell (1593).

This stream, up which the boundary line goes, is mentioned in some later records but is un-named – not to be confused with 'Blakewille' – See Deryck Seymour's *Torre Abbey*.

3 Boundstone at SX 7270 7225, 1837.

'Follow the said stream or the original bed of it, as far as the drive from Ausewell Marshes to Buckland, where stands a Bond stone marked 4th May 1837'. The inscription reads 'B/ MAY. 4th 1837/A on the three appropriate sides, being on both Buckland and Ashburton bounds, a Bastard stone of rectangular shape with cut-away corners at the top.

4 Boundstone at SX 7280 7230.

Situated in Muswell Woods, this point is recorded as 'Musowell' in 1613. The 1837 survey records 'a Bond stone marked K.H. and called King's Head'. The Ordnance Survey 1881 Boundary Report Book says 'marked Kingshead May 4th 1837 A B', it is actually inscribed:

MAY 4
B/1837/A
KINGS
HEAD

on the three appropriate sides, and does not have such pronounced cut-away corners at the top as the previous stone.

5 Ashburton Stone (1613).

'A Great bond stone called Ashburton Stone', about 150 yards below the Blyndwell Spring, on the line of an ancient wall, there is a roughly hewn stone approximately 6ft x 2ft x 1½ft, quite unlike the rest of the walling, which might well be the stone referred to – see reference to 'one other long stone' below.

6 The Throsholl Stone, at SX 7334 7266.

In the 1613 document we are instructed to go 'to one other long stone standing adjoining upon the highway that leads from the towne of Ashburton towards Buckland'. This has been the Roswolstone in 1593, and in 1709 became the Drosell Stone. Throstle is the

Anglo-Saxon for a song-thrush from the Germanic Drossell, so that it would appear that this stone was a point from which cock birds may have declared their territory. The 1837 Bastard survey gives a very clear description of its situation, though by an entirely different name, saying 'In the Road leading from Buckland village to Ashburton and opposite a Gate commonly called or known by the name of Awswell Gate and which said gate leads into the Plantation of Edmund Pollexfen Bastard Esq ... stands a Bond Stone called Ward to the Key Post which stone separates the Parishes of Buckland and Ashburton, and which said stone stands at the end of the Boundary Wall of Mr Smerdon which separates his land from that of E.P. Bastard'. The term 'Ward to the Key' suggests the locking side of the gateway. In 1683 it was Thrytle Stone, in 1698 Drossillstone; unfortunately it no longer exists.

6A Gray Mare.

From the Throssoll Stone all the sixteenth–seventeenth-century accounts take us north to Gray Mare; the eighteenth–nineteenth-century accounts also recording a reference to Stidwell, which clearly shows that Gray Mare was once to be found to the south of that spring. It is clear from all these accounts that the set upright stone near the Welstor enclosure wall just below Buckland Beacon, and which we have known as Gray Mare from William Crossing's reference in his *Guide*, is there misnamed, and is in fact the next boundary point going from south to north, a Longstone, described in 1613 as 'a long bondstone standing near the top of the hill'. The 1837 Survey, the only one to go from north to south, mentions nothing except the Welstor wall 'and thence to a well of water commonly called or known by the name Stidwell, thence to a Bond Mark or where a

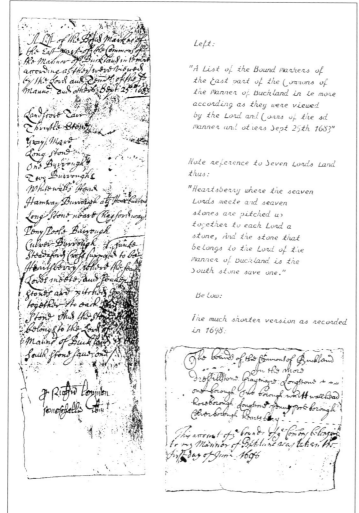

Fig. 36 List of Bound markers on Buckland Common.

Bond Mark formerly stood and known by the name of the old 'Gray Mare'. It is suggested that this, the true Gray Mare, disappeared during the construction of the Welstor wall.

7 Stidwell Spring, SX 7350 7294.

'Blind Well' circa 1200; our next reference is in 1771 when it is described as a 'well to be divided', that is between the commons of Ashburton and Buckland, the 1771 description of the bounds at the court case which took place in that year clearly shows that nothing has been done about it. It stated that 'the said Tozer and Abraham shall at their own expense fix a Moorstone Trough to be Eighteen inches deep and which trough is to be fixed in or near the well and to contain at least thirty gallons and we order it to be so fixed that one half of the trough shall be on the Buckland side of the wall for the benefit of the said William Bastard and his tenants...'

8 The Longstone, SX 7355 7303.

This is the plain standing stone referred to in 6A, incorrectly known as the Gray Mare in recent times.

9 One Borough (1709), Hems Burrow (1837).

As we climb to the crest of the rise from the Longstone, called Greenway Head in 1593 and Green Hill in 1613, the boundary line follows the Welstor wall, and this was built on the line of a series of Bronze Age burial cairns – can we assume that the most southerly of these was One Borough? (SX 7357 7324). The Buckland Archaeological Checklist records the findings of Quinnell and Turner and say that this was cut by the wall.

10 Wolstorrburrough (1593); Two Burroughs (1613); similarly in 1709 and 1771.

Quinnell and Turner record 'the arc of a stone kerb – cut into by two cairns (Buckland Checklist) – at SX 7358 7352.

11 Whitewallshead.

'From Wolstor Burrough to Whitewallshead' (1721 copy of the 1593 description); 'thence to an Great Heap of Stones called Whitewalls Head' (1709 and 1771) – just outside the Welstor wall there are the remains of a large cairn. Does the term 'Whitewalls' refer to the parallel reaves running up to the Buckland ridge from the two enclosed settlements nearer the Ruddycleave Water?

12 A Plain small set boundstone at SX 7368 7378.

This stone is just outside the northern extremity of the Welstor enclosure. The 1837 viewing of the bounds, going from north to south, says 'from Hurrah Burrow (see No.14) in a southerly direction to a stone by the fence wall which separates Buckland from Welstor, where there was a gate, thence follow the wall (the wall being in the parish of Ashburton)'. It obviously pre-dates the erection of the 1837 E.P.B. stones.

13 E.P.B. set boundstone at SX 7368 7377.

This is the most southerly of several set stones, Manorial stones erected by Edmund Pollexfen Bastard in 1837 subsequent to the 4th May survey of that year – they are not mentioned in that perambulation, where all points of reference are either to old stones or

'Burrows'. This example is not, as are others, set on the remains of a cairn or barrow. It is inscribed, as are most of the other similar stones, 'B' on its west-facing side, 'EPB/1837' on its south-facing side, and 'A' on its east-facing side. It is only a couple of feet from No.12.

14 Hore Burrough (1593), Worraborrough (1709), Hamburrough otherwise Whoraburrough (1771), Hurrah Burrow (1837).

All the different spellings derived from the original 'Hore' indicate an ancient boundary point, 'Hore' or 'Hoar' being a word often associated with such. Here we have another of the E.P.B. set boundstones set upon the remains of a cairn or barrow, recorded in the Parish Checklist as having a diameter of 16 metres. Its position at SX 7373 7390 is confirmed by the 1837 description of this part of the Boundary thus 'from thence [Ham Burrow] crossing the road from Newton to Widecombe [i.e. just west of Cold East Cross and going south] and over Ham Hill in a line nearly South West to Hurrah Burrow'. (N.B. a stone to be placed on Ham Hill which will be seen from Ham Burrow)! Obviously once fallen and re-erected, Bastard inscription facing east.

15 E.P.B. set stone at SX 7376 7392.

This is the only example without the date '1837' and appears to be on the remains of a small cairn. Is this the additional stone referred to in No.14?

16 E.P.B. set stone at SX 7391 7415.

This is possibly on the meagre remains of a cairn, inscribed in the normal way with '1837' date.

17 Ham Burrow, SX 7399 7428.

Here there are the remains of a cairn of some 20m diameter upon which is another E.P. Bastard set stone.

18 Mr Woodley's Post, SX 7395 7446.

The first mention appears to be 'Long Stone near Chagford Way' in 1698 when it would have been uninscribed. In 1837 'a long Moor stone now lying on the ground and marked 'PW 1746' separating Buckland from Ashburton, thence to Ham Burrow, from thence crossing the road from Newton to Widecombe'. The 'PW' stands for Peter Woodley of Halsanger Manor.

19 E.P.B. set boundstone at SX 7389 7473.

Not on a cairn. 'E.P.B.' north side, presumably re-erected.

20 Pennypowls Borrough (1721 copy of 1593), SX 7384 7498.

Penny Poole Burrough (1709), Penny Pole Borough (1771), Penny Pie Burrow

(1837). On the remains of this cairn or burrow there is now a parish boundstone, letter 'B' to the west and 'A' to the east, presumably of post 1837, nineteenth-century erection for there is no mention of it in the 1837 survey or earlier. 'A' and 'B' similar in style to those on 'E.P.B.' stones.

21 The Crooked Stone (1613), Bun Burrow (1837) at SX 7378 7498.

From the Gray Mare, the next point of reference in 1613 is the Crooked Stone, 'and thence to a fford called Rudarlay fford', i.e. Ruddycleave or Blackslade Ford. It is thought that the ancient parish set bound-stone is what is intended, which from a certain angle appears to have a twist to it. At this point the direction of the boundary line changes through 60°. It is on the remains of a cairn just north of the Tunhill Track and referred to in 1837 as 'thence to Bun Burrow where there is a Bond Stone'. It is inscribed with the letters 'B' and 'A', large elongated letters suggesting that it is of some considerable age. It is quite possible that it dates from the early years of the seventeenth century, just prior to the time that the Woodleys sold Buckland Manor to the Bastards, i.e. 1614, in spite of the fact that the later records all copy the earlier description of the bounds as given in 1593.

22 Culverhousburrough (1593).

Culver Burrough (1683), Colverborough (1696), Culver Burrough (1709) and 'which is adjoining or near to the wall built by Mr Woodley' (1791). Buiscate Burrow (1837) at SX 7370 7511. Also Ruddaclay Ford (1613), now known as Blackslade Ford. The barrow is now surmounted by an 1837 'E.P.B.' boundary stone.

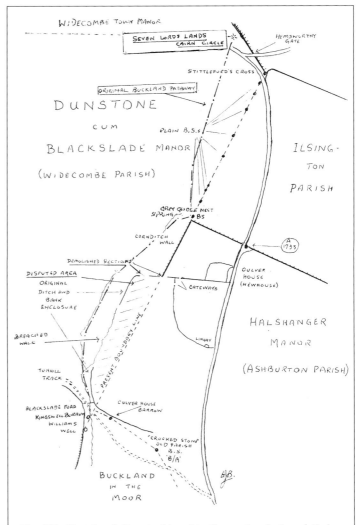

Fig. 37 Sketch of disputed land to Seven Lords Land Cairn.

111

Culverhouse Borough is on the bounds of Buckland and the ancient Manor of Halsanger in Ashburton parish, the original name indicating the fact that there was once a house or wayside inn long pre-dating Newhouse, perhaps on the same site. It must be remembered that the perambulation of 1837 not only viewed Buckland's bounds in their entirety, going in a clockwise direction, reaching 'Culverhouse Burrough', i.e. Biscate Burrow, via William's Well, but also that all other perambulations had only been concerned with Buckland's eastern boundary, viewing it from south to north.

The 1837 document only lists the points north of Culver Borough as a tailpiece, and it is plain that they only claimed a right of access through the Halsanger enclosed land to reach their object, Seven Lords Land Cairn. The relevant sections of the various descriptions of the Right of Way are as follows:

23 1583 (1721 copy): to Stoddy fford and there cometh in Hansanger and others which go to Horsditch where seven several Lordships meet.

1613: from Ruddaclay ford northwards on the water comes in another fford called Giles fford also Holsford also Stiddsonfford and from thence to a certain bond called Goose Eye and from thence northwards to certain bondstones standing round together called Hornberry near the highway which leads from Ashburton to Chagford all of which from Ruddaclay fford aforesaid to Hornberry aforesaid are the bond between the manor of Ashburton and the parish of Withecombe.

1683 Stoadaford Cross supposed to be sunke – Heartsberry where the seven Lords meete, and the seven stones are pitched up together to each Lord a Stone. And the Stone that belongs to the Lord of the Manor of Buckland is the South stone save one.

1698 Heartsbury only.

1709 from Culver Burrough – Harts Berry – Grey Goose Nest – Williams Well, in that order.

1837 'Bounds of the Halter Path claimed by the parish of Buckland to the Grey Goose Nest, and from the Grey Goose Nest to the Seven Lords Land. From Kingswell New Take Burrow up through new take common (the property of Mr Woodley) to a spring of water called Gray Goose Nest and from thence in a straight line to Seven Lords Land, being a Burrow of Stones, where the Parishes of Widdecombe, Ilsington and Ashburton meet'.

Ashburton certainly did not extend thus far in 1837, but may have done so until 1793. Culver House, a Woodley property, may have been established a couple of centuries earlier than 1593, on the then busy Ashburton–Chagford road. A point of far more interest is the fact that whilst the earlier records define the upper reaches and head mire of the Blackslade/Ruddycleave Water as being the then boundary line between Halsanger and Dunstone with Blackslade, along which the Lords of the Manor of Buckland were allowed to pass through their ancient rights, all later accounts from 1698 make no mention of the fords except that at Grey Goose Nest, which is outside the Woodley enclosures. Grey Goose Nest is the name now applied to the most southerly of a line of boundstones running from the spring of that name to the Mallock Stittleford's Cross, defining the extent of the Dunstone with Blackslade boundary. It seems unlikely that there was ever a cross at 'Stoadaford' though the name may have possibly given rise to the name Stentiford's Cross to the Mallock boundstone.

Once the references to fords over the Blackslade were omitted from subsequent perambulations it is not surprising that a straight line was taken between Culver Borough and Grey Goose Nest, originally just a spring, leading the Lords of the Manor of Buckland to think that old ditch and bank enclosures, upon which the Woodleys had erected a low stone wall, were infringing upon their ancient rights. In 1771 they took the Woodleys to court over the matter, winning their case, at one and the same time getting the Woodleys to breach their walls and establishing the present day straight-line boundary. The Woodleys protested against this judgment, rightfully in the opinion of the author, into the last century, but the straight-line boundary was then too well established. That this court case had gone against the Woodleys was not forgotten, being brought up again in the first decade of the last century by Mrs Woodley and her son, another Peter, but the arbitrary straight-line boundary was by then well established, and they got nowhere.

24 Hoartsberry (1683).

'Where the Seven Lords meete and stands stones so together to each Lord a stone and the stone that belongs to the Lord of the Manor of Buckland is the South Stone'. Besides using the cairn circle, each Lord had his own specific 'seat' – one can not get more conclusive than that!

Today we are accustomed to our parishes but before many of these were formed, the shires were subdivided into 'Hundreds' in late Saxon times, at the administrative centre of which the Hundred Courts were held adjudicating on matters beyond the powers of the individual manors.

The Kerswell Hundred, later to become the Heytor Hundred, was, as were several other Hundreds, divided into two sections, the administrative centre being in the larger part centred around Kingskerswell. It is known from a reference in the Cartulary of Torre Abbey that the Sworn Men of Kynges Carsuelle used to meet in the open, on the summit of Kyngesdone or Kingesdon at a height of 500 feet on a monthly basis according to Anglo-Saxon law to discuss business relating to their part of the Hundred. This was the meeting point of four parishes: Cockington, Torre, Kynges Carsuelle and Collaton (Shiphay) at SX 8785 6505 near Gallows Gate. The smaller portion was on Dartmoor, but in spite of its name did not include Haytor itself, this being within Teignbridge Hundred. The separate moorland section of Heytor Hundred comprised all the Widecombe Manors, Widecombe Town (earlier known as North Hall and thought to be the Wideacoma listed in Domesday), Natsworthy, Spitchwick, Dunstone with Blackslade, Blackaton Pipard and Dewdon or Jordan, plus Buckland in the Moor (a William de Bocland being one of the 'twelve Sworn Men of Haytorre Hundred' in 1274/75, enquiring into transfers of estates and encroachments). Dewdon/Jordan is listed at Domesday as part and parcel of Cockington, but seems to have been treated as a separate manor in some respects, in spite of references to it in the sixteenth-century Cockington records.

The Gallows Gate/Kingesdon site near the Torquay ring road–Marldon Lane junction had become quite overgrown and neglected over a time, but has been converted into a picnic cum viewpoint area. This, at a cost of £10 000, was opened to the public on 22 July 1994, when besides a plaque showing the

Old Cockington Gate, Gallow's Gate. SX 8790 6490

various points of the compass, another describing the historical importance of the area was worded as follows:

Gallows Gate Picnic Area

This site is where the Parishes of Marldon, St Marychurch, Cockington and Kingskerswell meet. The name probably derives from the practice of erecting gallows at Parish boundaries. This is said to be the place where the Ancient Hundred Court of Haytor was held.

The popular legend is that of a man who stole a sheep which he tried to carry away hanging by a rope over his back.

When climbing over the high gate the sheep carcass fell on one side and the robber on the other, with the result that the stolen property hanged the thief.

This picnic area was opened by the Worshipful the Mayor of Torbay, Councillor J.H. Nicholls on the 22nd July 1994.

A Torbay Centenary Committee project in Association with the Borough of Torbay and Devon County Council.

On clearing the site an old Cockington Manor gateway was found, together with an early twentieth-century Torquay Town Council boundstone, erected when Cockington became part of Torquay. Only certain manors had a right to erect a gallows, try a man and hang him if found guilty of a crime demanding his life. The fable of the sheep-stealer hanging himself occurs in many parts of the country.

ASHBURTON

Prior to the Tithe Commutation of the late 1830s early 1840s and the fixing of parish boundaries by the appointed Commissioners, there were many boundary disputes or anomalies, both Manorial and Parochial, and the moorland part of Ilsington, Ashburton and Manaton parishes appear to be no exception.

In 1566 we see that Lord Dynham, Lord of the Manor of Ilsington, claimed that his boundary extended northwards as far as the Halwell or Holwell Brook, now within the parish of Manaton, but the ancient bounds of the sub manor of Holwell are unknown. Matters are further complicated by the fact that Ashburton was given a market in 1310 or earlier and had had the status of a Borough from at least 1298, and as such was allowed to return members of Parliament, elected by all householders up until 1707, and after that date by freeholders having land or tenements within the Borough. The bounds of the Borough are hazy and unclear in respect of the limits, and on this subject in his Presidential Address to the Devonshire Association in 1924 J.S. Amery puts forward the suggestion that there were perhaps outlying settlements, separated from the rest of the Borough by commons or waste which were later enclosed, which were formerly accounted as parts of the Borough, but are now part of an adjoining parish. All that is known is that the Borough was larger than the town itself but smaller than the parish.

In 1710 it was resolved that the freeholders of the lands and tenements of Halsanger and Holwell, 'lying within the Borough of Ashburton and subject to a Burough rent' had the right to vote to appoint members of Parliament and Amery records that 'The Exeter Inn' was in the Manor of Holwell; can we take it that this is the former inn at Swine Down or Swallerton Gate, on the old Ashburton–Chagford track? On Halsanger we have remains of Newhouse, another inn, in earlier times known as Culver House. Later in 1761 it was declared that Halsanger Manor

was outside the Borough of Ashburton, though it was within the parish, 'except for a certain parcel of land', and the Tenement of Mountsland which is in Ilsington. The 'certain parcel of land' which was adjudged to be part of the Borough allowed one vote in respect of the appointment of a member of Parliament, and a similar privilege was accorded to Holwell, though Holwell now lies entirely outside the parish of Ashburton. All very confusing!

Dated boundstones are not common, the 'A/1793' stone which lies flat at the foot of the wall forming the boundary of Ashburton (Halsanger Common) and Ilsington certainly has an individual character. Another dated stone has been set up in Ashburton beside the old railway, now a public right of way and known as Bulliver Way after the name of the engine used on that line. This stone is just below Chuley Bridge, where the Ashburton/Staverton parish bounds join and follow the River Ashburn, and is inscribed 'A/1977'.

Ashburton: Grey Goose Nest.
SX 7399 7580

Rock inscribed A 1793.
SX 7410 7575

1977 near Chuley Bridge on the Ashburton/Staverton Bounds.

In 1987 the Bounds of Ashburton were to be beaten, but unfortunately the following is taken from the 'recce sheet' and there is no information on the actual proceedings. It was to start at Cold East Cross and go on a clockwise route, following the Buckland in the Moor/Ashburton boundary stones to Blackslade Ford, then keeping the Mire on their left, went upstream to the stone called Grey Goose Nest. Across to the road and the 'A/1793' rock, then outside the wall of Halsanger Common, crossing the headwaters of the River Ashburn, continuing on the east side of Langworthy Brook and following it down to Langworthy Bridge. Next the right bank of the Brook into Halsanger Wood, to join the road on the north side of Owlacombe Bridge. The boundary follows the river, then the River Lemon, and zig zags in a southerly direction to the new A38 dual carriageway to the boundary near Bickington Cross. There then comes a stretch through fields (Gale Road, Combe Cross to Whistley Hill) – here the road was to be taken back to Whistley Hill Cross. South down the road to a gate, to a track, which was to be followed, then the Chuley Brook to join the road at Chuley Hill, and down to Chuley Bridge.

LUSTLEIGH

The age old custom of 'Beating the Bounds' languished for many years but is once again being performed at regular intervals by most parishes, but quite often only a portion of the bounds at any one time, with youngsters being 'bumped', ducked in a stream, or rewarded as the custom requires, to impress on young memories the exact boundary, a hangover from the days when most people were illiterate. Even now, with many bounds some hundreds of years old, there are changes and new boundstones erected to strengthen the marking of old boundaries. In 1975 Lustleigh erected a stone that they took the care to date at SX 7490 8470 and more recently three more on their bounds with Bovey Tracey at Slade Cross (SX 799 812), at East Wrey on their bounds with Moretonhampstead (SX 780 830) and on their boundary with Manaton on Lower Terrace where the boundstone is set within a shallow miners' gully at SX 7685 7970. In addition, in May 1980 Lustleigh also set up, most unusually, a wooden boundary post at the point where the three parishes of Lustleigh, Manaton and Bovey Tracey meet on the western edge of Yarner Woods (SX 770 789) which has the relevant letters cut upon it together with a small plaque reading 'Lustleigh/Beating of the Bounds/May 1980'.

A startling example of how some parishes allowed their beatings of the bounds to lapse also relates to Lustleigh; a sixtieth-anniversary reproduction of the Torbay *Herald Express* dated July 1925 carrying an article headed 'Ancient Custom', which went on to say that after remaining in abeyance for a period of eighty years, the southern portion of their bounds were beaten, the northern section having been beaten the previous year.

HOLNE

William the Conqueror gave many manors to those who had given their services, and he gave Holne to William de Falaise, Domesday recording:

William has a manor called Holle which Alwin held on the day on which King Edward was alive and dead, and it rendered geld for one hide and a half. This can be ploughed by twelve ploughs. Of this William has in demesne half a hide and one plough, and the villeins have one hide and 5 ploughs. There William has thirteen villeins and seven bordars, and eight serfs, and one packhorse, and six head of cattle, and six swine, and fifty-two sheep,and one wood one leuga in length and the same in breadth, and pasture one leuga in length and breadth. This is worth sixty shillings, and it was worth as much when William received it.

Alwin, Alwyn or Aelfwine was the Abbot of Buckfast from 1040 and still living in 1066. This manor did not include the Stoke farms in the northern part of the parish, North Holne or Estocha. By the thirteenth century (Testa de Nevil) it is recorded that Falco de Breaute held the Manor of Dertintun (Dartington) by assignment of the King and 'the same also holds the Manor of Hunne by the King's assignment, and it is worth four pounds', i.e. North Holne. It later passed into the hands of the Bourchier family, the Earls of Bath, until 1654, thence through marriage to the Wreys and later to the Hon. Richard Maitland Westenna Dawson. Since the Second World War, Holne has only beaten its moorland bounds three times, in 1951, in 1977 and in 1990, not, as is the usual practice, at seven-year intervals. On the last Beating on Sunday, 16 September 1990, a notice outside Court Farm read:

The Court Baron of the Manor of Holne's earliest recorded date is 8 October 1790. Holne Commoners have decided that 1990 is a suitable occasion to beat the moorland bounds. According to the Manor Court Book the bounds

have been beaten regularly (every generation) since 8 October 1790, the last occasion being 25 September 1977.

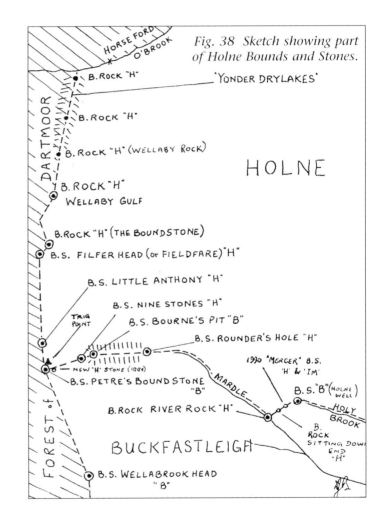

Fig. 38 Sketch showing part of Holne Bounds and Stones.

Holne Parish is bounded by the Mardle and Holy Brook to the south as far as Shuttaford Stream (thence) to Staddiscombe where another stream just inside the boundary flows into the Dart to the south-east of Park Wood. The Dart is the east boundary to Dartmeet, and Week Ford where the O Brook enters Dart acts as the west boundary'.

A History of Holne, a book published by the villagers in 1977 as a memento of the Jubilee Celebrations, defines the boundary followed on 9 June 1951, in the Court Roll thus:

The boundary of this manor then runs from Brimble Ford in a straight line up the valley to Roundhole where there is a large boundary stone with the letter 'H' on it, thence in a straight line up to Outer and Western Gulph to a place called Nine Stones and then in a straight line to a place called Peter on the Mount, thence to another boundary stone called Little Anthony, and thence to another stone marked with the letter 'H' called 'The Boundstone'.

This was going in a clockwise direction, but in 1990 they went anti-clockwise, starting from Combestone Tor, the party having been taken there from the village by tractor and trailer, following the Holne Moor Leat (alternatively known as Hamlyn's Leat) to its take-off point on the O Brook, where they met the boundary proper, common to Lydford, the Forest of Dartmoor, and Holne Parish. At Horse Ford there used to be an inscribed stone marked with the letter 'H', one of the slabs formerly paving the crossing point of the O Brook on the Monastic Way between Buckfast Abbey on the east side of the moor and the Abbeys of Tavistock and Buckland on the western side, but this was washed away in a severe flood in 1965 and has not been seen since. Crossing records that it was on the eastern side of the stream, and the Ordnance Survey

Fig. 39 Ryder's Hill Boundstones.

Holne: Near Horse Ford, commemorating Arthur Brown. SX 6635 7120

sketch in the Boundary Remark Book of 1880 records that 'The top of this rock is level with the surface of the ground'. In the late summer of 1995 a commemorative stone was erected nearby, but not strictly on the Holne parish boundary, in memory of Arthur Brown, Foreman of the Manor Jury in 1949, and Reeve from 1962 until his death in 1993. The stone is simply inscribed 'H', beneath which are his initials 'AB'.

We now follow the O Brook to the higher of the two gullies known as Drylakes, Yonder Drylakes Girth on the Ordnance Survey sketch, where the Holne Forest bounds leave the O Brook to follow the gully southwards, and where tinners' waste abounds. But dry it is not, though parts of the stream are subterranean. Almost as soon as we leave the O Brook a large slab of stone on the left bank of Drylakes was noted to bear the letter 'H' at SX 6605 7095 – it is not shown on the Outdoor Leisure Map. The next highest stone on the O.S. 1880 sketch is also shown to be on the west side

Drylakes, near head. SX 6606 7050

Drylakes. SX 6605 7095

of the gully, but may not be there now. A stone at the position shown is fractured and could, with imagination, be said to show part of the letter 'H', but the author recalls that many years ago a small stone embedded in tinners' waste in the middle of the gully was seen to have a clear letter 'H', but could not be found at a later date, and a member of the 1990 party had the same recollection! We proceed ever upwards, and on top of the small 'scarp' see a prominent rock at SX 6606 7050, which they called Wellaby Rock, and which is inscribed 'H' on its eastern side. This too is unmarked by the O.S. on their 1:25 000 map. Here in 1990 the youngest member of the party, a two-year-old boy, was held on his head over the stone and presented with a new penny. On again southwards to a very small, but well bedded rock, marked 'H' known as Wellaby Gulf at SX 6595 7010, now on the 1:25 000 map, and again southwards ever upward to where the boundary line crosses the Sandy Way, a track coming up from Michelcombe. Here there are two boundary markers, one on either side of the track. That on the northern side is a natural boulder and called 'The Boundstone', marked 'H', and on the higher southern side there is a set boundstone similarly lettered 'H'. This latter is known as Fieldfare or Filfer Head. In the 1977 book a photograph of this stone appears on page 60, there erroneously described as 'Peter on the Mount', which we shall come to later.

We now make our way yet further southwards and upwards again towards an east–west line of tinners' workings associated with the scattered gerts of Ringleshutes Mine on Holne Lea, on the northern side of which we find our next boundary marker, a set stone called Little Anthony lettered 'H' as usual, at SX 6596 6925. It was speculated whether the name could have been derived from the fact that there was once a monk from Buckfast Abbey called Anthony, and that Buckfast did at one time have rights on Holne Moor, and did claim rights within the Forest too. From Little Anthony we climb more steeply to the highest point of Ryder's Hill as it is known today, called Battyshull in 1240 and Knattleburrowe or Natting Borough in the seventeenth–eighteenth centuries. Within the scant remains of the 'cairn' on the summit there is now a triangulation point, and it is contended by the Holne Commoners that this is set upon the original site of the next former boundary marker, Petre-on-the-Mount, called Peter-on-the-Mount today. In making a claim to this in 1990 they bumped a child on the trig point, which is known to have been erected in the spring of 1937; about 13ft to the south there is a nine-teenth– twentieth-century Buckfastleigh boundstone inscribed 'B', and this is called Petre's Boundstone, at SX 659 690. For many years a fragment of a Holne 'H' stone, bearing that letter was to be found either leaning against the Buckfastleigh stone or in the immediate area, in all likelihood the last remains of Petre on the Mount. As late as 1983 this unsecured stone

measured about 2ft 6in in all, and had been reduced to about 2ft by 1985; by 1986 it had disappeared entirely, not to be seen again.

1983.

Petre on the Mount and Petre's Boundstone, 1985. SX 659 690.

Many parish boundstones are inscribed with two or even three letters or sets of letters indicating that the point in question is, or was, acknowledged as being on their common boundary by all parties concerned, but some other parishes tended to ignore the stones set up by their neighbours even though they were on the common boundary. This situation still applies to the Holne/Buckfastleigh bounds and in the periodic beating of their commons boundary Holne makes reference only to those stones bearing the letter 'H'.

The claim by the Holne Commoners that the trig point on the summit of Ryder's Hill was set upon the site of one of their old boundary stones led me to look further into the matter, revealing several facts hither-to unrecognised, and changing quite radically our appreciation of what has actually taken place here over the last one hundred and fifty years or so. Ryder's Hill was not always so called, as we have observed, and what must be an early reference to a marker stone here is one in the Buckfastleigh Manor Court Book, where in 1795 reference is made to 'Nottingborough Stone'. A complication is that not only is the boundstone called 'Peter' or 'Petre on the Mount', but the term is also used for the summit of Ryder's Hill itself. However, the Holne Tithe map of circa 1838, the Tithe Apportionment for the parish having been settled in that year but the map being updated, clearly shows 'Bound Stone. Petre on ye Mount' and another boundstone nearby to the north 'Bd Stone. Little Anthony', so that it is quite clear that both references were to a stone. But by 1809 the Ordnance Survey had published their first one inch to the mile map of Devon, where they record it as 'Peter's Bound Stone', and their later six inch to the mile maps refer to the stone there as 'Petre's Bound Stone', together with their symbol for a Bench Mark, both in 1884 and 1906, and marking the spot as 'Cairn'.

The summit of Ryder's Hill is certainly crowned by the scant remains of what appears to be a cairn, and within the circumference of this there is, besides the triangulation point, a Buckfastleigh boundary stone bearing the letter 'B' on its east face. This must be of nineteenth–twentieth-century erection as it has been shaped by the feather and tare method of splitting stone, not introduced until just after 1800. This is the boundstone that is called 'Petre's Bound Stone' by William Crossing. On page 362 of his famous *Guide*, written not later than the first decade of the twentieth century, and possibly observed at any time between the 1880s and 1909, it states:

There is a small cairn on the summit, but it is very dilapidated. On this are two stones, a rough one about two feet high having the letter 'H' cut on it, and another more carefully worked and about four feet high with the letter 'B' graven upon it. These represent Petre-on-the-Mount and Petre's Bound Stone.

This latter now stands some 4ft 8in above ground level, somewhat in excess of Crossing's estimate. We are also fortunate in being able to refer to a rather dark photograph of the two boundstones still in place as Crossing describes them dating from circa 1930, and appearing in the Rev. Hugh Breton's *Forest of Dartmoor*, Part 1, where he enigmatically says: 'Ryder's Hill (1695ft). Also called 'Petre-on-the-Mount. This is the highest point on this part of the moor… On its crest is a bond stone known as Petre's Bound Stone…', this in spite of the fact that his photograph showed not one but two stones, the more northerly one the small Holne Stone, and the more southerly the much taller Buckfastleigh one, the estimated distance apart being approximately 13ft.

At this time it was assumed that both stones were in their original positions, but Hemery's brief reference to a letter he had had from the Ordnance Survey caused the writer to get in touch with them leading to a revelation that the author had not suspected. Their letter said:

Ryder's Hill pillar (trig point) was indeed built in March 1937, as with many of our Primary Triangulation pillars it was constructed over the site of the original survey station of the Principle Triangulation (1783–1853).

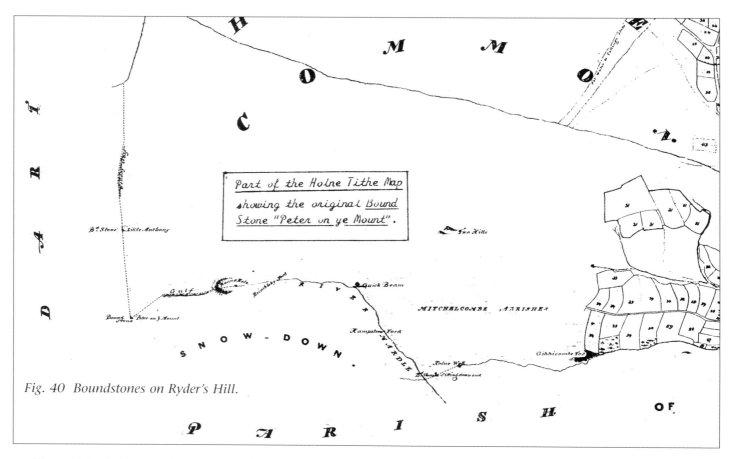

Fig. 40 Boundstones on Ryder's Hill.

The original observations were taken between 26 July and 22 August 1845 by Sergeant Donelaw RSM. The station mark was actually 2ft 6in below ground level and on completion of observations filled with gravel stones level with the surface. A turf pile 12ft in diameter and 13ft in height was erected above it to mark the station. These markers enabled the pre-war surveyors to find the many Principle Triangulation stations almost one hundred years later. In the more remote areas cairns of rock and stone were built, and when dismantled caused much debate as it was assumed the Ordnance Survey was defiling ancient monuments.

It went on to say that to interfere with boundstones would have been most improper, and indeed against their own interests as such markers were an invaluable aid to them. At a later date they sent me a full copy of the letter that had been sent to Eric Hemery in 1974, mentioned in his *High Dartmoor*, which shows that he had completely overlooked the valuable information offered, for it read:

In reply to your letter dated 26 February 1974, the triangulation pillar on Ryder's Hill, Dartmoor (N.G. Ref SX 659 691) was built in March 1937, exactly over the old, buried, triangulation mark.

The following reference from the 'Account of the Principle Triangulation, 1858' may be of interest to you – 'Ryder's Hill … the station is on the summit of the hill and is well known by the name of Peter on the Mount by the inhabitants of the South Dartmoor. About 12ft south from the station stands a stone with the letter 'H' rudely cut on it, to mark the limit of the parish of Holne in this direction; the parochial authorities in their annual perambulation describe the stone by the name Peter on the Mount.

In 1953 we fixed the positions of two stones for use with aerial photography. These were described as:
1. Upright slender rock. National grid bearing 166º. Distance 4.3 metres from the pillar.
2. Boundary stone. National grid bearing 353º. Distance 131.3 metres from the pillar.

We have no later reference to these stones.
Signed M.D. Bulpett Supt. Survey Services

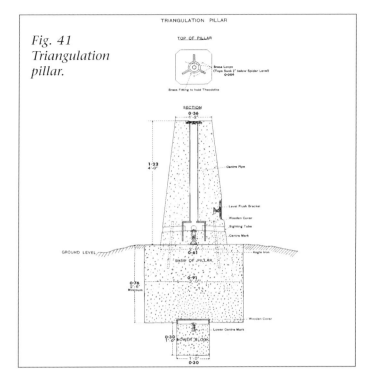

Fig. 41 Triangulation pillar.

This letter clearly shows that in 1858 the stone 'about 12ft to the south' of the original O.S. station was the old Holne one, whether we call it 'Petre on the Mount' as did the Commoners or 'Petre's Boundstone' as did the Ordnance Survey, and this answers a host of former anomalies. The later 1953 reference shows that the tall 'B' Buckfastleigh stone was then occupying the same site, as is demonstrated by angle and measurement given from the O.S. station, the second boundstone being Little Anthony to the north, another old Holne stone shown on their tithe map but not on either the first or second editions of the O.S. six inch maps except by way of the bench mark on it which they show as 'BM 1680.2↖'. It shows too:

1. that the O.S. have applied the same name to two different boundstones, albeit two successively occupying the same site.
2. that they did not disturb any boundstones when making their initial survey in 1845, though they possibly did so when erecting their pillar in 1937.
3. that Crossing's description of the scene as he saw it was not the original one, as he must have thought, and led us to believe. The change could have taken place at any time between 1858 and 1909 when the first edition of his *Guide* was published.
4. that the Holne Commoners were in error in thinking that the trig point occupied the original site of their boundstone, again due to the substitution.
5. that this fact resolves my doubts about the present line of the Holne/Buckfastleigh bounds east of Ryder's hill – it was the stones that changed, not the boundary line.

It seems prophetic that photographs taken by the author in the 1980s showed the remnant of Petre on the Mount leaning against what the O.S. call Petre's Boundstone, and that the Dartmoor National Park made a wise choice erecting the 1992 'replacement' for Petre on the Mount on the present boundary line near but east of the 'B' stone.

After all this involvement with Ryder's Hill, we continue our perambulation.

DNPA replacement - Petre on the Mount, 1992 (see p120).

We now turn eastwards leaving the Forest bounds, following those of Holne and Buckfastleigh, and go down towards more tinners' workings, but before reaching them come to an old tinners' reservoir and a group of rocks within which is a rough set stone bearing the letter 'H'. This is Nine Stones at SX 6610 6918. We continue down to the tinners' gert at the top end of which there is another Buckfastleigh set boundstone called Bourne's Pit at SX 6620 6920, but which the Holne people ignored, continuing down to the lower end of the gert above Mardle Head, where their next 'H' stone, known as Rounder's Hole, at SX 6648 6924 is to be found.

Towards the end of 1996, the author was advised that a recumbent stone inscribed with an 'H' on the underneath side had been found at SX 667 695, but no information has come to hand as to why it was in this position off the current boundary line.

The boundary now follows the Mardle downstream to Michelcombe Arrishes where a natural rock on the left bank, partially in the water, is marked 'H', and called River Rock at SX 6772 6857. This marks the point where the bounds veer away from the Mardle in a north-easterly direction to the head of the Holy Brook and between River Rock, marked 'B. Rock' by the O.S., and the next B.S. marked by them, a Buckfastleigh stone, there are two more Holne stones. The first we meet is a small natural stone at SX 6782 6860 at Sitting Down End, where the Commoners used to have their lunch at the perambulation, or viewing, of the bounds, marked as usual with an 'H', not shown by O.S. The other is brand new at SX 6785 6867, a rough set stone which appears to be part of a gatepost for it has one drilled hole in it. It was only 'unveiled' at the 1990 Beating of the Bounds, when Ian Mercer, the then Dartmoor National Park Officer, and acting Steward of Holne Manor on behalf of Devon County, was asked to remove a covering of bracken to reveal it.

Right: River Rock. SX 6772 6857.

Below: Re-erected Rounder's Hole. 17.9.2000. SX 6648 6924

Stone erected to Ian Mercer, 1990. SX 6785 6867

It is inscribed with an 'H' on its northern side, with his initials 'IM' below it in sans-serif letters, as a token of the Commoners' appreciation of all he had done for the moorland farming community, and Dartmoor in general, for so many years. He was ceremoniously 'bumped' on the stone, being lifted by several Commoners.

Reaching the Holy Brook, this was followed downstream, where another 'B' Buckfastleigh stone, lying recumbent, was

Recumbent 'H' stone found 1996. SX 667 695. (Courtesy Mr and Mrs R.Vane).

Re-erected Nine Stones. 17.9.2000. SX 6610 6918.

The stone at Hapstead Ford dedicated by Prof. Ian Mercer. 17.9.2000.

The above stone erected at Hapstead Ford 17.9.2000. SX 6710 6925.

observed having recently been found in the hedge. The bounds continue down the stream, but for ease of passage a higher route was taken through the edge of Gibby Combe Wood to join the right of way into Michelcombe, thence down to Watery Lane and Langaford Bridge, where the boundstones were not found [but reported to have been seen in 1998], and back through fields to the village, as the transport arranged for Langaford Bridge did not meet them there.

Arriving back at Court Farm, an attractive spread was laid before the perambulators in a barn, and presentations made to all the juniors who had completed the seven-plus-mile walk. In addition to the traditional giving of a new penny when the youngest member was bumped on a boundstone, all those under the age of fourteen, who completed the walk, were given one of the recently issued new 5p pieces. The rest of the bounds, along the West and Double Dart, etc., was undertaken later.

On 17 September 2000, Holne beat part of their bounds, from Combestone to Horse Ford and up to Ryder's Hill, where the Buckfastleigh Beaters were met. The bounds were followed to Rounder's Hole which had been re-erected for the Millennium, and taken to Hapstead Ford, where the recumbent stone mentioned above had also been erected for the Millennium and was dedicated by Ian Mercer, the ladies present having a glass of sloe gin whilst the men had whiskey to toast Holne's 'new' Millennium Boundary Stone. The Mardle was followed to Sitting Down End, then to Michelcombe, Watery Lane and Holne, where the participants enjoyed another superb spread at Court Barton Farm.

BUCKFASTLEIGH

Part of the boundary of Buckfastleigh parish is conterminous with that of Dean Prior, and in the Buckfastleigh Manor Court Book of 1781 to 1914 the bounds as beaten on 17 July 1902, embracing the manors of Buckfastleigh, Brook, Button, Mainbow and Holne Bozum, are detailed as follows:

Beginning at Rowden Cross and on the right side of the road to Linhay Cross and thence to Hawkmoor Head and thence down the road to Brook Mill Bridge and thence up by the River Merdle on the eastern or right side therefore to the south-east corner of Hepney's Wood on the right side of the same to the road leading to Holne, thence up the road on the right side and into a wood called Kiln Park being part of Burchette and on by the right-hand side of the western hedge of Kiln Park Wood into Langford Wood part of Burchetts and on by the same side of the hedge down to the road leading to Retreat, thence to the bottom, or west corner of Hawson Lower Meadow thence through the water on the right side of the brook under the new bridge, thence beside Hawson Lower and Higher Meadow around Redaclay Little Orchard on the north side of the stream to a bondstone* in the lane leading to Holne and across the road to Aller or Watery Lane, thence up by the right or northern fence of that lane to the stone* in the road hedge at the east corner of Odey Bridge Meadow up by the river to Weir in the said Meadow and from thence on the northern side of the hedge to the lower end of Gibbeycombe Tor, thence up by the right side of the stream

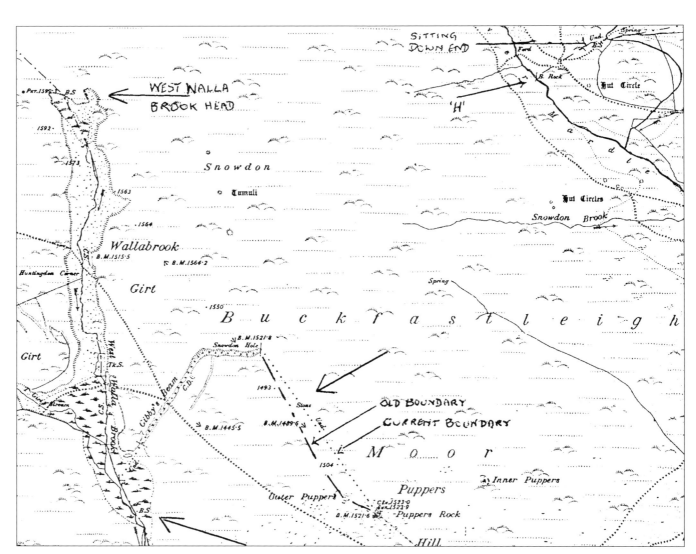

Fig. 42 Buckfastleigh Moor.

Buckfastleigh: B.S. at Sitting Down End. SX 679 688

The Wellabrook Stone. SX 665 686

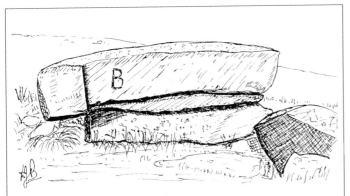

Fig. 43 Outer Pupers Rock.

outside of Scorriton Down Hedge to a Bond Stone and to Sitting Down End, and thence over a flat and down the gully to a Boundstone on the eastern side of the River Merdle and up the Holne side thereof to a stone in Rounder Hole, thence up the Gulf to Bourne Pit, and from thence to a stone called Peter in the Mount, and from thence to a Bond Stone to the northern corner of Wellbrook and from the head of Wellbrook following the water to a Bond Stone* at the end of the Gulf at Huntingdon Wall and thence up by the Great Gulf to the higher end thereof, and thence by a Bond Stone* to the Outer Pupers Rock and thence to the Inner Pupers Rock[†] and from that by a row or ridge down to Watersoak corner and thence on by the wall of Lambsdown from thence down on the right side of the fence between the Manors to the river by Larkham Coppice under Hollow Green thence down by the right bank of the river Dean Bourne to the bottom of Larkham Coppice, from thence up by the fence on the east side of Larkham Coppice, and on the left side of the fence bounding Wallaford Down to the lower corner of Thornpark by Wallaford Lane, thence on the road close to the right-hand fence thereof taking in the wastes and oak trees to Wallaford Cross, from thence on the side to the head of Ranscombe thence into Ranscombe...

* None of these were found; all appear to be missing. [†] = Pupers Rock

This very detailed line, even to the side of the river or hedge, follows that of today except in the area of Pupers Rock. It no longer touches Outer Pupers, but goes directly from the head of Gibby's Beam, the Great Gulf, to Inner Pupers as per their description, now called

Pupers Rock by the Ordnance Survey – both Pupers Rock and Inner Pupers appears to have been applied to this boundary marker (see Crossing's *Guide* p.362).

On its southern edge the letter 'B' is inscribed. The older Ordnance Survey six inch maps show a 'B.S.'at Huntingdon Wall as stated in the bounds quoted but nothing is to be seen today, and a 'Stone' is also shown about a third of the way between the top of Gibby's Beam and Outer Pupers but there appears to be nothing with an inscription there either. The direction from 'Inner Pupers' – 'by a row or ridge', obviously refers to the reave which runs from the O.S. 'Pupers Rock', called a burgh or barrow in medieval times, remains of the Bronze Age cairn surrounding it still recognisable as such, to Water Oke Corner.

The boundary stones at Sitting Down End, Boundary or River Rock and Petre on the Mount are Holne stones. No reference is made to either Peter's Stone, the Buckfastleigh stone at Bourne's Pit or the Buckfastleigh one on the summit of Ryder's Hill, known as Petre's Boundstone.

A contemporary article in a Totnes paper dated 19 July 1902 gives a little more insight into this Beating, as follows:

> After a lapse of ten years the Bounds of the Manors of Buckfastleigh, Brook, Button, Mainbow and Holne Bozum of which the Earl of Macclesfield is Lord, were surveyed or beaten on Thursday under the direction of the Steward, Messrs Michelmore and Son. The starting point was Rowden Cross, where at 8.30a.m. assembled a number of persons on foot, as well as a number of horsemen, determined to face the arduous toil under a burning sun, of nearly 26 miles of rough moorland. The initial glass having been taken, the first move was to Linhay Cross thence to Hookmoor Head including Five Oaks, and down the road to Farmer Rowland's property. There at Brook Mill Bridge the wall was scaled and the party proceeded up the eastern side of the river Merdle around Hepny's Wood across the road, through Burchett's and Retreat to a point named 'Steart' where Mr H.M. Firth's (the lord of the Manor of Holne) steward was met. A short consultation showed that the river was the boundary and we proceeded upstream to Red-a-Clay Bridge and thence to Langford Bridge, Aller or Watery Lane with its deep undergrowth and overhanging hedges, not excepting half a foot of water, was next waded through, bringing the party to Odey Bridge. Gibby Combe Bottom with its rough boulders and semitropical vegetation was painfully beaten and all were extremely glad to arrive at Scorriton Down in sight of the refreshments. At Sitting Down End host J.F. Bowerman had prepared for us and a much needed meal was indulged in, the appetite being greatly sharpened by the former hard work. After luncheon a bond stone near Merdle was found, and another up at the head of the stream, named Rounder Hole. Bourne Pit and Peter on the Mount were next reached and here the Duchy Steward was found, the Holne friends leaving. A good walk downhill brought us to Huntingdon Wall where Mr W. Penellum (Lord Churston's representative) of Dean Manor, joined the band. A grievance respecting a bond stone was aired, but satisfactorily settled, and the party proceeded to

Pipers Rocks, thence down the ridge to Lambsdown Corner. Here the horsemen left, the party on foot going over the terrible ground of Larcombe, which was the stiffest pull of the day, up to Wallaford Down, arriving at 2p.m. where greatly needed refreshments were again found. After a short rest, races were indulged in, the event of the day being a pony race, which was hotly contested, and won by a lady, who had challenged the company in the first instance. Leaving Wallaford Down with its refreshing breeze, we went down the road to Wallaford Cross, thence to Fullaford Pool, around by Half Moon to Deanbourne Bridge. To cool themselves the foot party had now to walk down the Deanbourne river which runs down at the back of Buckfastleigh to Croppins Park. There a number of children greatly increased the party and we proceeded around Long Wood, the Churchyard and Deepey, arriving at our starting place, Rowden Cross, about 6p.m. Cheers having been given for the King, the Lord of the Manor and Mr and Mrs Alfred Michelmore, a very enjoyable day was brought to a close. Amongst those who traversed the whole of the wide area of the boundary were noticed: Messrs Egremont, Gwynne, J. Bickle, Jas. Chaffe and his sons (William and John), E. Barnicoat, W. Weeks, F. Rowlands, R.P. Tarring, L. Arscott, E. Butland, Head, J. Dunn and others, while a special mention should be made of two youngsters, Messrs Gerald Bowerman and Hubert Bickle, who also stuck to the band throughout and received the old custom at the boundstones after being held on their heads on the tops. Quite a day for all concerned!

BUCKFAST ABBEY

Buckfast Abbey is not included in the parishes which touch upon the Forest, but had rights on parts of both Buckfastleigh and Brent Moors, so it seemed sensible to include it here. It was also involved with Buckfastleigh and Brent Manors.

As a Benedictine and then a Cistercian house it was re-founded in 1018, having been originally founded circa 760. In Domesday there is no mention of the abbey's rights on Dartmoor but these appear to be confirmed by King Henry II, though John confiscated the abbey 'and all ther landes and Godes unto hys tenyur' some time between the years 1208 and 1214. In 1280, having recovered their former properties, the abbey, in common with all other land and property owners, was obliged to satisfy the Commissioners appointed under the 'Quo Warranto' as to their rights of ownership of their estates, and Abbot Robert's rights on Dartmoor were contested by the Jurors of the Hundred of Stanborough, who alleged that the abbey had made purpresture (*encroachment*) 'of a certain great waste of the Common moor in the south part of Dartmoor, to the injury of all the country, because, in the time of Henry III, Howard, the Abbot, and the convent of Buckfastleigh, appropriated to themselves the aforesaid waste, to the yearly damage of 40 shillings'. Tried at Exeter in 1281, the finding of the court was in favour of the abbey, and on several subsequent occasions, when the same subject was raised, the abbey was again found to be within its rights. They did, however, allow the Commoners to depasture their animals on the abbey's moors without charge.

In 1446 a John Ford made a search for their title 'and the right of theyre saide monastery to theyr three mores ajoynyng to the southe parte of the kynges Forest of Dertmore in Devon parcell of the Duchie of Cornewayll of whyche seid iij mores the one of them is called South-Holne more, parcell of the maner of Bukfastleigh, and the iijde more is parcell of the manor of South Brent yn the seid shere of Devon'.

The Buckfast Abbey ledger book contains a record of their former 'moor of Buckfast', a copy of which, made in 1610, reads thus:

Hec sunt de la mora de Bucfastr a hurburnwelm descendendo versus aystr n usque ad la ffen forda, a la ffenforde ascendendo versus occidentum usque ad Blackover, a Blackover descendendo ad versus occidentum, ad Smallbrokesfote, a Smallbrokesfote ascendendo versus boream p'Avon versus ulteriorem

Blackover or Blacouer. SX 687 645

Welbrokesfote, ascendendo boream usque ad caput de ulteriori Welbroke capite girando versus orientam usque ad Popaburgh versus austr n girando versus Bowrone usque ad Docaston, a Docaston usque ad Hurburnwelm.

The line here described is taken from Harbourne Head, going first to 'ffen forda', i.e. Dockwell Hole, thence up over the ridge westward, the crest here called 'Blackover', and down the west side to Smallbrook Foot, up the Avon to Wester Wellabrook Foot, and thence up that stream to its head. There we appear to go directly eastwards to 'Popaburgh', Pupers Rock and still on the bounds of Buckfastleigh parish. From that point the boundary turns south to Bowrone, most probably Water Oke Corner, and thence to Docaston, the longstone or menhir above Harbourne Head, and down that stream to our starting point.

Today there is a line of boundstones marking the boundary between Dockwell Hole and Smallbrook Foot, one near the former being called The Goose. They are all uninscribed, some appear to be older than the ones with feather and tare. The bounds described here encompass not only what is still the moorland part of Buckfastleigh parish but also the moorland part of what is now Dean Prior, and bordering on to Brent to the south, also the abbey's property prior to the Dissolution, and embracing two bequests of land made during the earlier and mid-thirteenth century.

In 1223 Hosefenne, now known as Hawson, passed from Urglas de Holne to Nicholas de Laya with common rights on moors 'which land is in the Manor of the Lord of South Holne', formerly the property of

Sir Reginald de Valletort, the Purchaser to give the vendor 12½ marks of silver, and annually 1lb of wax for a candle. Later de Laya sold the property to Robert de Helion, again with the 1lb of wax proviso, who made a gift of it to the abbey some time between the years 1237 and 1244. This was later confirmed by Ralph de Valletort, Sir Reginalds's brother and heir. The bounds were described as being:

A capite de Smalebroc per descendum eiusdem Smalebroc usque in aquam de Avene, et per aquam de Avene ascendendo usque ad Hutters Welebroc; et ab Huttere Welbroc ascendendo usque ad caput eisdem Welebroc, et ita directe usque ad Pubbaburgam, et Ita a Pubbaburga oer dictum Ruherewe versus austrum usque in directum capitis predicti Smalebroc.

Contrary to the previous document, this boundary takes us from the head of Smallbrook, not the Harbourne, but otherwise follows the same line as far as Puper's Rock, and thence by the major reave (ruherewe) running south-east – but this does not go to Smallbrook Head but to Water Oak Corner and beyond, so was the Harbourne intended not Smallbrook? Later Ralph de Valletort also gave additional land to the abbey including Hembury Woods, but attached a proviso to this too concerning the annual supply of wood by the abbot to a Sir Stephen de Beauceyn, later to be spelt 'Bozum' or 'Bozon'. This proviso proved to be an embarrassment to the abbey due to the trespass and removal of wood by Sir Stephen's tenants. Killed in battle in 1257, his estates then passed to his brother Richard, who, in about 1260, made another bequest to the abbey, bounds of an unspecified date being:

from la Haven to Bremelford (*Brimble Ford*), and so by the water of Miriles (*Mardle*), ascending to Driavilsford (*Hapstead?*), and so lineally as far as Gnatesburg (*Ryder's Hill*), and thence lineally to the head of Wester Walbroke, until it falls into the Avon.

A document of unknown date, but possibly of fourteenth-century origins, in the Buckfast Cartulary defines their bounds on Brent Moor as follows:

Hec sunt de la Mora de Brenta ad illo ubi due Glast concurrunt ascendendo versus boream usque ad caput Glaste, a capite Glaste, ad huc descendendo versus boream p' la Rowerewe usque ad media de. Triberie burge. A Triberie burge girando versus boream usque ad ulterioram Whitaboroughe, ab ulteriori Whitaboroughe versus orientam usque ad Bucklandforde descendendo p' te occidentale p' Avon usque ad

Buckfast Abbey: Two Stones, Rowerewe. SX 6565 6218

Ermington Manor. SX 6510 6320

Smallbrookfote a. Smallbrookfote ascendendo p'
Avon magis versus orientam ad Blakoueran, a la
Blakoueran versus orientam usque ad ffen forde.

This Latin text takes us from the Glazemeet to East
Glaze Head where there is still a boundary rock,
thence to 'Rowerewe', the major reave, to the centre
cairn of Three Barrows. Near the southern end of the
reave there is now a boundstone set within a gap in
the reave known as 'Two Stones'. From Three Barrows
the line now goes to Western Whittabarrow, although
'ulteriorem' – 'ulter' on the Platte de Dertemore
map – might well imply Eastern Whittabarrow, which
the Duchy still insist is on the Forest Bounds. On this
part of the bounds there are two named points, a
boundstone at the northern end of the reave known as
'Ermington Manor', and on Quickbeam Hill is
'Meynell's Bank', where an attempt was made in the
nineteenth century to enclose Brent Moor by Francis
Meynell, then of Brent Moor House. From Western
Whittabarrow we go to Buckland Ford and down the
Avon as far as Smallbrook Foot, thence up that stream
to 'Blakoueran' on the divide between the Avon and

'ffen forde', or Dockwell Hole, on the infant
Harbourne. This word is spelt 'Blackover' elsewhere in
the Buckfastleigh bounds.

At the Dissolution of the abbey in 1539, the abbey
manors and all its other lands had an annual value of
£430. 19s. 7d. Shortly afterwards Sir William Petre
purchased some of this property, but not the abbey
buildings themselves, including the Manor of Brent.

DEAN PRIOR

The Buckfastleigh/Dean Prior boundary line as we
know it today is most interesting in that between the
West Wellabrook and Pupers Rock it follows the line of
an early open cast tin working, or beam, known as
Gibby's Beam. This type of surface working was
pursued by the tinners after the alluvial deposits had
been worked out, following a lode by opening up the
surface, before shaft working had been introduced to
any extent. The fact that this boundary changes
direction abruptly to follow this tinners' gully poses
the question both as to the age of the tinners' 'beam'
and the age of the present boundary line following it.
Beam working is generally considered to date roughly
from about the fifteenth century to as late as the
seventeenth or possibly even the beginning of the
eighteenth, and the bounds of Dean Prior parish were
certainly very different to those of today in 1613,
especially on the open moorland and did not follow
Gibby's Beam. The document defining the bounds in
1613 is in the archives of the Bishop of Exeter and
reads thus:

From the grabtree being a place betweene the
lane end leading from Dene church towards

Totnes and the newe house and from thence towardes the south as the hedge goeth betweene the moore pke and Christopher Heddes tenement and so from then untill the souther corner of Beare p'ke and from thence along the lane called Greenlane untill Marley ford water called Harborne and from thence towardes the north west along by the said water of Harborne almost untill a gate called little yeat neare about Dockwill pound, and so from thence by a ditche or rewe towardes the north west untill the corner of the said ditche or rewe lying a little bewest of a rounde rynge made of stones being on the west side of the aforesaid water of Harborne and so from the said corner through the said ringe of stones towardes the north as the aforesaid ditche or rewe goeth untill the north corner of the said rewe or ditche wch. lieth neere by Harborne well being a bond of Buckfast moure and from the corner to long stone and from thence to Lenisdon corner and from thence by Lenisdon untill it come to the water of Denbourne at the utter end of Holagreepe and so by the said water untill ye come to Larcome hedge or wale and from thence towardes the north east by the said hedge until Wallaforde yeate and so from thence towardes the north east by the way untill Wallaford Crosse and from thence by the way that leadeth towardes Buckfastlee towne untill or neare about Coxhill yeate and so by the hedge on the north side of Coxhill untill ye come to the north Voulanford als Voulaver poole and ffrom thence by the waie that leadeth towards Deanetowne untill Denbourne bridge and from thence down by the water of Denbourne untill the hedge below the Tucking mill and from thence towardes the east by the said hedge untill the higher end of Whitaclay woode and from thence towardes the south directlie as the hedge runneth by the Barton of Court untill Rasthorne yeat and so from thence as the way leadeth towardes Totnes untill the aforesaid Grabtree.

Thus the line of the moorland section of this old boundary went up the river Harbourne, passing through Harbourne Well, or Dockwell Hole as it is now more often called, where it is confirmed that the latter was once on the bounds of Buckfast moor and Dean Prior, not that of Brent and Dean Prior as it is today. It then went up to the menhir known as 'The Longstone' above Harbourne Head to Lambsdown Corner, around the Lambsdown Farm enclosures to Hollow Green (see Buckfastleigh bounds) and the Dean Burn, following the stream downwards off the moor. Nowhere does this boundary approach Inner Pupers or Gibby's Beam nearer than Holagreep (Hollow Green) above the head of the Dean Burn.

In the T.D.A. Vol. 52 the Rev. Oswald Reichel, under the title 'The

Dean Prior: The Longstone above Harbourne Head. SX 697 651

Origin and upgrowth of the English Parish', describes how in 1270 Dean Prior was appropriated to Plympton Priory by Bishop Bronescombe, his address to the Prior and Convent of Plympton setting forth:

> Wherefore beloved of Christ, we being minded to further your humble devotion with paternal affection, in order to relieve the necessities of the poor and of strangers that flock to you, with consent of the Dean and Chapter of our Church of Exeter ... give and confirm to you in full right the Church of Dene with its fruits and obventions ... to hold for ever to your own proper uses saving a suitable portion for the vicar to be canonically presented to us and our successors by you.

Forever, however, was not to be, for in 1539 all the local monastic institutions were to be dissolved by the Crown.

SOUTH BRENT

A report of Beating the Bounds dated 15 August 1903, states that at that time the moorland boundary had not been beaten since 1871. About 100 horsemen and pedestrians then attended, gathering at Corringdon Ball Gate, a Mr John Edmonds being the guide. The report reads:

> Proceeding from Glasscombe Corner, the bounds between Ugborough and Brent were traversed, the former named parish satisfied as to the line taken. It was decided to mary (*mark*) a stone at the Head of Glaze, and the boundary as marked by stones was examined right up to Peter's Cross. From thence some difficulty occurred as to the real right of the Brent representatives. Eventually Mr W. Hull produced a map which decided a straight line from Peter's Cross to Buckland Ford was the right direction to take, and the Ordnance Survey map confirmed this. Mr Pearse, keeper of Huntingdon Warren, disputed the right of Brent to a portion of the land traversed but he could not sustain his point in the face of evidence produced. Luncheon was in readiness at Huntingdon Cross, having been provided for by subscription. Mr J.R.T. Kingwell of Great Aish, South Brent, produced and read the Minutes of the last meeting held on the moor eleven years ago. He stated that the Ordnance map showed the true position of their claim now as it did then. Questioned as to the right of rabbits on the moor, it was shown that a person, although having a right to grazing, had no right whatever on that account to the rabbits. Mr W. Knapman of Brent according to custom sang a song 'Brennan on the Moor'. Some interesting documents relating to various perambulations were read by Mr Hull. It was noted that the same courses that traversed in 1871 had been gone over. Several water courses were inspected, and no diversions were found to exist since that destroyed eleven years ago. The west bank of the Avon was followed down to Smallbrook and fording the river, a deal of excitement was caused. The old custom of 'dipping' the newcomers was carried out amid roars of laughter, several visitors being put under water in mid stream. The route was then from the bondmarks to Dockwell Hole Mires, and then to Brent which was reached about 5.20p.m.

This report is interesting in so far as it states that a period of no less than thirty-two years had elapsed since the previous beating and that the leader had to refer to the Ordnance map to be sure that they were taking the right line from Petre's Cross on Western Whittabarrow. The age old controversy of the true and correct line of the Forest Bounds once again raised its head with the keeper of Huntingdon Warren trying to enforce the Duchy line to Eastern Whittabarrow as of old. What were the 'diversionery' water courses destroyed in 1892, in other words a leat? Now it is impossible to follow the course of the Avon along the whole of Brent's bounds due to the construction of the Avon dam marking the exact line of Brent's bounds, and which is inspected at the Beating of the Bounds and was so viewed in 1987. Another report of the beating of the bounds, as recorded by the *Western Gazette* on 7 August 1919, is worthy of repetition:

> On Bank Holiday, the septennial ceremony of traversing the moorland boundary of Brent Moor was carried out by invitation of the Parish Council, about thirty horsemen and the same number on foot assembled at Corringdon Ball Gate at half past ten and proceeded along the western boundary to the Abbot's Way vicinity, Peter's Cross, Bush Meads, Huntingdon Warren, Ford of the Avon, thence down the river (right bank) to the ford leading over the Dockwell Ridge to Dockwell Gate. The perambulation occupied about four hours, and no difficulty occurred with neighbouring owners concerning the claims of the parishioners of Brent as had formerly occurred. Mr T.W. Colley attended with regard to the rights of Ugborough parish

> and the Misses Carew. There was nothing to repair until Dockwell Ridge was reached, and here three boundary stones had to be re-erected. Before leaving the moor, the party of about 70 partook of luncheon, provided by the arrangement of the clerk of the Parish Council (Mr J.H. Stanbury). He was suitably thanked on the proposition of the Chairman (Mr E.W.Mead).

The article goes on to record some of those present, and that a couple of hours were spent in impromptu racing, etc. at Yelland (Yalland). It is interesting to note that 'foreigners', i.e. representatives of other parishes, accompanied the South Brent parishioners along their respective boundary.

BRENT MANOR

After the Dissolution of Buckfast Abbey, Sir William Petre acquired the lands of the Abbey, including Brent Manor. Anxious to confirm his rights to the moorland attached to Brent Manor, a search was made of the documents in the Abbey Cartulary which brought to light the 1531 finding in favour of the abbey and thus confirming his entitlement. Even so, the precise bounds were still in dispute, and this in turn led to a further inquisition by Commissioners in 1557. The line of the bounds was finally settled by a panel of Jurors, but this entered the ancient line of the Forest; to mark the bounds once and for ever four crosses were erected, one each at Three Barrows, Western Whittabarrow, Buckland Ford on the Avon and at the junction of the Avon and the Wester Wellabrook. The inquisition that took place on 25 August 1557 gave the bounds as:

The aforesaid moor or waste of Brentmore extends itself, ascending from a certain valley or place where and in which two waters called Les Glases run together into one and from thence towards the north to Glase Head, and from Glase Head ascending towards the north by a long 'conger' of stones called Le Rowe Rewe to a certain great heap of stones by the name of Tryberie Boroughs, alias Tre Boroughs, being the middle heap of three heaps of stones there, thence towards the north by the waste of Uggbroughe Moor adjoining, as far as Further Whiteborough otherwise Wester Whiteborough (where) the Forest of Dartmoor adjoins on the north side, thence towards the east by the Forest of Dartmoor aforesaid to the Ford of Buckland called Buckland Ford, near Bishops Mead otherwise Busshe Mead, descending by the Forest of Dartmoor aforesaid as the Water of Avon runs, as far as Welbrook Foot, and from Wellbrook Foot aforesaid towards the east by the Avene aforesaid as far as Smallbrook Foot, at which place called Welbrook Foot the aforesaid Moor of Brent, called Brentmoor, and a certain moor called Buckfastleigh Moor lie adjacent to the aforesaid Forest of Dartmoor.

As has been said earlier, the Duchy never accepted that the Forest bounds went to Western Whittabarrow as described above; it is also interesting to note that at that time the moors of Brent and Buckfastleigh both touched upon the Wester Wellabrook at its foot, not Brent and Dean Prior as they do today.

The sixteenth-century map of Dartmoor has the 1240 Perambulation points of the Forest of Dartmoor shown upon it, the captions reading from the west, and also much of the southern moors, where the captions are read at right angles to them. This leads one to believe that it was either prepared for, or used to, delineate the bounds of this manor of Brent, for clearly marked upon the map are 'Brente More' and 'brent moore', together with other points of reference, including the heads of the East and West Glaze Brooks and the legend 'Brente in Grounde' for the enclosed land.

Robert Burnard, writing in *Dartmoor Pictorial Records* (Vol.1 p.47) quotes from yet another source 'upon a heap of stones called Triborough a cross is erected bearing the words "Bunda de Brentmoor".' Spence Bate reported the finding of a mutilated part of this cross, the top part of the head together with one arm, as he said 'in all probability the remains of one of those set up in 1557'. Other later sightings have been reported, the last the writer heard about was in 1957 but a photograph of this was hardly convincing. The question has been raised as to whether this cross was prepared to mark the Brent Moor bounds, or whether there was once a proper cross standing where we now see Hobajohn's Cross, removed from that site and utilised to mark Brent Moor at Three Barrows. However both crosses depicted on the sixteenth-century map, Syward's and Hobajohn's, whilst shown thereon as conventional crosses standing upon plinths or calvaries, must be depicted only in a symbolic manner, the present Hobajohn's being the original 'cross', merely an inscribed cross upon a small standing stone, and that the lost cross formerly standing upon the centre cairn of Three Barrows was a conventional one.

The next cross on Brent's bounds was set upon the summit of Western Whittabarrow cairn, and still exists in part, but mutilated almost beyond recognition. The shaft has been re-erected in an inverted position so that now the tenon formerly fitting into a socket stone is uppermost. It was not until 1847 that workers associated with the naptha works at Shipley Bridge made a shelter from the vast amount of stone comprising the cairn, utilising the cross shaft as a lintel for their chimney piece, having first knocked off the arms. The re-erection was the work of Francis Meynell, on the bounds of whose property it was situated, after the naptha works failed. It is known as Petre's Cross.

Nothing at all appears to remain of the third cross in the series which used to stand at Buckland Ford on the Avon, although the late Mr Codd of Gisperdown Farm maintained that the cross head found on his land once belonged to it. This head bears an inscribed cross on both faces (now set into the wall at the entrance to the farm), similar to another set into the wall of the cottages at Swallerton Gate in 1988 and may just be another remnant of a wayside cross.

The fourth example, on the other hand, was the only one to remain intact until early September 1990, when it was found recumbent, broken off at ground level. It was replaced by the Dartmoor National Park Authority quite quickly, and stones were placed around the bottom in an endeavour to stop animals rubbing themselves against it. This is sited just within the Forest at the foot of the Wester Wellabrook below Huntingdon Warren as it falls into Avon. William Crossing (*Guide* p.367) comments that 'although we know Huntingdon Cross was standing in 1557, there is no mention of it in the survey of 1609, which however is

hardly to be wondered at seeing that the Wella Brook forms the forest boundary, and that the point given by the perambulators of 1240 was the confluence of that stream with the Avon'. The cross is mentioned in the later 1786 Survey presented at Lydford Castle, and it is also recorded as being a tin bound of Huntingdon Mine, dating from 1759. No sign of any inscription can be seen on this cross, though George Oliver's *Monasticon Diocesis Exoniensis*, probably the source of Burnard's reference to an inscription on the Three Barrows example, records that the 1557 Inquisition repeated a reference to an insciption being made on each of the four crosses, here worded '... ac etiam ad predictum locum vocatum Welbrokesfote quarta crux erecta est in qua etiam eadam verba, videlicet, "Bunda de Brentmore" – insculpta sunt'.

The mention of 'Glaze Meet' on these sixteenth-century bounds has already been made. Before the Dissolution of all monastic houses at about that time, a small parcel of land situated between the East and West Glaze Brooks belonged to the Canons of Torre Abbey. A document of circa 1250 cedes a triangular piece of land to the canons from William de Lestre of Langforde Lestre Manor, bounded by these two streams from Glazemeet as far north as a point called 'Nywapitte' on the West Glaze. There is still a wall around this land with an entrance from the left bank of the West Glaze via a ford. Inside are the remains of two small rectangular buildings, the remains of Glascombe Farm. Whilst Torre Abbey held the property from the thirteenth century, there was a dispute in the early fourteenth century between Joannis de Rous, Abbot of Torre (1305-30) and William atte Slade, Abbot of Buckfast Abbey (died 1327) over animals at some point where their estates adjoined each other,

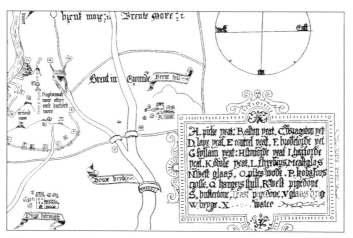

Fig. 44 Sixteenth-century Map showing Harford, Ugborough and Brent moors.

which may well have been here, where, on the East Glaze, they did so, Buckfast Abbey owning Brent Moor to the east. There was certainly a settlement near Glazemeet from very early times. The sixteenth-century map of Dartmoor shows the wall extending from the West Glaze to the East Glaze, the land so enclosed being coloured dark brown. This property gave the Canons of Torre the advantage of the right to pasturage on the moor, Torre holding the land not as an outright gift but as an exchange, the abbey having returned to de Lestre a ferling of land at Ingsdon, within Ilsington parish, which his father had given to the abbey. One of the points of the bounds was called 'Wyrttrum' at the 1557 Inquisition, said to be interpreted as 'tree roots or a clearing'.

In general, the boundaries of parishes when first formed were based on, and followed the same line as,

those of a manor or group of manors already established, and it is known from documentary evidence that in the thirteenth century the land between the East and West Glaze Brooks belonged to the Manor of Langforde Lestre, this lying within the parish of Ugborough, as were the Manors of Ulgeberge, Pech Coma and Lodebroc. In the sixteenth century, when the bounds of Brent Moor adjoining Ugborough, were re-defined for Sir William Petre in 1557, after his purchase of Brent Moor following the Dissolution of Buckfast Abbey, the bounds thereabouts were the same, going from Three Barrows to East Glaze Head and thence to Glazemeet, etc. as they do today.

However, Crossing in his *Guide* (p.380) relates the tale of the finding of a dead body on the open moor, supposedly on Brent Moor, which the Brent people refused to bury, leading to the Ugborough Commoners doing so and thus claiming the land in question, as was the custom. He says that in a document dated 1812 in which 'the acreage of the commons and waste of the manor of South Brent are set forth' there is an entry referring to the Glazes, which is stated to consist of over 64 acres and to be situated 'between Easter and Wester Glazes'. He goes on to say that this piece of land was 'formerly said to be in the parish of South Brent' and that it 'now pays rates and taxes to Ugborough'.

If there be any truth at all in the tale regarding the body on the moor, it could only be accounted for by South Brent burying it and claiming the said piece of land from Ugborough, rather than the other way around and that at some time between the sixteenth century and 1812 Ugborough had reclaimed their original and historic boundary.

UGBOROUGH/HARFORD

Ugborough and Harford are two of the most elongated parishes of all those bordering on to the Forest, in places no more than a quarter to half a mile wide. There has been some controversy and confusion at various times since the late eighteenth century over their boundaries. From 1782 to 1784 there had been a dispute between a Humphrey Savery of Stowford, the old Domesday manor of 'Estaforda' in Harford parish and abutting on its eastern side to Ugborough Moor, and a Thomas Lane of Cofleet, owner of the adjoining manor of Langford Leister or Lestre within Ugborough parish, Savery alleging that Lane:

> with force and arms broke and entered the Close of the said Humphrey called East Harford Moor and with his feet walking trod down trampled upon consumed and spoiled grass of the said Humphrey there lately growing to the value of £20 and with divers cattle eat up depastured trod down trampled upon and spoiled grass of the said Humphrey there also growing to the value of another £20 and with the wheels of carts wagons and other carriages crushed squeezed damaged and spoiled the grass there also lately growing to the value of another £20 and tore up turned up rooted up subverted and spoiled the soil there and cut dug up and raised divers quantities of turves and blackwood upon and from the said close to the value of another £20 and took and carried away the same and converted and disposed thereof to his own use and other wrongs to the said Humphrey there to the great damage of the said Humphrey and against the peace of our Lord the now King.

Ugborough/Harford: Recumbent Longstone. SX 6543 6065 *Longstone re-erected in 1991.*

In the court case resulting from these allegations which were not settled until 1803, possibly due to the poor health of Savery, a Mr John Andrews acted on Savery's behalf, a solicitor from Modbury who had some knowledge of the moor, and who in 1799 with a Richard Willis as guide, made a survey of Erme Plains and East Harford Moor. He had made several perambulations of the moor since 1788, including a visit to the Cranmere Pool at his second attempt to find it in 1789. He had an ancient sixteenth-century map of Erme Plains, but was a competent mathematician and able to make his own survey, which in the T.D.A. of 1941 Richard Hansford Worth praises for its accuracy. Many of Andrews' original notes for the case were found by chance when they were sent as salvage for the Second World War 'War Effort' and reproduced and commented upon by Worth in an article entitled 'Dartmoor 1788–1808'.

At the time of Andrews' survey, it appears that there were no boundstones along the Harford/ Ugborough boundary, and that only natural or Bronze Age objects were used to define it, but he had no notion of the true purpose of stone rows, and in a comment made in September 1800, referring to a then recumbent menhir or Longstone, re-erected in 1991, says:

> From the Middle of Long Stone towards Hobajones Cross there is a Row of Stones which seem plainly to have been intentionally laid, and probably for the purpose of a boundary and Mr Rivers consents to consider it as such, and instead of going in a direct line from Hobajones Cross to Three Barrows, to go from the Cross to Long Stone, and from thence to Three Barrows...

This was the then considered boundary of East Harford and Langford Lestre but in July of that same year a William Tozer stated that 'all the Moor which adjoins East Harford Moor on the east, from Prowse's Rock to a long stone beyond Hobajones Cross, belongs to the Manor of Torpike, and not to the Manor of Langford Lester'. Suffice it to say that when in September 1803 a number of boundary stones were erected, 'some revision' of Andrews' map had to be made. Not only was the stone row running north from Butterdon Hill used to mark the boundary, but Worth states that 'fifty-five boundary stones were erected in August and September 1803, of which fifty-one are marked on the opposite sides with the letters 'H' and 'U'. These were set to indicate

Prowse's Rock. SX 648 573

the boundary between Harford and Ugborough Moors, not necessarily the parish boundary.

His statement regarding the marked boundstones is patently an error, for the only 'stones' inscribed 'H/U' are from the Forest boundary southwards: the outer 'U' stone at SX 643 664, a slab of stone having the letters on the same plane with an inscribed line between them; the 'U' stone, formerly at Stony Bottom at SX 644 650 but now missing; above Dry Lake Head at SX 645 638; on Piles Hill at SX 653 610; near Sharp Tor at SX 651 618; on Western Beacon at SX 655 575; and Prowse's Rock, though this is a natural boulder not a set boundstone, at SX 648 573, which is inscribed with the appropriate letter on its east and west sides. Thus it must have been intended to read '51 unmarked'!

Hobajohn's Cross is not a true cross, but an upright stone somewhat larger than most others in the stone row associated with it, having an inscribed cross on its south-western face. Its base is set within a small platform of stones and at the time of Andrews' survey he commented:

> The stone called Hobajones Cross (or post), which leaned considerably before, has lately been thrown quite down, but it is not removed from its place and the socket is very distinct. It went but a little way (say not more than 6 inches) into the ground. It is like the Frustrum of a Pyramid, the Bottom being much broader than the top.

Fig. 45 Hobajon's Cross

Later on he records that (6 September 1800):

> The stone called Hobajones Cross which had been thrown down by some means unknown, was again fixed exactly in the place where it had stood. Present Messrs Geo Rivers, Jno & Rd Andrew, Rd Willis...

Rivers was then the representative for Stowford, but more interesting is the nature of the tenon of the cross. The sixteenth-century map in the D.R.O. (Fig.44) shows both 'Hobajon's Crosse' and 'Syward's Cross', both depicted as standing upon a plinth or calvary, but this must be purely a symbolic representation, and there is no doubt in the author's mind that what we see today is the original Hobajohn's Cross, and that the one erected on Three Barrows in 1557 had no connection with it.

Andrews also turned over the fallen Longstone at SX 6543 6065 to see if it bore any inscription on its underside (it did not), and set up a plain stone beside it, the point at which he had proposed to take the manorial bounds to Three Barrows. After the 'award' of 1803 and the settlement made, by 1867 an agreement had been made whereby the boundaries agreed upon were again ignored by a deed drawn up between the Duchy of Cornwall, the Earl of Chester and Henry Rivers of Stowford.

The Ordnance Survey also had their troubles with the Harford/Ugborough boundary. There are two large cairns of stone on Butterdon Hill associated with these bounds where it veers from a northerly direction to one to the north-east before resuming a northerly direction again. On the original six inch scale map of 1889 they marked these two cairns or

Marntory Rock. SX 6560 5945

tumuli as 'Mound of Stones' (the more southerly one) and 'Heap of Stones', together with a third point more to the north-east which they called 'Pile of Stones'. This latter was, in fact, the cairn circle at the southern end of the Butterdon stone row. However in their Second Edition of the six inch map of 1906 the O.S. place a 'Stone Circle' north-east of the Pile of Stones, together with the stone row running east of the Harford/ Ugborough boundary line, and meeting this parish boundary between Marntory Rock and another cairn to the east of it, thus apparently duplicating the Cairn Circle, for there are only two cairns on the height of Butterdon Hill itself. Later they corrected their error, marking only these two cairns or tumuli and the 'Stone Circle' where they had formerly marked the 'Pile of Stones', taking the boundary along the stone row.

ERMINGTON MANOR

There is also a manor having rights upon Dartmoor, yet whose bounds do not touch upon the commons. William Crossing mentions this fact when referring to the bridge over the Erme at Ivybridge, where formerly the boundaries of the parishes of Harford, Cornwood, Ermington and Ugborough met, pointing out that the Lords of the Manor of Ermington have rights on Erme

Plains, which tract of land, formerly in the Hundred of Ermington, now lies within the parishes of Harford and Ugborough. At Domesday Ermington, the chief Manor of the Hundred, was acquired by King William, together with Blackawton, in exchange for Bampton which had been held by King Edward. The house at Flete was built in Tudor times by the Hele family, and was inherited in 1716 by James Bulteel who had married Mary Crocker, from his great friend Richard Hele. The Bulteels continued to live there until 1863 when it was sold outside the family to a retired Australian sheep-farmer, who had originally come from Devon, William Francis Splatt, at a time when it was also the ancestral home of Georgiana Bulteel. Miss Bulteel married Henry Bingham Mildmay, who re-purchased the house for Georgiana in 1876, and it was only during the brief interlude when the house was not in the possession of the Bulteels, that an ancient ceremony inaugurated as early as 1603 was reinstated in 1878. This custom claimed the Manor's right to fish the whole length of the river Erme, from source to mouth and beyond, a perambulation taking place every seven years, a proclamation being made at several points on the river, together with the casting of nets. The 1878 Proclamation read:

> Manor of Ermington; All persons whom it may concern take notice, that a perambulation of Erme Plains – on which tenants of this manor have a right of common pasture – will this day be made, by order, and on behalf of the Lord of the said Manor, according to the bounds and limits following: viz.,

> Beginning at a small heap of stones near Left Lake Head, at the end of the ridge of stones which

proceeds north-west from the Middle Borough of Three Boroughs, thence by several bound stones and a ridge of stones to outer Whitaburrow (Western Whittabarrow) passing a little to the south-west of the cross called Petre's Cross, and so on to Abbot's Way, otherwise Jobber's Path, and from thence to Red Lake Head, and by the same lake to the river Erme, thence by the said river to the foot of the Left Lake and thence by the same lake to its head, and so back to the small heap of stones first above mentioned. Take notice further that, by the same authority, it is also intended to view the said river Erme from its head to the sea, and to fish therein and do other acts in order to assert and maintain the right of fishery, and other rights belonging to the said Manor of Ermington. And be it known that the Lord of this manor asserts as belonging to in respect thereof a right of free fishery in and throughout the said river and that is intended on this occasion to use a net and other means for taking fish therein for his use, in order to maintain such right. And that he also asserts the like right to all wreck and goods found, either jetsam, flotsam, or ligan, within the said river, and from the mouth thereof seawards as far as an umber or tar barrel can be seen.

The starting point of this perambulation was marked on John Andrews' map of 1799 where it was described as 'A Small Heap of Stones at the south-east Corner of Erm Plains, where the Perambulators thereof usually begin'. This is just beyond the northern end of 'Rowerewe', the major reave north and south of Three Barrows, and where we now find a small boundstone ringed by stones known as 'Ermington Manor' (SX 651 631). This boundstone was mistakenly marked as 'Hobajohn's Cross (remains of)' by the Ordnance Survey on their 1889 six inch scale map, made as the result of a survey undertaken in 1886. However they compounded two errors in doing this, for it is the next boundstone north-wards, between Ugborough and Brent moors that fortuitously somewhat resembles a rough cross, seen from a certain angle, at SX 651 632, and to which they had erroneously intended to apply the description. Be that as it may, these boundstones are, as stated, on the Ugborough/Brent bounds, not on those of Harford/Ugborough where the true Hobajohn's Cross is to be found. It is also interesting to note that whilst reference was made to Petre's Cross on Western Whittabarrow, there is no mention of any cross on Three Barrows in this declaration, presumably dating from the 1878 reintroduction of the custom, suggesting that there was even then no sign of it. The *Western Morning News* of the time records that Lord Blachford, who also had rights on the Erme, made a good-humoured observa-tion to the Ermington people landing fish on his right bank of the river at Ivybridge, his rights of fishing the river being advertised in 1986 when the Blachford Manor Estate was put up for sale.

CORNWOOD

Cornwood together with nearby Lutton comprises a large parish, 6000 of its acres being moorland. Their Bounds were beaten in 1981 (anti-clockwise) and again in 1991 (clockwise), led in both instances by Len Copley.

In 1981 16 members of Cornwood Church gathered at Slade Lawn at 7.30a.m. on 10 September, to cover 22 miles. They walked along Slade Drive, Stert Bridge, Little Stert, Marks Bridge, Cadleigh, Stibbs Cross and New Waste. Next to the Erme, when the rain came, the Stone Row, reaching Broad Rock for lunch, after-wards over Langcombe Hill to Shell Top, through Dendles Wood to Higher Hele and back to Slade.

On 8 June 1991, 24 people started the walk by Quick Bridge, up through the right of way past Cholwich to Penn Moor. The first boundary stone near the clay works was not found, but the second on the way up the hill to Shell Top was. Next along the col – an area more often than not wet under foot – with lunch at Erme pits in the rain. Down the Erme until the stone row was reached and followed to the Dancers, over Stall Moor to New Waste and through the lanes to Cornwood, where tea was kindly supplied at the Vicarage.

CHOLWICH TOWN

Cholwich Town farmhouse was a superb example of a late-medieval building but is now much neglected and isolated, the word Town here applied to a single settlement, won from the open moor at a time when people were having to go further and higher into the moor to find unoccupied land [some repairs were carried out during 1998]. It is now completely sur-rounded by china clay waste, the old approach lane with its massive boulders now closed off by English China Clays who own the whole area.

The Ordnance Survey records in 1881 show the site of a former boundstone just north of the former Tolchmoor Bridge over the Torry Brook, now lost under the waste, inscribed 'C/PM' – probably Cholwich and Penn Moor.

BLACHFORD MANOR

Blachford Manor, in the parish of Cornwood, is another ancient manor, recorded in Domesday. In the Exon version it is spelt 'Blacheorda' and in the Exchequer Domesday spelt 'Blacheurde'. In a Tax Roll of 1302-03 it becomes 'Nitherblachesworthy' and was often referred to as Blachworthy rather than Blachford from the seventeenth century. The rebuilt manor house had been in the same family's posession from 1694 (the Rogers) until the estate was sold in June 1985, but back on the market in December (W.M.N. 7.12.1985). The estate covered some 700 acres including much moorland with fishing rights on both the Erme and the Yealm, the bounds extending as far into the moor as the Forest Bounds at Erme Head. The manor bounds have been marked by several boundary markers running from the 'A/Head' rock to Broad Rock at SX 6185 6735 which used to have a pole marking its position. The rock is inscribed 'BB/Broad Rock',

Yealm Head. SX 6155 6475

Blachford Manor: Langcombe Hill. SX 6204 6630

the letters 'BB' standing for Blachford Bounds, these letters being used on other boundstones belonging to this manor. Those on the Cornwood parish bounds are marked on the 1:25 000 Ordnance Survey map at Langcombe Hill (SX 6204 6630) and now repaired with cement, on Langcombe Hill (SX 6175 6583) and at the junction of Penn Moor, Lee Moor and Blachford bounds, which is lettered 'BB/L/P' on its three sides (SX 6150 6545) and not 'B/LP' as recorded elsewhere, the 'L' and 'P' having distinctive serifs. This latter stone is, in all likelihood, that mentioned by W. Burt (Carrington 1826) as being on the Forest boundary, though it is not, and where he records it as being inscribed 'B.B.L.B.' Below Yealm Head there is another 'BB' stone at SX 6155 6475, and there used to be another inscribed 'L.P.BB' near the Torry Brook but this has been lost through the extensive china clay workings that have taken place in that area over the past hundred and fifty years or so. Two other stones on the old six inch Ordnance Survey map, one in Dendles Wood at SX 616 626 and another at SX 621 615 may also be, or have been Blachford 'BB' stones.

SHEEPSTOR

The earliest document the author has come across regarding Sheepstor is one dated 1626, in the WDRO, as follows:

The first Bound is Portlane Head from thence West and North West by the hedge between the lands of Walter Elford Esqr now the Lord of this Manor and free hamlet of Sheepstor and the lands of Nicholas Slanning Esqr called Yeo to a rock called Oxentor lying between Mr Elford's wood and Mr Slanning's wood from thence by the hedge between the said woods to the river of Meavy and so ascending that river to the tayle bound of a tinwork called Broadmead and so by the bounds of the said tinwork and the bounds of another tinwork called Sandymead in Bounsalls pits to another bound in the highway between the said tinwork lying between the House called Mullacraught and new bridge from that bound to the head bound of Broadmead which lyeth in Furzeham a little by the west side of the gate and from thence between the bound of the said Sandymead and the bound of another tinwork called Woodsidemead again to the River of Meavy ascending to the head bound of Woodsidemead and from thence to the flood hatch at the head wear of Plymouth leat where another of the ancient bounds stood and so ascending the said river by the ancient course there of to the fall or foot of Denbrook and because the said river of Meavy hath in times past been diverted by tinners out of its said ancient course and in such places yet remaineth so there be (ancient?) bounds which were formerly set by a view and (- - -)

parishioners of Sheepstor and Walkhampton and the (- - -) both sides for many years since and now review(ed) (by the?) jury and others and shewed to younger people which (does?) truely manifest where the ancient course of the said River (- - -) and from Denbrook (foot) ascending by the hedges of Middle (Worthy) and West D(ean)ccombe (where) the ancient course of the said brook was in times past to the foot or fall of another brook and so ascending that brook of Crecombe between Heathmead and Leedon on the east side and Oldmead Down on the west side to Berricombe Gate and from thence by the outer hedges or corn ditch of Nattor Blackland Colleytown Holditch and Blackhay next to Ringmore Down unto the said (first?) bound of Portlanehead.

A list of the jury and of those who we present at the view of the bounds of the Manor and free hamlet of Sheepstor in the year 1626

The jury	
John Elford	William Dundridge
John Andrew	William Barrett
Nicholas Bickford	William Watts
Richard Bounsall	William Northam
Hugh Stuttaford	Bernard Baylie
Richard Brocke	Sylvanus Lowde

And those here under named ancient persons then and there likewise present John Woollacombe. Richard Woollacombe. Richard Bounsall. Barnard Elford. Walter Dunderidge. Stephen Knight. Charles Stuttaford et al Concordat cum originale Testante J W et al

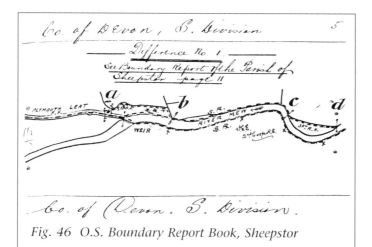

Fig. 46 O.S. Boundary Report Book, Sheepstor

Sheepstor/Walkhampton B.S. at Copythorne Rushes. SX. 5910 6870

Reverse (showing 'W' for Walkhampton).

Now known as the river Meavy, it was in Crossing's day more usually referred to as the Mew or Mewy. In this early 1880s' extract from the Ordnance Survey Boundary Report Book slight changes in the Sheepstor boundary are shown, together with the weir at 'Headweir', take-off point of the Plymouth, or Drake's Leat, dating from the sixteenth century. The whole of the part of the river shown is now inundated by the Burrator Reservoir, opened in 1898.

The only boundary stone known to the author is at Copothorne (or Copythorne) Rushes, engraved with an 'S' for Sheepstor and 'W' for Walkhampton, at SX 5910 6870.

BUCKLAND MONACHORUM

Although, again, not a parish mentioned in the 22, it is nevertheless of interest as Isabella de Fortibus held the Manors of Buckland Monachorum, Bickleigh and Walkhampton, and it seems appropriate to include it before Walkhampton.

At Domesday the Manor of Buckland Monachorum was described thus:

In the time of King Edward the Confessor, Ulveve held Bokeland, and it was taxed for 1 hide and 1 virgate of land and 1 firling. The land is 8 plough lands, there are in demesne 2 plough lands and 5 bondmen and 10 villeins, and 4 bordars, with 5 ploughs. There are 6 acres of meadow and 6 acres of wood and 12 acres of pasture. Brismar also held Bokeland, in the time of Edward the Confessor, and it was taxed for 3 hides and 1 virgate of land and a half. The land is 25 concales. The demesne are 3 concales and

15 bondmen and 24 villeins and 10 bordars with 7 ploughs. There is a salt pit and a fishing rendering 10/-, and 8 acres of meadow pasture 1 mile long and the same in width. Wood 4 miles long and 2 furlongs broad. Formerly it was worth 50 shillings, now it is worth 100 shillings.

In the thirteenth century the Manors of Buckland Monachorum, Bickleigh and Walkhampton were given by Amicia, Countess of Devon, to found the Cistercian Abbey of St Benedict at Buckland Monachorum. These manors she had acquired from her daughter, Isabella de Fortibus, Countess of Albemarle, the Charter of Confirmation allowing the transference of the property to Amicia, and for the right to assign it to the foundation of a religious house reading as follows:

Edward, by the Grace of God, King of England, Lord of Ireland, and Duke of Aquitaine. To all to whom this writing shall come greeting. Know ye that we have conceded and confirmed to Amicia, Countess of Devon, the manor of Buckland, with the hamlets of Columpton, Walkhampton and Bickerley, together with all and singular their appurtenances wheresoever situate; To have and to hold to the same Amicia according to the form and tenor of the deeds which she had from the gift of Isabella de Fortibus, Countess of Albemarle, her daughter; And if it shall happen that the said Amicia should wish to give and assign the said manor and hamlets with all their appurtenances whatesoever to religeous men, and with them to found a new religeous house, know ye that we for ourselves and for our heirs, will consider and

accept that gift as acceptable provided that the said house, after the decease of the said Amicia, shall be held of us and our heirs 'in capite' And we faithfully promise to confirm it, when founded or appointed, in pure and perpetual alms. In Witness, etc.

Witness myself at Odiham, 8th day of August, in the 4th year of our reign.

The fourth year of the reign of Edward I puts this document as being signed in 1276, and the charter is dated 1278, but a second charter was drawn up later by Isabella de Fortibus after Amicia's death in 1291. The Deed of Amicia, Countess of Devon, and the 1291 Charter of Isabella de Fortibus, describe the 'metes and bounds' of the land granted to found Buckland Abbey (Fig. 47) thus:

the manors of Bocland, Bykelie, and Walkhampton, according to their metes and divisions, that is to say, from the Lobbapilla, on the western part of Bocland towards the north and east, through the middle of the water of Tavy, and from Walkhampton to the boundaries of Dartmoor, on the northern part of Mistor, and thence towards the south by the boundaries of the Verderers of Dartmoor, that is to say, by Mistorhead, and by Hysfochres, and by Siwards Cross and Gyllesburgh and Plymcrundla to the Plym towards the west to Yaddabrook, and so by the bounds which surround Rydemore and Smalacumba, that is to say, by the old ditch to the angle of the ditch of Yllalonde, and thence by Hurtwallen to Smalacumbacrosse and Smalacumbalak, and by the water course of

Meavy to Olvak, and by the ditch to the road which leads from Plympton to Schitestorr, and so by the stone bounds to Biricombaford and by Crewecumba, and Denebrok, and (along) the course of the river Meavy to Schollaford, and so by the old boundaries to Yanedoncrosse, and thence by the bounds to Stoford and Lake and Churcheford, and by the divisions between Elleford and Crosseton to Elfordlak and to the course of the river Meavy, and so to the place where the Meavy falls into the Plym, and along the Plym towards the divisions of Hescombe, and to the cross roads beyond Purpris, and thence by passing along the way which leads from Cadworth Bridge to Plympton through the land of the Schagh towards the east as far as Shitaburgh, and thence by old bound-stones to Haneketorr, and thence towards the west and north through the land of Farnhill to Maynstonktown and Maynstoncross and Horingbrook to Pudehel, including Southpudehel, and so along the bounds towards the east to Horsford, and thence along the ancient metes to Writewille and Horyngbrok, and to the Plym and to Wolewille Cross, and thence by the road which leads from Sutton to Tavistock at Copriscrosse, and thence towards the north along the antient ditch to Bycacumbayoneda, and so along the antient bounds to Lobbapilla.

The deed continues, giving 'the lands and villeins of Torr at Schitestor, adjoining the manor of Buckeleye' and 'the Hundred of Roborough with all profits from thence arising', the Abbot of Buckland becoming Lord of the Manor of the whole.

Starting at 'Lobbapilla', now Lophill, near Maristow on the river Tavy, this was, according to Spence Bate, the head of the salt-water creek at the mouth of the river. On the sixteenth-century map of Dartmoor there is just one word written on the face of it in a later style to the rest, and in the same hand as the copy of the 1240 Perambulation written on the reverse side. This is the word 'Lobbapilla', written within the breadth of the river Tavy opposite a drawing of Bickleigh church. Towards the north we then go up the Tavy and the Walkham as far as the Forest boundary. Then in a southerly direction, following the Forest bounds to Mistorhead, or Mistor panna, the rock basin on the eastern edge of the tor, thence to North Hessary and South Hessary tors, Syward's Cross and Eylesbarrow. All this is plain sailing, but next we come to 'Plymcrundla' again, a variation of the 'Plym Crowndel' already referred to, and which Crossing equates with a spring or well at Evil Combe, and which is shown on the sixteenth-century map within a circle and given the same standing as all the other major points of reference on the Forest bounds of 1240. It is now thought to be not Evil Combe but the Crane Lake, another small right bank tributary of the Plym, a short distance upstream from Evil Combe, and which is still on the Forest boundary line. Following the Plym downstream now, we leave it again at 'Yaddabrook', the Legis Lake, following the present boundary, and thence around Ringmoor Down via 'Yllalonde' and 'Hurtwallen', the locations of which are unknown to the author. However the next two points, 'Smalacumbacrosse' and 'Smalacumbalak' are more identifiable, at least the latter, today's Smallacombe, flowing into the Meavy near Yeo Farm. We are on the right line, but which cross was the original 'Smalacumbacrosse'? And where was it originally situated? Marchant's Cross nearby may have been the one referred to, but equally this may still be on its original site where the ancient track from Tavistock divided, to Plympton, and across the moor to Buckfast. Formerly it stood 8ft 2ins in height but in 1937 it was knocked down by a car, when a short piece of the lower part of the shaft was broken away, thus when re-erected it was shorter by a few inches. The socket stone was found to be perforated right through, unlike most other Dartmoor examples. It has a large incised cross on each face. This was suggested as being Smalacumbacrosse by both Masson Phillips and Crossing. Hansford Worth at first agreed, but later opined that this was unlikely and leaned towards the only other cross extant in the immediate area, that now set up outside the Lych Gate of Sheepstor church, sometimes known as Roman Cross. In the last century it was in a field near Burrator House acting as a rubbing post for cattle, and it was not until 1910 that it was suggested that it be re-erected as a commemorative gesture to celebrate the Coronation of King George V. The damaged arms were sympathetically repaired and the whole set upon a new three-tiered pedestal. The shaft bears a cross in relief on both faces, the shape of which suggests the origin of the name 'Roman Cross'.

We now bear eastwards and encircle Sheepstor in an anti-clockwise direction and by the track from Plympton to Sheepstor, Portland Lane, we arrive at Biricombaford, i.e. Burracombe Gate under Gutter Tor on the Eylesbarrow mine track. 'And by Crewcumba' to the Deanbrook, and back on present bounds down to the Meavy to 'Schollaford' on the old road into Sheepstor now under the waters of the reservoir, thence up to Yennadon Cross, possibly that re-erected

at the junction of the Princetown–Yelverton road with a lane from the Meavy valley at SX 545 695. This, only re-erected in the late 1970s, has chamfered edges and an incised cross on both faces. We now go westward

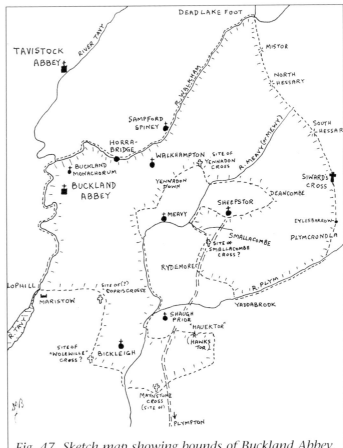

Fig. 47 Sketch map showing bounds of Buckland Abbey.

to Lake and Elford and down the Elford Brook to the Meavy once again, following it downstream to Shaugh Bridge where it flows into the Plym. 'Purpris' would seem to be identifiable with Purps Farm, and the crossroads beyond Beatland Corner. 'Haneketorr' or perhaps 'Haueketorr' is Hawks Tor, so is 'Shitaburgh' synonymous with Saddlesborough? Through the Fernhill Waste in the Wotter area we next go to Maynstone Cross. This was formerly thought to have been to the west of the river Plym, but Masson Phillips states that it was to the east of the river, not the west, and 'thus it cannot be near the present mainstone'. He then records the opinion of Dr M. Spooner (T.D.A. 1987) who contends that Brownie Cross at SX 545 558 is the most likely to fit the bill, on the Tavistock–Plymouth road. Sadly all that remains of this cross is the old socket stone, octagonal in shape together with a few other stones that may well have once formed part of the pedestal.

Wolewille Cross is thought to be the 'Greatcrosse' shown on the late sixteenth-century map of the Plymouth Leat (Drake's Leat). In 1769 a survey of the Lopes estate shows a 'Great Cross' at the point where the drive of Woolwell leaves the Tavistock–Plymouth road at SX 502 613. The last cross on this extensive boundary is Copriscrosse. Once again the former candidate for this cross was thought to be that belonging to the fine socket stone in the hedgebank of the Bickleigh road at its junction with Leigh Lane, but Masson Phillips records the view of Dr Spooner, who is of the opinion that it was formerly sited at Axter Gate at SX 496 630, near a farm called 'Coppers' anciently 'Coperesland', and probably associated with the de Coppere family in the fourteenth century. This just leaves us with the problem of where the Leigh

Lane socket stone came from. From Copriscrosse we return to our starting point at Lobbapilla via the Milton Brook.

WALKHAMPTON

The following Beating of the Bounds was very recently found by Mike Brown in the Maristow Estate documents, gratefully received in mid-October 2001, and as Dave would have appreciated its inclusion, it has been added. Mike mentioned that the document is very badly stained with damp and mould in a large patch in the centre of one side, so the first few words of many of the lines in the central part of the text are lost, but not so many that the meaning intended cannot be understood.

Beating of Bounds of Walkhampton
30–31 July 1821

The Boundaries of the Manor of Walkhampton. Be it remembered that on Monday the Thirtieth Day of July in the year of our Lord 1821 Sir Mannasseh Masseh Lopes Bart, Lord of the said Manor of Walkhampton with divers of the Tenants of the said manor and others whose names are hereunto subscribed, together with numerous other persons, perambulated and viewed the meets limits and bounds of the Manor aforesaid, and found them to be and they were acknowledged to be as hereinafter set forth and described. Due notice of such view having been previously given in writing to the several Lords of Manors, Landholders and others whose Estates or Commons adjoin to the said Manor of Walkhampton. Began near the village of Horrabridge at a place where the back Water from Horrabridge Mills and a small stream that comes down the bottom from Horrabridge through the Filley falls into the River Walkham, and ascended by the said united stream to the corner of an Orchard belonging to the said Mills, and then along by the hedge of Lord Ashburton's Lands keeping the said hedge on the right hand till we came to the lane leading from the Village of Horrabridge to Knowl Down, where we turned short to the left and followed the Hedge to the corner of a Dwelling House now held on Lease by Walter King where a small stream of Water comes across the Road and enters the Land called Filley, then ascending by the said stream of water keeping the Hedges on our right hand until we came parallel to the Hedge that parts Mill pool Tenement from Ellis's Tenement, there crossed the hedge into the lower meadow of Ellis's Tenement and kept on with the Hedge on our left hand up through Ellis's ground and two closes of Land called … to G…ford and … kept on by the north side of the Hedges that separate the Grounds … until we came to the head of the first meadow belonging to William Snell's Gnatham where … hedge on our right, until we came to an Ash tree which we found cut in the Bark W B 18.. … did cut the figures 1821, there returned short to the right and kept on by the Hedges on the north side … ground and three fields belonging to Binkham until we came to a place commonly called … the Lane to Walkhampton Town and a lane leading to Lake intersect the Turnpike Road … we there crossed the said Turnpike Road and took the Lane to Lake, keeping under the … Plymouth

Leat crosses the said Lane, there we passed over the right hand hedge which we followed … Water called Gnatham Brook, where there is a pretty wide space of Road or rather a piece of Waste … Buddle there of the said Brook we turned on our left and crossed the said piece of Waste to … of the same Bank and in doing so went over a stone that in time past appears to have been sunk into the ground … mar… where it was now proposed a Post should be set upp. We broke over at the said upper buddle … sides of … that divides John March's Estate of Lake from Mr Thomas Harris's Lake for a space of two fields … Angle in the Hedge and there we passed over to the North side of the Hedge in John March's higher meadow, and from thence pursued our course on the north side of the Hedges to the lane that leads from Walkhampton to Meavy, crossed the said lane by the small stream of Water there, entered the lower field of Doustilands and ascended on the north side of the Hedge that divides Doustiland from Mr Harris's Lake until we came to the field of Doustiland commonly called Starve park where we crossed over to the south side of the Hedge, and from thence kept along on the south side of the Hedges of Doustiland through Mr Harris's fields and up over Meavy Yennadown till we came to the higher or eastern corner of the great Dousiland where we passed over to the north side of the Hedge that divides little Yennadown from Meavy Yennadown and kept on that side of the Hedge until we came to the place where the Road divides into two branches, the one leading to Lowery and the other to Sheepstor Bridge, there we crossed over to the southern side of the northern Hedge of the Lane leading to Sheepstor Bridge, and descended by that hedge till we came to the corner where the Hedge of the Higher Woodland meets Lowery hedge, there we broke over Woodland Hedge and descended on the south west side of Lowery hedges until we came parallel with the higher hedge of a piece of Land called the Pitts belonging to Lowery, there crossed over to the East side of the Hedge of the said Pitts and descended on the same side of the Hedges (and crossed the Plymouth Leat) until we came to the Hedge that divides Crecoby from Longstone Pitts where we turned short on our left, and kept on in the ditch on the north side of the last mentioned hedge until we came to the Head Weir Pool of the Plymouth Leat in the River Mew. Crossed the River at the Weir Head, and ascended on the south side of the said River until we came to a certain large Rock therein where we began to ... north side of the River under the fences of Vinneylake Pits, and continued along by the side next the River of Vinney lake fences until we came to where Dean Brook otherwise Deancombe Brook falls into the said River Mew, there we crossed the said River Mew ... by the north side of Dean Brook up through Middleworth Pitts and Middleworth Estates until we came to a certain meadow called West Mead belonging to Deancombe Estate, where we took on the southern side of the fences, this course brought us to a Gate at the bottom of Deancombe Lane, there were turned on our right and presently came to Deancombe Steps which are large stones thrown into Dean Brook to enable persons on foot to cross the said Brook. We then turned on our left and ascended on the southern side of the exterior hedges of Deancombe and Coombeshead Estates until we had passed Coombeshead Buildings and came to the ... of a piece of Land commonly called Wort Hill, from whence we took a straight line to Ellisborough through Coppa... and in doing so passed a stone post that appeared to have been set up many years since, whereon is engraved a W ... side and an S on the other side thereof. From Ellisborough took a north easterly direction in a straight line to Sywards Cross or Nuns Cross. From then is a straight line to South Hisworthy Tor and from South Hisworthy Tor in a straight line to North Hisworthy Tor but when we came to the Turnpike Road that leads from Plymouth to Moretonhampstead we halted .... On the morning of Tuesday the Thirty-first of July assembled at the Turnpike Road where we left off the preceding... pursued our line to the North Hessary Tor. From North Hessary Tor in a straight line to Mistor otherwise Mistor pan, and from Mistor in a straight line to Didlake otherwise Deadlake foot where the said Didlake otherwise Deadlake falls into the River Walkham, there crossed the said River Walkham and descended on the northern bank thereof (taking in all the Islands thereof) from thence to Merrivale Bridge, Ward Bridge, Huckworthy Bridge and to the point near Horrabridge where the said Bounds ... ...

The document was signed by those who attended the boundary beating(s) – Sir M. Lopes, Ralph Franco, George Giles, Charles ..., William

Shillibeer, Walter King snr, Abraham Giles, John Edmunds Giles, Philip Pearse, Peter Reed, Walter King, Thomas Greep, John Damerell, Robert Damerell, Henry Pearse, Richard Pearse, John Pearse, Henry Toop snr, Henry Toop jnr.

[It is interesting to note that they went down the *north* side of the River Walkham from Deadlake Foot].

As has already been stated, the Commoners of many parishes have, over the centuries, pushed back the Forest Bounds to their present position but at Walkhampton at least there was genuine doubt as to the correct line. The bounds of Walkhampton Manor and parish were conterminous with that of the Forest of Dartmoor from a point opposite Deadlake Foot on the river Walkham to Mistor, and thence to Plym Head via North and South Hessary Tors and Eylesbarrow Boundary Rock to Crane Lake, a right bank tributary of the Plym. The manor had been one of those given by Amicia, Countess of Devon, to form the foundation of Buckland Abbey in 1278, and in the nineteenth century was the property of the Lopes family of Maristow, who begged to differ with the Duchy of Cornwall on their interpretation of the Forest bounds where it abutted on to Walkhampton. The question had been raised by the Rev. James Mason in a letter written by him to the Rev. J.P. Jones, Vicar of North Bovey, an interested antiquary, dated 5 October 1844, when he wrote:

I have referred to the Charta Isabellae de Fortibus of Buckland Abbey 'aqua de Tavie et de Walkamp', with the intermediate bounds which are correctly described, to 'Eyllesburgh et Plymcrundla ad Plymna'. In the description of the charter which you have lately obtained is there a different wording as to the part I have referred to? There is a great rock on the north side of the Walkham River named 'Hanging Stone', close to which is Kingford; viz the bound between the forest (Lydford) and Walkhampton; but the lord of that manor would go higher up the stream before he turns south, and from Eyllesburgh he would go to Plymhead. Now Plymcrundla and Plymhead cannot be the same, for 'ad Plymna' would not follow. The forest line is from Eyllesburgh to Plymsteps.

Whilst he states that the line taken by the Duchy was to Hanging Stone and Plym Steps, he was obviously in some doubt about the position of Plymcrundla, going on to assume that it was Plym Steps, and invites both Jones and a Mr E. Smirke (Vice Warden of the Stannaries) to view the bounds with him. In the Plymouth West Devon Record Office there are a number of documents relating to the Maristow Estate, including copy letters which refer to this dispute. The ealiest found was dated 14 March 1850, addressed to the Right Hon. Earl of Morley at Saltram and written from Jump, the old name for Roborough by Sir Ralph Lopes as follows:

I am sorry to say that I cannot get any decisive intelligence amongst the people at Sheepstor as to the boundary between that Parish and the Forest of Dartmoor, some of them contending from what they have heard from old men, now dead, that it went from Aylesborough to Plym *Head*, while others assert they have heard it ran from Aylesborough to Plym *Steps*. The old

Richard Northcote, of whom I spoke, is become so very deaf nothing can be learned from him…

A later letter from his secretary at Jump to Sir Ralph, then in London, is dated 14 July 1851, and again raises the same question of their bounds:

I hope that we shall not have to go over the parts again that we did last year, but that the centre of the Torrs will be admitted by the Duchy in each instance, except Mistor, where I do wish the Pan or Rock Basin as mentioned in the Forest Records could be established as this point instead of the centre of that torr, which it is not an easy matter to determine from the widely scattered, and irregular mass of rocks.

On 23 August 1851, there is a further letter, this time to George Pridham, Solicitor, at Plymouth, in which Geo Giles, Sir Ralph's steward writes on his behalf:

I am well aware that a few years since a question was in dispute between the Duchy of Cornwall and the Earl of Morley as to the boundary between Lee Moor and the Forest of Dartmoor – the question was, whether the line of demarkation should be from Ellisborough to Plym *Head* or to Plym *Steps*. Sir Ralph is now involved in a similar question on the same parts and I am to meet on Friday next the Duchy Surveyor, Mr Watt, who asserts that Lord Morley has yielded to the claim of the Duchy, and agreed to Boundary shall be considered from Ellisborough to Plym *Steps*.

The Earl of Morley, having conceded to the Duchy on this point, we next have another letter from Geo Giles to Sir Ralph dated 30 March 1852:

I enclose sketches of the boundaries between your commons and the Forest which I hope will give you an idea of the points in dispute, from Mistor on the north, and from Ellisborough on the south. Our contention is for Deadlake foot from Mistor, and Plym head from Ellisborough. If these would be determined, the sooner the Bound Posts were prepared & fixed the better.

Later that year, on 10 September, Mr A. Ferguson, the Duchy Agent, writes to Sir Ralph stating that he had had Mr Shillabear, the Duchy Surveyor, erect flag poles in holes drilled in the summits of South Hessary Tor, North Hessary Tor and Mistor. However it was not until 10 August 1867 that a Deed of Agreement was drawn up between the Duchy and Sir Massey Lopes and matters were finally resolved, with Lopes paying the Duchy £250. The agreed boundary was stated to be:

From Deadlake Foot in a straight line to the summit of Great Mis Tor to be marked by an iron cross; thence in a straight line to North Hessary Tor (iron cross); thence similarly to South Hessary Tor (iron cross); thence similarly to Nuns Cross; thence similarly to Eylesborough (iron cross); thence similarly to a post erected at the confluence of a small stream with the Plym on its right bank near Crane Hill.

These four iron 'crosses' (Fig.49) were approximately 18ins tall but more resembling a cobra with a flattened head, and are recorded in the Ordnance Survey Boundary Remark Book of 1881, where sketches show

Above: *Fig. 48
Eylesbarrow 'cobra'
iron boundary marker*
Left: *Walkhampton:
Iron B.S. South
Hessary Tor (West
side). SX5975 7238*

they were found to be 'in a satisfactory condition'. The line of this section of the Forest Bounds and Walkhampton is, of course, that still current until 1987. In the case of North Hessary Tor, its summit is now covered by a concrete triangulation point and at Great Mis Tor no sign of the iron post remains – by the mid-nineteenth century the boundary point became the centre of that same rock pile where the Army had erected a flagpole to warn the public when firing was taking place.

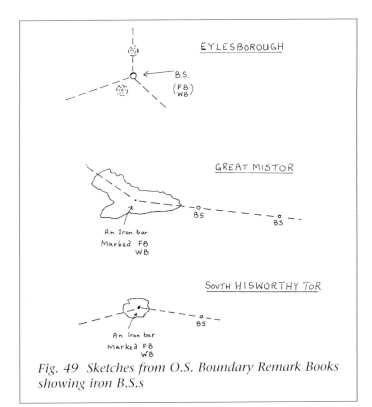

Fig. 49 Sketches from O.S. Boundary Remark Books showing iron B.S.s

the exact location of each of them as does the Boundary Report Book of 1883; the one at Eylesbarrow (Fig. 48) was not set into native stone but into a rock sited between the two cairns on the crest of the hill. In early summer, 1991, this was found to be loose in its socket, so the iron bar was removed by the Dartmoor National Park Ranger and affixed in another rock which was later replaced on the original site. The only other extant example is that on South Hessary Tor. They were all originally inscribed with the letters 'FB' for Forest Bounds on their east-facing sides and 'WB' for Walkhampton Bounds on their west-facing sides. The west-facing sides are now so corroded that little can be seen but the eastern sides, less exposed to the prevailing wind and rain, still retain the identifiable letters 'FB'. The Lopes correspondence mentions an inspection of these Boundary Posts which took place in 1903 when

PETER TAVY

There have been many changes to the parish boundaries on the northern side of the Tavistock–Merrivale Bridge road, those of Peter Tavy, Whitchurch and Walkhampton. (See Fig.50.) From Collaton Lane, near Moorshop, the present boundary of Peter Tavy and Whitchurch follows a line of no less than seven small boundstones, or portions of them, eastwards, each lettered 'RB' following a reave and old field boundaries. The line then bends north-eastward to a Boundary Rock near Beckamoor Head at SX 5345 7595 called Flat Rock or Black Rock bearing the letters 'P' and 'W' on the appropriate sides of its flat top. It then turns more east-north-east to Picke Rock, another natural boundary rock similarly inscribed and passes between Great Staple and Roos Tors, and in the col between these two tors there is now a set boundstone, also inscribed 'P' and 'W'. However the first six inch O.S. map of the 1880s does not show this, although by the time it was published this boundstone must have been erected, showing only the boundary rock to the north-west of it. The erection of the set stone was the result of a settlement being made between the Commoners of Peter Tavy and Whitchurch after a disagreement over the correct line to take. William Crossing in his *Guide* refers to this, saying:

> This was once the scene of a quarrel which terminated in the manner usually associated in our minds with the slight misunderstandings that occasionally arise at Donnybrook Fair. The men of one of the parishes named were viewing their bounds, the operation being watched by the men of the other, when a dispute arose

about a bondmark. Heated arguments followed, but failed to be convincing…

This must have been the then newly erected stone, for it was erected in 1882 but apparently not inscribed until later, after Peter Tavy had formerly claimed a line from the Picke Rock directly to the corner of Shillapark wall, whilst Whitchurch claimed that it went to Roos Tor itself and followed the Roos Tor reave down to Shillapark Corner, each party claiming a line most advantageous to themselves.

It was the Duke of Bedford who suggested that 'substantial granite posts' be erected to mark the new compromise line, including one at the point where the line met the Roos Tor Reave, but nothing appears to have been done about this latter, the one in the col being the only stone to be erected. However the Duke's agent in correspondence called the now dry Wheal Fortune Leat 'the Duke of Bedford's leat', and on the bank of this leat, where it cuts through the Roos Tor Reave near the Shillapark Wall, there is a stone similar to Flat Rock marked with the deeply incised letters 'P' and 'W' which appear to be late-nineteenth century and, in addition, it also has the letter 'P' in relief sideways on its southern end, this letter being similar to that on the boundstone at the end of Collaton Lane, on which the letters 'W' and 'T' also appear. The problem with this letter 'P' is that it only shows clearly on occasions depending very much on the 'correct' light. This old, and apparently forgotten boundary rock was in all likelihood tipped on its side when the tinners cut their leat late in the eighteenth century, or possibly earlier if this leat was originally cut for another purpose and only adopted by the tinners at Wheal Fortune, i.e. it may have been the original Brook Mill Leat.

158

In 1923 there were two parishioners, the Parish Clerk, W. Williams and J.H. Bray present who were attending their fourth consecutive viewing, the report appearing in the *Tavistock Times* of 22 June 1923 being as follows:

At 10a.m. the horsemen and pedestrians moved off to the foot of the Coombe Brook (which flows into the River Tavy). Following the south side of the Tavy (where stones were thrown in to claim half the river) to Mine Water, where we crossed to Hoyle's Meadow. Keeping to the north fence to the gate across the lane we recrossed the river at Clam Bridge to the south side of the river, and to Devon United Mine, West Wood, and Walter's Wood. Following the hedge up-hill towards Cudlipptown Road, we entered the road opposite the stream flowing down the Brake. Crossing the road and hedge of lower land marks we negotiated the hill to Smeardon Down through higher land marks, up to Boulder Hole, Boulder's Tor and Twist Gate, where the first halt was made... The party then journeyed on to Twist Lane, keeping on the Moor path. Here we halted to inspect the stone marking Stephen's grave, where tradition has it 'That this man, who committed suicide at Lower Godsworthy, in 1785, was buried at the crossroads with a stake through his body, as was customary in the olden days'. Passing on to the ancient tombstone or menhir, and on to Lanson Moor Post, which was re-erected several years ago by the Duke of Bedford, and keeping on the left hand path where moor path divides Lanson Moor, through Jaddy Grip, on to New or Longbettor Hedge, where a halt was made for luncheon... The party then resumed their journey towards Sandiford Road on to Whitebarrow, over Cock's Hill, through Didlake Wells to Didlake Foot, down River Walkham by the right hand side, on to Hanging Stone, where we claim half of the river. Up the hill by the right hand side of Park's Hedge, outside boundary of Shilla Parks, to the New Bond Stone, Picke Rock, and Flat Rock, on to the head of Blackamoor Coombe, to the right boundary stone, Dog Hill, down the path through Collaton Down Gate to Collaton Down Lane, to back of Glanville Meadow, on by right hand hedge of same, into lane to the parish stone, on road leading to Moor Shop, following the road towards Harford Bridge, up the River Tavy by left hand bank to foot of Coombe Brook, the point of our departure, where we arrived at 5p.m.

The Bounds were beaten in 1867, 1882, 1899 and 1923, the approach to Whitebarrow being the same route taken in 1990, but no stones were thrown into the river to claim half of it, and lunch was not taken until the party arrived at Whitebarrow, but it is the designation of the points of reference on the bounds from Whitebarrow that are of particular interest. If we look at various reference to the Walkham 'Hanging Stone' or 'Hanging Rock', it appears that the name has been given, over the past one hundred and fifty years or so, no less than three different locations.

From Whitebarrow the Peter Tavy Commoners went first to Cock's Lake, then to Deadlake Wells and Deadlake Foot, and down the Walkham 'by the right hand side, on to Hanging Stone where we claim half

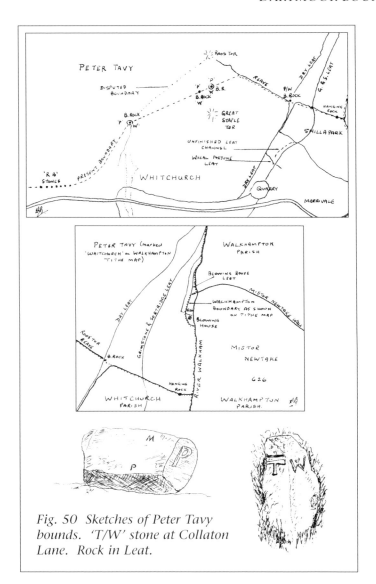

Fig. 50 Sketches of Peter Tavy bounds. 'T/W' stone at Collaton Lane. Rock in Leat.

the river. Up the hill by the right hand side of Park's Hedge…' This indicates that they left the river at the corner of Shillapark Enclosures, and the 1801 and 1833 Whitchurch accounts agree, saying (going in the reverse direction) 'to Roolstor, from thence by the remains of a Stone Wall or Fence to Hanging Stone, from thence to Walkham River', the 'Stone Wall or Fence' being the reave on which the outer Shillapark Wall was later built, incorporating the huge rounded boulder known as the Hanging Stone – this is the lowest of the three sites so named.

From the Shillapark Wall, the Peter Tavy people went on to the 1882 'New Bond Stone', but both the O.S. 1888 and 1907 six inch maps only show a 'B.Rock', Picke or Picket Rock somewhat to the west of it. We will, too, have already passed the other Boundary Rock already mentioned on the bank of the old Wheal Fortune Leat at SX 548 763 which is not remarked upon by either parish.

Peter Tavy: Boundary Stone. SX 5430 7630

160

Boundary Rock. SX 5420 7627

North-west of the 'New Bond Stone' at SX 5420 7627 we come to the next point of reference, on line to Beckamoor Head, this is a large boulder in the clitter of Great Staple Tor, which has the letters 'P' and 'W' inscribed on its northern and southern sides respectively. It is recorded as the 'Picke Rock' or piked rock, a term usually applied to a pointed rock. This rock, whilst it cannot be called pointed, is nevertheless

Flat Rock, Beckamoor Head. SX 5346 7597

prominent amongst other rocks in the clitter, especially when viewed from lower ground. The 1833 Whitchurch boundary did not touch this point.

Next Peter Tavy records the 'Flat Rock', a very apt description, for its upper surface is very like that of the stone near the Shillapark Wall, and bears the usual 'P' and 'W' on opposing edges of it. It is beside the old Wedlake track at SX 5346 7597. This stone is marked on the early O.S. six inch maps. Here, coming up in the other direction, Whitchurch in 1801 and 1833 refer to a 'burrow of stones', a ruined cairn perhaps, and a 'rush bush beyond Backamoors Head' before going apparently to Roos Tor itself, the rushes above Beckamoor Head are no longer on the boundary.

Continuing in our north-westerly direction, Peter Tavy next go to 'the head of Blackamoor Coombe, to the right boundary stone', what did they mean by 'right' – right as opposed to left, or 'right' as opposed to 'wrong'? Note that they say 'stone' and not 'rock', suggesting a set stone. As we come down the Wedlake track, where it crosses another to Coxtor and Youlditch, we see not one but two set boundstones, one to our left hand, and another to our right. They are both 'RB' stones and that to our right is on the Peter Tavy/Whitchurch parish boundary, but that on our left is not, merely marked as 'Stone' by the O.S. not 'B.S.' Thus the word 'right' is applicable in either context, though it is now fallen. We continue to follow the track to Collaton Moor Gate, and through the lane to the Moorshop–Peter Tavy road, where we find the 'Parish Stone', lettered in relief on three sides respectively 'P' (Peter Tavy), 'W' (Whitchurch) and 'T' (Tavistock). In the Whitchurch account it is referred to as 'a Cross or Bond Mark' but is not, and never has been a cross.

Crossing the Tavy above Harford Bridge. 10.9.1994 Bound Beating.

A Beating of the Bounds took place on 2 June 1990, lunch being taken at Whitebarrow, the bounds being the same as 1923 as far as Collaton Moor Gate. From this point the Harford Bridge road was taken, turning left past Nutley Farm, then right along the Old Tavistock Road, with its detour around the quarry, the participants having fun scaling down the side of the quarry through the trees, then paddling through the rivers Tavy and Burn, in the case of the latter walking upstream under the main Tavistock–Okehampton road via Half Bridge, recrossing the Tavy upstream to arrive back in Peter Tavy.

From all the foregoing, it will be seen that from the corner of the Shillapark enclosures on the river's edge upstream, we have Walkhampton Parish to the east (left bank) and Peter Tavy to the west (right bank), but the Walkhampton Tithe Map shows an interesting deviation from this line, that parish's bounds being shown to extend to and beyond the west bank of the river to encompass a small area south of where the Mistor Newtake wall meets the river at its north-western corner (see Fig.50). When Hansford Worth was describing the third, right bank, tinners mill above Merrivale Bridge (T.D.A. 1931), he says that it 'lies about 233 yards south of the point at which the newtake wall crosses the river', and this is the very area on the tithe map shown as being within Walkhampton parish, and has ascribed to it the same Field Number as that given to Mistor Newtake itself, i.e. 626. But there is no wall to be seen above the right bank of the river there, the only possible demarkation lines being either a steep scarp immediately down-stream of the Mistor newtake wall or this and the mill leat, but with other inaccuracies on the map it is difficult to know exactly what the incursion was intended to refer to. If it did not encompass the blowing house site, there seems no advantage to be had by Walkhampton in claiming this small piece of land. Certainly Peter Tavy did not define its commons on its tithe map, only the enclosed land, so that there was some ambiguity or uncertainty here. The Walkhampton tithe map shows Whitchurch parish extending far up the right bank of the Walkham at least as far as Hanging Rock (SX 5550 7774), which is not supported by the Whitchurch map, who then took the same line as they do today. Of course at the period in question, namely the 1840s, the Duchy were still claiming that the Forest Bounds went from Mistor to Hanging Rock (SX 5550 7774), near which, above the right bank, there is an earth-fast boulder inscribed with the letters 'PT', in all likelihood standing for Peter Tavy. This difference of opinion was not settled until

1867 between the Duchy and the Lord of the Manor of Walkhampton, and the bounds of Merrifield Bridge Mine, Wheal Fortune or Staple Tor Sett, in June 1859 were on the north side stated to be 'a straight line drawn Eastward from the said corner of the hedge (Wedlake) to a place called Hanging Rock near Kings Ford where the Forest Boundary intersects the Wallcombe or Walkham River'.

Peter Tavy parish bounds follow Collaton Lane, thence to Beckamoor Head but the enclosed lands are below the Godsworthy road, and here at SX 530 769 on the corner of the enclosures there is a boundstone bearing the single letter 'P', possibly defining their enclosed land.

On 13 June 1992, on a hot and sunny day, the Peter Tavy Commoners beat the northern section of their extensive bounds, starting at Hill Bridge, but having assembled in the village. They proceeded in a clockwise direction as is customary, following a small tributary of the Tavy up through Chilly Wood to Lower Town and on to near the Wheal Jewel Reservoir, thence across the Wheal Jewel leat via One Stone Bridge to WD44 and W.B. at Down Pool, WD45 at Tin Pits, WD46 and W.B. at Ring-o-Bells and thence to a three-sided modern boundstone formerly near the now demolished Army huts, the junction of Peter Tavy, Mary Tavy and Brentor parishes, inscribed 'P/M/B'. They then struck east to Prescombe Corner (WD4) and followed other WD stones to Nos 10 and 11 at Lissicombe Head. Now instead of going down to the Wallabrook they kept going eastwards to circumnavigate the Bearwalls enclosures, a change of boundary line made in 1987, when several isolated farmsteads were taken in by adjoining, more enclosed parishes, in this instance Lydford. Joining a tributary

of the Wallabrook, they kept to this for a short way before crossing to the Wallabrook, following it to the head and WD18, and on to Haytor Bound (WDl9), Deadlake Head (WD20) and Foot (WD21) to Rattlebrook Foot, up the Tavy to Wester Redlake Foot (WD22), following the stream in dry conditions for the area to WD23 and WD24 and beyond the head to WD25. From this latter a southerly course took them just east of Lynch Tor on to Limsboro Cairn and finally to White Barrow, where the southern part of their bounds had been beaten in June 1990. Liquid refreshments were much sought after, having been brought up the track from the village, and a return made to the village, along the track or by tractor and trailer, about 15 miles in all.

WHITCHURCH

Copies of the bounds of Whitchurch prior to the Tithe Commutation are available, those for 1801 and 1833 being virtually identical except for the spelling of the odd word. That dated 10 September 1833 reads:

Parish of Whitchurch

Be it remembered that the Meets Limits and Boundaries of the said Parish of Whitchurch were Surveyed Viewed and acknowledged the 10th day of Sept 1833 by William Courtenay Esquire, Lord of the Manor of Walreddon in the said Parish, George Pridham Gentleman Steward to John Harris Esquire Lord of the Manor of Whitchurch in the same parish and the several tenants of the said Manors and Parishioners of the said Parishes whose names are hereto subscribed with several other Persons (due notice of such View having been given in writing to the Parishioners of the several Parishes whose Boundaries are adjoining to the said Parish of Whitchurch) and that such View was conducted as follows:

Commenced our Perambulation at Skoynes Tenement bounded by the River Tavy from thence to Brook Bounded on the North by Moons Ground in the Parish of Tavistock (NB Hedges dividing Brook and Moons Ground are included in the Survey) from thence to Crelake Bounded by one other Crelake in the Parish of Tavistock from thence to Challacott bounded by the before mentioned Crelake in the said Parish of Tavistock from thence to Whitchurch Down Bounded by the Hedge of Thorns Crelake and Witheridge ground in the said Parish of Tavistock on to a Cross or Bond Mark on the said Down from thence on the said Whitchurch Down Bounded by Tor Land and great Tavyton in the said Parish of Tavistock on to Little Down from thence around Little Down Bounded by the Bank or Mound of the said Down in the said Parish of Tavistock on to a Quarry or Pit adjoining the Turnpike Road from thence across the said Turnpike Road to a Bank or Mound dividing the said Parishes of Tavistock and Whitchurch from thence to Broadmoor Bounded by Kingford and Nutley in the said Parish of Tavistock from thence on the road towards Peter Tavy to a Cross or Bond Mark opposite Collyton Lane which said Cross or Bond Mark divides Whitchurch Parish from Petertavy and Tavistock from thence through Collyton Lane to the Potwater Shoot from thence through Higher Collyton Meadow to the lane leading to Coxtor from thence to the said lane to Moor Gate Bounded by part of Higher Collyton

and Tartown in the said Parish of Peter tavy and thence to the north east on a Path leading to Wedlake in the said Parish of Petertavy on to a Burrow of Stones in the said Path from thence on the said Path to a Rush Bush beyond Backmoors head from thence to Roolstor otherwise Rouge Tor from thence by the remains of a Stone Wall or Fence to Hanging Stone from thence to Walkham River which said River divides Whitchurch from Walkhampton from the Commons on to and through Heckwood which is imbounded by the Parish of Sampford Spiney to Heckwood Gate from thence by the Market Road to Mason Gate from thence through Dreary Lane to New house from thence through the Mousey Pieces to Plaister Down from thence to Wimmaton Corner on to Wimmaton Lane End from thence by Monkshill Hedges on to Jourdern Lane from thence to Horrabridge Bond Mark on the Bridge from thence by the River Walkham to Sortridge Estate Bounded by part of the said Estate in the Parish of Peter tavy on to a Bond Mark in the Turnpike Road from thence through the Leases of the said Estate to Beat Lands through Beatlands to Sortridge Lake (Lake included) on to Sortridge Water Shoot from the Shoot to a Bond Mark in the Kitchen from thence to Walkham River (by the Lake through the said Sortridge Estate) from thence the said River divides the Parish of Whitchurch from the Parish of Buckland Monachorum to the extreme west part of west from Walreddon Downs where Walkhampton River drops in the Tavy from thence the said Tavy imbounds Whitchurch to Skoynes Tenement where the survey began.
(NB there were present at the above Views the

following Boys being Sons of the Parishioners of Whitchurch – namely – Richard Easterbrook Charles Gill William Nicholas Thomas Mitchell William Bicknell Joseph Berriball Nicholas Glanville junior)

Witness our Hands

John Roskilly Willcock	Nicholas Symons	John Berriball Junr
Joseph Willcocks	Thomas Berriball	The mark X of Richard Davy
The Mark X of John Smith	Walter Toop	The mark X of George Hockings
Nicholas Glanville	Robert Gurydn	The mark X of John James
Gregory Nicholas	The Mark X of Thomas Mutters	Signed William Courtenay
	William Gill	Geo Pridham

Whitchurch Beat their Bounds in three sections on 1, 10 and 31 May 1992. A brief account follows:

On 3 May the start was at Merrivale Bridge. The Walkham was followed to Higher Shillapark enclosures, then by the wall to Roos Tor Reave, across the col between Roos and Great Staple Tors to Beckamoor Head following the RB stones to Collaton, via Moorshop and Redlands to the Taviton Brook which had to be crossed either by a makeshift bridge or carried by a

Above: *Whitchurch, against the Vixen Tor Wall. SX 541 743*

Above right: *Boundary Stone and Rock. with Feather Tor beyond. SX 537 742*

Right: *Boundary Stone. SX 523 726*

Below: *Double Waters. Bounds Beating 10.5.1992.*

Crossing the Taviton Brook. Bounds Beating 3.5.1992

couple of men in wellies! On to the junction with Tavistock Urban and Rural Districts on the Golf Course, south-east to Budghill, Anderton Mine and to the finish at Anderton lay-by.

10 May. Start at Anderton lay-by. Through farm and fields to River Tavy which was followed to Double Waters, up the River Walkham with lunch at Grenofen Bridge. Along main road and through fields above Magpie Cottage, around Sortridge fields and passed in front of the Manor, along right of way to a long wet lane to Riland Plantation, and followed three WB stones across Plaister Down to the end of this section.

31 May. Again started at Merrivale Bridge, walked down to Heckwood Quarry (on private land, but the owner was with the group) and along to see the BS in Mansell Wood, with lunch being taken near Pew Tor Cottage. The boundary stones in Beckamoor Coombe were then followed with the finish being on Plaister Down.

SAMPFORD SPINEY – WHITCHURCH

Sampford Spiney parish, though not actually divided into two parts, only hangs together 'by a thread'. It is one of the few parishes on Dartmoor, like Harford, that does not have a central village, the main part being south of Pew or Pu Tor, and formerly extending to Horrabridge to the south and bounded on the east by the river Walkham. In addition to this there is a small block of land centring around the Beckamoor valley between Barn Hill and Vixen Tor which is almost totally encompassed by the parish of Whitchurch, locally sometimes referred to as 'The Ace of Spades'; it is joined to the rest of the parish only by a thin ribbon of land running along the Heckwood track, the wall itself forming the eastern boundary, and with Heckwood Tor in Whitchurch. In addition to the Sampford Spiney 'SS/P' current boundstones in the Beckamoor and Pew Tor areas and the old 'S' stones near Horrabridge, there are others, both set boundstones and boundary rocks which are inscribed with the letters 'SB' for Sampford Bounds, not commented upon elsewhere (see Fig.51). They extend north and west from a set boundstone in the wall near Vixen Tor (SX 541 743), bearing the inscription 'SB' and 'WB', this still on the Sampford/Whitchurch bounds. Near this at SX 541 744 there is a huge earth-fast boulder simply inscribed 'SB' on its west-facing end, and at SX 541 748 is another equally large boulder which forms part of an old enclosure just below the present course of the Grimstone and Sortridge leat which bears the same inscription, again on its west-facing side. Below the leat on the lower east slope of Barn Hill there is a set boundstone with 'SB' only, inscribed on its east-facing side at SX 536 745.

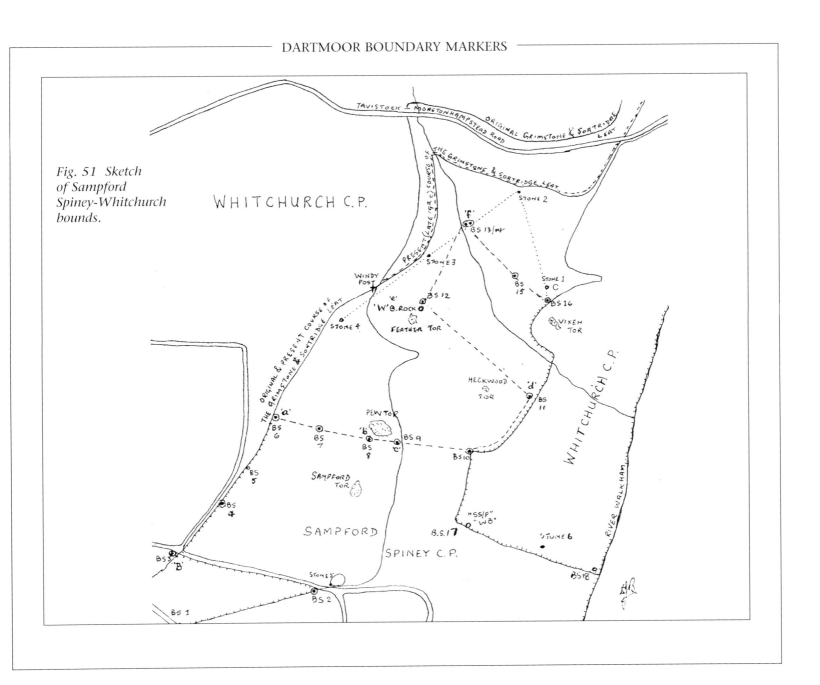

Fig. 51 Sketch of Sampford Spiney-Whitchurch bounds.

Set Boundstones on Putor Common (Whitchurch/Sampford Spiney)

No.	Inscribed	Designated point		Other Comments
1	'SB' and 'WB' –	–		in wall of enclosed land
2	'SS/P' only –	–		
3	'SS/P' only	'B'		
4	'SS/P' only –	–		on 1884 O.S. and SX57 but not on Outdoor Leisure. Still there.
5	Not known	–		on 1884 O.S., now missing.
6	'SS/P' & 'WB'	'a'		
7	'SS/P' only –	–		
8	'SS/P' only	'b'		
9	'SS/P' only	'c'		
10	'SS/P' only –	–		
11	'SS/P' and 'WB'	'd'		
12	'SS/P' and 'WB'	'e'		pre 1845 'W' B.Rock 10yds south of B.S.
13	'SS/P' and 'WB'	'f'		now broken, replaced by No.14
14	'SS/P' only –	'f'		replacement for No.13
15	'SS/P' and 'WB' –			
16	'SB' and 'WB'	–		in wall of enclosed land, probably a point agreed in 1834
17	'SS/P' and 'WB' –			on O.S. SX57 Blue map but not O.L.
18	'SS/P' and 'WB' –			Lazy 'S's and cruder than all others, not on O.S.

Set boundstones south of No.1 in sketch defining boundary points in enclosed land are all lettered 'SB' and 'WB'. Boundstones bearing the letters 'SS/P' and 'WB' only occur on that part of the boundary amended in the Award. Those inscribed 'SS/P' only were probably erected later by Sampford Spiney to strengthen the definition of the amended line.

'Stones' on the original Sampford Spiney bounds as claimed by them:

1	'SB'	'C'		Saddle Rock, a huge natural boulder, not shown on any O.S. map

2	'SB'	–	another huge natural rock, marked on 1906 O.S. six inch map, possibly referred to in 1834 suggested boundary
3	'SB'	–	set boundstone inscribed on east-facing side. On O.S. six inch maps
4	unknown	–	shown on 1884 O.S. six inch map, not traced
5	unknown	–	shown on 1906 O.S. six inch map, missing by 1980s. 'Little Field'?
6	unknown	–	shown on 1906 O.S. six inch map

All these six 'stones' were probably inscribed by Sampford between 1834 and 1843, but unrecognised by Whitchurch.

Above: *Sampford Spiney: One of the oldest boundary stones simply lettered 'S'. Near the bridge at Horrabridge.*

Above right: *Lettered SS/P, near ford over the Beckamoor.*

Right: *Lettered SB. Not now on the bounds. Barn Hill. SX 5360 7425*

It is possible that there are or were other examples of rocks or set boundstones similarly inscribed, for the first edition of the Ordnance Survey six inch map shows another three Stones, one on the common between Feather Tor and the Grimstone Leat at SX 5325 7410, another within a small enclosure at SX 5307 7278 and another in private grounds in Mansel Woods at SX 5440 7285. In addition to these a 'B.S.' was shown near Oakley Cottage which has now disappeared.

The Parlby family, Lords of the Manor of Sampford Spiney, claimed rights over the whole of Pewtor Common, extending to some 382 acres, but this was strongly contested by William Courtenay, Lord of the Manor of Walreddon who owned Whitchurch Common adjoining. At the Beating of the Bounds of these manors in 1833, both claimed Pewtor Common, Courtenay stating that 'nearly the whole of Pewtor Common was within and part of his Manor of Walreddon'. On 9 July 1834, at a Vestry meeting of Sampford, it was resolved that due to the difficulties in defining the bounds between Whitchurch and

Sampford near Pewtor Commons it was agreed that 'stones be erected bearing the initials 'WB' and 'SB' and placed according to the arrangement entered into by William Courtenay Esq as Lord of the Manor of Walreddon and the Parish of Whitchurch, and the Devisees of Humphrey Hall Esq on their parts as Ladies of the Manor of Sampford Spiney which stones or Bond Marks shall for ever be considered as forming the Division of the two parishes'. If it had only been that simple, for later Courtenay contested the siting of some of these boundary markers inscribed by Sampford without giving due notice to them, saying that they were not on the agreed line. Thus we have the early 'S' stones of Sampford, the 'SB' markers of the 1830s, some still in use but others ignored, and the later 'SS/P' boundstones.

The original boundary of this area as drawn up by the Tithe Commissioners was not accepted, although at a Vestry Meeting on 19 January 1845 Sampford Spiney said that 'Lines on Plaister Down and Pewtor Common as now shown by the Bond Stones placed on these places are the ones which have always (been) taken by the parishioners of Sampford Spiney in their Manor's bound viewings and are the ones handed down to them by their ancestors as the correct and proper boundaries of this parish from Whitchurch, this vestry will not consent to any alteration whatever being made...' and that 'in the opinion of this vestry the map of this parish which has recently been taken by Mr Palmer under the provision of the Tithe Commissioners, is a true and correct map of this parish and of the commons attached thereto...' The Commissioners were requested to 'inquire into, ascertain and set out' the bounds of Whitchurch, it being finally agreed that 'Great Pewtor be henceforth annexed to and to form part of the Parish of Whitchurch and Manor of Walreddon and Little Pewtor being henceforth annexed to and to form part of the Parish of Sampford Spiney and Manor of Sampford and a line to be drawn from the northern corner of Hecklake defined on Mr Courtenay's map by the letters 'WB' on one side and 'SB' on the other side, along by the southern foot of Great Pewtor down to the stream which runs to Grimstone to a point opposite Oakley and that part of Pewtor Common lying south of the line to be in Sampford Spiney and the part west of the stream down to Moor Gate is to be in Whitchurch'. The boundstones marking this part of the bounds of the two parishes were lettered 'SS/P', some being marked 'WB' by Whitchurch. The Parlbys retained 201 acres and Courtenay acquired 181 acres.

Granite had been worked in this area for some time, and a notice in 1817, issued by William Courtenay, forbade the removal of stone from Pewtor Common without his consent. In 1844 it had been proposed that Courtenay and Mrs Parlby should define 'a boundary line on Pewtor Common without reference to the boundaries of the parishes of Whitchurch and Sampford Spiney, or of the Manor of Walreddon and Sampford Spiney, beyond which line each of the above parties to agree not to take a claim for Stone, Quarries, Mines or Minerals or other ancient rights, but to confine himself or herself for those purposes within the agreed boundary line'. Desperate measures!

The working of the granite was the over-riding consideration and in February 1862 we see a *Duchy* notice offering for tenders, either as a whole or split into three parcels:

Little Pew Tor. 2 parcels, being unenclosed land in Sampford Spiney Parish.

Great Pewtor. The portions of Whitchurch Common south of the road leading from Tavistock to Merrivale Bridge.

Staple Tor. The northern side of the road within the parishes of Whitchurch and Peter Tavy.

The Revised Findings of the Tithe Commissioners was precisely worded as follows:

This is to certify that I James Jerwood an Assistant Tithe Commissioner have on the day of the date hereof made and published my Award concerning the Boundary of the Parish of Whitchurch in the County of Devon and particularly concerning that portion of the said Boundary between the said Parish of Whitchurch and the Parish of Sampford Spiney in the said County of Devon and that I have thereby found adjudged and determined that the said Boundary continues and extends from the point where the South fence of Jourden Lane joins that of Plaister Down which point is 88 yards or thereabouts distant from the South Easterly Angle of the close called Crocken Field part of Grimstone Farm belonging to John Collier Esquire being the point marked with the letter A in the map to my said Award annexed along by the South fence to the said part of Plaister Down to the point which is 7 yards or thereabouts distant from the South Easterly Angle of the said point to Plaister Down thence along in an imaginary line in the said part of Plaister Down at the said distance of 7 yards from the said Easterly fence to the extremity thereof thence along in an imaginary line in the said Plaister

Down at the same distance from the Southerly fence thereof until it meets the road leading from Tavistock to Hockworthy Bridge thence along in an imaginary line in the same direction across the said road to the end of the southern fence of the said Plaister Down until it meets the Western fence of the road leading from Tavistock to Sampford Spiney thence along the said westerly fence to the said road in a southerly direction to the South East Angle of the close called Mousey Piece part of Coom Hill Farm belonging to Humphrey Halls Trustees being Sir George Pownall Adams and John William Spicer thence along in an imaginary line in an Easterly direction across the said Road to the end of the South fence to Dreary Lane along by the said Southerly fence of the said Lane to the fence across the said lane thence in a Northerly direction by the said fence across the said Lane to the South West Angle of the close called Little Field part of the New House Tenement belonging to William Lux John Lux and Nancy Brooks thence along by the North fence of the said Dreary Lane to the South fence thereof adjoining the close called Brake part of Mason Gate Farm belonging to Sir Thomas Trayter Fuller Elliott Drake thence along by the South fence of the said close to the extremity thereof thence along the North fence at the end of the said close to the extremity thereof thence along in a Westerly direction by the south fence to Putor Common until it meets the stream or Brook called Grimstone Leat and forming the point marked with the letter B in the said map to my said Award annexed thence along by the South side of the said Grimstone Leat to the point which is 812 yards or thereabouts distant from the aforesaid point marked with the letter B as aforesaid in the said map measured along the said Grimstone Leat the said point is marked with a small letter 'a' in the said map to my said Award annexed thence along in an imaginary line in an Easterly direction on the said Putor Commons to the point which is 396 yards or thereabouts distant from the aforesaid point marked with the letter 'a' in the said map and 25 yards or thereabouts distant from the West end of the Rock called Great Putor the said point is marked with the small letter 'b' in the said map to my said Award annexed thence along in an imaginary line in the same direction on the said Putor Common to the point which is 122 yards or thereabouts distant from the aforesaid point marked with the letter 'b' in the said map and 32 yards or thereabouts distant from the East end of the said Rock called Great Putor the said point is marked with the small letter 'c' in the said Map to my said Award annexed thence along in an imaginary Line in an Easterly direction on the said Putor Common to the point which is 10 yards or thereabouts distant from Hecklake Corner thence along in an imaginary line in the said Putor Common at the said distance of 10 yards from the South fence of the said Common adjoining the close called Higher Tor Park part of Hecklake Farm belonging to Sir Thomas Trayton Fuller Elliott Drake to the extremity thereof thence along in an imaginary line in the said Common at the same distance from the South fence thereof to the point which is 14 yards or thereabouts from the North East Angle to the close called Outer Middle grounds part of Heckwood farm belonging to Mary Ann Windeatt being the point marked with the small

letter 'd' in the said map to my said Award annexed thence along in an imaginary line in a North Westerly direction to the said Putor Common to the point which is 518 yards or thereabouts distant from the aforesaid point marked with the letter 'd' in the said map the said point is marked with the small letter 'e' on the said map to my said Award annexed thence along in an imaginary line in a Northerly direction in the said Common to the point which is 568 yards or thereabouts distant from the aforesaid point marked with the letter 'e' in the said map the said point is marked with a small letter 'f' in the said map of my said Award annexed thence along in an imaginary line in a South Easterly direction in the said Common to the Middle point of Saddle Rock which is 506 yards or thereabouts distant from the aforesaid point marked with the letter 'f' in the said map thence along in an imaginary line in the same direction in the said Common to the point in the South fence thereof which point is 70 yards or thereabouts from the point of the aforesaid Saddle Rock 11 yards or thereabouts distant from the point where the said South fence meets the East fence of the close called Tor Park part of Vixen Tor farm belonging to Mary Ann Windeatt being the point marked with the letter 'C' in the map of my said Award annexed And I do hereby certify that the red dotted line in the said map to my said Award annexed is the Boundary Line which I have set out and described and which I have adjudged and determined to be the true Boundary Line of the said Parishes of Whitchurch and Sampford Spiney between the aforesaid several points respectively. In Witness whereof I the said

James Jerwood have hereunto set my hand this fifth day of May 1845.

Signed James Jerwood

So here, amongst all the legal phraseology, we have the present Whitchurch/Sampford Spiney boundary line, defining the corridor allotted to Sampford joining the main southern part of the parish to that part known as the Ace of Spades in the Beckamoor valley area, and retaining the use of the author's Boundary Rock No.1 at SX 5415 7440 and naming it Saddle Rock.

Fig. 52 Saddle Rock.

BRIDESTOWE

There was a report of Bound Beating at Bridestowe on Whit Monday in the T.D.A. of 1936, as follows:

An ancient custom that still obtains at Bridestowe is 'beating the bounds' of the Parish, or the side which extends over Dartmoor. This is a necessary proceeding, or the bounds would before long become obliterated or undefined, it is followed by all the parishes on the confines of the moor. It is supposed to take place once in three years, usually on a Whit Monday. An early start is made from the village by as many of the parishioners as elect to be at the trysting place. These proceed in a body, joined as they go by others, to the moor and there follow the boundary line of the Parish, verifying and examining each landmark. At certain points they meet the 'bound beaters' of adjoining parishes, and stop for refreshments, which have been conveyed whither by carts – piles of sandwiches, bread and cheese, etc., also drinks and, above all, buns. In former days it was customary to take out the boys of the parish and beat them at every landmark, thereby impressing it on their memories! but in these (1938) soft and degenerate days, to that same end they stuff the lads with buns! Wherefore the minds of the lads have become confused as to terms, and their name for the custom is 'beating the buns', or the 'bun beating'.

BRIDESTOWE/LAMERTON

There were changes on the west side of the moor also, the parish of Lamerton becoming much truncated, with the redistribution of parts of it to other parishes in that area. In the past Bridestowe had been split into two parts, with another parish intervening, as had been the case with some of the old Hundreds; in this instance even the village itself was partially within Lamerton parish and partially in Lew Trenchard, giving rise to the couplet quoted by Crossing 'Lamerton and Lew Cut Bridestowe in two' (*Folk Rhymes of Devon*, 1911). Describing this anomaly he refers to then recent changes in the bounds of various parishes to rectify this situation under the title 'A Divided Village'. There he explains that a small part of Bridestowe, situated half a mile below the well known White Lady waterfall on a tributary of the Lyd and Ox Clam Bridge was cut off from the remainder of the parish by parts of Brentor and Lew Trenchard, and that much of what is now Brentor formerly belonged to Lamerton.

BRIDESTOWE AND SOURTON

Neither Bridestowe nor Sourton parishes have a boundary in common with that of the Forest, and yet they enjoy the same privileges as the 'in venville' parishes by reason of that area of land known as Bridestowe and Sourton Common, held jointly by them, which does have boundaries conterminous with both Lydford and the Forest. This extends on its western side from Nodden Gate, SX 530 864, approached via the Fox and Hounds Inn on the Tavistock–Okehampton Road, northwards on the line of the King Wall and King Way. At Nodden Gate for some years there had been a fallen boundstone lying across the gateway and showing the letters 'BS' on its upper face, but not marked on the O.S. maps. At the Beating of the Bounds of the newly formed Lydford

Above: *Fig. 53 Bridestowe-Sourton B.S. at Higher Dunnagoat.*
Left: *Marked 'P' on left bank of West Ockment at Sandy Ford.*

Bridestowe and Sourton: B.S. fallen stone at Nodden Gate. Re-erected 1988.

At Dick's Well, showing 'L' for Lydford. SX 5515 8610

parish in 1988 it was decided to have it re-erected and this was done in August of that year, setting it up beside the west side of the gateway. When lifted, it was found to bear an 'L' for Lydford in addition to the 'BS' for Bridestowe and Sourton. North of the King Wall, and on the ancient King Way, south-west of Sourton Tors, there is another boundstone inscribed 'ꟼ0/B', i.e. 'OP/B' (for Okehampton and Bridestowe) at SX 5445 8970 on the outer bounds of that common and situated between substantial old boundary banks, known as Iron Gates, to which is attached a story or legend. It is said that the body of a dead man was found there centuries ago, which the Commoners of Bridestowe and Sourton refused to give a proper burial, on whose land it then lay, leading to men from Okehampton carrying out the task and claiming the land in question, which led to squabbles between the two parties for generations. Finally the Bridestowe and Sourton folk gave way, but not before contesting Okehampton's claim at each successive beating of the bounds until recent times. There is no actual gate, or likelihood of there ever having been one in the immediate area, but the name Iron Gates appears to be associated by Crossing (*Guide*, p.59) with another point nearer to the col between Sourton Tors and Corn Ridge, though he mentions a 'bond-mark'. Hemery too (Tracks) places Iron Catch Gate north of the bondstone, but is specifically not referring to the pair of widely spaced stone posts on the northern side of the col at SX 5470 9004, 'a certain stone mark called Iron Gate' is also referred to in proposed, but unadopted, bounds for the Sourton Ice Works in 1874 which might well be these posts. From Nodden Gate, the southern bounds of Bridestowe and Sourton Common goes due east up the slopes of Arms Tor, where there are two more boundstones, to Dick's Well (SX 5515 8610) where there is another 'BS/L' stone, and on to Higher Dunnagoat where the stone is marked 'BS' only, thence through the mire at Rattlebrook Head above Bleak House to another 'BS/L' stone on the Forest Bounds. The line now veers north-east, on the Forest boundary, to Stengator boundary rock. From this height we have a very good view of the West Ockment, and drop down to that river at Sandy Ford, where on the left bank (west side) there is a small boundstone lettered 'P', said to represent 'Parish', in other words, the outer bound of Bridestowe and Sourton Common, as opposed to the Forest. We now follow the West Ockment downstream as far as Vellake Corner and back to Iron Gates.

The bounds of Bridestowe are beaten on Whit Monday, as are several other parish bounds.

WILLSWORTHY MANOR

Willsworthy Manor house has completely disappeared, the site being marked on the old 1:25 000 map at SX 535 815 but omitted from the more recent Outdoor Leisure one. The manor pound, however, is still well preserved nearby where a lane branches off the Horndon road to the open moor, known as Willsworthy Lane. Before the turn of the century Willsworthy had been in Lamerton parish, and in the Boundary Remark Book of the 1880s mention is made of a boundstone by the bridge over the Sounscombe Brook, a tributary of the Lyd, on the Okehampton–Tavistock road as being on the then Lamerton boundary at SX 518 840; Willsworthy being described as 'the Hamlet of Willsworthy, Lamerton'. The bounds of Willsworthy Manor (Fig.54), are described by Crossing as follows:

> from Buddla Corner on Black Down, by the boundstones running by Down Pool, Tin Pits, and the Ring-o-Bells to Prescombe Corner; thence to Sounscombe Head and Sounscombe Foot and Beardon Gate; thence to Lissicombe Head and down the hill to Lissicombe Foot; thence to Greenwell, and across the marsh to the Walla Brook, and up that stream to a bond mark in Doe Tor Bottom from Walla Brook Head to a cairn between Hare and Sharp Tor, thence to Tavy, and up the Tavy to Red Lake Foot; up Red Lake nearly to the head, and thence to a pile of stones thence to the head of the Baggator Brook, and down the brook by Bagga Tor farm and the Hare's Double to the Tavy; thence down the Tavy to Hill Bridge, and up by the stream on the edge of Chilly Woods to the enclosures, and thence to Buddla Corner.

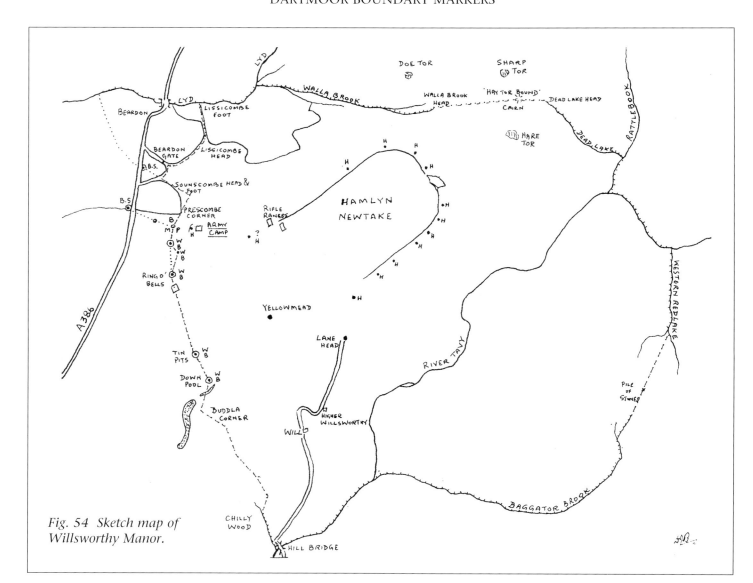

Fig. 54 Sketch map of Willsworthy Manor.

The former manor lands, now belonging to the Ministry of Defence, have two distinct classes of boundstone, those marking the manorial bounds which are referred to above, and those erected by the Ministry, or rather the War Department as it was in 1900. There is also a series of old 'H' stones relating to the Hamlyn family who enclosed a large area to the east of Willsworthy army camp stretching to under Ger Tor and Lane End, and incorporating part of the old Redford farm. Some of this enclosure is walled but much is merely defined by a broken bank or reave, around which on the open moor side there are a number of rough set stones inscribed 'H', twelve in all, with a possible thirteenth which is unapproachable as it is inside a wired enclosure on one of the rifle ranges.

Later than the Hamlyn stones are those running across the crest of Black Down between One Stone Bridge over the Wheal Jewel leat and Willsworthy Camp, past

Nineteenth century W.B. stone on the crest of Black Hill.

A broken W.B. stone, re-erected near the Lookout in 1988.

Down Pool, Tin Pits and the Ring-o-Bells. These are of nineteenth-century origin and inscribed 'W/B', bearing the marks of feather and tare. They are sited at SX 5260 8183, 5235 8228, 5215 8185 and 5222 8310. This latter is shown on the old six inch map but for many years had lain broken in two pieces; it was re-erected in 1988 by the Dartmoor National Park. Two of the sites are common to the War Department's stones (see The Army).

The cairn between Hare Tor and Sharp Tor is known as 'Hay Tor Bound', an old map of Willsworthy Manor referring to Hare Tor itself and Little Hare Tor as 'Great Hay Tor' and 'Little Hay Tor' respectively, a corruption of 'hey' or high as at Haytor on the eastern side of the moor, formerly spelt Heytor'.

Willsworthy Manor: two of the Hamlyn stones

OKEHAMPTON

At Okehampton they used Ascension Day for Beating their Bounds in the past, and in *A History of Okehampton* there is recalled a custom called 'Spurling Day' when, on perambulating the bounds 'quantities of apples, nuts, etc. are thrown into certain miry places, as the beaters proceed, where the boys, who always follow, scramble for them', and thus remember that place as a boundary point. Okehampton was a Borough at the time of Domesday, when it had a market and four burgesses, the Manor of Okehampton belonging to Baldwin de Brionys, Sheriff of Devon. Up until 1556 the Lordship of the Borough was held by the Courtenays, thereafter passing into the hands of four heiresses and their descendants. From the year 1600 fractions of the Borough were purchased by the town, and in 1623 (21 James I) Okehampton obtained a Charter of Incorporation which allowed a Court of Record. In 1628 a 'Moytie of the borough of Okehampton' was purchased 'of the Right Hon. John Lord Mohun, Baron of Okehampton, for which was payd £XX and an yearly rent charge of £V11 in ffee'. In 1682 it was ordered that the charter be surrendered to his majesty, which order was complied with in the following year, leading to a new charter being granted, and it is recorded that on 3 September 1684 Mr Richard Shebbeare 'now sworne mayor of the town, borough and parish of Okehampton, by virtue of the new charter, which was this very day brought home, accompanied by Sir George Carey, Knight, the Recorder, Sir Amos Pollard...'

Under the Municipal Act of 1882, the Corporation became extinct, and in 1885 application was made for a new charter which was granted in 1886, the govern-ing body consisting of Mayor, 4 Aldermen and 12 Councillors, creating a Municipal Borough. The bounds remained the same as those obtaining in 1623, which were then defined as 'the libertie lymitts and points of the Towne and Borough of Okehampton shall extend every where throughout the whole Towne and Borough. And alsoe by the space of halfe a mile from the Crosse in the middest of the same Towne', but the 1882 reference stated 'from the place where the Cross was formerly erected' so that it had obviously disappeared by that time. However it was still there in 1696 for it is recorded that on 26 October 'Lord Justices proclamation made at the town hall, at the Crosse and at the markett house...' – the cross was in Fore Street. This 'circle' is marked on the current O.S. maps and on it are marked a series of eight boundstones set up in 1935 inscribed 'OBB/1935'. However there are others remaining from an earlier period – one on Castle Hill at SX 5835 9440 approximately 3ft 6in in height inscribed 'The/Bounds/of the/Borough', shallowly cut and probably dating from

Fig. 55 Okehampton Borough Bounds stone on Castle Hill.

Fig. 56 Okehampton Borough Bounds 1935.

around the 1880s. Another older stone simply lettered 'B' on the borough bounds is on the 'Old Road', now closed to traffic, at SX 581 947 (see also Introduction re Bench Mark on another that has now disappeared).

Some other early references to the Bounds of Okehampton Commons are as follows:

1610. Mr Richard Bowden, Vicar of Oke-hampton, is mentioned as being present 'on a perambulation of boundaries' in that year.

1672. 13th May – This day Mr Mayor, with many of the inhabitants of this town, together with Mr Hussey and Mr Randall, schoolmaster, and divers both young and old, viewed the bounds of Dartmoor Commons belonging to this parish.

1689. 1 Gul.111 – Mr Thomas Squire, Mayor 30 Sept., The Commons not viewed untill Tuesday in the afternoon.

1885. Sept. William Crossing: 'About 10 o'clock in the forenoon a party of over 100 persons on foot, together with some 25 horsemen, headed by a band of music, set out from the town for the commons, and after viewing the various boundary marks the company repaired to the slopes of Yes Tor and partook of refreshments, which had been provided, the expenses of the day being defrayed by subscription. Most of the perambulations of the commons on the moor have some particular custom pertaining to them. That which was formerly observed when the one in question took place was the throwing of apples and nuts into the boggy places, as the bound beating proceeded, for the boys who followed to scramble for'.

In *A History of Okehampton* (revised edition 1889), additional notes include 'Marginal Notes made by the Rev. H.G. Fothergill' to the original Bridges edition, and these include the following:

Place names of such antient bounds in the Common of Dartmoor, belonging to the Borough and Parish of Okehampton: 'Imprimis. It begins at a certain place called and known by the name of Symon's Ditch corner, near about the middle of the south-east hedge of Pudhanger, and from thence south-west unto a bound stone. And from thence unto a bound stone on the west side of the way (standing fast by the way) that leadeth from the moor gate, soe called to Blackator, and from the said bound stone west unto another bound stone, and from thence to the top or highest point of Rowtor, and lineally from thence to the Middle Tor, alias Miltor, to the highest part thereof, and from thence lineally to the Top or highest part of Eastor alias Highest Tor, and from thence lineally to a certain rock called or known by the name of High Willows, and from thence to Fosborne lodge, and from thence to Sanders Ford, the which is in the river of water that flowethe nere the west side of a certain wood called Blackator's Wood.

In another chapter, contributing additional information, Crossing relates somewhat similar bounds as obtaining in 1885, going from Fitz's Well. He says 'On reaching the farm (Pudhanger, later Pothanger and now the site on which we have Moorgate Farm), and passing through the yard, we shall enter by the gate upon the Common at Halstock Down'. Now 'Pudhanger' is an ancient name, and is recorded in the Rentals of

Okehampton Manor of 20 November 1593, where under Free Tenants there is listed 'Edmund Ffurse, for Pudhanger alias Symon's parke VId.' Crossing goes on to say 'Turning left along by a wall in a short time we reach a point where an old gully is situated on its furthest side which may not improbably at some time have been a rough track. This is Symon's Ditch.' This point is still used as the starting or finishing line for the viewing of the bounds of Okehampton Common.

The boundstones mentioned by Fothergill, of which there are four, are those that run from the roadside near Pudhanger (Moorgate) Corner west towards the Moor Brook, not marked on the O.S. 1:25 000 maps. Three bear an 'L' (south side) for Lydford i.e. the Forest, and they are obviously of nineteenth-century erection for they bear the marks of feather and tare. Crossing, in a footnote, tells us that 'for some distance to the westward of the corner of Pudhanger Farm the boundary of the common is marked by a row of stone posts, the portion of land between them and the park wall (to the north, now the boundary of the Army Camp) having been given up to the Lord of the Manor, in 1866'. It was in 1780 that the 1300-acre Okehampton Park had been purchased by Charles Luxmoore, and by the 1880s 80 acres had been leased to the War Department for a period of twenty-one years. Another of these 'L' stones is to be found at Stone Ford – SX 600 919 – above Cullever Steps, and another plain stone post stands hard by the southern wall of one of the fields of Higher Halstock or Bowden Farm which may well serve the same purpose of defining this nineteenth-century boundary line.

A Beating of the Bounds of Okehampton Common, or Okehampton Hamlets, took place on Wednesday, 22

August 1990, when a party of almost 300, including 17 horsemen, took part, starting at Meldon Village after a short prayer, traversing the same route as that taken in 1933, when a newspaper recorded:

The Okehampton Commoners yesterday (5 September) followed a route along the line taken by the twelve knights (of the 1240 Perambulation). They made Sandy Ford – 'that ford which lieth on the eastern side of the Chapel of St Michael's of Halstock' (according to old documents still extant) – their first objective, and from that point surveyed the whole boundary, with the exception of some detours caused by difficult configuration of the ground. Normally the process of beating the bounds is carried out every seven years, but to compensate for the derangement caused by the Great War the last interval was one of five years... This ceremony was more orderly than it used to be, although the procedure of smiting the boundstones as a sign of claim to the enclosure land was performed as methodically as before. There was none of the horseplay as in earlier times. In pre-war days it was not unusual for riders to be jostled into the ditches besides the bumping of youngsters on the boundstones, held by their legs. The following boundstones were beaten: Iron Gate, Sandy Ford, Outer Dinger, Dinger Ridge, Inner Dinger, Curtory Clitters, New Bridge, Rough Tor Combe, Hartor Corner, Cullever Steps, Alstock Corner, and finally Simon's Ditch.

Now, as we are aware, the boundary thus described was not that of the 1240 Perambulation, for in the

Above: *Old OP/B1697/SP/B/1697 stone on the Crediton road near Webber Hill Farm. SX6095 9670*

Left: *Mirror image of OP/B for Bridestowe on reverse. At Iron Gate. SX 5445 8970.*

Vellake Rock – in the river just above Vellake Corner. SX 5550 9050.

intervening years it had changed considerably. Nor were they correct in saying that Sandy Ford was the ford 'east of St Michael's Chapel'. The 1990 perambulators entered the moor via the gateway near the Prewley Treatment Works at SX 5500 9060, where it was asserted by some that this was Iron Gate. Whilst there is no evidence to support this, photographs were taken of a youngster being bumped on the gatepost, thence taking a south-westerly course to the true Iron Gate boundstone.

The custom of setting a child upon the stone and repeating the stone's name was performed on this and all the other ones in due course. The party now turned north-east to drop down to Vellake Corner, crossing the West Ockment via the footbridge there, following the right bank of the river upstream, calling two uninscribed rocks in the river Vellake and Black Tor respectively. Although there had been disputes as Okehampton used to claim the left bank of the river, to support this there is an old inscribed natural rock at SX 5695 8852 having the usual 'OP/B', and a small set boundstone above the left bank of the river at Sandy Ford lettered simply 'P', perhaps standing for Parish. These were paid a visit at the later 1995 Okehampton beating. Eddie Hain, the former Park Ranger, says that a farmer called Worden was one of the most vociferous in the former disputes.

The next boundstone proper was that at Sandy Ford, the name being first mentioned in the 1608 Perambulation of the Forest, where above the right bank we find it to be inscribed 'OP/B'. We do not go to Forsland Ledge, the Rev. Fothergill's 'Fosborne lodge' but to another boundstone to the south-east of it, after a stiff climb, known as Outer Dinger, inscribed as before, and thence

Another, larger, rock below Black Tor Copse. SX 5665 8885.

continued north-east to a Boundary Rock, similarly inscribed 'OP/B'. This was, at first, erroneously called Inner Dinger – its correct title is Dinger Ridge.

North-east again brings us to the true Inner Dinger, another set stone, or rather two, a broken portion of an old small stone and the more modern replacement, and likewise north-east again to the Curtery Clitters where there is also the remainder of an older smaller set stone and the nineteenth-century replacement. These are at SX 5906 8962, not that nearest to where the O.S. mark Curtery Clitters. Next is New Bridge at SX 5940 9022. Here the party had lunch provided by the town, a tent having been erected to the east of the Black-a-ven and the army road on what is Duchy land. Returning to the boundary line after their welcome repast, and continuing in the same north-easterly direction, they next came to the boundstone known as Rowtor Ridge, which was not recorded in the bound beating of 1933, but nevertheless is shown on an O.S. map of 1931. It differs from all other Okehampton stones in that the three letters 'O', 'P' and 'B' are each on a different face, the east side facing towards the Forest being blank. To our right we can see the remains of a ruined wall, part of what is known as the Irishman's Wall, built in the nineteenth century to fence off the commons from the Forest and to which the Commoners objected, tearing it down, as an infringement of their rights of common, from Rowtor Ridge B.S., to follow the true current bounds, we should have

taken a course due east to Harter Ford on the East Ockment, this line having been established in 1987 with the formation of Dartmoor Forest Civil Parish, but we continue on the earlier boundary to another stone marked 'Middle Ford' on the O.S., the stone being known as Rowtor Combe. In fact there are, once again, two stones, a complete older small one, beside which the more prominent nineteenth-century one has been erected, both lettered with the usual 'OP/B'. At our next two ports of call, Harter Corner and Cullever Steps, there are similar pairs of stones. From the latter point the parish bounds go down the river, but we make our way up above the left bank, skirting the enclosure walls to Halstock Corner on the bounds of the commons, where there is another boundstone lettered 'O/PB', not on their parish bounds. Crossing in his *Guide* records an 'L' stone as having once been at what he calls Kelly's Corner, part of the 1866 line previously mentioned. From Halstock Corner the party proceeded to Symon's Ditch, as of old, and thence to East Hill, where there were games and races.

A little mystery – above Cullever Steps on the left bank a few yards west of the Okehampton boundstones, is a natural boulder apparently set on its edge, which bears the inscription 'MAD' on its south side and 'RA/TH' on the top – their significance being unknown to the author.

Finally, there is a late seventeenth-century stone to be found at Chichacott Cross to the east of Okehampton at SX 6095 9670. On the bounds of Okehampton and Sampford Courtenay, this roadside stone bears the inscription 'SP/B/1697' on its east side and 'OP/B/1697' on its west side, with an incised line on the otherwise plain north side.

Left bank of the Ockment, opposite the higher end of Black Tor Copse. SX 5695 8852.

Rowtor Ridge with O, P and B on separate sides. SX 596 908.

Above left: *Middle Ford, showing the old small stone and the taller replacement. SX 5985 9122.* Above right: *Harter Corner. SX 6015 9190.*

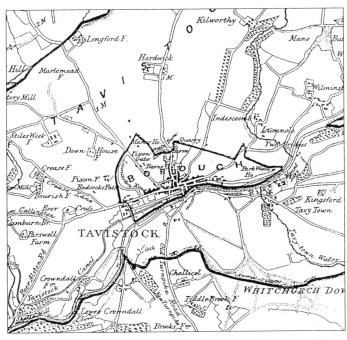

Fig. 57 Early nineteenth century Ordnance Survey map showing the eighteenth-century bounds of the Borough of Tavistock.

TAVISTOCK

Although outside not only what is considered to be Dartmoor proper, but also the Dartmoor National Park, one can hardly ignore the town of Tavistock, a former borough, and which has long associations with the moor being one of the three original Stannary Towns of Devon dating from 1305. The Domesday Book reads:

Land of the Church of Tavistock: Tavistock Church holds Tavistock Manor. Before 1066 it paid tax for 3½ hides. Land for 40 ploughs. In Lordship 5 ploughs; 12 slaves; ½ hide. 17 villagers and 20 smallholders with 14 ploughs and 1½ hides. A Mill which serves the court; meadow, 16 acres; pasture 10 furlongs long and wide; woodland 2 leagues long and 1 league wide. 1 cob; 26 cattle; 12 pigs; 20 sheep; 30 goats.

The foundation of the abbey dates from 974AD in the name of Aethelred the Second, and lay mainly in the Hundred of Lifton until an ecclesiastic Hundred of Tavistock was created. The original manor extended for eight miles in length, but by the early part of the thirteenth century 325 acres were detached from the rural manor to form a borough at a time when tin was starting to become an important factor in its prosperity.

With the formation of the Borough, the original manor of Domesday had been split into two parts, the half square mile borough around the town, of which the abbey itself was not part but an enclave, and the rural district composed of the Manor of Hurdwick, the word 'heordwic' signifying that it was the demesne farm of the abbot. From 1682-1688 there was an Incorporated Borough, as there was at Okehampton, but by the Reform Act of 1885 Tavistock was deprived of its municipal status. A description of the bounds of the Incorporated Borough as surveyed on 7 August 1738, from a board formerly hung in the old Guildhall in 1848, read thus:

The said boundaries begin at the end of the Channel of Water running under Coney Bridge; at the foot of West Bridge. From thence up the said Channel as far as the Trough or Shut, in the lane adjoining to Chapman's Garden. From thence up the same lane to a Bridge called Cole's Bridge, at the end of Ford Street and up the North side of the said Bridge as far as the Shut, or Buddle, near the Beer Cause way. From thence to the Buddle House in the adjoining field called Bolt's Meadow. From thence to the gate leading from the said Meadow into Pixon Lane. Near which gate there is now a Post marked B.B.* From thence to the head of Pixon Lane (the said Borough being bounded by the South hedge of the said Lane) and from the end of the said Lane into a field directly opposite called the Parish field bounded by the Southern hedge of the same field. And then a little more than half way down the next field on the same Southern hedge where there is another Post erected marked B.B.† From that Post immediately over the said Hedge to a stone Post in the middle of the next field called Middle Park in Drake's Means. From thence over the next Hedge to a stone post in the middle of the Field called Wyatt's Long Field (being Saunder's Land). From thence over the North East hedge unto a Stone Post in a field called Cleak's Field or Long Meadow. From thence down Wyatt's Lane to a Stone Post in the bank near the Buddle. From thence Eastwards thro an Orchard of Charles Davies adjoining to the bottom of Waddon Lane to an Oak tree in the lower Eastern Corner of the next field called Lower Waddon. From thence to a tree upon a Rock at the bottom of the next field called the East Waddon. From thence to a tree in the North Hedge in the next field called Bulteel's Lower Waddon. From thence to a Sycamore Tree situate in the South side on Bannawel Meadow to a tree in the East End of Higher Culver Meadow. From thence over Vivian's Meadow to a Post in a field called Billingsbear Wood. From thence over Crebear Cross to an oak in the South West Hedge of a field called Tolland's Field. From the said Oak directly thro the middle of Old Woods and bounded by the Hedge dividing the Higher and the Middle Old

Above left: *Tavistock: Tavistock 8/Okehampton 8 Cast Iron marker. SX 5265 8701*
Above right: *In 1986 whilst looking at the metal boundary marker at Hurdwick, I felt a stone, which was later dug up and erected by Simon Ford, the then local Park Ranger, which turned out to be inscribed 1/T/1755 with 15/O on the reverse.*
Left: *Milestone near Lydford Church inscribed 8/T/9/0 (8 miles to Tavistock and 9 miles to Okehampton).*

Woods. From thence into Exeter Lane to a Borough of Stones near a Crossway in the same Lane near Kimber's Mead. From thence to Olivers Park Wood in which there is a Post erected. From thence directly to an Oak tree in a Meadow next beyond the Barn Field. Part of the Park Wood now in possession of Mr Richard Cudlipp. And from thence directly to the Head Ware of the River Tavy the North Banks of which river are the Boundaries of the

said Borough from the West Bridge where the survey began.
* *broken lower part still in place*
† *still in situ and inscribed BT NOT BB*

The other 'Stone Posts' may be unmarked and still in position too. Totnes, another ancient borough, still has similarly marked boundstones lettered 'BB' (Borough Bounds).

Today, around Tavistock, we have a number of cast iron boundary posts defining the bounds of Tavistock Urban District Council (T.U.D.C.) and Tavistock Rural District Council (T.R.D.C.). It is known that the ancient Manor of Tavistock extended beyond the bounds of Lifton Hundred, later the Tavistock Hundred, into Roborough Hundred, and it would appear that the 'Collaton' boundstone might be so placed.

STICKLEPATH

At the higher end of the village of Sticklepath there is an ancient and most unusual stone, a pillar now approximately 4ft 6in in height bearing various symbols whose original purpose remains shrouded in mystery, but which is now used as a boundary marker, formerly by the parishes of Belstone and Sampford Courtenay but since 1987 by the newly formed parish of Sticklepath. Standing above and overlooking Ladywell on the round of the down under which the Skaigh road passes, it was first placed there in 1829 when the Okehampton–Exeter road was improved, presumably having previously been in the path of the road at the time. It is shaded by a small tree so that the symbols are somewhat difficult to see and decipher, but what is certain is that it has been re-erected since Lloyd Page described it in *An Exploration of Dartmoor* (1899), and since it was photographed by Chapman of Dawlish for the subject of one of his 'real Photograph' postcards. The stone is now set so that the two adjoining sides bearing symbols are facing in the opposite directions to that either described or shown, i.e. that formerly facing north now faces south, and that formerly facing east now faces west. The latter bears incised symbols with a 'St Andrew's' cross at the top, under which is an hour-glass, figure '8', symbol, and under that is another cross. However before it was re-erected in relatively recent times there was a further symbol below this cross, a double-lined 'lazy S' which is now below ground level, and which Chapman's photograph shows very clearly, without the funnel-shaped top depicted by Masson Phillips (T.D.A. 1987 p.247), nor does his photograph show a bar to the 'hour-glass' symbol though this too is very clearly defined. The south side has what Page describes as a 'Latin cross surmounted by a boss'. He comments that the stone 'marks the venville bounds of Belstone and Sampford Courtenay, and that when the bounds are beaten once in every seven years, a flag is hoisted on the post immediately behind the so called cross to celebrate the event'. There is still a flag-pole there today higher up on the down, marking the spot where John Wesley once preached.

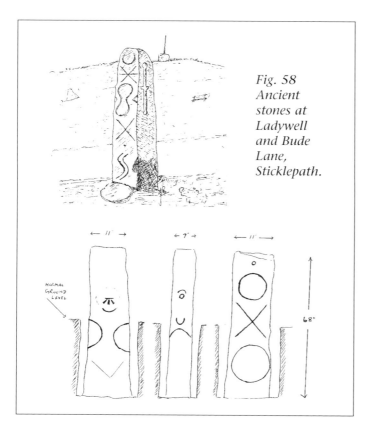

Fig. 58 Ancient stones at Ladywell and Bude Lane, Sticklepath.

A second, somewhat similar stone also on the former bounds of Belstone and Sampford Courtenay, but now on the bounds of Belstone and Sticklepath, stands at the junction of the old Okehampton–Exeter road and a lane leading down to Bude Farm. Until very recently with only about 3ft of its length exposed, a 'near miss' by a car which damaged the plastic roadside bollards beside it (seen Oct 1990) resulted in the Dartmoor National Park Authority digging a narrow trench around the stone to reveal its true size and the formerly hidden parts of its inscriptions. It then stood to a height of 68in within the hole, having a width of 11in at the top and about 15in at the base, and edges approx 7$\frac{1}{2}$in across. Later

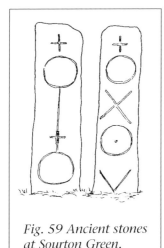

Fig. 59 Ancient stones at Sourton Green.

in the spring of 1991 it was re-erected on a firm base at the same site. The north side has a small circle inscribed near the top, followed by another larger circle beneath it, and below that a St Andrew's cross, under which is a third circle larger than the other two. Half of the cross and the lower circle were formerly below ground level. The south side bears an Ordnance Survey bench-mark, formerly just above ground level, which has now been cancelled by them thus ⋇, below which there is now revealed a small arc. Below that again there are two half circles as per sketch, one on either side of the face. The third inscribed face is the eastern side, bearing a short arc above a small circle, with another device below that. Both Crossing and Ruth St Leger Gordon call this stone 'The Honest Man'. Whatever the original purpose of these two stones may have been, possibly memorial cum boundary markers, they are not the only ones, for a few years ago a third example was found not so far away at East Linnacombe Farm near Sourton which has been set up by the D.N.P.A. on Sourton Green with an explanatory plaque, assigning it to the tenth century. Here two opposing sides bear similar inscribed circles and crosses to the Sticklepath examples with additional 'St George's' crosses at the top.

1987 BOUNDARY CHANGES

1 April 1987 saw not only the creation of another four new parishes in the Borough of West Devon, but also the disappearance of boundary lines that had remained constant since the first perambulation of the Forest of Dartmoor in 1240, together with separate status for both the Forest of Dartmoor and Lydford. As long ago as the compilation of the Domesday Book in 1086 it was recorded that 'The King has a Borough of Lidford. King Edward held it in Lordship', etc., with no mention whatever of the Forest of Dartmoor, though it was an appurtenance to that borough, due to the fact that it was not taxable, the prime concern of Domesday being to assess the value of estates for that purpose. Now we see the creation of individual civil parishes for Dartmoor Forest, Lydford and Sticklepath, which has necessitated several boundary adjustments that affect Dartmoor, together with Gulworthy which changes boundaries around Tavistock.

On the north side of the moor the formation of Sticklepath parish involved the taking in of part of Sampford Courtenay and to a lesser degree parts of Belstone and South Tawton, and the formation of Dartmoor Forest parish saw two changes, a loss from the old Forest of Dartmoor to Okehampton Hamlets and a gain of a substantial part of Walkhampton parish. The formation of Lydford parish involved changes in the parish bounds of Brentor, Bridestowe and Peter Tavy; other small adjustments were also made at the same time. All these new boundaries utilised rivers and streams as of old, together with enclosure walls, roads and the course of the old Princetown railway.

To take Dartmoor Forest first: the most northerly point of the old Forest retreats once more. Originally it was taken to the ford east of the Chapel of St Michael, Halstock, then in the nineteenth century to Cullever Steps. Now it retreats once more to Harter Ford near East Okement Farm, the new bounds running from the Okehampton boundstone between New Bridge and Middle Ford, to skirt the southern end of East Okement Farm via the track there to Harter Ford, thence running down the East Ockment river to a point immediately west of the Belstone boundstone below Higher Tor, and then going east to the point on the old bounds. All that former part of the Forest north of this line is now relocated and has become part of Okehampton Hamlets.

Dartmoor Forest C.P.'s gain is that part of Walkhampton parish north of the Longash Brook, being all that area from Deadlake Foot on the Walkham Down to the Longash Brook, thence eastwards along the course of that stream to its head, then around (outside and to the south of) the Yellowmeade Farm enclosures and Foggington Quarry, and thence along the course of the track of the Princetown railway until it meets the old Forest bounds. Thus those ancient boundary points, Great Mis Tor and North Hessary Tor are no longer on a boundary at all. In all of these changes there is only one boundstone, that at Merrivale Bridge, which is affected, formerly on the bounds of Whitchurch and Walkhampton.

The newly formed Lydford C.P. boundary was beaten for the first time in June 1988, the old Borough bounds having last been beaten in 1754, that is that part of the old parish of Lydford lying outside the Forest. At a view and perambulation of the 'Commons

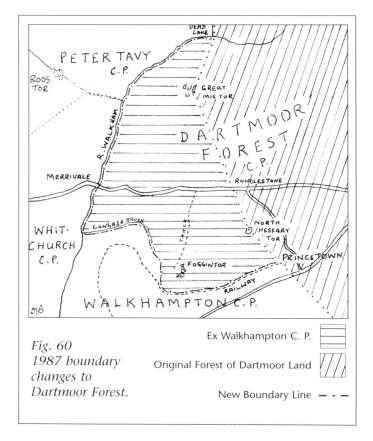

Fig. 60
1987 boundary
changes to
Dartmoor Forest.

Ex Walkhampton C. P.

Original Forest of Dartmoor Land

New Boundary Line — · — ·

of ye Borough and part of ye Parish of Lydford' the bounds recorded on 14 October 1754 were as follows:

Firstly, from Kew Lane End the right hand hedge bounds the parish as you go from the east of Kew Lane to the End thereof, and turning North East by Longford gate, from thence by Hollow Com Lake leading by the hedge to Down Town

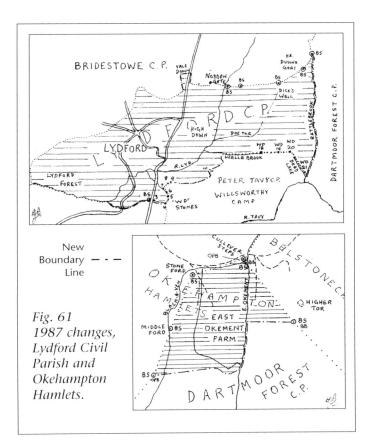

New Boundary Line – - -

*Fig. 61
1987 changes,
Lydford Civil
Parish and
Okehampton
Hamlets.*

with LB cut in the turf and an heap of Stone.
Thirdly, From thence to a little below Lid head to a little to the East of Woodcock Hill in a direct line to the West of Hunter Torr and from thence directly down to Rattle or Raddle Brook where was cut in the turf LB and some stones set up.
Fourthly, From thence down by Rattle or Raddle Brook about South to Curbeams where by the ditch was cut LB and an heap of stones from thence to Dead Lake adjoining to the Boundary of Mr Tremaine's Commons.
Fifthly, Another bounds a little to the North East of the Road leading from Dead Lake towards Lydford.
Sixthly, From Thence to Sharp-a-Torr Borrow, and down in a direct line to Black a Brook head, and so on to the River Lyd, under the Tenement called Bare Walls.
Seventhly, From thence bounded by the River Lyd to the east till you come to Cleaves Foot and thence by Raddon Lake till you come to Slow Gate.

Lane End. From thence about South east by the right hand hedge to Fernworthy Gate.
Secondly, The Bounds cut with LB and an heap of Stones thrown up near Fernworthy Gate as near as possible out of the highway. From thence by Kingwall Hedge along the high road near the hedge till we come to the Eastmost part of the hedge where the bounds were renewed

In part the new boundary takes the course of this old 1754 Borough one, following the Forest bounds, but diverges at other points. 'Curbeams' or Kerbeam is an old tin mine on the right bank of Rattlebrook at SX 559 857, and the so-called 'Road towards Lydford' but a mine track. 'Sharp a Torr Borrow' must be the cairn situated between Sharp and Hare Tors, known as Haytor Bound and where the Army have erected a boundstone to define the boundary of Willsworthy Range, one of several on this Lydford boundary but of which more under the appropriate chapter. 'Black a Brook head' has to refer to what is now designated the Wallabrook, and Wallabrook Head, where the

189

Willsworthy boundstone No.18 is situated. There are now thirteen of these Willsworthy Range boundstones on Lydford Civil Parish (1987) bounds.

The new 1987 boundary now takes in the habitations at Vale Down from Bridestowe. On the southern boundary it still follows the left bank entrant to the Lyd which ends in that spectacular waterfall known as the White Lady, and follows that line as far as Willsworthy Gate, where changes have been made; at that point there is, on the west side of the road, a Tavistock Turnpike Trust boundstone, long since obsolete inscribed 'Mary/Tavy' on whose bounds it still is, and 'Lam/erton', not on the bounds of this parish for many a year. From Willsworthy Gate the Lydford bounds now largely follow the line of the Willsworthy Army Range and their boundstones numbered through from 3 to 11, first to Prescombe Corner, then around the Beardon and Bearwalls enclosures to the Wallabrook, thence up that stream to its head and beyond eastwards via the cairn to Deadlake Head as before, down that stream to its foot and up the Rattlebrook to its head, where there is a Lydford parish stone in the mire inscribed 'L'. The only two boundstones affected by the 1987 changes are two that have never appeared on the Ordnance Survey maps; these are replacements for stones destroyed by the Americans during the Second World War near the Army camp. One is uninscribed, the other bearing the letters 'P', 'M' and 'B', at 518 836, the meeting point of the parishes of Peter Tavy, Mary Tavy and Brentor.

Brentor's bounds, too, were changed in 1987, but parts are still those of Saxon origin. A Beating of the Bounds took place on 1 May 1989 when four boundstones were located on the present boundary at SX 470

1987 Boundary Changes: 3-sided Parish Boundstone, modern replacement for one destroyed by American Forces in the Second World War, bears P, M and B (Peter Tavy, Mary Tavy and Brentor). Not on O.S. and no longer on these bounds. SX 518 836

794, SX 469 797, SX 467 802 and SX 467 805. The 1987 changes involved the loss of a portion of land to Lydford north of the River Lyd, and the acquisition of a thin strip of land on its eastern boundary.

Sticklepath parish was the other parish newly formed in 1987. Here it takes in a tiny part of Belstone at the upper end of the village around the mill, the boundary then crossing the river Taw at the weir. The new boundary still incorporates the two ancient stones at Ladywell and Bude Lane, following the A30 past the latter junction to beyond Tongue End to Chicacott Lane. Here Sticklepath's newly created boundary follows that of Sampford Courtenay but for a short distance only, as far as the dual carriageway road, thence following this eastwards back to the river Taw. It then ascends the river and encompasses a few houses that are not part of South Zeal, but which were formerly within the parish of South Tawton, east of the river, and at the point where this boundary crosses the A30 there is a boundstone inscribed 'ST/S' on the east side of the road near the Okehampton 4-mile stone. No doubt other new boundstones will be set up in the future as the need arises.

HORRABRIDGE

Some parish bounds have changed over the last century or so to create new civil parishes, as was the case in the formation of Horrabridge and Ivybridge.

Horrabridge had had an ancient chapel of St John the Baptist in the parish of Buckland Monachorum until the dissolution of Buckland Abbey, after which it was allowed to fall into decay, and it was not until 1893, with the help of Sir Massey Lopes, that the present church was built on the site of this old building. However, in 1833 an unused nonconformist chapel was bought and made a chapel of ease to Buckland Monachorum, as the Chapel of St John had been three hundred years earlier.

Something has already been said about the bounds of Walkhampton parish and the difficulties of Sir Ralph Lopes in establishing the correct line of his bounds where they were conterminous with those of the Forest from the Walkham to the Plym. Originally the ecclesiastic bounds were one and the same as those of the civil parish but with the formation of the Horrabridge Consolidated Chapelry in 1867, Horrabridge became an ecclesiastic parish in its own right. Parts of the surrounding ecclesiastic parishes of Peter Tavy, Whitchurch, Sampford Spiney, Buckland Monachorum and Walkhampton were ceded to Horrabridge in the hope that the status of a new civil parish would follow, but it took until 1 October 1950 for this to happen.

The bounds were beaten in that month, but this was not repeated until 14 September 1991, forty-one years later.

Horrabridge: Horrabridge Consolidated Chapelry, No. 3.

The bounds of the Horrabridge Consolidated Chapelry, later to become those of the civil parish, were marked by a series of eight numbered boundstones, each inscribed 'HCC/1867/No...', with the appropriate number (see Fig.62).

Before the formation of Horrabridge Civil Parish, the old bridge over the Walkham, from which the village takes its name, was the meeting point of the bounds of the parishes of Sampford Spiney, Buckland Monachorum and Whitchurch. The bridge is ancient, in the opinion of Henderson (*Old Devon Bridges*, 1938), 'of three arches, pointed, far more ancient than Huckworthy Bridge', having arches with double arch rings and recesses for pedestrians over the cutwaters, and a span of some 16 yards. In 1345 it was known as 'Horrebrigge', 'har' and 'hor' being prefixes frequently associated with old boundary markers as it is here. To mark the precise point at which the three parishes met, there is a stone set into the downstream parapet,

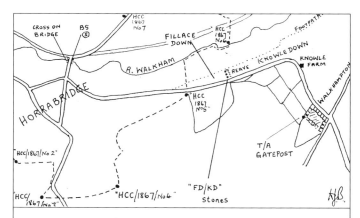

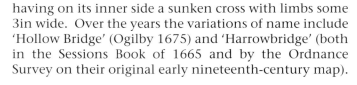

No. 1 : marked 'BS' on the Outdoor Leisure map at SX 499 705 on bank
of Walkham at the Mill.

No. 2 : also marked 'BS' on the map above Horrabridge Station at SX 505 695

No. 3 : in corner of field opposite Sadlers Retreat, SX 512 688

No. 4 : on the track to Gnatham Barton where stream crosses it at SX 517 689
covered in moss

No. 5 : inside field south of the back road running across Knowle Down at
SX 523 697

No. 6 : above the north bank of the Walkham opposite Knowle Down at
SX 525 701

No. 7 : inside field opposite house called 'California' at SX 5161 7020
(not now on the boundary)

No. 8 : at corner of Rilland Plantation on the Plaster Down road at
SX 516 714

*Fig. 62 Boundary stones
around Horrabridge.*

having on its inner side a sunken cross with limbs some 3in wide. Over the years the variations of name include 'Hollow Bridge' (Ogilby 1675) and 'Harrowbridge' (both in the Sessions Book of 1665 and by the Ordnance Survey on their original early nineteenth-century map).

Nearby just beyond the north-eastern edge of the bridge there is another boundstone, a Sampford Spiney one, waterworn and bearing the letter 'S' only. Another Sampford stone is to be found near the entrance to 'Foxhams' on the Horrabridge–Sampford Spiney road. Also on that road, at a point where the present Horrabridge boundary crosses it at SX 5235 7030 there is what must be a modern Horrabridge/Sampford Spiney boundstone, a rough slab having on its top surface the inscription 'H/P' and 'SS/P' set within an incised border panel – it lies in the hedge bank. Though it must only date from the 1950s, when first found it was covered in moss and algae.

FILLACE AND KNOWLE DOWNS

Mention might be made of some other boundstones outside Horrabridge. On the road from Horrabridge towards Walkhampton, there are stones defining the bounds between Fillace Down and the adjoining Knowle Down to the east. Formerly there were three stones, two are set on the west side of a reave between the road and a river path, and one being on this path. About 3ft in height, they bear the inscriptions 'FD' to the west and 'KD' to the east. A field bordering the down is called 'The Fillace', no doubt deriving from 'filacer', which *Chambers Dictionary* defines as 'An officer of the Court of Common Pleas who formerly filed original writs and made out processes on them', in other words a document confirming ownership.

Fillace and Knowle Downs: 'FD' with 'KD' on reverse side. SX 528 698.

IVYBRIDGE

Ivybridge Civil Parish was formed as late as 1894. Here we see the bounds of the newly created parish formed from parts of Harford and Cornwood to the north of the bridge, and Ermington and Ugborough to the south of it, the bridge spanning the Erme. Ivybridge has from very early times been on the route from Exeter to Plymouth, in fact until the dual carriageway was constructed and bypassed the village. Records show that there was a bridge at this crossing of the Erme as early as 1280 when it was called 'Ponte Ederosa'. By 1291 it was recorded as 'Ive Bridge' and in 1313 'Ivybrygg'.

Set beside each end of the downstream parapet of the present bridge are boundstones, rounded pillars, on the west side (right bank) inscribed 'Ermington' and that on the east side (left bank) 'Ugborough'. Another similar 'Ugborough' stone is still at the point where the Glaze Brook is crossed by the old A38 road. As at Horrabridge a boundary that was to

become the Ivybridge civil parish boundary was defined in the third quarter of the nineteenth century when a number of short, round-headed boundstones were set up inscribed 'ILB'. These are generally no more than 12in to 15in in height, and refer to the then newly formed Ivybridge Local Board of Health, formed in 1873 as a direct result of the fact that the village had grown at the junction of the four parishes, with some part of the community in each of them making it very difficult to get anything done. A poster of the time shows the cause of concern as being the disposal of sewage, dated 8 October 1870. This reads:

Sanitary Act 1866

Whereas in pursuance of the 49th Section of the Sanitary Act 1866 and of a Memorial duly presented by ratepayers in the village of Ivybridge, in the County of Devon, complaining of the state of the Sewage of that village, addressed to the Right Honourable Austin Bruce M.P., as one of Her Majesty's Principal Secretaries of State, praying him to institute an Inquiry as to the default of the Sewer Authority of the Parish of Ermington, in providing therein a proper system of sewage, Inquiry has been directed as to the subject matter of such Memorial:

Notice is hereby given, that on Monday, the 24th day of October, 1870 at Eleven o'clock on the Forenoon, at the London Hotel, Ivybridge, Robert Morgan Esq., the Inspector appointed for the purpose, will then and there be prepared to receive the evidence of all persons entitled to be heard before him upon the subject of the said 'Inquiry'.

This enquiry led to the formation of the Ivybridge Local Board of Health who first met in January, 1873 to attend to this matter, but which eventually took over other local functions such as the responsibility for lighting, water and finance, until in 1894 the Board became the Ivybridge Urban District Council. In 1935 the Ivybridge Urban District Council was amalgamated with that of Plympton St Mary. The 'ILB' boundstones are still to be found at various locations around the boundary of the present parish. Some are shown on the 1:25 000 scale Ordnance Survey map at SX 6364 5750, on Henlake Down at SX 6285 5735 and on the bank of the Erme (right bank) at SX 6364 5750. Another at Woodland near the housing estate seems to have disappeared, and there is one marked on the O.S. near the sewage works. There are also two more, unmarked by the O.S. on the old A38, quite near together to the east of the centre of the village at SX 6430 and 6440 5635.

Ivybridge: Ivybridge Local Board set up in 1872. At SX 6364 5750

3

OTHER MISCELLANEOUS BOUNDSTONES

1 The 'RB' Stones on Peter Tavy/Whitchurch parish bounds, SX 5240 5280 to 5240 7545.

On the 1:25 000 Ordnance Survey maps there are, between the eastern end of Collaton Lane, north of Moorshop, and the boundary rock at Beckamoor Head, three boundstones marked on the Peter Tavy/Whitchurch parish boundary. They are not, however, parish stones, and examination of the larger scale six inch to the mile maps shows that they recorded there no less than seven 'BS's on this boundary and another 'Stone' to the east of these off the parish bounds. These are all inscribed 'RB', or part thereof as a couple have had their tops broken off, but most westerly of them all recorded by the O.S. is not now to be seen. This is the single example shown by the O.S. to have been west of the Godsworthy road, the line extending eastwards along a reave. Two are set at points where ancient field banks branch off the east–west reave southwards.

William Crossing, in *One Hundred Years on Dartmoor*, relates the story about the introduction of wheeled vehicles to Dartmoor, and of a farmer in Peter Tavy parish who was the first to use a cart to collect peat from his ties. The farmer was, he believed, one William Reep of Cox Tor Farm. With the cart unstable, and overturning on the rough ground, he was ridiculed by his companions who were still using packhorses, and so, the story goes, unhitched his pony

and put the cart in the tie and buried it in the peat, leaving it to rot in disgust. This was at the beginning of the nineteenth century. At that time he was at Cox Tor Farm, later at Hill Town, and died about 1860. The Reep family had farmed in the area since the fourteenth century, and at the time were accustomed to run their sheep on Little Cox Tor, just to the south-west of the main tor, up to the end of the nineteenth century, and hence the 'RB' stones were associated with the family since Little Cox Tor was locally known as Reep's Tor, but as they were only tenant farmers, it seems far more likely that the 'R' on the boundstones relates to the manorial Lords, the Radcliffes of Warleigh, who were considerable landholders in the area from the late sixteenth century. The Radcliffes owned not only Cox Tor Farm and Hill Town, but also Collaton and Dennithorne, Godsworthy, Horndon and Longstone; William Reep being recorded as paying rent to Longstone in the early part of the nineteenth century.

The boundary stones are as follows:

No.1 marked on O.S. but now disappeared though a few humps of the west–east reave remain at this western end of the Godsworthy road.
No.2 is fallen, face upwards, at a junction of the west–east reave with another running southwards.
No.3 is still upright and set, inscription facing south.
No.4 also still upright and set, inscription facing

north, at the corner of the west–east reave and another running southwards.

No.5 is fallen but the inscription is still uppermost.

No.6 is broken but the lower part is still set, and shows the lower part of the letters, only a few inches high.

No.7 is fallen, inscription again uppermost and visible.

No.8 the most easterly example, this is *not* on the Peter Tavy/Whitchurch parish bounds and is the one marked 'Stone' by the O.S. on their six inch scale map, set where a track comes over the side of Coxhill to join the Tavistock road. Still set, the top portion has been broken off so that only the legs of the 'R' are visible and most of the 'B'.

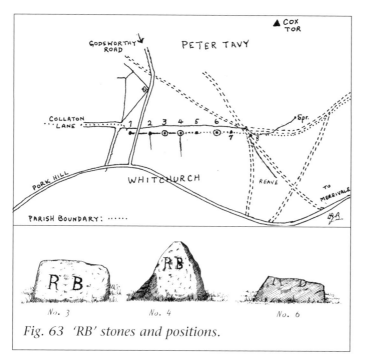

Fig. 63 'RB' stones and positions.

From No.8, in a south-westerly direction, there is a shallow gully running downhill to the Tavistock road, and in the gully, about half way between No.8 and the road, there is a plain set boundstone, unrecorded by the Ordnance Survey, possibly associated with the 'RB' stones.

2 Creason Woods, Mary Tavy

Between Hill Bridge leat and the river Tavy, and much nearer the latter, there are two boundstones only a few yards apart. That nearest the river at SX 5280 7989 is a very rough set stone inscribed with the letters 'IG' on its north-facing side. It has been said that the land between the line of this stone and Horndon Lane was given to help support the needy of Horndon. The second stone at SX 5279 7989, only a few feet away, is also a set stone of approximately 3ft 6in and in line with the first mentioned stone, but further from the river, being inscribed with what appears at first sight to be a reversed letter 'S' and a 'C' on its south side and the letter 'B' on its western edge.

This latter stone is most interesting and seems to be an example of an adaptation, and re-use, of an old stone, for the letter 'B' on its edge has been cut on a chiselled-out smooth plane, probably standing for Buller, or perhaps just 'Bounds'. Buller was a considerable landowner with extensive mining interests, but it is the adjacent side that is of the most interest. A possible theory as to the origin of this is that the stone was formerly one of a series of pre-turnpike milestones from the Okehampton–Plymouth road via Harford Bridge where there is still another milestone inscribed 'P/15' along by Moorshop and across Plaister Down. One at Hurdwick was discovered a few years ago and re-erected, that bears the date 1755. All these

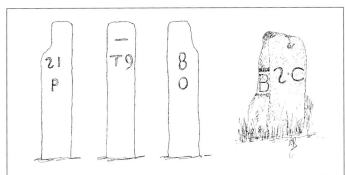

Fig. 64 Milestone at Lower Downtown/Creason Woods.

On 11 August 1993 a '12' mile stone, which had been discovered in Tavistock, was erected at the Royal Standard Arms, but is not the 'tombstone' type used in this area.

3 Cholwell Farm, Mary Tavy

This farm is situated on the eastern side of the Tavistock –Okehampton road near the famous Wheal Betsy lead/ silver mine, whose engine house is a well-known landmark.

The enclosed land on this farm is not very extensive, and the higher, east boundary is only defined by a post and wire fence along the line of an old reave on the bank. Beside the gateway to this enclosure on this eastern side there is a small boundstone (pictured above), approximately 18in in height, on which are the letters 'B' facing east to the old workings of Wheal Betsy on Kingsett Down, and 'C' facing westwards towards the farmland. This latter no doubt stands for Cholwell, and the letter 'B' for Buller – a connection between this and the 'B' on the stone in Creason Woods? And the next stone?

milestones simply bear the figures of miles and the initial letter of the town concerned inscribed upon the face of the stone, i.e. 'T.9' and 'O.8' at Lydford between the church and prison in the wall, Tavistock 9 miles, Okehampton 8 miles. At Lower Downtown there used to be another of this series, and a few years ago the author had the opportunity to examine drawings of this stone, which no longer exists, made by the late E.N. Masson Phillips, which bore the inscriptions '-/T9', '8/O' and '21/P' on three of its four faces. The resemblance of the figure '2' and the same reversed 'lazy 2' of the Creason Woods stone is remarkable. Earlier it had been brought to the author's notice that the '12 Mile' stone from Okehampton that used to be sited near the Mary Tavy Arms was missing, so with the resemblance in mind, and the fact that the edge of the Creason Woods stone had been chipped away to make a flat surface on which to inscribe the letter 'B', it is very possible that a figure '1' was cut away in the process and that this was the '12' milestone, with the apparent letter 'C' being what remains of the 'O' for Okehampton.

4 Higher Willsworthy, Mary Tavy

Now acting as a gatepost on a branch of the Lych Way between Cataloo Steps and Higher Willsworthy in the ancient lane sometimes called Corpse Lane, at SX 538 814, there is a stone inscribed with the letter 'B' but is probably not on its original site.

5 Henscott, Mary Tavy

At SX 510 825 there is yet another boundstone bearing the letter 'B'.

6 Spooner, Lydford

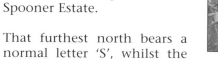

On the higher path through, or rather above, Lydford Gorge, there are two boundary stones in Watervale Woods relating to the Spooner Estate.

That furthest north bears a normal letter 'S', whilst the more southerly one (pictured) nearer the stream which falls down the gorge in a cascade (not the White Lady waterfall), bears a reversed 'Ƨ'. This is at SX 5035 8360.

7 Peter Tavy

Within the parish bounds of Peter Tavy at SX 5298 7690 and just outside the enclosure wall, there is a boundstone bearing the letter 'P', above Higher Godstone Farm.

8 Butterbury, Peter Tavy

The first edition of the six inch Ordnance Survey map (1890) for this area shows a series of no less than nine 'Stones' associated with reaves or banks to the north of the Langstone Moor menhir, one of them apparently on the line of the short stone row associated with the menhir.

Higher and Lower Butterbury farms, both now deserted, are ancient settlements recorded as early as 1330 and it is to nineteenth-century occupants that we can associate the above mentioned 'Stones' which are/were inscribed with the letter 'H' (Fig.65). It appears that in 1877 a William Maddick Hill and his brother Walter 'of Butterbury and Little Butterford' set up these granite posts illegally enclosing and claiming rights to common land, but were sued by John Reddicliffe of Middle Wapsworthy Farm, the case being reported in the *Devon and Exeter Gazette* on 25 October 1897. At that time it was stated that the boundary posts had been taken down and replaced by 'hedges' or banks in 1895, there yet remain at least three examples, two of which were 'standing', and still are, and a third which was re-erected by National Park Rangers in the late 1980s, having been found lying recumbent on its original site. Another, or even others, may still be there for the finding. The most easterly of the three erect stones at Daw's Corner, SX 555 790, is 5ft in height and has been drilled as a

Right: H5, re-used as a gatepost, not on its original site.

Below: Butterbury: H1 on sketch.

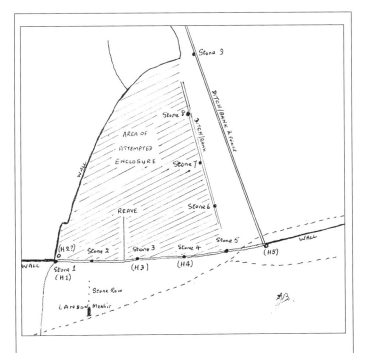

Stone 1 (H 1): 30" tall, used later as a gatepost of which only the top remains.
Stone 2: site of only, a recumbent gatepost near H 1 may possibly be it.
Stone 3 (H 3): approx 4ft tall, this was recently re-erected by the D.N.P. were found lying recumbent on the site of Stone 3, 340yds from H 5.
Stone 4 (H 4): approx. 190 yards from H 5, at the site of Stone 4, there is a recumbent stone, almost certainly the 'H' stone.
Stone 5 (H 5): Stone 5 is not on its original site but H 5 is probably it, later used as a gatepost - has two drilled holes. It is approx. 5ft tall and stands at the terminus of the ditch.
Stones 6 to 9: all are now apparently missing, Nos 6, 7 & 8 were sited in a gully running parallel with the present fence at a distance of approx. 100 yards.

Fig. 65 Butterbury boundary stones.

gatepost. It is not on the site of any of the original stones, and the most westerly example is but the top section of another that has formerly been used as a gatepost too, with drill marks. Both bear the letter 'H' on their south sides as does the re-erected stone (see sketch).

Hemery refers to the Yoledon Brook as rising in Daw's Newtake under what he calls Arthur Hill, and that in 1780 the Land Tax List showed a Stephen Madeford as chargeable for two tenements at 'Butaford alias Butworthy' – the now deserted Higher Butterbury and Lower Butworthy (Little Butaford), both within the Manor of Cudlipptown.

9 Roskilly, Willsworthy

On the Peter Tavy/Mary Tavy parish boundary and on the bounds of Willsworthy Manor at SX 5267 8155, near the Willsworthy Army 'WD' stone No. '42', there was a fallen boundstone bearing the letter 'R' which has now been re-erected by the National Park. The Roskilly family farmed Willsworthy for several generations and are still in the area.

10 Vinney Lake, Walkhampton SX562 694

Below Crossgate, on the west side of the road, where the Vinney Lake enclosures come up to the road, there is a former gateway, the more easterly gatepost bearing the letters 'LG' – a former tenant of the farm?

11 The Rattlebrook Peatworks, Lydford

The Rattlebrook Peat Works are first recorded in 1868, and in 1878 the West of England Compressed Peat Co. Ltd were granted a lease to work an area of approximately one square mile, taking the peat mainly from the slopes of Amicombe Hill.

Just under Great Links Tor there is a plain granite post (pictured) which one supposes relates to their bounds at SX 551 867. Crossing also records another where the Western Redlake falls into the Tavy, but this the author has failed to find.

12 Coryndon Luxmoore, Okehampton

On the common above the old glassworks at Meldon, and above the right bank of the Red-a-ven Brook, there is a boundstone inscribed with the letters 'CL' at SX 5690 9205.

This stone relates to the Coryndon Luxmoore family who purchased an eighth part of the Manor of Okehampton in 1759, including Okehampton Park, and who held the Manorial Rolls of the Court of Okehampton for the years 1581 to 1759. Their tenants included Holstocke, Cleave, Potthanger (Moorgate Farm), East Bowerland Alferton, and the tenements of Garstin, Richard Boyer, Warring and Staddon, all these last being situated in Meldon. In the years 1790 to 1796 Coryndon Luxmoore was Mayor of Okehampton, and other members of the family held that position between 1720 and 1794.

13 Saxongate, Okehampton Park

At SX 582 933 a 'Stone' is marked on the old six inch to the mile Ordnance Survey map, and later editions also show the legend 'Chapel (Remains of)' nearby. Investigation of the area revealed no inscribed stone but this site is but one of several medieval deserted settlements thereabouts, here with raised enclosure banks and ancient drove ways.

The chapel remains consist of two complementary shaped stones forming a half circle, which appears to have been the head of an old archway or doorframe; only a few yards away there is another worked stone of more recent manufacture – a half of a millstone. In the raised bank to the north of these objects there are a few stones protruding from the turf, the largest of which may well be the 'Stone' referred to by the O.S., and which may relate to the Coryndon Luxmoore boundary of their ⅛th portion of Okehampton Manor which included Okehampton Park.

14 Hartyland, Postbridge, Lydford

Apart from the ancient tenements in the area, Postbridge as such developed only from about 1780, when several grants were made by the Duchy of Cornwall and many new enclosures built, the name 'Postbridge' being derived from the old clapper bridge but not used for the village until early in the nineteenth century. One of the ancient tenements was Hartyland, first recorded as such in 1521, which by circa 1750 held not only copyhold land, that is to say land held 'from time out of mind', but also certain 'newtakes', land permitted to be enclosed by ancient custom by those owners of tenements who had held the farm concerned for two generations. These newtakes were only supposed to be of 8 acres in extent, for which a rent or fee of 12d was paid, but this was supposed to exclude bog and rock so that the privilege was much abused and enclosures made many times this acreage. The Hartyland boundary of 1750, as per sketch map, has at least nine boundary stones or boundary rocks on its north and north-eastern sides between the East Dart river and the Sheepfold, which is of later origin, comprising four natural boulders and five naturally shaped but set boundstones, all being inscribed with the letter 'B'.

It was not until some time after 1750 that a Mr Paterson leased some 3000 acres of land from the Duchy to found Stannon Farm, but later sold the leases to Thomas and John Hullett who enclosed Great and Little Stannon Newtakes. At the time of the Napoleonic Wars with France an attempt was made to produce starch from potatoes but this was short lived, and later the Scotch Sheepfold, a most impressive structure, was built to over-winter sheep – feather and

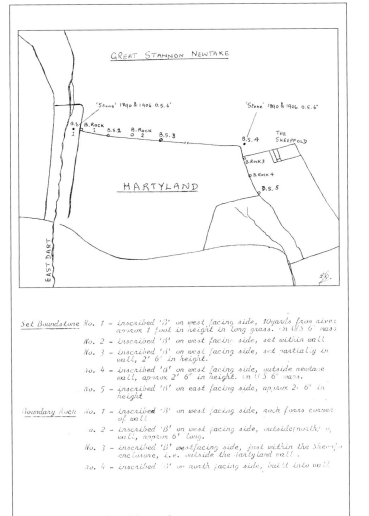

Set Boundstone No. 1 – inscribed 'B' on west facing side, 10 yards from river approx 1 foot in height in long grass. In O.S. 6" mass.

No. 2 – inscribed 'B' on west facing side, set within wall

No. 3 – inscribed 'B' on west facing side, set partially in wall, 2' 6" in height.

No. 4 – inscribed 'B' on west facing side, outside newtake wall, approx 2' 6" in height. In O S 6" mass.

No. 5 – inscribed 'B' on east facing side, approx 2' 6" in height

Boundary Rock No. 1 – inscribed 'B' on west facing side, rock forms corner of wall

o. 2 – inscribed 'B' on west facing side, outside(north) of wall, approx 6' long.

No. 3 – inscribed 'B' west facing side, just within the Sheepfo enclosure, i.e. outside the Hartyland wall.

No. 4 – inscribed 'B' on north facing side, built into wall

Fig. 66 *Hartyland boundstones.*

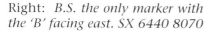

Above: *Hartyland: Boulder showing 'B'. SX 6395 8095*

Right: *B.S. the only marker with the 'B' facing east. SX 6440 8070*

tare in the impressive walls show this to be of nine-teenth-century construction. Leases to Stannon and Sheepfold passed to the Rev. Vollans and thence to J.N. Bennett who built Archerton in 1851. The dwelling built into the Sheepfold was sadly burned down in 1830 and was still empty in 1839 when the Tithe Apportionment described it as 'Cott, House and Garden Chargeable to Stannon'. Ridge and furrow marks may still be seen near the Sheepfold where presumably the potatoes were grown.

At a later date the Duchy repossessed several estates, so that today the house and garden of Hartyland, a relatively modern building on the site of the old longhouse, is a private residence, with the rest of their former land again in the hands of the Duchy and leased to Middle Merripit Farm with the Little Stannon newtake and the Sheepfold leased by the Duchy to Yardworthy Farm, Chagford. So when were the 'B' boundary markers set up and/or inscribed? The boundary rocks could have been marked before the

wall was erected. Only two 'Stones' are shown on the 1890 and 1906 Ordnance Survey six inch maps, one the set stone designated 'B.S.4' on the sketch and the other towards the river (East Dart) below 'Boundary Rock No.1' on the sketch, this latter 'B.S.1' being a small set stone hidden in long grass. Of the nine known boundstones and boundary rocks, eight have the letter 'B' inscribed at right angles to the line of the boundary, all facing westwards, the ninth facing eastwards. They were possibly erected by the Duchy.

15 Routrundle Lane, Walkhampton. SX 5525 7184

Built into a wall of what must have once been a smithy, opposite to a farm settlement known as Babyland, marked 'Homestead' on the Ordnance Survey Outdoor Leisure Map, in Routrundle Lane, there is an inscribed stone bearing the letters 'JW'. [Not found in 1998, possibly due to poor light.]

In the Tithe Apportionment List of 1839 the then occupier of Routrundle Farm was a John Westlake. Might this possibly be a boundstone or marker of his? Several drilled holes are to be seen in rocks at this site, indicating the sharpening of tools for the nearby Ingra Tor quarrymen of that period.

16 The Ecclesiastical Commissioners and the Glebe House, Princetown

Even before the prison for prisoners of war was built between the years 1806 and 1809, at what was to become Princetown, it had been proposed to erect a

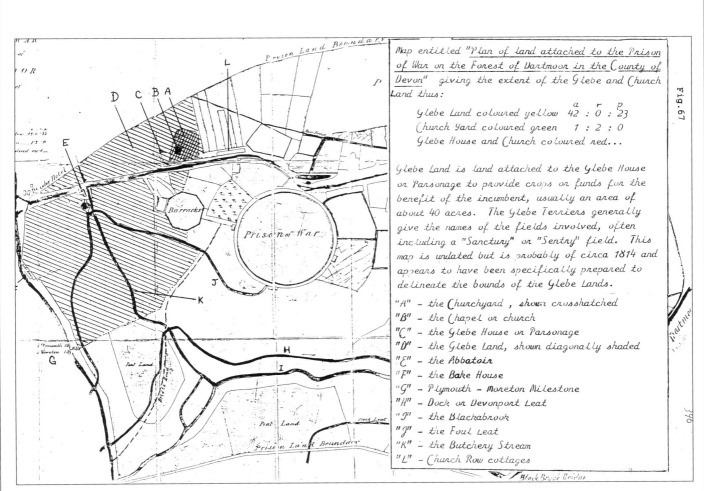

Map entitled "Plan of land attached to the Prison of War on the Forest of Dartmoor in the County of Devon" giving the extent of the Glebe and Church Land thus:

Glebe Land coloured yellow   42 : 0 : 23
Church Yard coloured green   1 : 2 : 0
Glebe House and Church coloured red...

Glebe Land is land attached to the Glebe House or Parsonage to provide crops or funds for the benefit of the incumbent, usually an area of about 40 acres. The Glebe Terriers generally give the names of the fields involved, often including a "Sanctury" or "Sentry" field. This map is undated but is probably of circa 1814 and appears to have been specifically prepared to delineate the bounds of the Glebe Lands.

"A" – the Churchyard, shown crosshatched
"B" – the Chapel or church
"C" – the Glebe House or Parsonage
"D" – the Glebe Land, shown diagonally shaded
"E" – the Abbatoir
"F" – the Bake House
"G" – Plymouth - Moreton Milestone
"H" – Dock or Devonport Leat
"I" – the Blackabrook
"J" – the Foul Leat
"K" – the Butchery Stream
"L" – Church Row cottages

Fig. 67 Map of Prison showing Glebe and Church lands.

chapel at 'Prince's Town', the name given to the settlement by Thomas Tyrwhitt, by the then Prince of Wales at his own expense. However nothing came of this at the time, though the Register of Births dates from 1807, denoting services performed at private residences. But once the prison was in use, some of the French P.O.W.s of the 'La Laborieux' class were prepared to work for the 6d per day offered to them, to enable them to supplement their meagre rations. They were put to work constructing an additional two prison blocks, cottages and also the chapel, the latter being started in 1810 and the shell finished in 1814, later to be internally furnished by American P.O.W.s in 1814-15.

Brooking Rowe (T.D.A. 1905) says that three cottages were originally made into the Glebe House quite early on, but it has now been established that this small gentleman's residence was built as such in 1813 and is not a conversion. An undated map, thought to be circa 1814, confirms this.

The map also shows the extent of the Glebe Lands extending over an area of some 42 acres from the prison boundary to the west, to the 'Plymouth 15/ Moreton 13' milestone to the east on the Princetown–Two Bridges road, much of this land being where the town was later built. The map shows the P.O.W. bakery, the Duchy Hotel, initially built to house the prison officers until the barracks could be completed, the prison abbatoir, the Glebe House, the 'Church', Church Row Cottages and the prison buildings as they then were. The 'chapel' was originally called Dartmoor Church but soon designated 'Dartmoor Chapel' since it was indeed a chapel of ease to the parish (Lydford) church of St Petroc. From 1816 until his retirement in 1860, the Reverend James Holman

Mason was vicar of Widecombe-in-the-Moor, under whose jurisdiction the chapel came. The chapel closed between the years 1816 and 1831, during that period the prison was empty, but it was re-opened in 1831. It was not until 1860 that Princetown was declared a separate ecclesiastical chapel, and in 1868 that the parsonage or Glebe House was conveyed by the Duchy of Cornwall to the Ecclesiastical Commissioners under the Church Buildings Act 'to be appropriated as and for the residence or site for the residence of the Minister who may serve the Church of Princetown'. This was purely the house and garden, now a private property, and was an enclave within the land leased from the Duchy by the Prison Authorities.

The boundary was defined by four boundstones, approximately 9in² in section, having the letters 'EC' (Ecclesiastical Commissioners) carved in relief within small sunken panels. That at the south-west corner of the grounds is about 3ft in height, that at the north-east corner only about 1ft in height and that at the north-west corner about 2ft in height. The fourth example may be hidden under a pile of stones and turf in the south-east corner!

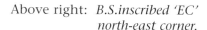

Above right: *B.S.inscribed 'EC' north-east corner.*

Right: *B.S.inscribed 'EC' south-west corner.*

17 The Stark Family and Yardworthy Newtake

No.1. on map.

Within Yardworthy Newtake to the west of the Fernworthy road between Tawton Gate and the Metherall Brook, there are a number of small set bound-stones bearing an inscribed letter 'S', eight having been observed, with the inscribed side facing in various directions, extending from the right bank of the South Teign at SX 674 848 and up the Metherall Brook to the road and others in a line to one beside the roadside wall at SX 676 843.

It is thought that these boundstones probably refer to the Stark family. Robert Stark was a successful sculptor and painter in the late-nineteenth–early-twentieth century, originating from Torquay, who had empathy with Dartmoor, especially around the South Teign. He first went to the area on holiday and on his

marriage, he rented Berrydown as his first home, later he designed and built Scorhill House. After buying a 275-acre estate in the 1890s, he also built the substantial properties of Ford Park and Great and Little Frenchheer. He later sold Ford Park to the Duchy in 1912 but retained seven acres of land near the Teign. This might well be the area defined by the boundstones and possibly suggests that he had earmarked it as the site for another house, having a frontage on the Fernworthy road and an ample supply of water from the Metherall Brook. Some of the ground is rather boggy and a few exposed stones bear feather and tare marks.

Whilst he was building the houses he rented a property known as Shallows. Thomas Fairbank who, after the Second World War, lived there for a time after running the peat workings in the Amicombe Hill area, published a book in 1956 entitled *The Log Hut* which is the name the building then went by.

His daughter Freya Stark spent her early years near Chagford, became a writer and traveller, exploring much of the Middle East. She lived to be a hundred and died in 1993.

18 Belstone Consols, Sticklepath

Ivy Tor Mine, on the southern side of the River Taw in Belstone Cleave, was worked for copper from about the 1840s, though there are no records of ore obtained in spite of driving down to 42 fathoms by 1865. In 1866 it was amalgamated with Belstone Consols, a sett on the northern side of the river, which had been started in about 1829 privately, later being called variously Greenhill, the shaft being adjacent to a farm of that name, the Copper Hill Mine (1874), the

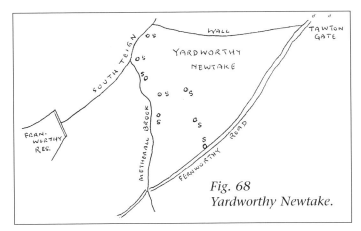

Fig. 68
Yardworthy Newtake.

Belstone Consols: Rock in-scribed 'A'. SX 6360 9380   *Rock inscribed 'B'. SX 6332 9384. (Photos taken 1992)*

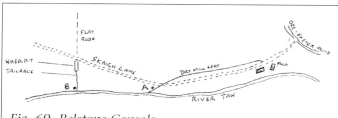

Fig. 69   Belstone Consols.

Mid-Devon Mining Co. (1878), etc. The shaft was eventually taken to almost 100 fathoms, and to de-water it, a 70ft wheel was erected just south of Skaigh Lane, the leat from the Taw near Birchy Lake being laundered over the road, the wheel driving about 2000ft of flat rods. The tailrace feeds the water back into the Taw, and just upstream of this point there is a slab of stone set flush with the ground inscribed 'B' at SX 6332 9384. At first this was thought to be a possible Belstone parish stone, the left bank of the river being the boundary, but the finding of another rock inscribed with the letter 'A', beside the bank of the dry mill leat at SX 6360 9380, suggests that the bounds of the sett were thus marked in a similar fashion to Yeoland Mine (see No.24). Others may exist to the north of the shaft, etc. near the Tongue End–Belstone road.

19 Haytor Down

In addition to the 'Templer/Somerset' stone already noted on Haytor Down at SX 765 779, there is another broken boundstone under the south side of Smallacombe Rocks at SX 7544 7817, which, whilst no longer 'set', must have once been erect near its present position. As regards shape, it is almost identical to the 'Templer' example, having a rounded top, 13½in wide and 9in in depth, the broken shaft being 20in long. It has laid for so long in its present position that the top surface is level with the ground, on which there is a shallowly engraved 'C', and upon lifting it, with difficulty, one finds a reversed letter 'S' on the other side.

It is not unlikely that this stone relates to the bounds of John MacCarthy who worked a sett granted by Somerset in 1824, having an agreement with Templer that he could run his own wagons over the tramway on payment of a royalty.

Smallacombe Rocks: Recumbent stone inscribed 'C' on one side and a reversed 'S' on the other. SX 7544 7817. (Photos taken early 1990s)

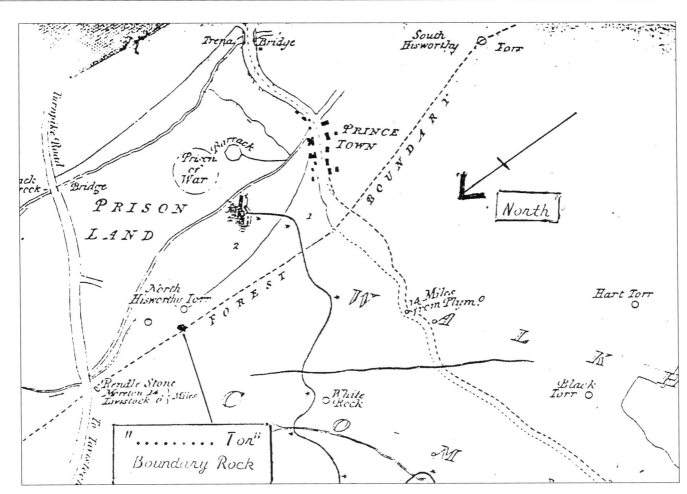

Fig. 70 Tyrwhitts map of North Hessary Tor area.

20 North Hessary Tor

During the period early-eighteenth–mid-nineteenth century the Duchy were still in conflict with various adjoining landowners, and an inscribed boundary rock discovered in the late 1980s would appear to indicate that the Duchy were in that period of time claiming it to be on their bounds. This rock or outcrop (pictured) is somewhat to the west of North Hessary Tor, but is no more than about 5ft in height, still bearing the inscription 'Tor' at SX 574 743. Several letters preceding the word 'Tor' have quite obviously been professionally chiselled away, and it has been suggested that these were either 'N. Hisworthy' or 'N. Hessary', for on a map accompanying a booklet by Sir Thomas Tyrwhitt, the Forest boundary line is shown to pass through the site of the boundary rock to the former 'Rendle Stone' on the Tavistock road, with the true 'North Hisworthy Tor' shown well to the east, and thus depriving Walkhampton of quite a few acres of common. In other words, did the Duchy create a boundary point that was later declared to be incorrect and erased?

21 Inscribed Stones at Stover Country Park and the Haytor Tramway

In 1980, when the Devon County workmen were cleaning up a series of old silt traps on the Whitelake, which feeds Stover Lake, they found that various stone artifacts had been used including an uninscribed post and two other smaller posts roughly square of section, both bearing the same inscription, a single letter on each side 'H/T/W/B/'. These were set into the bank of the stream near where they were found and now stand at 6ft, 3ft 3in and 2ft 4in respectively (pictured below). In the author's opinion they refer to Haytor Tram Way Bounds, and that they originally came from Brimley where the tramway crossed the Newton Abbot–Drumbridges–Bovey Tracey road. It is known that the Tramway leased a corridor of land 32ft in width through all the enclosed land that it crossed, and that in 1825 they paid Viscount Courtenay the sum of 5 guineas for that year for crossing Lower Down.

It is not known when the inscribed stones were uprooted, but the Moretonhampstead and South Devon Railway, formed in 1866, used practically the same contour between Ventiford and Brimley, and was incorporated into the South Devon network in 1872. The bridge carrying this railway over the road at Brimley was demolished when the Bovey Tracey bypass and the present roundabout were constructed.

It is suggested that one of these inscribed stones once stood at either side of the Tramway Bounds where it

crosses the road. The taller 6ft post may also have come from the roadside. Whilst not inscribed it has a drilled hole in its top. A similar stone still stands beside the point where the tramway crosses Higher Terrace Drive, the road from Haytor to Manaton, and may have once been used in some way as a warning device to road traffic of oncoming tramway wagons with but a wooden brake. Other worked stones from the tramway have been used in the outfall of Stover Lake.

22 Yennadon Down – the Meavy Iron Mine

There is now little to be seen, but the abortive efforts to work this mine in 1836 are recorded in a copy of the lease of that date, showing the prescribed area marked by a series of no less than 11 boundstones. Only one appears to remain, a plain stone, but the ground is covered in gorse, etc. so there could be others. This is at SX 5489 6833. George Stone Baron or Barton had the original lease, a gentleman adventurer who was also unsuccessful with his sett working for clay on Walkhampton Common at about the same time.

23 Assycombe, Fernworthy

There is an upright pillar standing on the scant remains of a cairn on the summit of Assycombe Hill just outside the outer Fernworthy wall at SX 665 820, shallowly inscribed with the letter 'D' on its west-facing side. It was thought that this 'D' referred to the Duchy in spite of most of their boundary stones being marked 'DC', either when the Forestry Commission planted trees (c.1918) or when the Torquay Waterworks Authority acquired land in the area for the Fernworthy Dam.

Since then two further examples have been found further west actually in the wall and similarly inscribed. It was in about 1802 that a Sir John Davie extended his holding at Fernworthy, and it has been suggested that the 'D' stands for Davie, which seems to be the more likely answer.

24 Yeoland Mine, Roborough Down

The first edition of the six inch Ordnance map of this area shows 'Yeoland Mine (Tin disused)' at SX 510 662, and on Roborough Common nearby to the east marks four stones between the Yeoland Farm enclosures and the old Great Western Railway track, 'Shaft (dis)' is also marked on the current Outdoor Leisure map.

Tinning had been carried out in this area at least since Elizabethan times – in 1600 Sir Walter Raleigh was having trouble with the tinners diverting water to 'certain clash-mylls upon Roborough Down to work the tynn'. Reports on this mine are rather confusing, but it would appear that East Yeoland was first reported in 1848, West started in 1851, and at some time the four stones mentioned above must represent the area leased to James Yonge, Joseph Square and Ponsford Fisher by Lord Roborough in 1847, as follows:

All that part and portion of Roborough Down … bounded on the eastern and western sides by the hedges and fences of lands already inclosed, and on the northern side by a straight line to be drawn from a Granite Post inscribed A set up on the western side of the said Down to another Granite Post inscribed B set up on the eastern side … and on the southern side by a strait line to be drawn from a Granite Post inscribed C set up on the Eastern side of the said

down to another Granite Post inscribed D on the western side.

Stone 'A' and Stone 'C' are still there, but the other two presumed to be lettered 'B' and 'D' could not be found.

The mine was put up for sale in 1857 after operations had ceased, in spite of having raised £13 000 worth of black tin in 1856. I have an unconfirmed date of 'about 1890' for the final closure of the Yeoland mines.

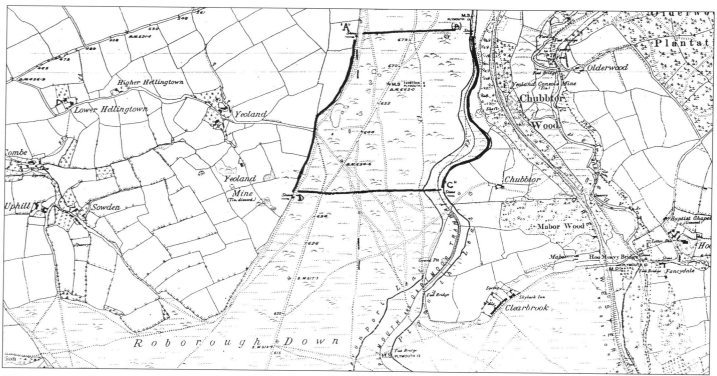

Fig. 71 Map showing boundary of Yeoland Mine.

4

THE ARMY

Today we have the army in what appears to be permanent occupation of a large part of Dartmoor, on their ranges at Okehampton, Willsworthy and Merrivale, together with 'dry' training exercises taking place elsewhere, but long before the then War Department bought Willsworthy Range outright and acquired leases from the Duchy of Cornwall on the other two, with new leases for a further twenty-one years being granted by the Duchy in 1991, there had been many earlier exercises and camps under canvas from the late eighteenth century, generally in times of peril, and even by Volunteers from Elizabethan times.

The army trained on Ugborough Down as early as 1794, and an encampment was set up on Hemerdon Ball at about the same time, under threat of invasion by Napoleon, and on Butterdon Hill there are the probable remains of a Militiaman's hut dating from that period. Such was the threat of invasion, and the activity of spies, that early Ordnance Survey maps of the Plymouth area, only published in the early 1800s, were withdrawn from public sale as security was tightened. Other early indications of rifle practice on Dartmoor and its surrounds date from the 1860s, when Britain was again under threat, with ranges sited at Okehampton near the golf course, at Belstone, under Hartor south of Devil's Bridge near Princetown, north of Butterdon Hill where there were four targets, and on Welstor Common just within Ashburton parish. Range markers of between 100 and 700 yards

are still to be found on the Hartor and Butterdon Ranges, on the latter upwards of 65 range markers have been noted with double rows for each of the four butts.

It was the army manoeuvres of 1873 on Yennadon Down, at Ringhill and at Roborough that were the forerunners of, at first, a regular annual summer camp of six weeks' duration from 1875, when the Duchy of Cornwall agreed to the establishment of camp at Okehampton Park, and artillery firing took place over an area of some 3000 acres. From 1877 regular summer camps were held at Okehampton, and in 1892 a 99-year lease was granted, renewed in 1991, on this range, 80 acres having been acquired from Okehampton Park Estates in 1891 on which to set up a permanent campsite. In 1895 the entire northern sector of the moor was leased to them and over the years they have increased their hold so that today they own or lease a total of

The Army: 'No 7/W.D./ ' near Anthony's Stile. SX 586 925

some 33 000 acres. The remains of obsolete rifle and artillery ranges on the Okehampton Range are numerous, many of which the army, a few years ago, offered to dismantle. One of these, however, caused some disagreement between the National Park Authority and the Dartmoor Preservation Association, the former preferring it to be retained as part of Dartmoor's past and the latter wanting its complete removal. This is a mobile target range comprising a narrow gauge railway with a loop at either end, points and a 'bunker' for the engines, of which there were two, under the east side of West Mil Tor. Unique to Dartmoor, it is worthy of saving, this relic of the past misuse of Dartmoor is just part of what makes the whole area so fascinating. That is not to say that a close watch and control should not be kept on future proposals.

The bounds of the original 80 acres granted to the War Department to set up the permanent camp at Okehampton are defined by a series of eight boundstones, inscribed 'No.1/W.D/-', etc. There are at least two others within Belstone parish simply inscribed

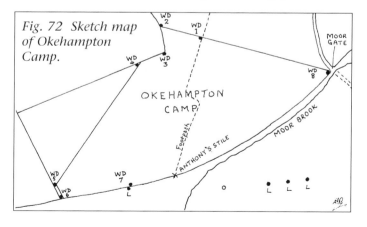

Fig. 72 Sketch map of Okehampton Camp.

'WD'. Above the right bank of the East Ockment river between Scarey Tor and Winter Tor, each of these two stones appears to be one half of a granite window sill, at SX 6070 9233 and SX 6075 9210. The other well marked boundary is that around the Willsworthy Range (Fig.74), which was purchased outright in 1903. The line of this boundary virtually follows that of the old Willsworthy Manor, with some slight variations, about 3200 acres being purchased from the Calmady-Hamlyn family.

The boundaries were, according to Hemery, cut in the 'locality of Nattor Down' and taken to their sites by a Fred Palmer of Lane End Farm. They are generally about 2ft in height, square of section and bear the marks of feather and tare. The face is inscribed with the letters 'W.D' beneath which is the appropriate number, the series running from No.1 to No.46.

Their sites are as follows:

1   on Black Hill at SX 5185 8258
2   on the Tavistock/Okehampton roadside at SX 5175 8314
3   at Willsworthy Gate at SX 5180 8350
4   at Prescombe Corner at SX 5217 8345
5   at Sounscombe Head at SX 5220 8360
6   on the Sounscombe Brook at SX 5215 8370
7   at Sounscombe Foot at SX 5200 8380
8   at Beardon Gate, south side, at SX 5207 8393
9   at Beardon Gate, north side, at SX 5208 8396
10 at Lissicombe Head, west side, at SX 5237 8415
11 at Lissicombe Head, east side, at SX 5238 8415
12 at SX 5237 8427
13 at Lissicombe Foot at SX 5228 8442
14[†] left bank of Lyd at SX 5266 8448 and via the

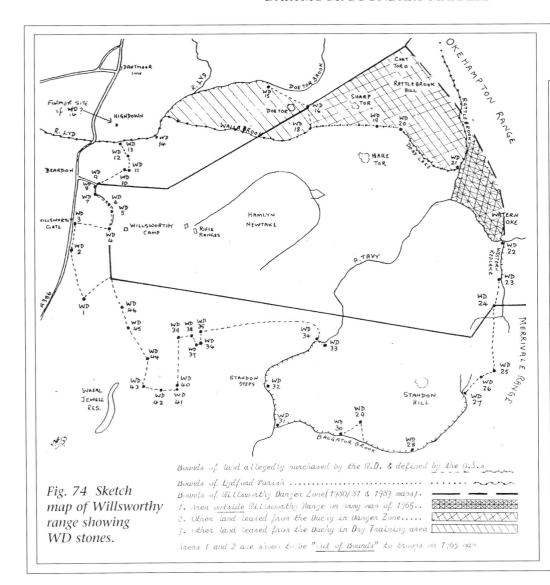

Fig. 74 Sketch map of Willsworthy range showing WD stones.

Bounds of land allegedly purchased by the W.D. & defined by the B.S.s
Bounds of Lydford Parish ....
Bounds of Willsworthy Danger Zone (1980/81 & 1983 maps).
1. Area outside Willsworthy Range on Army map of 1765..
2. Other land leased from the Duchy in Danger Zone.....
3. Other land leased from the Duchy in Dry Training area

Areas 1 and 2 are shown to be "out of Bounds" to troops on 1765 map

Fig. 73 War Dept No.6 B.S., at Camp and WD stone near Scarey Tor.

River Lyd and Doetor Brook

15 at Doe Tor Bottom near Tavistock Water Intake at SX 5413 8506
16 near Cist east of Doe Tor at SX 5445 8495
17 see following paragraph
18 at Wallabrook Head at SX 5447 8455
19 near cairn north of Hare Tor at SX 5517 8457
20 at Deadlake Head at SX 5547 8460
21 at Deadlake Foot at SX 5610 8405

† all these stones, except for Nos 14 and 17 are shown on the six inch O.S. map in their present positions, just marked 'Stone'. What appears to have been No.14 is marked at High Down (SX 5218 5467) so when was the boundary changed and the stone moved?

22 via the Tavy at Western Redlake Foot at SX 5662 8322
23 midway up the Western Redlake at SX 5656 8280
24 near Western Redlake Head at SX 5652 8250
25 near the head of the Baggator Brook at SX 5650 8173
26 ditto at SX 5638 8160
27 ditto at SX 5616 8140
28 at the north-west corner of South Common Plantation at SX 5550 8075
29 at the north-west corner of Baggator Woods at SX 5495 8115
30 at the south-west corner of Baggator Woods at SX 5478 8997
31 at Cataloo Steps at SX 5403 8114
32 at Standon Steps at SX 5395 8155
33 on the left bank of the Tavy at SX 5460 8204
34 on the right bank of the Tavy at SX 5446 8207
35 on the edge of Yellowmeade enclosures at SX 5313 8222
36 ditto at SX 5318 8213

37 ditto at SX 5316 8210
38 ditto at SX 5303 8220
39 ditto at SX 5292 8220
40 at Buddla Corner, north side, at SX 5288 8162
41 ditto, south side, at SX 5289 8160
42 on the edge of Willsworthy enclosures at SX 5270 8155
43 ditto at SX 5248 8162
44 next to 'W/B' memorial stone at SX 5259 8186
45 next to 'W/B' memorial stone at SX 5238 8220
46 on the crest of Black Hill at SX 5227 8250

One would have thought that there would be a complete set of these numbered boundstones 'in situ', and that these would define the precise boundary of the land actually purchased by the War Department, but it appears that this is far from the case. The Ordnance Survey six inch to the mile map shows only 45 such 'Stones', with 'W.D/17' conspicuous by its absence. A statement made by a former Willsworthy Warden indicated that he understood that the army bounds once went up to, or included, Sharp Tor, though he did not know exactly when this was, and that they were later amended to go directly from 'W.D/16' east of Doe Tor cairn to 'W.D/18' at Wallabrook Head. So why was this amendment made and when? Did the War Department follow the Doe Tor Brook in error when they should have followed the Wallabrook, formerly called the Black-a-Brook?

Further complications arose when, during the beating of the bounds of the newly created Civil Parish of Lydford in 1988, another stone simply inscribed 'WD' was found lying recumbent only a yard from 'W.D/20' at Deadlake Head. At first it was thought that here we had the stone intended for No.17 at Sharp Tor, but closer inspection showed that not only was it un-numbered but that the letters 'WD' were cruder and without the normal stop after the letter 'W', and contrary to all other examples there was no dash below those letters.

Part of the answer to this apparent amendment of the bounds can be gleaned from a 1980/81 Ordnance Survey map of a scale of 1:50 000 of Dartmoor prepared for the army and which was overprinted to show what the army then considered to be the bounds of all their ranges, both for dry training and Danger Areas, a copy of which the author found on the moor some years ago, abandoned, and a later one dated 1983. In the case of

'W.D.14' on left bank of Lyd near Bearwalls.
SX 5266 8448

Willsworthy Range, the 1980/81 map showed the boundary under High Down following first the river Lyd and thence up the Doe Tor Brook to a point near the Tavistock Water Intake, 'W.D/15', and thence to 'W.D/16' east of Doe Tor cairn and on to 'W.D/18' at Wallabrook Head,

'W.D/19' near the cairn at Hare Tor, etc., thus excluding Sharp Tor from the area so encompassed. However the map does still show that Sharp Tor was within a 'Danger Area' associated with the Willsworthy Range, which extends beyond the area defined by the numbered 'Stones'.

Yet more information regarding the Willsworthy bounds has also appeared in the Dartmoor Preservation Association newsletter for December, 1988 (No.108, page 11), wherein Lady Sayer is stated to have declared that she:

Left: 'W.D.20' at Deadlake Head, showing recumbent stone marked 'W.D.' found on the perambulation of the Bounds of Lydford C.P. in 1988. SX 5547 8460.

Right: 'W.D.44' sited at Down Pool, beside one of the 'W/B' (inscribed on reverse side) Willsworthy Manor B.S. SX 5259 8186.

has been able to prove beyond doubt that ... 330 acres of the Willsworthy Range is held from the Duchy of Cornwall under the Okehampton Licence. This consists of land in the north and north-east of the range. It includes land in the Danger Area as well as Dry Training land in the Doe Tor area. The Danger Area under Duchy licence includes Sharp Tor and part of Rattlebrook Hill and further south includes Watern Oke.

So was 'W.D/17' removed from Duchy land at their request? But this 330 acres of Duchy land outside that purchased by the army in 1900, but utilised as part and parcel of the Willsworthy Range under a licence due to expire in 1991, comprises not only the land in the Danger Area from east of Doe Tor up to a point north of Chat Tor on Rattlebrook Hill, and then bending south-eastwards down through Watern Oke before crossing the Tavy and following the Western Redlake (marked 'Danger Area Sub Division' on their map), but also all that area between the Doe Tor Brook and the Wallabrook, for the true boundary line of the land purchased by the War Department appears to follow the latter watercourse rather than the former, as did the Willsworthy Manorial bounds. This means that 'W.D/15' and 'W.D/16' are also incorrectly sited and on Duchy land, though No.15 is shown on the army map as being on the bounds of the Dry Training Area and No.16 at the junction of the Dry Training Areas. As long ago as 1938 the War Department had sought to increase the Danger Area by a further acquisition of 550 acres on Doe Tor Common, contested by Lydford parishioners, the Wallabrook here defining the parish boundary.

Another earlier Ordnance Survey map prepared for the army and showing the then considered boundaries of all three ranges, published in 1965 (Scale 1:25 000) also shows the area bounded by the Doe Tor cist to Rattlebrook Hill, around to Deadlake Foot and thence up the Deadlake to its head, to Wallabrook Head, as 'Out of Bounds' even to the troops, and the Willsworthy Danger Area did not extend southwards through Watern Oke to the east of the Rattlebrook as is shown on later maps. So what is the true position? Whereas the Calmady-Hamlyn purchase was said to be about 3200 acres, more recent figures given for the extent of this range are 3400 and 3450 acres.

In 1991 the Duchy approved and granted the army further 21-year leases for Okehampton and Merrivale Ranges, but firing was to take place on a reduced number of days per year, giving the general public more access, and to phase out the use of explosive shells at least by 1998. On Willsworthy Range the army have promised free access on all days when there is no firing, but this only maintains the status quo. Their plans to demolish the somewhat untidy and obtrusive huts on the moor, to replace them with a purpose-built, single-storey block at Higher Beardon Farm, were approved and to cost an estimated £500 000, were officially opened on 12 May 1995. Changes also took place in the bounds of danger zones taking Great Mistor, Roos Tor, White Tor and Watern Tor outside the live firing ranges, thus giving the public unrestricted access to them, though 'Dry' training will continue.

Warning:
Do not pick up any metal objects within the firing ranges, but notify them to the authorities.

Always make sure that there is no firing taking place on the range or ranges on the day of a proposed visit. Relevant information is always available, published in the *Western Morning News* on Fridays for the following week, and is also available from Police Stations and the Dartmoor National Park Headquarters, Parke, Bovey Tracey, and also their Information Centres.

Red Flags will be flying when firing is taking place, from prominent points on the range in question, and one is warned that one is entering a range by a series of red and white striped poles.

5

BRIDGES, ROADS AND RAILWAYS

Yet another aspect of boundaries, or more correctly boundaries of responsibility, relates to county bridges. Early river crossings had been accomplished on Dartmoor and its environs by means of fords, or in many cases by those rude structures known as 'clapper' bridges, drystone built of slabs of natural moorstone, a single slab over the narrower and smaller streams, or with piers to carry it across the wider streams and rivers. These sufficed where the river had cut a channel below the level of the river bank by only a few feet but where it had cut a deep chasm or gully, as is sometimes the case, it was necessary to construct a special type of bridge to allow the strings of pack-horses carrying wool and other commodities to cross safely. In medieval times trade had increased to such an extent, both in wool and tin, that strings of such pack-horses numbered up to as many as 30 or so animals, carrying their wide loads on a pair of 'crucks' across their backs. Thus whilst most such bridges were narrow, they were generally highly arched to clear flood-water levels, with low parapets to allow the loads to project over them. Mainly of fourteenth-century construction and later, they were built either by the church, great bridge builders, and by the manorial Lords in earlier times, or later by the parish or county, graceful structures with their piers and cutwaters, above which there were 'refuges' for those pedestrians caught unawares by the pack trains.

Those bridges either constructed by the county, or taken over by them and henceforth maintained by them and sited within the County of Devon, had set 'C' stones erected on either side of the bridge to acknowledge the County's responsibility for their upkeep. In a Statute of Henry VIII dated 1531 it was stated that unless it could be proved that 'a Hundred, Riding, Wapentake, City, Borough, Town or Parish nor what person certain, or Body Politick' should by right maintain a Bridge then a shire or county were obliged to maintain them. In Devon the County's responsibility for the maintenance of a bridge was marked by the erection of these 'C' stones, which date from 1841. At the Michaelmas Quarter Sessions of that year it was resolved that 'Bound Stones', made of a durable stone – and most of those around Dartmoor are of granite – and of a height of 2ft, be set up on both sides of all bridges that were their responsibility, at a distance of 300ft from such bridges, for they were responsible not only for the structure of the bridge itself, but also for the immediate approach, or cause. They are said to have cost 7/6d each to erect. At about the same time, more attention was paid to the height of parapets, some of which were dangerously low and without guard rails. Fortunately many of these older bridges have retained their 'C' stones by virtue of the fact that the roads on which they stand have been relegated to secondary or an even more minor status, so that if they have been widened they are still, in essence, the original bridges. There does not seem to have been any hard and fast rule, but most of these stones are to be found on the right-hand side as one approaches the bridge, but several are to the left.

The author has noted the following:

Bellever Bridge: on the East Dart at SX 658 774. Both 'C' stones remain on this early nineteenth-century replacement for the old clapper bridge.

Cadover Bridge: on the Plym at SX 555 647. The 'C' stone on the old Cornwood road remains, but there were originally three stones; the other two are now missing.

Cockingford Bridge: on the East Webburn at SX 717 751. The west side 'C' stone remains. A 'modern' bridge.

Dart Bridge: on the Double Dart at Buckfast at SX 745 667. In spite of being widened twice and a dual carriageway constructed nearby, the west side 'C' stone remains. There are two tablets set into the down-stream parapet dating the widenings to 1827 and 1929.

Dartmeet Bridge: on the East Dart at SX 673 733. Both former 'C' stones are now missing but the bridge has a tablet on the upstream side declaring it to be a county bridge, inscribed 'County Bridge 1792'.

Gulwell Bridge: over the Ashburn in Ashburton on the Old Totnes Road, one 'C' stone remains.

Harford Bridge: on the Tavy at SX 507 768. Both 'C' stones remain. The bridge has a dated tablet '1892', the date of rebuilding after being partially demolished by floods.

Hill Bridge: on the Tavy at SX 532 803. Both 'C' stones remain.

Holne Bridge: on the Dart at SX 730 706. Both 'C' stones remain but that on the southern side of the bridge must be that formerly shown on the old Ordnance Survey six inch map on the old route which passed near the lodge and went through North Park Woods, and re-routed to its present course in the early 1900s. The old section of roadway is still unpaved, the surface bedrock in places, and on the old Tavistock/ Ashburton pack-horse track.

Horrabridge: on the Walkham at SX 514 699. Thought to be one of the oldest bridges around Dartmoor, it retains both 'C' stones; earlier known as Harrow Bridge. Formerly at the junction of the bounds of three parishes, Sampford Spiney, Whitchurch and Buckland Monachorum. A stone set into the downstream parapet bears an inscribed cross to mark this point.

Huccaby Bridge: on the West Dart at SX 659 729. Both 'C' stones remain.

Huckworthy Bridge: on the Walkham at SX 531 705. Both 'C' stones remain but since both are on the same side of the road one has probably been re-set.

Ivybridge: on the Erme at SX 636 564. Both 'C' stones remain, both to the

Bridges: 'C' stone on the east side of Huccaby Bridge. SX 6595 7290

south of the bridge. There are also Turnpike boundary stones for Ermington and Ugborough beside the downsteam sides of the bridge. Former junction at the parishes of Ermington, Harford, Ugborough and Cornwood.

Langham Bridge: on the Yealm at SX 608 592. Both 'C' stones remain, that on the south side having the letter inverted (pictured). The stone has a rounded top and the letter has serifs, so it must have been inscribed thus originally and not set, or re-erected, in an inverted position.

Merrivale Bridge: on the Walkham at SX 550 751. In the re-alignment of the road in the 1950s one 'C' stone disappeared but the other on the Dartmoor Inn side remains. Bridge built by the Tavistock Turnpike Trust in the 1770s, replacing the old clapper, (c.1774).

Ockery Bridge: on the Blackabrook at SX 595 743. There are two bridges here, the old clapper of two openings and the modern road bridge, but the single remaining 'C' stone, left side on approach from Two Bridges, relates to neither of these, but to Trena Bridge, replaced by the present road bridge in 1901.

Piall Bridge: on the Piall Brook at SX 596 604. Both 'C' stones remain. In the mid-nineteenth century the Delamore Estate was owned by William Mackworthy Praed, who was instrumental in the improvement of various roads and bridges around the village of

Cornwood. He had Piall Bridge built at his own expense in 1844 and then handed it over to the county for maintenance. Thus we have both a tablet inscribed 'This Bridge erected at the Cost of William Mackworthy Praed Esquire was accepted by the County of Devon', and the two 'C' stones acknowledging the county's acceptance of the responsibility of maintaining it. Many other bridges formerly maintained by parishes or other bodies were also taken over by the county in the nineteenth century.

Ponsworthy Bridge: on the West Webburn at SX 702 604. Both 'C' stones remain. Inset into the upstream parapet there is an upright stone bearing the dates '16/66' (1666) and '1911', ancient and relatively modern repair dates. Many bridges are known to have been repaired just after the mid-seventeenth century. In 1664 this bridge was described as 'Ponsworthy Bridge in Withycombe, near the foot of the Moor', when it was in a state of disrepair and £30 was needed for its repair.

Shipley Bridge: on the river Avon at SX 681 628. Both 'C' stones remain, these on the left-hand approach on both sides.

Ward Bridge: on the Walkham at SX 543 720. The present bridge is relatively modern, the old bridge having been washed away in 1890. Built into the downstream side of the present bridge is the only surviving stone from the earlier structure, dated 1687, together with another relating to the re-building dated 1891. The 'C' stone on the east side is to the left, an old rough stone, but that on the west side is to the right and of a completely different character, having a wide inscribed letter of what appears to be late-nineteenth century origin. This latter was recently thought to have been a boundstone by a Mr Collier, a local landowner, who removed it, but it has since been replaced on its former site.

At Norsworthy Bridge over the Meavy at SX 568 694 there is the only example known to the author of the letter 'C' being cut on a native rock, rather than using an erected set stone. This is on the west side of the bridge. Another must have once existed nearer the remains of the Bal Mine, for a boulder there, obviously formerly projecting into the roadway, has had part of it cut away, and is marked as the site of a 'C' stone on the old Ordnance Survey six inch map. Nearby at Sheepstor, the inundated bridge still under the water of the reservoir had 'C' stones as is shown by the old maps – the parish bounds still follow the line of the river through the reservoir. A bridge of some interest is that on the old Exeter/Plymouth road of turnpike days, passing through Harbourneford. There used to be a ford for wheeled traffic, but beside the site of the ford, where a pipe now takes the water under the road, there is a 4ft wide footbridge of clapper construction. This was the butt of caustic comment by James Green the County Surveyor in 1809 when he made an inspection of all the bridges under his jurisdiction, saying that it was 'across a ford which is never dangerous for horses and carriages, and it appears very extraordinary that the County, by taking upon themselves the repair of this bridge should support 200 yards of road on one of the most public Turnpikes in the Kingdom'. In other words, it should have been maintained by the turnpike. Both 'C' stones remain, of granite though the local stone there is not granite, that on the west side appears to be blank at first glance.

Left: *Norsworthy Bridge, Earthfast boulder showing 'C'. SX 568 694*

Below: *Steps Bridge, dated 1816 (the upper curve of the 6 is very indistinct) on the downstream parapet. SX 804 883*

Many rivers and streams constitute a part of a boundary of numerous parishes, and bridges on these rivers are sometimes marked to denote that fact.

Steps Bridge on the Teign is a bridge bearing boundstones,, this early-nineteenth-century ashlar-built bridge bears the date of its construction, 1816, on a stone on the downstream parapet, and on separate ashlar blocks forming the upstream parapet, two are inscribed, 'Dunsford' and 'Bridford'.

Staverton Bridge, which is over the Dart, but not in Dartmoor country, is nevertheless of interest. It has seven pointed arches, and has on the upstream side some pedestrian refuges, the most southerly having coping stones inscribed 'D' for Dartington and 'S' for Staverton. Also acting as a coping stone on the downstream side there is part of the shaft of the old churchyard cross, having chamfered edges, the cross in the churchyard has a modern replacement. Only recently the old socket stone, too, was rediscovered.

Hundreds were the forerunners of parishes, but some Hundred Courts persisted into the seventeenth century, with presentments being made regarding roads and bridges, and levies imposed for their repair. The Constables made these presentments to the Grand Jury at the Sessions and there are records of no less than 48 constables making well over 125 such presentments in Devon in the period 1660 to 1670. Most references to bridges were reports of them being 'in decay' as, up to that time, they were not regularly maintained but just allowed to deteriorate until something had to be done before they collapsed. Repairs were speeded up in the second half of the seventeenth century, and it is of this period, primarily the 1660s, that we see a number of tablets inserted into the parapets of bridges repaired by the County, acknowledging their responsibility, the forerunners of 'C' stones. At the Sessions of 1647 'Sparrowe Bridge' was reported to be 'in decay', this is Spara Bridge over the Teign in the Teign Valley on the edge of the Dartmoor National Park. The very fragmented tablet set into the upstream parapet reads 'This Bridge was New Builded at The Covntyes Charge Anno 1660'. Was this a completely new bridge or a rebuilding? The latter, one feels. In 1667 one Richard Osborne was treasurer for both 'Spera' and Christow Bridges, and had the responsibility of collecting funds for their repair, needing at the time the sum of £170. With

Spara Bridge 'new builded' in 1660 it seems that the £170 was needed for Christow Bridge, but this was never a stone bridge and is described in the Sessions of 1643 as being of timber but had stone abutments and a stone pier, and that 'Christow Bridge be repaired by the people of Christow and (is) not a county charge', in other words the Parish's responsibility. Bow Bridge over the Lemon at Bickington, on the road through the village on the Exeter/Ashburton and Plymouth road, at SX 795 725, is another that has a tablet and both its later 'C' stones. The County Tablet is rather fragmented, set into the downstream parapet. In a good light most of the inscription is legible, reading 'This Bridge Repared By The Covnty in anno 1688...' The remainder is almost impossible to decipher but may continue 'Mi...e Gre...d Yovle .Ustis'.

Drakeford Bridge over the Bovey at SX 789 801 near Lustleigh has a superb tablet reading 'This 168Ƅ Bridge Was Repared by the County', the figure '4' reversed. In his inspection of bridges in 1809, James Green commented upon Drakeford to the effect that it then had a single arch to carry an 8ft roadway, but that it should be rebuilt. When this was done it was widened by a further 6ft on the upstream side under the 1803 Bridge Act which gave the county the power to do so. Another nearby is Wilford Bridge, also over the Bovey at SX 799 798. This is a rarer eighteenth-century example reading '1750 This Bridge Was Repa Red By The County'. Subsequently the date '1914' was added below, perhaps when the old stone bridge was swept away to be replaced by the present roadway carried over the river on iron girders. All that remains of the stone bridge are the abutments. There were many other later repairs to Devon's bridges during the years preceding the First World War, a number having iron

Spara Bridge fragmented tablet. SX 8430 8410

Wilford Bridge, over the Bovey.
SX 799 798

Bow Bridge on the Lemon at Bickington. SX 795 725

Drakeford Bridge, Lustleigh.
SX 7895 8012

rods put through them to give added strength, which usually have a Devon County Council end-plate which is dated. Gulwell Bridge on the Old Totnes Road out of Ashburton has a coping stone, obviously from an earlier bridge, inscribed 'CCS/1775/SP'. This may well refer to a repair at that date.

It was not until relatively recent times that 'roads' were anything but rough tracks, though some sort of firm footing was given to the approaches to bridges, and on some of the busier routes by the use of loose stones which became embedded into the mud below without any real foundation as had been the case in Roman times. Stones were broken up to pass through iron rings, usually of either 2in or 4in diameter and, with the setting up of turnpike trusts in Devon from the middle of the eighteenth century, some of their 'main' routes saw some improvement, though many trusts were not financially successful and thus often skimped repairs. In their earlier years trusts usually used existing roads, but later sometimes took on the task of building new alternative ones. On the verges of Dartmoor, several turnpike trusts were formed between the years 1755 and 1826. The Ashburton Trust covered the main Exeter/Plymouth road from Chudleigh to South Brent and dates from 1755, followed by the Plymouth Eastern Trust formed in 1758 from South Brent into Plymouth. On the western side of the moor there were two trusts, the Okehampton Trust formed in 1760 and the Tavistock Trust formed in 1762. On the eastern side there was the Moretonhampstead Trust formed in 1772, as was the Tavistock Trans Dartmoor Act.

All these trusts erected their own milestones as they were obliged to do, and also 'Parish' stones where their roads crossed parish bounds; each trust's stones being in a style peculiar to that trust only. Many turnpike trust roads terminated at the boundary of the parish in which they commenced, radiating out from that town, but others extended to the further boundary of the adjoining parish. Thus in an Act of George IV (1823), paragraph 119, it was stated that Turnpike Trustees:

> shall cause Stones or posts to be set up or placed in or near the sides of every Turnpike road, at the distance of One mile from each other, denoting the distance of any and every such stone or post from any Town or Place and also such Direction Post at the several roads leading out of any such road, or at any Crossings, Turnings or Terminations thereon, with such inscriptions thereon denoting to what Place or Places the said roads respectively lead ... and shall also cause stones to be put up marking the Boundaries of Parishes where such boundaries shall cross any Turnpike Road.

Unlike ordinary parish boundstones, all the turnpike trust ones have the names of the parishes concerned inscribed in full, rather than the usual initial letter. The Tavistock Turnpike Trust was meticulous in erecting these, where we have four examples extant, obtusely angled slabs of granite, of which one at Rundlestone on the Tavistock/Exeter road has already been mentioned, incorrectly sited on what was then thought to be the Forest bounds, and inscribed 'Walk/hamp/ton' and 'Lid/ford'. Other similar stones are at Merrivale Bridge inscribed 'Walk/hamp/ton' and 'Whit/church' on the Tavistock/Okehampton road at Half Bridge, lettered 'Tavi/Stock' and 'Mary/Tavy', and

Above: *Turnpike Trusts: On the Exeter–Moreton-hampstead road outside Ducksmoor Cottage at SX 784 872.*

Left: *Where the parishes of Walkhampton and Lydford (The Forest) meet at Rundlestone, on the 1772 Tavistock Turnpiked road.*

By the General Turnpike Act of 1772, Turnpike Trustees were permitted to relax a law restricting the number of horses allowed to draw specified types of wheeled vehicles. This concession was to help preserve the road surface on certain hilly sections of road, a concession whereby the hitching up of an extra horse or horses was permitted without the payment of extra toll charges up to a specified point, some of which were marked by 'Take off' stones. These are rather rare but it is known that Exeter once had some on the outskirts of the city, of which there is now no trace, and one is still extant on the Cornish side of the Liskeard road, but in the Tavistock area we still have no less than four examples relating to the Tavistock Turnpike Trust.

In 1800 Thomas Hasker was the Surveyor and Superintendent of Mail Coaches, and gave an instruction to all the Mail Coach Guards as follows:

> You are desired to leave two or three of the enclosed Bills at every village you pass through in your journey, and request they may be posted up in some conspicuous Place – leave a bill or two also at the Houses you stop to water at, you need not leave them at the Post Offices, as they will be sent there.
>
> Yours etc., Thomas Hasker

Enclosed with this directive was a caution to waggoners, a Governmental publication being issued on 20 March 1800 giving the limitation on the number of horses which may be used with a specified breadth of 'tyres' on Turnpike Roads, and refers to an Act of 13 Geo 3, C84 thus:

at Willsworthy Gate lettered 'Mary/Tavy' and 'Lamer/ton', though this has not been on the Lamerton bounds for many years. It was repositioned in 1990 a couple of yards from its original site when a new cattle grid was installed, just north of the gully in which it had formerly stood. Another may have stood near Moorshop on the Tavistock/Two Bridges road on the bounds of Tavistock Hamlets and Whitchurch at SX 5114 7460. It is still shown on the O.S. 1:25 000 scale map but now appears to be missing.

Breadth of Wheel		No. of Horses
Four-wheeled carriages	9 inches	8 horses and no more
" " "	6 "	6 " " " "
Less than " "	6 "	4 " " " "
Two-wheeled Carriages	9 "	5 " " " "
" " "	6 "	4 " " " "
Less than " "	6 "	3 " " " "

And the Wheels to roll on a Flat Surface

W. Buckingham was Clerk to the Trustees of the Exeter Turnpike Trust for a period of almost twenty-five years, and in 1885 wrote and had published a booklet entitled *A Turnpike Key*, an account of that trust. In this he records that in 1807 'Posts were ordered to be put up, shewing where the extra horses might be put on, and should be taken off, in drawing up hills', to clearly define the extent of a concession given to carters on certain sections of hilly turnpike roads. This wording implies that extra horses were permitted to be hitched up on both ascent and descent of these sections of road, though all marker posts set up to define the limits of the concession appear to be inscribed 'Take Off'. The Exeter Trust's Take Off stones were on the Okehampton and Plymouth roads. He says of this concession that:

> The General Turnpike Act regulated the Weights which might be drawn on the roads in Summer and in Winter, the number of Horses or other beasts which might be used for drawing, or might be driven when in pairs or when singly, except during Snow and Ice, when any number might be used, and empowered the Trustees to allow an additional number to be used when the

Hills rose more than 4 inches in a yard (i.e. 1 in 9 gradient), with a variation according to the width of the wheels, e.g. not exceeding 10 for wagons with 9 inch wheels, or 7 for 6 inch wheels, but carriages moving on wheels of 16 inches, with flat surfaces, were allowed to be drawn by any number of Horses or cattle.

Thus we have a comparison between the normal number of horses allowed with a certain width of wheel, and that allowed on hilly stretches of road with a gradient of not less than 1:9. Obviously the wider wheel, the less wear and tear there was on the road surface. It is not known exactly when the Tavistock Trust erected their 'Take Off' stones, nor how many there were originally, but they well may date from the mid-1820s. All Turnpikes, having the right to grant such a concession under the General Turnpike Act, were they then allowed to put them where they liked, subject to the hill being at least the minimum specified gradient? What is certain is that many of the local roads in the Tavistock area would have qualified for the concession especially before new routes were introduced to more accommodate wheeled traffic.

The example at Beardon, on the Tavistock/Okehampton road, has been known to us for many years, thanks to the writing of William Crossing. It is the only known example still in situ beside the road, on the verge, at a point near where the old original turnpike road went down to Roman Bridge to cross the Lyd, the higher Skit on Kitt's Bridge having been built on the early 1830s to lessen the incline. It is only about 18in tall, having a rounded head and rectangular of section, inscribed 'Take off' in two lines in upper and lower case letters. In the opinion of the late E.N.

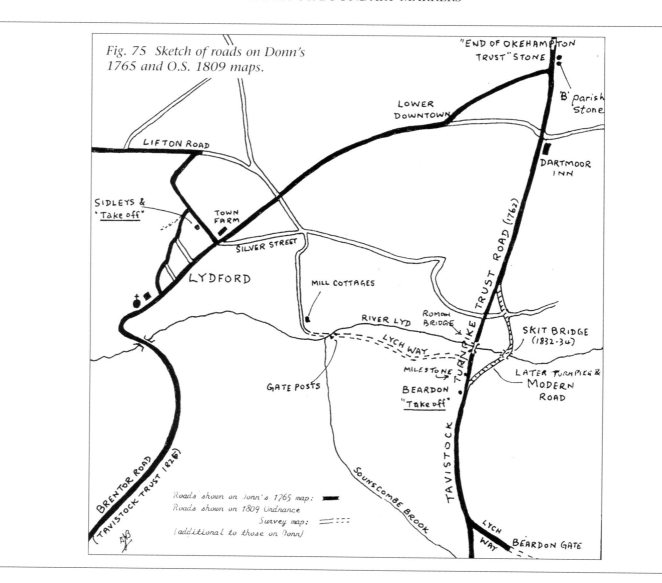

Fig. 75 Sketch of roads on Donn's 1765 and O.S. 1809 maps.

Masson Phillips, the ringed stones now set beside it have no relevance to the Turnpike Trust and the unhitching of the extra horse or horses – they were certainly placed there in the 1950s by the farmer Mr Friend, and his father, but since other sites of such 'Take Off' stones are also known accompanied by them, it is just feasible that, whilst used on the farm in more recent times, they may have originally been the tethering stones.

Not far below the Beardon stone on the old route down to Roman Bridge there is one of the old Tavistock Turnpike milestones, shaped something like a rudimentary cross, inscribed 'From Tavistock 7-miles, Oakhampton 8, Truro 57', and near this a gateway. The track through this gate is part of the ancient Lich Way and this may well have been one of the approaches to Lydford via the Okehampton turnpike between 1762 and 1825, crossing the Lyd at a ford and climbing up to Silver Street past the old Mill Cottages, in spite of the fact that most travellers would have used the Hurdwick/Brentor old ridge road, this only turnpiked as far as the Brentor Gate until 1825. This had been important enough a route to have had a series of pre-turnpike milestones erected along its length, from Tavistock to Lower Down Town, known to have been set up in 1755, for that outside the entrance to Hurdwick is so dated. Now set against the garden wall of Hurdwick farm, there is another 'Take off' stone, that no doubt originally came from lower down the Brentor road which rises steeply from the town. This was originally found acting as a gatepost to a field to the west of the farm. It is about 4ft in height and 1ft across, with the inscription, in the same style as that at Beardon, in one line across the top of the stone. It still retains one of the gatehangers.

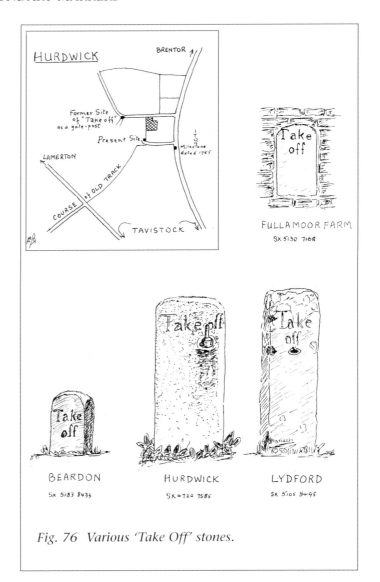

Fig. 76 Various 'Take Off' stones.

Yet another is in the garden of a house in Lydford called 'Sidleys', off an unmade track opposite the top end of Silver Street. It is similar in size to the Hurdwick example, and it too has formerly been used as a gatepost – this has the inscription in two lines, and retains an iron ring. The writer was told that it had been 'found quite close by', but this was probably a re-use of the stone and not its original site. It is most likely to have come from the top of the rise into Lydford from the bridge, and if so, since this part of the road was not turnpiked until 1825, dates from that period, in fact the similarity of the inscriptions suggests that they were all carved by the same hand and are the same date.

The most recent find, a fourth example, is a 'ringer' for the Beardon stone, now set into a reconstructed slate-stone wall outside Fullamoor Farm on Plaister Down, an unlikely site for a 'Take Off' stone but accounted for by the fact that it was found in a job lot of stone purchased in Tavistock, thus we cannot attempt to guess where it might have come from except by examining inclines on other turnpike roads, though by 1825 the Plymouth road was not part of the Tavistock Turnpike Trust, having been found to be unprofitable, but reformed into the Plymouth and Tavistock Trust.

It seems that a possible site for this, or a fifth example, may have been on the old Tavistock/Launceston road, where the former Uppaton Toll House came to be known as the Round House. It has been reported that this latter name arose from the fact that that it 'took two horses to pull even a light wagon up the steep and winding road from Chillaton to the toll house. There the horses turned around and went back down the hill to await the next pull up. To locals it was the turn-around house which in the way of all vernacular was quickly shortened to 'The Round House'. (Tavy & Tamar, July/August 1990)

Okehampton Turnpike Trust marked the points at which their responsibility ended on the various roads radiating out from Okehampton. These either ended at the parish bounds of Okehampton Hamlets or, passing through the adjoining parish to its further side, ended on those parish bounds. At each of these points they erected a slab of stone approximately 18in² bearing the inscription 'End of Okehampton/Trust'; there were seven of these originally, that nearest Dartmoor proper being on the main Okehampton/Tavistock road near the lane to Downtown, a short distance from the Lydford turn-off – it is about 20 yards towards Okehampton from the lane junction, in the

Fig. 77 End of Okehampton Trust and 'B' Parish boundstones.

eastern verge at SX 5235 8568 – usually covered in herbage and/or mud! Beside it there is another stone, a boundstone bearing the letter 'B', not another example of a 'parish' stone erected by a turnpike trust, in accordance with their obligations, but a proper Parish one – one presumes that this was formerly on the Bridestowe bounds, many changes having taken place hereabouts since the close of the nineteenth century.

Looking for other examples of Okehampton 'End of Turnpike' stones, the author found that the one on the Holsworthy road appeared to be missing and, making enquiries, found that it had been snapped off at ground level by a reversing lorry and had been taken into a garden of Railway Cottages. This was on Maddaford Moor near Thornton Cross at SX 532 940, originally set outside the gateway to the cottages. Contacting the local authorities, they were only too happy to have the stone re-cemented to its base where it had formerly been set, but it is not, nevertheless, the original site, for when the Holsworthy railway and railbridge were built circa 1878 both the 'End of Turnpike' and a '4 miles' stone were re-erected (T.D.A. 1936 *Okehampton Turnpikes* by E.P. Bund). Others were on the Launceston, Exbourne, Jacobstowe, Hatherleigh and Exeter roads. The example from the Jacobstowe road is now in the Museum of Dartmoor Life, Okehampton.

Two boundstones, one either side of the bridge over the Erme at Ivybridge inscribed 'Ermington' and 'Ugborough' have already been mentioned. These were set up by the Plymouth Eastern Turnpike Trust formed in 1758, as was another inscribed 'Ugborough' where the Glazebrook crosses the A38. There are also two more erected by this trust at Lee Mill Bridge, which had their faces cemented over in 1940 as a security precaution! These were inscribed 'Ermington' and 'Plympton/St/Mary' – the latter is still legible. It would appear likely that the 'Chagford/North Bovey' stone opposite Bennett's Cross and on the Moretonhampstead Turnpike road was also a turnpike example. Unlike stones erected by the parishes themselves, they are only ones that have the names of the parishes spelt out in full. That at Steps Bridge is another.

Railway companies also marked the bounds of their property. The only line to be constructed over the moor proper was, of course, the Princetown line, taken over by the Great Western Railway Co. in 1883, and closed in 1956. This followed almost the same course as its predecessor, the old Plymouth and Dartmoor Rail Road inspired by Sir Thomas Tyrwhitt and constructed from 1823 for the Swell Tor Quarries, and later extended into Prince's Town to what is now the Devil's Elbow public house, formerly the Railway Inn. The railway company owned land across the green to this establishment and on the green there are two, three being there previously, metal boundary markers of the standard Great Western Railway pattern; circular, 5in in diameter, of cast iron, and set almost flush with the ground. The top bears the legendary 'Great Western Railway Co - Boundary' around the perimeter, and dated '1895' in the centre. Other later markers relating to the railway are situated in the mire at the head of the Meavy, south of the former station. Two are hidden in rushes between and extending the line of two Plymouth Corporation Water Works boundstones dated 1932. There, set upon the top surface of short concrete posts approximately 15in in height and 5¹/₂in x 6¹/₂in in section, are bronze plaques approximately 3in² lettered 'B T C' in relief. On 1 January 1948, the British railway system was nationalised, and it is suggested that these boundary markers were set up subsequent to that date when the extent of their property was surveyed and marked where appropriate. Posters relating to the nationalisation were all headed 'British Transport Commission', i.e. 'B T C'.

The Moretonhampstead & South Devon Railway was formed in 1866, a branch line from Newton Abbot, but by 1872 it had been incorporated into the general South Devon system. However, it left its mark by way of a boundary marker which used to be sited on the approach to Lustleigh Station inscribed 'M & SDR', behind the Cleave Hotel, another was reported at SX 7861 8224, and no doubt there were others. Similar rectangular stones of the later 'South Devon' period are still to be seen outside the main entrance to Parke, the Dartmoor National Park Headquarters, inscribed simply 'SDR', the line having formerly passed through the grounds of the house. Near Grenofen Tunnel there are also boundstones relating to the South Devon & Tavistock Railway Co., founded in 1859, inscribed 'SD & TR'. On the disused railway between Clearbrook and Yelverton there still remain a couple, and there are possibly others still in situ.

Fig. 78 British Transport Commission markers, Princetown.

Above left: *After the South Devon and Princetown Railway Act of 1878, the Great Western Railway Co. took over the old line of the Plymouth and Dartmoor Rail Road from Yelverton to Princetown. There used to be three, now only two, standard G.W.R. cast iron circular boundary markers dated 1895 on the Green.*

Above right: *One of the two South Devon Railway boundstones outside the entrance to Parke, the D.N.P.A. headquarters, through whose grounds the railway used to run.*

6
CHINA CLAY COUNTRY

Many millions of years ago decomposed feldspar crystals, a constituent of granite and the present day source of china clay, were washed down from the granite uplands of Dartmoor into what was then a huge lake, the Bovey Basin, where the kaoline was deposited to produce a very fine 'ball clay' up to several hundred feet thick. On Dartmoor itself, principally on the south-western borders around Lee Moor, the rotting granite was not displaced but simply lay undisturbed until the nineteenth century when the same kaolinised feldspar crystals were exploited, the 'china clay' being extracted by means of pressure hoses which separated the clay from the mica in a suspended solution, which represents but a small proportion of the original mass, usually about ten to fifteen per cent, the rest made up of mica and quartz, the composition of the huge waste tips that only of late have been greened over with tree lupins, etc. in these more conservation conscious days.

It was in 1830 that Lord Morley, the landowner, first leased out land on Lee Moor to John Dickens and John Cawley to extract clay. These small beginnings were taken over by William Phillips in 1833 at a fee of £75 per annum, further developing the undertaking, joined by his son John in 1835. The Phillips leat is now dry but once carried the essential water supply needed from the Lannacombe, or possibly the river Plym itself above its confluence with that stream, to wash out the clay. Later the old Bottle Hill Mine leat was used, taken off the Plym at Ditsworthy weir. This is still in use, supplying a reservoir known as 'Big Pond'. William died in 1861 and the business was taken over by John. Although being involved in the venture since 1835, John had a lack of business sense, and the whole enterprise was put on the market on 25 October 1862 by the Lee Moor Porcelain Company, which was floated in 1852, offering the property on a 21-year lease, and advertised thus:

> The property includes the clay bed and right of water, the clay works and the brick and tile works, the railway, Laira Wharf with house, stables and stone thereon, the proprietor's house of four sitting and nine bedrooms, with stables and two servants' houses, 17 workmen's houses including 2 suitable for foremen, a carpenter's shop and smithy, and the farm of 140 acres of arable and 3500 acres of open moorland.

3500 acres is about six square miles and could easily have extended up as far as the Hanging Stone and the Cholwich Town Reave.

On 27 November 1862, Mrs Rebecca Martin of St Austell purchased it, and on her death not long after, her son William took over, and on his death in 1885 his brother Thomas followed him to Lee Moor House to run the business. The Martins virtually built the village of Lee Moor including a Wesleyan Chapel,

Reading Room, the New Church Mission Room, School, etc. The Martins had also developed Cholwich Town and Whitehill Yeo pits but by 1901 had abandoned Wotter as uneconomic, and the latter was bought by C.H.R. Sellick & Sons, becoming the Dartmoor China Clay Company in 1906, now also absorbed into the English China Clay group, as were all other small family enterprises excepting Watts, Blake & Bearne who still own the Headon Works and Shaugh Lake in addition to their extensive ball clay interests in the Bovey Basin.

In April 1919 English China Clays Ltd was formed through the amalgamation of Martin Brothers (established in 1837), the West of England and Great Beam Co. Ltd and North Cornwall China Clay Co. Ltd.

The best view of the china clay area is to be had from the top of Penn Beacon or Shell Top. Shell Top has been used as a boundary marker and bears a small incised cross on the southern side of the topmost layer of rock. On the upper surface of this, too, there is an incised triangular device with the letters 'AR' and 'WR' either side of it, once the site of a flagpole used when army field exercises were taking place in the vicinity. South-west of Shell Top there were three massive boundstones which were on the boundary common to Penn Moor and Lee Moor, all inscribed 'PM' and 'LM' on opposite sides. The Ordnance Survey 1:25 000 map marks two of them at SX 5929 6337 (quite recently this lower example has been removed, perhaps by E.C.C.) and SX 5908 6318, but the third has fallen and remains unmarked higher up the hill at SX 5954 6360. They are on the Cornwood/Shaugh Prior parish bounds, as well as separating Lee Moor from Penn Moor.

The other boundary running down from Shell Top is that dividing Lee Moor from Shaugh Moor; it follows a line to the head of the Blackabrook, where at SX 5760 6380 there is an old gatepost, complete with drilled holes for the hangers, and which has been set up there to act as a boundary marker. It is almost, but not quite, on the line of the nearby double stone row, and a short distance from the southern end of it. On the old six inch scale map the Ordnance Survey mark this post 'Stone', as is their practice for those boundstones that are not on a parish boundary. In the Transactions of the Devonshire Association for 1936, however, there is a report of an excursion made by the Plymouth Branch, where they mistakenly describe the boundstone as the 'blocking stone' of the stone rows. The opinion then expressed on examining the gatepost, was that the holes had been made for the gatehangers in anticipation of its removal, obviously in ignorance of its true purpose, this boundary line on it being marked in the nineteenth century as is shown by other dated boundstones. From the old gatepost the boundary follows the Blackabrook downstream for about half a mile, where there is a set boundstone on the left bank of the stream in a very wet and boggy situation, inscribed 'LM/1835' to the south and 'SM/1835' to the north, the date perhaps significant as it is at just the time that Phillips was developing the china clay industry. The grid reference to this boundstone is SX 5695 6382. There the boundary line leaves the Blackabrook, going westward to another similarly inscribed stone on the edge of the former Cadover Bridge – Cornwood road at SX 5693 6340. It then continues westwards to Emmet's Post, another boundstone set on the remains of a cairn at SX 5665 6318, similarly lettered to the other stones but undated. In the Maristow copy letter books (W.D.R.O.)

there is a reference dated 30 September 1837 from Sir Ralph Lopes's secretary to W.T. Stentiford, Land Surveyor, which says 'I now send you the Deed of Partition between Lord Morley and Sir Ralph Lopes as to Shaugh Commons.'

Whilst Lord Morley owned Lee Moor, and leased the clay rights to Phillips and later clay enterprises, the Lopes family owned Shaugh Moor, but Crossing in his *Guide* appears to get himself in a bit of a muddle, describing the inscriptions on these boundstones. From Emmet's Post the boundary cannot be followed any more, for we are on the edge of recently developed pits almost to the foot of Saddlesborough, 'Stones' are shown on the old six inch maps of this area but are now lost to us. Eventually it is the intention of English China Clays to make one huge pit, joining up Cholwich Town, Whitehill Yeo and Lee Moor, which will extend for 2½ miles.

Not very far westward from Saddlesborough are Hawks Tor and Collard Tor, both of which have remained outside the clay workings. Here there are monolithic boundstones associated with old reaves and field boundaries, all bearing the letter 'H', which may possibly relate to the use of the land so circumscribed by Huxton Farm. The most southerly boundstone is set upon a mound in the fork of the roads at Beatland Corner at SX 5490 6220. A second is at SX 5512 6225 on the corner of a reave amongst the remains of the Second World War anti-aircraft gunsite. The third is more or less recumbent and more difficult to find, but probably still on its original site, just below Hawk's Tor 'shelter', at the terminal point of a north/south reave and on an east/west 'wall' at SX 5526 6250. The fourth is some distance away on a

China Clay: 'H' stone set on a mound from which a reave goes north in the direction of Hawk's Tor.

wall running eastwards from Collard Tor at SX 5575 6225. All appear to be either on or very near to the ancient boundary line of the land bequested to Buckland Abbey by Amicia, Countess of Devon, for its foundation in 1278 (Fig.47). Another recumbent stone inscribed 'WH/B' is nearer Collard Tor at SX 557 622. Several investigations into the reave systems and their development on Shaugh Moor have taken place in recent years and one, *Field Systems and Boundaries on Shaugh Moor and Wotter* by John Collis mentions these 'H' stones, describing them as being on boundaries re-formed in post-medieval times after older field boundaries were re-made, but all devolving on the major Saddlesborough reave. Another report entitled 'The Shaugh Moor Project; Third Report – Settlement and Environmental Investigations' by several contributors, contains a quote from the Strode papers, where a deed of 1562 defines the boundary of Fernhill north waste as follows:

yn the est part of the Stonye Rew that ledyth from knyll to hawkystor and so north as the Rew ledith towardes Settleborow and from thens towardes the est by a rew or Banck of stones untyll ye com to Wotter Water and so doune as the Water Runneth.

When Cholwich Town was granted to Benedict, son of Edryke Syward, by Guy de Bryttavilla circa 1200, the bounds were clearly stated in the charter as follows:

all my land of Cholleswyht in free, pure and perpetual socage, namely from the ford in the paved road over that water which comes from Bromwiht (*Broomage*) and falls into Pial. And thence from that ford along the paved highway above Torizhete and so westwards as far as the water of Toriz. And then up the Toriz as far as the stream by the north of Blacaorde (*Blachford*) and so along the aforesaid stream as far as the spring which is at Pial head. And so along the Pial descending as far as the water of Bromwiht and thence up to the aforesaid ford. And I grant to the said Benedict, his heirs and assigns, common pasture in all my moor and waste belonging to my demesne of Cornwood beginning at the north at the headwater of the Toriz in a line eastwards as far as Yalumphauede (*Yealm Head*) in woodland, open land, ways, and paths, and all other easements, freely to the said land of Cholleswiht in dry and wet, and to take there hay, turves, coal, furze, and all other necessary commodities.

This clearly indicates that the original thirteenth-century boundary around about two hundred acres went

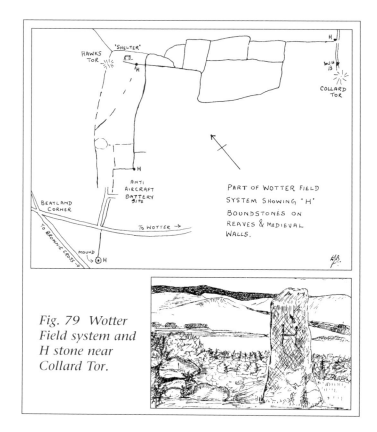

Fig. 79 Wotter Field system and H stone near Collard Tor.

up the Tory Brook (*Toriz*), but nowhere is there any reference to Cholwich acquiring land to the west of the Tory Brook, in what is Shaugh Prior parish, although later in the fifteenth/sixteenth centuries their land did extend eastwards as far as Rook Moor. The Cholwich documents referred to by W.G. Hoskins (*Old Devon*) are concerned with Cornwood parish only, but in the adjoining parish of Shaugh Prior near Hexton Tor there is, set near a Bronze Age Cross Dyke, a menhir or

Figs. 80 and 81 'CB' and 'BC' stones on Lee Moor.

Standing Stone known as the Hanging Stone or Leaning Rock at SX 584 637. It is inscribed on its eastern face with the letters 'C' and 'B', one below the other, which it has been suggested might refer to Cholwich. Considering its position, this would seem most unlikely as it would have crossed parish bounds, unless, of course, the parish bounds themselves have changed at some time. The present boundary line rises from the Tory Brook to Shell Top.

The 1991 finding of a fallen boundstone near, and south-east of, the Hanging Stone bearing the same two letters as are inscribed on that stone, but in reverse order, i.e. the letter 'B' above the 'C', and the shape of those letters, leads one to think that they mark the same boundary line, whatever that might be, as the letters in each case are similarly shaped, the 'B' larger and better formed, the 'C' small and somewhat 'crabby'. This fallen boundstone is situated at SX 5858 6352 and about 145 paces from a nearby cairn. It is only approximately 2ft in length, so that when set would not have stood more than about 18in tall.

Another fallen boundstone has since been reported to the author, lettered 'B/C' at approximately SX 593 635. Others may still exist, but with the extension of Cholwich Town china clay pit and linking it up with the Lee Moor one, they may have already disappeared.

A far more rational explanation of the purpose of these boundary markers is that they define the bounds of the original clay sett, 'C' standing for clay. We have other examples of boundstones that bear letters related to their purpose, 'CW' on Walkhampton Common defining the bounds of another clay sett, and a stone on Peter Tavy Common inscribed 'PT/G1', 'G denoting granite.

Today the excavations of the English China Clay Company on the skirts of Dartmoor at Lee Moor extend for some five miles, and is the most easterly of workings of a similar nature in the St Austell area of Cornwall. The commodity is in such demand that the company have succeeded in trading at a time when all other forms of mining – tin, copper, etc. – and the quarrying of granite had failed.

Somewhat further south are a number of other clay workings, many now abandoned, which can be explored from either Tolchmoor Gate or Hemerdon. These would be outside the bounds of the National Park but still within the granite area. From Tolchmoor Gate, SX 581 616, the right of way to Broomage, an abandoned farmstead, should be followed to Crownhill Down, and a small tor of the same name. From a stile two leat channels can be seen, one to Broomage and the other probably to the nearby Mumford Cottage. Proceeding further towards the Torycombe valley a third leat channel is encountered which can be followed for almost a mile. This is the now disused section of the old Bottle Hill Mine leat, the upper part of which has been taken over by the Lee Moor clay works as mentioned earlier. The Bottle Hill mine chimney is still a prominent landmark, the mine being opened in 1715 and produced varying quantities of tin, arsenic, copper and mispickel. Just below the dry leat across Crownhill Down there is a series of boundstones, seven of which bear the inscription 'LM/1887', defining the boundary of Lee Moor as, no doubt, the working became more extensive. The marked stones are in the general area SX 569 606 to 577 612. Another unmarked stone of the same period is at SX 576 608, with yet more further south amongst the disused workings.

Lee Moor Boundary Stone.

Nearer Hemerdon there is another at SX 578 595 bearing the inscription 'H' and 'V', whose origin and purpose is not known to the author. The whole area has been long abandoned, though there was talk of re-opening Hemerdon from which tungsten was obtained in the past. Several boundary points on Heddon Down are marked by 'Piles of Stones'.

Wigford Down also sports its share of boundstones. The down has Bronze Age remains – cairns, reaves, hut circles and a cist, this latter still unmarked on the O.S.

maps, though known for many years, at SX 544 644. The Outdoor Leisure map shows a green line running across the Down marking the northern boundary of land owned by the National Trust, centring around the Dewerstone its quarries and Goodameavy. Along this line there are six boundstones dating from the nineteenth century bearing the letter 'L' for Lopes. However they follow the line of a much older boundary marked by natural stones or, nearer the crest of the Down, by a reave. There is a similar seventh stone near the roadside outside Higher Beliver Farm.

Recently (c.1990) a letter relating to the erection of these 'L' stones was found in the Maristow papers when George Giles, the Maristow Estate Steward, writing to William Stentiford, a land surveyor, on 18 February 1841 said:

> I have been with Sir Ralph Lopes and Mr Scobell on Wigford Down this day – they both returned to my office to inspect the plan, and ultimately agreed on an equal division of the 393a 3r 15p, the boundary to be shown by Granite posts, when the line has been traced – and that Mr Scobell's portion shall be that moeity next adjoining his inclosed lands or Urgles and Good-a-Meavy – beginning north from the corner of outher Diamond park (wherefrom you took your direction towards the Thorn) across towards Oxen Torr – or somewhere in that direction, wherever the line takes immediately from the corner of Diamond or a chain or two off towards the Thorn – but it must be taken up from Sir Traystow Drake's boundary of Greenwell Down – and should it fall upon Shaugh Prior boundary it must not be carried

across it. From this description I hope you will comprehend the nature of the arrangement came to, and be able, on your rough Plan of Meavy, to trace it … the line that will divide the whole equally, so that when you come down you will be able to go on the ground and shew it with facility.

This is a matter that requires your earliest attention. Sir Ralph and Mr Scobell will again meet on the locus in quo when you are prepared to shew the divisional line. This Job is to be at the joint expense of each party.

Much of Wigford Down is criss-crossed by reaves and later medieval abandoned field patterns (see *Settlement of Wigford Down* by D.G.Price, T.D.A. 1978). Two of the reaves form the boundary of a group of fields opposite to and now belonging to Durance Farm, one running north-west to south-east, on which a cornditch type wall has been built almost to the high-

A very rough set stone lettered 'BA', with an incised line below the letters. SX 5520 6535

Wigford Down: 'L' Stone near the Urgles/Goodameavy Road. SX 5380 6525

est point of the Down, and another running west-south-west to east-north-east, this latter defined only by the reave and a post and wire fence.

Near the point where the wall ends at SX 547 652 there is a set boundstone, approximately 15in high bearing the letters 'BA' on its eastern face, the letter 'A' having a bar at its apex, similar to some old Guidestones in the Holne area dating from the early eighteenth century. This may well date from circa 1793 when Durance is known to have been the property of the Drake family. At the very highest point of the enclosures at SX 5475 6515 there is a fallen boundary post, the letters 'BA' still visible. Part way down the west-south-west/east-north-east reave at SX 5515 6530 there is a large boulder, also inscribed 'BA', and at the lower corner of the enclosures there is another inscribed post at SX 5520 6535, the 'BA' facing north. The lettering on these three markers appears to be much more modern than the first mentioned one. John Somers Cocks, writing in 1967, says that when it was suggested to him that the letters stood for Buckland Abbey, he was sceptical as the lettering appeared to be too modern, in fact he learned that they were cut in living memory. This must, however, only apply to the three markers comprising the two stone posts and the boulder. He ascertained that in

1906 the Drake family still owned both the abbey and Durance Farm, and that the markers were Buckland Estate boundary markers, defining the extent of the abbey's land at Durance.

Past the modern Urgles Cross on the Goodameavy road, just before reaching the bridge over the Meavy, there will be seen in the wall on one's left an inscribed stone bearing the legendary 'JS/1832', referring to one Joseph Scoble, one time Lord of the Manor of Goodameavy. The stone is adjacent to the track leading to Dewerstone Cottage, now a public right of way on National Trust land. Enter the pathway towards these cottages and within a few hundred yards there is a railway embankment through which a tunnel passes, with another uncompleted embankment a short distance away on the other side of the river. This proposed railway was intended to link up with the nearby South Devon line, and thus facilitate the transportation of stone from the Dewerstone Quarry but, due to permission being refused to cross part of the route, the whole enterprise had to be abandoned. One wonders why so much work was carried out before the issue was raised.

Apart from the main sources of china clay in the Lee Moor/Shaugh Moor area, attempts have been made to obtain it from various other localities including the Red Lake, Left Lake and the Bala Brook area above Shipley, also Petre's Pits and Knattabarrow Pool on Brent Moor. Most of these small, and relatively short-lived enterprises did not have the success of the larger workings, due to the poorer quality of the clay, making them barely commercially viable, either due to insufficiently rotted feldspars or to contamination with either earth or other minerals. The deposits at Petre's Pits were worked spasmodically between the years 1855 and 1923 but earlier than any of these were those at Knattabarrow Pool, believed to have been started in the 1830s. In 1846/47 the Zeal Tor tramway had been built to carry peat to Shipley for processing and the extraction of naptha, but this soon failed and later on their old buildings were converted for use in the china clay industry. The first attempt to work the clay at Petre's Pits in 1855 was carried out by The China Clay Co. Ltd, but use of the old tramway was specifically denied them in the lease by the landowner, Francis Meynell of Brent Moor House. In 1872 another attempt was made by The Brent Moor Clay Co., this time adapting the naptha works. Crossing (*Guide* p.71) states that these buildings were 'put in good state of repair by a china clay company about the year 1872'; this phase was also of very short duration. At and above Shipley there are a number of plain boundary posts defining the areas within which these two companies were permitted to build their settling pits, mica drags, and dries, to the east of the Zeal Farm enclosures and extending down as far as the river bank (Avon).

Pockets of china clay are also found on Walkhampton Common and within the parish of Sheepstor, and there are several references to clay being found there in the nineteenth century and later. Indeed the deposits must have been known to Bronze Age or perhaps Iron Age man, for during the nineteenth century when the settlement of hut circles under Hartor, near Devil's Bridge, was investigated, a stone-lined fireplace was uncovered in one hut measuring 3ft in diameter and 1ft 3in deep, of which it was said 'the china clay in which it has been sunk was reddened with fire. Two wheelbarrow loads of charcoal and burnt stone were removed from this hole. Pottery was found on the left of the entrance … it was suggested by George French that the large pits full of charcoal had been baking places for pottery'.

During the nineteenth century china clay was found in several locations. In 1826 some was found at Eylesbarrow Tin Mine 'at various depths within the tin ore', and two casks were actually sent to potteries as samples, one each to Liverpool and Newcastle, and of which Burt, in his introduction to Carrington's Dartmoor poem, writes 'a quarter of a mile due north of Ailsborough Mine, (which is three miles south-east of the prison) … not equal to Cornish Clay, but superior to that of Bovey Heathfield, of which blue and white ware is manufactured'. He then goes on to mention other deposits within Walkhampton Common 'in some deep cuttings of the railway

between Swell Tor and King Tor'. In 1852 a man by the name of Babb is known to have formed a company, The Dartmoor Tile Company, working a clay bed just inside the Forest boundary near Princetown railway station, working an area near, and using the water from, the Butchery Stream which rises near the head of the Meavy but flows eastwards, going under the Princetown School to flow into the Blackbrook. In 1873, too, a map prepared for the Plymouth Water Base, or watershed, showed other 'Clay Beds' at Hartor Mire, Cramber Pool and Outcombe.

The author had long been intrigued by the reference to 'China Clay Works' at Yes Tor Bottom as shown on the William Wood's map dating from about 1850, and amongst a mass of papers from the Maristow Estate and now held by the West Devon Record Office, a lease has been found dated 19 September 1835, granted by Sir Ralph Lopes, to George Stone Baron, of Plymouth, permitting the digging of china clay for twenty-one years on 'certain lands in Walkhampton', dues payable to the landowner 2/-d per ton for the first 7 years for china clay, 2/6d per ton for the remaining fourteen years for china clay and $\frac{1}{12}$th on other clays. This compares with the royalty of 3/6d per ton asked by Lord Clifford for the best ball clays in the Bovey Basin at much the same time and 6d per ton only for his poorer stoneware clays. However the lease was surrendered on 1 January 1840.

The bounds of the Yes Tor Bottom sett are described as follows:

> From Little Kings Tor along Plymouth & Dartmoor Railroad on South side thereof to a

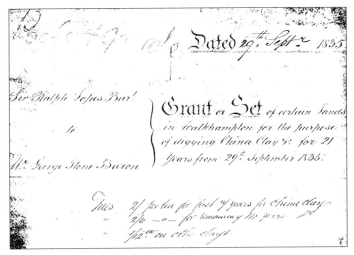

Fig. 82 Lease from Sir Ralph Lopes to George Stone Baron.

certain bound stone on said railroad near Princetown which bound stone is inscribed with 'W' on one side thereof and 'D' on the reverse side thereof and from the said bound on to another bound stone similarly inscribed at or near the high road until a post is reached denoting 12 miles from Plymouth on the said road and from the said milestone on a direct line to another bound stone inscribed 'CW1' near a hedge of a certain field called Furzepark part of a farm called Waytown, and from thence by the outside of boundary hedges of Waytown, Routrundle, Babyland, Stockington, Withill, Criptor, Yestor, Daveytown and Huckentorr to another bound stone inscribed 'CW/2' on the western side of Little Kings Tore aforesaid and from thence to Little Kings Tor where the said bounds began.

A further note states that:

> … about midway between Little Kings Tor aforesaid and first mentioned bound stone situated and lying on the northern side of the said railway and (compuied) within the limits distinguished by three bound stones these set up and severally inscribed 'CW/3' 'CW/4' 'CW/5'.

From the description of the bounds we can see that the boundary of the Walkhampton Clay Sett is largely made up of the Plymouth & Dartmoor Railroad track and the Princetown/Plymouth road, enclosing the watershed of the Yes Tor Brook, though it must have been of very short duration. Compare it with the size of, and success of, those on Lee Moor started by William Phillips at the same time (1833)!

The 'CW/2' boundstone is the only one marked on any Ordnance Survey map but that is not to say that others may not still be in situ, but recumbent, for the finding. From Little King Tor it will be noted that the boundary was south of the railway track, for by 1835 Fogginter Quarry had been working for a number of years to the north of it. North of the track between King Tor and the Royal Oak Sidings at Fogginter there are two plain boundstones, but these relate to the bounds to which the quarry was allowed to extend rather than anything to do with the clay works. It is only beyond Fogginter that the boundary line of the clay sett switches over to the north side of the railway track, where the boundstones 'CW/3', 'CW/4' and 'CW/5' were once located. The two boundstones inscribed 'W' and 'D' obviously refer to Walkhampton parish and the Duchy of Cornwall, and were sited on the Walkhampton/Forest Boundary. Walking up the Dartmoor railway, William Crossing (*Guide* p.84) says 'soon the Plymouth road is noticed where it crosses the hollow at Devil's Bridge and a short distance further on the station, close to which is one of the stones

'Plymouth 12 Miles Prince-town' (the Goadstone?), with 'Plymouth Corporation Water Works 1917' stone behind.

marking the Forest Boundary, is reached'. This was, in all probability, the first mentioned 'WD' stone in the lease, now in the garden of the old Station master's house. Again Crossing (*Guide* p.81), walking the Plymouth road into Princetown, says 'crossing Devil's Bridge the road climbs the steep ascent from the hollow, and soon after reaches the limits of the common in this direction and enters the forest. A granite post on the right of the way serves as a bondmark of the latter'. 'Walkhampton Bound Stones' are shown at these two sites on a 'Plan of Lease from H.R.H. The Prince of Wales to Mr Joseph Nicklin dated 18 November 1808'. In all likelihood this is our second 'W/D' stone, now replaced by one of the Plymouth Corporation Water Works stones erected in 1917.

Three miles west of Princetown, on the Plymouth road, we find the '12 miles from Plymouth' stone on the north side of the road, straddled by two later Plymouth Corporation Water Works ones, and which we are told was used as a boundstone for the Walkhampton clay sett. But is this what is known as the Goadstone? Crossing confuses us by assigning the name 'Goad's Stone' to two different stones. In his *Guide* (p.91) he says, referring to the 'Plymouth 12 miles' stone, 'Half a mile further on (i.e. westward) we reach the twelfth milestone from Plymouth. This is known as Goad's Stone, and on the upper half of the face are some markings, but they are not readily distinguishable'. However, much earlier in 1905, in a series of articles in the *Western Morning News* under the title 'Early Historic and Medieval Remains on Dartmoor', reprinted as a booklet by Quay Publications in 1987 (p.38) he says 'The Exeter road enters the Moor at Peek Hill, not far from Dousland, and is carried over the shoulder of the eminence. On its northern side, and on the left of the way going to Princetown is a stone, which may not improbably be one of these erected some two centuries ago by the Plymouth Corporation. It is known as Goad's Stone, and marks a point where a green track, coming up from Walkhampton, joins the highway. It is of small size and is usually regarded (as) being an old milestone; some faint markings may be traced upon it, but whether they are artificial is doubtful'. We now know that it was not a Plymouth Corporation mile or Guide Stone, and his reference to indistinguishable markings on both stones must point either to an error or a change of opinion.

Hemery (*High Dartmoor*, footnote to p.108) links the word 'Goad' to a West Country tinners' boundary mark, but does not state his source; however this may well have been in A.K. Hamilton Jenkin's *Cornish Miner* (p.49) where he quotes from an early writer in reference to marking the bounds 'Then make they Goad or rodd pard (*pared by slicing off the turf*) four square, being in length or shortness according to the number of workers in this Goad. Every one of these fellow workers shall have his place sketched out to him which they call that man's park'. Hamilton Jenkin goes on to say 'Goad – a land measure. It represents nine feet, and two goads square is called a yard of ground – E. Cornwall Glossary. N.E.D.' Hemery, was, of course, quite unaware that the '12 miles from Plymouth' milestone had indeed been used as a boundary stone, not by tinners but by the Walkhampton Clay Sett. The Ordnance Survey six inch maps of the 1880s and 1906 both show the track from Walkhampton going directly to the milestone on its way to Stanlake, crossing the highway as Crossing describes it; it is only the more modern maps that show the track from Walkhampton joining the highway further west opposite Goadstone

Pool, exactly where the older, rough unmarked stone is sited! More confusion, but the author thinks that this is what must be correctly called the Goad Stone.

Other references to the stone, whichever of the two it might be, call it the 'Goat's Stone' or Goatstone, and this is referred to in the census of Walkhampton parish for the year 1851, when the parish was divided into two 'Districts', district No.1 being 'All that part of the Parish of Walkhampton south of the main road from Little Horrabridge to Walkhampton Infants School from thence to Horn Hill and on to Green path to Goats Stone. From Goat Stone on the Morton road to the extent of the parish near Princetown which is marked by a bound stone. Including that part of little Horrabridge which is divided by the road...' Within this district No.1 were 'Horseyeats', 'Peek Hills' and 'Stenlake', whilst Waytown, Furstor and Eggworthy, etc. were in District No.2. By 1851, of course, the Walkhampton clay sett had failed and been abandoned. The boundstone 'near Princetown' would be the 'W/D' stone formerly by the roadside at the western extremity of the village, now replaced by a Plymouth Corporation Water Works one inscribed 'PCWW/1917'. The word 'Goat' also occurs in the 1786 Stannary Bounds of Ashburton Stannary in 'Dunnagoat', and Plympton Stannary as 'Dunnagoat Stone in Wellake Lawe', also referred to in the seventeenth century as 'Turnagott Stone in Woollake Haw'. Is this coincidence, or is there some long lost connection between 'goat' or 'gott' and a boundary marker? There are also the Higher and Lower Dunnagoat rock piles above the Rattlebrook – perhaps used as boundary markers by the tinners working in the Rattlebrook valley below.

Other later references to the search for clay on Walkhampton Common are to be found in the Maristow Papers in the form of copy letters for the year 1906. On 22 June of that year the estate secretary writes:

> Met Mr Nicholls and Captain Crowe of St Austell at Princetown with reference to their application for a lease to the china clay in this part of the estate, we went over the land around Routrundle towards Mistor, then through the valley east of the old quarries at Foggintor and on the other side of the railway above Criptor. The formation indicates clay ground in each of these places and formal application is to be made for a licence to sink trial pits. The whole ground inspected is outside the limits if the Plymouth watershed.

The 'valley east if the old quarries' was, of course, a reference to Yes Tor Bottom. The next letter dated 28 June says:

> Messrs Nicholls and Gavin met me in Mr Wolferstan's Office with reference to their application for a lease to the china clay in Walkhampton Common and Outcombe Newtake and Ringmore. Their proposal is to wash the clay and conduct it in pipes down to as near Dousland Station as practicable and there construct their drys.

However nothing appears to have come of these proposals, although on 30 September there is a passing reference to 'a man sinking pit for clay'.

7

GRANITE WORKING

The surface granite scattered over much of Dartmoor, known as 'moorstone', is the result of the gradual disintegration of the tors through climatic conditions over the millennia, and has been used extensively for building purposes since the Bronze Age as is evident by the number of hut circles still remaining, which run into several thousand, in spite of the vast amount of stone including cairns and circles, etc. that went into the construction of the miles of newtake walls in the eighteenth/nineteenth centuries. The moor has one of the most extensive accumulations of Bronze Age artifacts in Western Europe.

Even until relatively recent times, most moorland buildings were largely constructed of unshaped weathered pieces of moorstone. It was only at the beginning of the nineteenth century that the granite was drilled and cut for re-sale on a commercial basis, and a little later still that it was at all widely quarried. Until just after 1800 granite was split by cutting a series of slots along the line to be cut, into which wedges were inserted and hammered home until the stone split, hopefully cleanly. Shortly after 1800 a method known as 'feather and tare' was introduced whereby a series of holes about an inch in diameter were cut along the line required by means of an iron 'jumper', a metal rod with a wedge-shaped tip, this being rotated whilst struck with a sledge-hammer. When the holes were of the necessary depth, two 'feathers', thin pieces of metal, were inserted into each hole and between the 'tare', an iron wedge. The series of wedges were then struck along the whole length of the stone until it split.

The construction of the prison for Napoleonic prisoners of war between the years 1806 and 1809 at Princetown used local moorstone on Walkhampton Common taken without the permission of the landowner, Sir Masseh Lopes, who took the Duchy to court for the illegal removal of stone from his common in 1810. Burt comments on this, and that Lopes was awarded the sum of £500 'on a writ of enquiry against Mr Isbell for taking stone therefrom to build Dartmoor prison, without procuring Sir Masseh's leave'. In 1820 a lease was granted by Lopes to work the stone on Walkhampton Common, and Thomas Tyrwhitt was instrumental in forming the Plymouth & Dartmoor Railway Co. to transport this stone down to the original terminus at Crabtree Wharf, Plymouth. Opened in 1823, the line was later extended in 1827 at the moorland end into Princetown, and at the Plymouth end to Sutton Pool, but by then the working of the quarries had passed into the hands of the original contractors for the line, Messrs Johnson & Brice. Not only did they work Foggintor and that area including Swell Tor, but they also purchased the lease of the Haytor Granite Company in 1850 to eliminate competition, working the quarries on Walkhampton Common but trading as the Haytor Granite Company.

Many men were employed at Foggintor and there are the remains of several cottages which used to house these workers; Hill Cottages on the large spoil tip, known as 'Big Tip', being where they had their own chapel cum school, Red Cottages nearer the Princetown road and others around Rundlestone. The census for 1861 records 267 persons living in the Foggintor and Rundlestone area. The track from the Tavistock road went to the Plymouth & Dartmoor Railroad near the later King Tor Halt, and still has a number of setts remaining in situ from Yellowmead Farm (founded c.1860) south wards in spite of the fact that in the general strike of 1926 the apprentices at Swell Tor Quarry had to remove many of them from the Tavistock Road end to be broken up for road-stone.

Under Foggintor and north of King Tor there are four plain boundstones bearing feather and tare markings, defining the perimeter of the quarry's ground. Below North Hessary Tor and down to the quarry a number of pieces of moorstone bear both the marks of the earlier method of splitting the stone and of feather and tare, showing that the changeover of methods was by no means sudden, and that both here were being used concurrently, perhaps at the time that stone was being taken for the prison.

As the quarries on Walkhampton Common opened in about 1820, so George Templer opened his quarries on Haytor Down on the eastern side of the moor. He transported his stone down to Ventiford, a drop of about 1200 feet via a unique tramway constructed of granite rails or setts, gravity alone taking the loaded 'cars' down to a canal constructed by his father earlier for shipping Bovey Basin ball clay to Teignmouth. On

sections of the line from Holwell Tor and West Emsworthy it was necessary to use horses to pull loaded wagons before the gradual descent to Ventiford, controlled only by a hand-brake. However, with the additional handling of the stone from the wagons on to the barges and then its transference from barge to ship at Teignmouth, in spite of Templer's ingenious tramway, costs were such that they far exceeded those of his competitors and was one of the causes for the failure of the whole project. Much of the original tramway right down to Brimley is still in situ, the lower section of Templer's track having been utilised by the later railway company, in fact some setts were unearthed when the new Bovey Tracey bypass was constructed near the former Brimley railway bridge. The tramway can be followed for much of its length via a route waymarked by the National Park and designated 'The Templer Way', though access to certain sections passing through private land was not possible. Templer's quarries were worked on land owned by the 11th Duke of Somerset, who held the Manors of Ilsington and Natsworthy, leasing an area around Haytor extending to 600 acres, for which he paid a rental of £200 per annum. However he only worked about 90 acres. There only appears to be a single boundstone remaining to mark the extent of this land, north of the tramway at SX 765 779. It is a well shaped stone with a rounded top, and a reversed letter 'S' for Somerset on its east-facing side, a lazy or sloping letter similar to others on the Hole Stone and at Long Pool. On the west-facing side there is a well executed 'T' for Templer. By 1829 Templer was in serious financial trouble and was obliged to sell not only the quarries, tramway and canal, but also his residence at Stover, all of these being acquired by the Duke.

Tracing the track of the tramway one day, long before the Templer Way was thought of, the author walked the bridlepath between Reddaford Water and the Bovey Tracey/Haytor road to look for two plain boundstones mentioned by Hemery in *Walking the Dartmoor Railroads* as the tramway crosses this path. The stone nearer to Reddaford to the east of the path is undoubtedly free of any inscription, but the other nearer to the Haytor road is both of a different character, being shaped, and does bear an inscription on its west-facing side, not visible from the path. This reads 'Shewte Rights', an intriguing inscription, and a letter of enquiry to Mrs Scott of Shewte resulted in the receipt of a very nice letter of explanation, as follows:

Fig. 83 Templer Stone on Haytor Down.

It was originally marked as our grazing rights on what was once common land before it was enclosed, and, we believe, squatted on, many years ago. It would have been in that position because just recently we have pulled down a stone shed on the farm and have found that marker stones, or granite posts, were buried underneath and in one case used to make a step – and on one of them is written 'Lower Down of Yarner Down'. Once upon a time the whole will have been referred to as Yarner Down, then the piece below the railway as 'Lower Down'. It was just rough grazing when we first came here. This farm was once part of the Yarner Estate and when it was split up some of the rights were sold off separately. However, the late Mr Harold Retallick once informed me that it was still our right to graze on there and that we could take it up, but to try to demolish the present status quo would be unthinkable. This was twenty-five years ago before the land was divided up and reclaimed by Mr Holland.

The original first edition of the O.S. six inch map shows four 'Stones' relating to this boundary, that nearest the Bovey/Haytor road being the one inscribed 'Shewte Rights' at SX 7905 7825 west of the path. The next is a plain post bearing feather and tare. Beyond this the present right of way veers north-west, but formerly there also used to be a more direct path to the Bovey/Manaton road and it was along this route that the other two stones were originally placed. One suspects that the 'Lower Down of Yarner Down' stone was one of these. The only other boundstone relating to the Yarner estate known to the author, in spite of being on the Lustleigh/Bovey parish bounds, is unmarked by the O.S. This is beside the road on

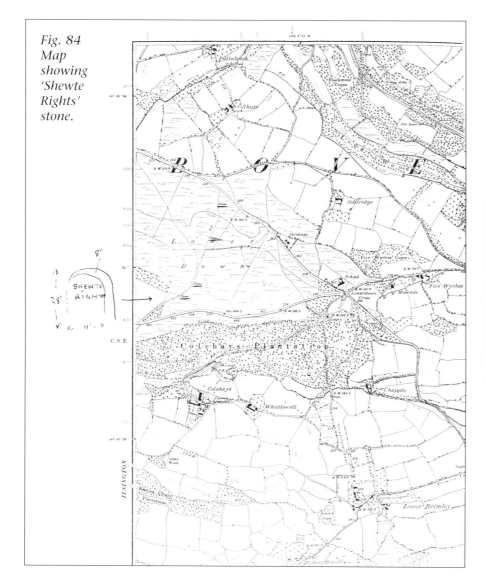

Fig. 84 Map showing 'Shewte Rights' stone.

Granite Working: 'Shewte Rights' B.S., SX 7905 7825

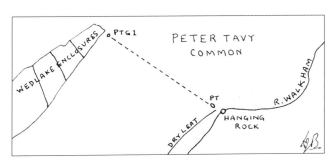

Above and right: *Fig. 85 Position of PTG1 and drawing of it before re-erection.*

Left: *Peter Tavy Granite 1, 'P.T.G.1' stone after being re-erected.*

Trendlebere Down, north side, at SX 7790 7923, a rough set stone inscribed with the single letter 'Y'.

On the western side of the moor much stone has been removed for building purposes, both surface moorstone and quarried stone, some being used in the reconstruction and rebuilding of Tavistock by the Duke of Bedford in the nineteenth century. It was on 1 November 1847 that the Duchy of Cornwall granted a licence to two Tavistock men, Joseph Edgcumbe, a chemist and druggist, and John White, a wine and spirit merchant, to take granite from within the Commons of Devon north and south of the Tavistock/Two Bridges turnpike road within the parishes of Peter Tavy and Whitchurch. The northern boundary line of this sett was defined as a 'straight line from a post marked "P.T.G.1" placed by the boundary of the Commons at or near Wedlake (Peter Tavy) to a stone post marked "P.T.G.2" on the west bank of the river Walkham at or near Hanging Rock.'

In late September 1987 the author and his wife found the Wedlake stone (Fig.85) not more than ten yards from the north corner of the Wedlake enclosures at SX 5475 7805. It was recumbent, an apparently unshaped piece of stone not much more than 3ft in length overall, wider at the head than the foot, and entirely covered in a thick layer of moss, the scraping away of which revealed the inscription 'PT/G1'. It was re-erected by the then National Park Ranger for the area. The Hanging Rock referred to here is a large fractured boulder lying in the river at SX 556 777. The river bank was searched in this area but produced no obvious fallen boundstone. However, directly in line with Hanging Rock and the stone at Wedlake, a 6ft

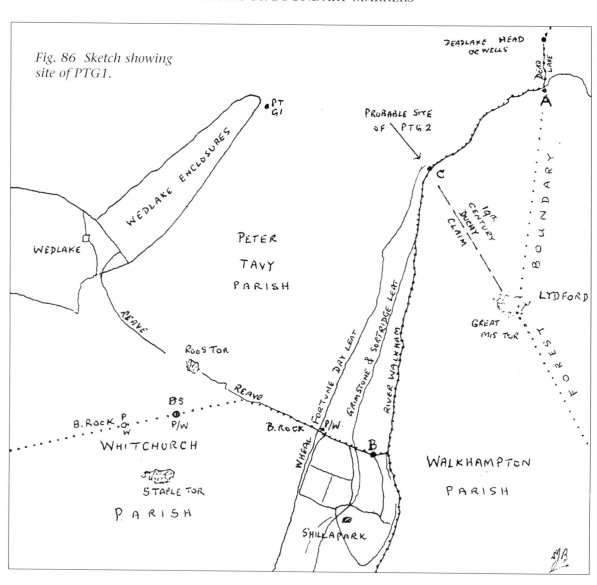

Fig. 86 Sketch showing site of PTG1.

long earthfast boulder was found, that had split naturally, with the letters 'P.T.' on the side of the larger piece, the former well formed but the latter more poorly executed due to the nature of the rock, together with what appeared to be 'TO' on the side nearest the river. However they were nothing like as well executed as the letters on 'PT/G1' which has serifs so perhaps there is another stone there waiting to be found.

Within the setts were Roos Tor and the Staple Tors to the north of the Tavistock/Two Bridges road, and Feather, Heckwood and Pew Tors to the south. The latter was particularly vulnerable to the onslaught of the stonemasons, being so near a road, making transportation very easy, so that a restriction was put upon the workmen not to remove stone from the tor itself, the limits of which they were allowed to approach being marked and defined by a series of nine positions, each a natural rock marked with an incised circle of ten inches diameter, quartered. This restriction was put into force in 1847, but infringements continued to be made and in 1879 a complaint against Mr Duke of Merrivale Quarry was made but was found to be untrue, as at that time the only work being carried out was at Little Pewtor, otherwise known as Sampford Tor, within Mr Parlby's land nearby. Concern for Pew Tor, described as Great Pew Tor on occasion, again reared its head in 1881, so that in August of that year a public meeting was convened by the Portreeve of Tavistock and held in the Guildhall. As a direct result of the public meeting a sonnet was written by Isiah Waterloo Nicholson Keys entitled 'To Pew Tor Devon', and published shortly afterwards on 17 September 1881, in the Plymouth *Weekly Mercury* as follows:

Beloved old Tor, fully fifty summers known
To me – though countless storms have o'er
thee swept
And lightnings fierce around thy crags have leapt,
Midst all unscathed still steadfast is thy throne!
Less happy me, the flight of time I moan.
Its numbing influence hath o'er me crept;
My feet, that once thy boulders nimbly stept
And scaled thy flanks, are now unsteady grown.
Yet thou'rt in peril, I am sad to see
Gangs of rough quarrymen thy form surround,
And, penetrating to the depths profound,
Block after block pluck forth with ruthless glee,
Rise, mighty Odin, rise, their fury check,
And Save, oh save, thy sacred Rock from wreck.

It seems that a wider protective boundary around Pew Tor had already been sought from the Prince Regent by the Vicar of Tavistock, and a promise obtained from him.

Originally granted in 1876, Mr Duke's licence to work granite had to be renewed in 1896 and it was at this time that a condition of the granting of the fresh lease was that Mr Duke should 'have marks cut on blocks of stone to define the limits'. By 30 December 1896 he had complied with this condition and it was remarked that 'he has had marks cut in some natural fixed stones to indicate new protection limits of Pew Tor, each mark being a circle with five holes about an inch deep to distinguish them from the original marks made by a cross within a circle'.

Whereas the old limits had been close up to the tor, and in a ten-sided shape, the new 1896 bounds took the form of a trapezium, with only four markers, one

All markings are on natural rock faces.

The Original boundary has 9 marked points, each having an inscribed symbol consisting of a quartered circle of 10 inch diameter, dating from 1847.

Marked on the sketch:

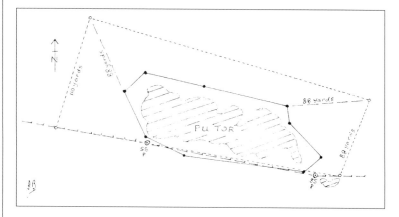

Pew Tor, 1847 Boundary Rock, 1 of 9 with a 10" circle quartered incised upon the stone.

The Revised Boundary of 1896 was quadrilateral in shape. Each of the four corners was marked with a circle of 6 inch diameter, having a hole drilled at the five points of intersection of the quadrants.

Marked on the sketch: ·······o······

Sampford Spiney Parish boundary and boundstones: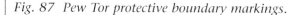

Fig. 87 Pew Tor protective boundary markings.

1896 Bounday mark, 1 of 4, 6" diameter, quartered but with five holes drilled where the circle and inner cross lines meet.

at each corner. These are even smaller than the 1847 ones, only about six inches in diameter, and difficult to find, in fact one still eludes the most diligent searches for it. When Helen Harris wrote her article (Nineteenth Century Granite Working on Pew Tor and Staple Tor, Western Dartmoor, T.D.A. 1981), only two of the four marked stones had been recorded, but since that time the one at the north-west corner of the protective limit has been found. This stone is marked with the symbol both on its horizontal and vertical faces, and is near to the small quarry. The author did hear that the one at the south-east corner was found in the early nineties, but no confirmation was forthcoming.

A somewhat similar arrangement of marked stones took place around Roos Tor (Fig.88) where the boundary line was marked at 14 points, again using fixed natural rocks. Here the symbol used was a bisected circle. These too are relatively inconspicuous, and to emphasise the points to which the masons were allowed to approach the tor, the then Duke of Bedford had a series of 14 set boundstones erected bearing his initial 'B'. These are approximately 4ft to 5ft in height, and are generally beside, or near to, the earlier marked natural rocks, but in one case on the western side of the tor the two complementary markings are a considerable distance apart. It would seem that the Duke of Bedford had had trouble and considerable correspondence with the Duchy about infringements of the boundary around this tor, and erected the boundstones so that the workmen had no excuse.

On the eastern side of the Staple Tors the main occupation was that of making setts for the

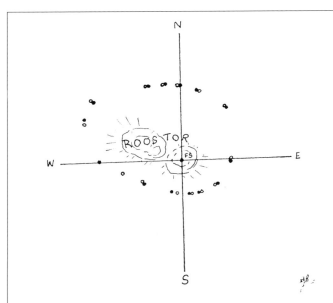

o *The original natural stones marked* ...... ⊖
• *The Duke of Bedford's set boundstones* ... B

Above: *Fig. 88 Roos Tor protective boundary markings.*

Right: *Roos Tor: One of 14 pairs of markings, a circle with a line across the middle, and the later stones erected by the Duke of Bedford, inscribed 'B'.*

nineteenth-century cobbled streets of Tavistock and elsewhere. There are numerous sett makers bankers remaining on the hillside, individual ones, doubles back to back, treble ones and groups of four back to back. Of only knee height, what weather these men must have endured, all for the princely sum of 1d per sett, their earnings about 5/- per day at most, many coming from Peter Tavy via the so called Quarryman's Path.

As a final footnote to this chapter, it is interesting to note that in a similar manner there are protective limits set out around three tors on Bodmin Moor.

These were marked out in 1864 and are still to be found on Stowe Hill, Bearah Tor and Kilmar Tor, protecting the skyline as the result of an agreement between the Duchy of Cornwall and the quarrymen.

All the markings are identical consisting of a fleur-de-lis approximately 10in x 8in. The number of marked stones far exceeds those on Dartmoor, there having been 17 around Stowe Hill, 31 around Bearah Tor and 54 around Kilmar Tor, making a total of 102! However some have disappeared but there are still no less than 88 positions recorded. They were once painted to make them more conspicuous.

Sett makers' Bankers, Staple Tor.

8
THE DARTMOOR PRESERVATION ASSOCIATION

Sharpitor, overlooking Burrator Reservoir, gives one superb views towards Plymouth Sound, to Brentor and Princetown, and across the Tamar to Kit Hill. It was formerly owned by the Plymouth Corporation, being within their water catchment area, and thus later became part of South West Water's property. It is situated on the major watershed reave between the Meavy and Walkham, designated the Walkhampton Common Reave by Andrew Fleming. Whilst owned by Plymouth Corporation, Peek Hill, adjacent to Sharpitor to the west, had been leased to the R.A.F. for a number of years as a 'Gee' station, to improve their navigational network; they erected a short mast and hut and the base of the small building and bunker are still there. After it became redundant, the Corporation considered using the site as a juvenile training centre in 1970, but fortunately nothing came of the proposal, rejected by Devon County Council.

In 1984 the Dartmoor Preservation Association was able to purchase 32 acres of land immediately around the crest of Sharpitor from South West Water with funds from the Lady Sylvia Sayer Land Fund, and on 22 June of that year five boundstones were erected around the perimeter of this land by the Dartmoor National Park Authority Ground Services Department. Although unfortunately not Dartmoor granite, but granite just the same, these boundary stones are machine-finished slabs having an arched top, with the letters 'DPA' incised within a slightly sunken oval panel on the side facing the tor.

In 1985 the DPA were able to acquire a further 50 acres of land at Swincombe, again from the South West Water Authority, that had formerly been the property of Paignton Urban District Council and the South Devon Water Board. This land comprised a site that had, since the 1930s, been the subject of several proposals to erect a dam across the river Swincombe to create a reservoir, capturing the waters of the Swincombe itself, the Strane and other minor streams. These 50 acres were purchased by the Association with

Dartmoor Preservation Association: Sharpitor, looking westwards.

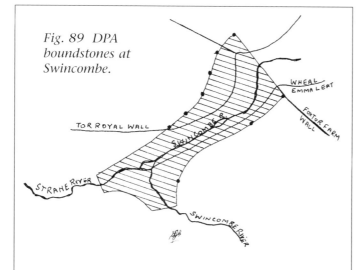

Fig. 89 DPA boundstones at Swincombe.

D.P.A. boundstones: •

Swincombe, plaque on the Swincombe acknowledging the generosity of Loveday Trehair of Dousland.

funds from a bequest specifically for land purchase made by the late Miss M. Loveday Trehair. This land comprises an area from above the confluence of the Swincombe and Strane rivers, downstream as far as the Fox Tor Farm newtake wall, and includes 8.89 acres of land actually within the Tor Royal newtake, land which had been sold by the Duchy to Paignton Urban District Council in the 1930s and which was thus South West Water Authority land. At first a small plaque was set into a large boulder on the left bank of the Swincombe near Sam Parr's house to commemorate the bequest, reading:

> This land (50 acres) was purchased for the Dartmoor Preservation Association in 1985 through the generosity of Loveday Trehair of Dousland who loved Dartmoor and cared for its preservation.

It had always been intended that boundary stones be erected to mark the bounds of this 50-acre site which included the 'Boiler' and the site of the proposed dams, and in July 1987 wooden poles were set up to mark certain points on the boundary. Five were noted by the author at the time, three within Tor Royal newtake, and two above the course of the old Wheal Emma leat on the southern side of the river. Subsequently a map was drawn up showing sites for five boundstones within the Tor Royal newtake and the two on the southern side of the river. However, in September 1987 revisiting the area, no less than nine boundstones were observed to have been erected, the five shown on the map within Tor Royal newtake plus another directly inside the wall at the old hunting gate, and three on the south side of the river. All are similar in shape and size to those set up around

DPA stone above old Wheal Emma leat at lower end of land purchased.

DPA stone above Swincombe/Strane Meet, looking towards Whiteworks.

Department of the Environment: 1972 concrete post on the road near Over Tor.

Sharpitor, but of a coarser grain and with the face left with a rough finish – the 'DPA' motif is identical.

Not connected with the Dartmoor Preservation Association, other signs of protection of the environment also exist. On Merrivale Hill there are a number of concrete markers very similar in shape and size to those put up by the Post Office Authorities (now Telecom) to mark their cables. These are inscribed 'D/O/E/AM/1972'; the letters standing for 'The Department of the Environment, Ancient Monuments'. One is just above the small quarry, another towards Over Tor, and others higher up the hill, all protecting the Merrivale antiquities. Another somewhat similar instance of protection being given to a specific area is to be found above East Rook Gate (Cornwood), towards High House Waste, (purchased by the DPA). In this case there is a cast iron notice reading:

This Ancient Settlement is protected as a Monument of National Importance under the Ancient Monuments Acts 1913-53.

Ministry of Works.

Ministry of Works, Ancient Monuments Acts 1913-53.
SX 607-619

9

PAROLE AND OTHER PRISON STONES

Dartmoor. Mention the name and in the minds of those not resident in the South West the first thought is often that of the prison at Princetown rather than of the moor itself, a 'resting' place for so many hardened criminals in the past, and now accommodating a wider range of less hardened offenders too. But the prison was, of course, originally constructed to house prisoners of war taken during the Napoleonic Wars with France and her allies. Hostilities had been going on for a number of years prior to the Peace of Amiens in 1802, but with the renewal of hostilities in 1803, the Napoleonic War proper, the volume of prisoners taken increased to such an extent that the former prisons at Millbay, Plymouth and elsewhere became quite inadequate. At first dismasted hulks unsuitable for repair were brought into use as prison ships, at Plymouth anchored out in the Hamoaze, and these comprised the *Formidable*, an ex-French 80 Gunner captured at Trafalgar in 1805; *El Firme*, a Spanish 74 also captured in 1805; the *San Ysidro* and *San Nicholas*, both Spanish 80s captured off Cape St Vincent in 1797'; two French 74s, the *Hector* captured in 1782 and the *Genereaux* captured in 1800; the *L'Oiseau*, a French frigate together with three old British vessels. These were capable of accommodating some 6200 prisoners, and there was also the *Le Caton*, an ex-French 74 which was used solely as a prison hospital ship.

Conditions on these vessels soon became no better than those in the prisons as numbers mounted, so alternative safe-housing had to be found. It was Thomas Tyrwhitt, the 'founder' of Prince's Town, Princetown as we know it today, who was the prime mover to get the purpose-built prison put on the moor so far distant from his estate at Tor Royal. Secretary to the Prince of Wales, later to become George IV, and appointed Auditor to the Duchy of Cornwall, Tyrwhitt was ever well placed to influence the powers that be of the benefits to the area that might accrue from such a scheme. Building commenced in 1806, and the first prisoners of war arrived there in May 1809. By 1812 there were 9000, in conditions hardly better than those on the hulks. However officers enjoyed the privilege of being able to give their word of honour that they would not attempt to escape, and live outside the prison 'on Parole'. They were billeted at Ashburton, Moretonhampstead, Tavistock and Okehampton in the Dartmoor area, together with Crediton, North Tawton, South Molton and Tiverton, these eight towns being those approved in Devon by the Transport Office. Such officers were given the freedom to travel a maximum of one mile from the outskirts of the town to which they were sent, and surviving relics of this restriction on their movements are the milestones erected for that particular purpose on roads leading out of Ashburton.

Residences were assigned to each officer prisoner allowed 'on parole', who was also given an allowance of 12/6 per week regardless of any private means that he might have, which was considerably more than the average wage of our farmworkers, then getting about 9/- a week. Officers were also allowed to trade in any business or occupation and some French prisoners at Ashburton are known to have taught modern languages, music and dancing. The American prisoners who came along later in the war formed a Masonic Lodge and wrote to the Grand Master in London complaining of their lot, begging for additional funds! The official notice sent to all inhabitants in towns selected as persons to accommodate these prisoners of war stated:

> that all such prisoners are permitted to walk or ride, on the great turnpike road within a distance 1 mile from the extreme parts of the town (not beyond the bounds of the Parish), and that if they shall exceed such limits or go into any field or Cross road they might be taken up and sent to prison and a reward of 10/- will be paid by the agent for apprehending them.

Ashburton is said to have erected seven stones set at a distance of '1 Mile' from the 'Extreme parts of the town' to define the limits to which the prisoners were permitted to walk or ride, but the roads so marked were far from being turnpiked roads in all cases. The only turnpike trust roads at that time in the Ashburton area were the Ashburton Trust, covering the main Exeter to Plymouth road from Chudleigh to South Brent dating from 1755 and the old Totnes road via Pridhamsleigh turnpiked in 1763. The '1 Mile' stones on these roads have now disappeared. However three examples still survive, 12 to 18in in height and simply inscribed '1 Mile', since they were not intended to be milestones in the normal sense of the word.

One was to be found on the Broadhempston road, approached from Whistley Hill and was photographed by the author. Unable to find it again, in 1989, it transpires that the owner of a recently erected house on the Woodland road, near the entrance to 'Hawkes', removed it and had it cleaned and re-erected by the roadside opposite his house. In June 1990 it was returned to its original site in a hedge, or at least to where it was found, for this

Parole Stones: Whitchurch Road, milestone inscribed 'Miles/From/ Tavk 1/Plym &/ Dock/X111'.

example is said to have been moved by the prisoners so that they could see around a corner in the road, a ruse perpetrated elsewhere with normal milestones. One also exists on Druids Hill near the entrance to Druid Cottage, sited a mile from Great Bridge, as is a third on the Holne Turn road opposite the entrance to Dart Vale, the latter only showing the figure '1' above road level. Two others are known to have existed, on the bank outside a house called Highgrove on the Buckland road and another on the Woodland road to the south of the town.

At Tavistock beyond the first milestone on the Whitchurch road there is an ancient oak tree used as a similar marker, called the 'Honour Oak'. It is but a

Honour Oak Tree, which is nearer Tavistock than the milestone.

shadow of its former self, a shell, strapped together with iron bands. It bears a plaque reading:

> Honour Oak Tree, marked boundary of French Prisoners on Parole in Tavistock from Princetown during the Napoleonic War (1803-14). Also where money was deposited in Exchange for food during a cholera outbreak in 1832.

It has been suggested that another '1 Mile' stone, which bears no indication where it is one mile from, on the Natsworthy road out of Widecombe-in-the-Moor, might also have been set up for the purpose of making a P.O.W. limit but Widecombe was never one of the 'approved' towns to which officers on parole were sent. Thus it must be purely a local milestone; however it is full of character and well worth seeking,

on the west verge with 'mile' spelt 'miol' in the broad Devon vernacular, one mile from the village and church.

Finally in respect of parole stones and limits, William Crossing refers to Ollsbrim Cross as one such, now reinstated in its rightful place at the junction of the Ashburton and Widecombe roads from Dartmeet at SX 685 735. Crossing writes (*Ancient Crosses of Dartmoor*):

> Mr Dymond informs me that, on the authority of old William French of the Higher Lodge, Spitchwick, who has spent all his life there, that this cross, when standing in its place on the moor (then in use as a gatepost at Town Farm, Leusdon), was fixed upon as the limit to which French Prisoners of War Officers detained at Princetown at the commencement of this century were permitted to extend their walks on parole of honour.

Special permission to extend a walk beyond the statutory '1 mile' could be obtained from the Transport Board for a specific journey, but to grant this privilege to an officer at Princetown just to take an extended walk, an officer prisoner who by his very presence in Princetown prison had probably refused to give his word of honour not to try to escape, seems most unlikely to say the least.

The majority of the prisoners of war, both French and American, had left Princetown prison by the end of 1815, and the sick by 1816. Thereafter the prison remained closed until pressed into service as a convict prison in 1850, except for a short period of time when some outbuildings were used as a naptha plant in

1846. The former barracks that used to house the troops detailed to act as guards were also used to house Foggintor quarry workers and their families from about 1820 to 1850.

There are two boundstones of coarse, red granite belonging to this period that are of interest, showing the grooves of feather and tare; one to the south of North Hessary Tor at SX 5834 7372, the other to the north between the Tor and Rundlestone Tor at SX 577 745. Each has an incised six inch arrow on its east-facing side (a letter dated September 1852 records expenses of erecting 'stone Posts' in this area), and which must relate to the then convict status of the prison. Both are, however, on the Forest bounds and are thus misplaced as the original bounds granted to the prison did not extend that far westward, but only as far as the enclosure walls at these points, though the Forest Bounds do enter the enclosures at another point. There is a second unmarked boundstone a few yards nearer the enclosure wall than the one to the south of North Hessary. This is remarked upon at being 'out of position', with the arrowed nearby stone marked 'B.S.' in the Ordnance Survey Boundary Re-mark Book of 1881. The

Prison B.S.s: Depicting just the arrow, south of North Hessary.

arrowed stone to the north of North Hessary is not shown on the 1.25 000 maps in spite of its being on the Forest bounds, though unintentionally so.

The original prison bounds encompassed an area of some 390 acres, granted on a 99-year lease by the Duchy, and follows the line of the wall on the west side to near North Hessary Tor, thence bearing eastward to Little Tor and on to the Two Bridges road as far as the Blackabrook Bridge, then following the course of that river down stream to Trena or Ockery Bridge, and back along the road to the Duchy Hotel. Later, about 1867, the prison extended its bounds by a further 1000 acres under a fresh lease, the whole then marked by a series of boundstones inscribed 'DCP/ ↑'. They are generally about 18in to 2ft tall, square in section, and with a peaked top, though several, probably replacements, do not have the latter feature. These boundstones extend from the west enclosure wall to near North Hessary Tor (north side) towards Mistor on or near the Mistor track to New Forest Corner, and around the New Forest enclosure to the Two Bridges/Princetown road. Between North Hessary Tor and Mistor these stones follow the line of the erroneous eighteenth/nineteenth-century Forest Bounds to cross the Two Bridges/Tavistock road exactly where the Rundlestone once stood, and where there is still the Walk/hamp/ton/Lid/ford Turnpike Trust parish bound stone. Set into the road-surface just outside the gateway to the North Hessary television mast there is a unique $8\frac{1}{2}$ inch square stone, flush with the road, marking the prison's boundary, similarly marked, but reversed, to their boundstones, '↑/DCP'. The author was told that this stone was formerly in the wall fronting on to the road, but when the road up to North Hessary was made up, the wall was set further

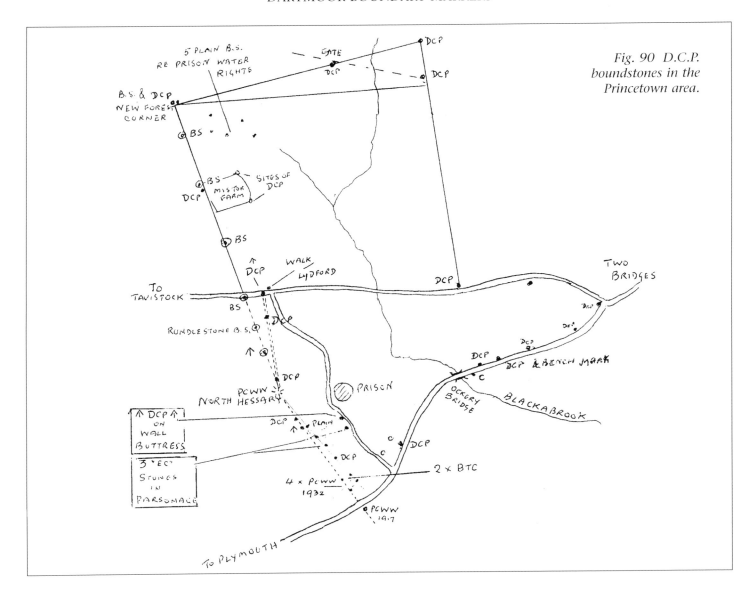

Fig. 90 D.C.P. boundstones in the Princetown area.

back, in the 1950s, when the television mast was erected. The letters 'DCP' refer to the Directors of Convict Prisons, not as was once supposed Dartmoor Convict Prison. This is borne out by the legends found on old maps in the possession of the prison authorities, 'Land held by the Directors of Convict Prisons', and other drawings that bear a similarly worded rubber stamp.

Also just within New Forest Corner, off limits to the general public, and in normally very boggy ground, there are five plain boundstones marking one of the early sources of the prison's water supply; they are shown on the old O.S. six inch map. Water drained into the prison leat via the Mistor Lake to supplement that coming from the Walkham and Spriddle Lake. The original reservoir opposite the main entrance gate on the west side of the road is now disused, but there is, nevertheless, a rather ornate commemorative stone there on the edge of the reservoir. It has a 'VR' and crown in relief at the top, beneath which there is a shield inscribed 'AD 1856' and beneath this again the letters 'GL'; possibly the initials of the stonemason who did the work on it. Other inscribed stones relating to the rebuilding of the walls on the roadside into the town include one which has 'V (crown) R' and the date 1853 beneath. Two others are dated 1852. Today the Prison Authorities are the largest single lessee of Duchy land, other than the army, holding no less than 1600 acres, largely the prison farm. The grounds of Princetown church and the former parsonage are, of course, outside the prison bounds. On the roadside where the north wall of the churchyard abuts on to the former Chaplain's House, there is a buttress which bears the inscription 'D.C.P.' to denote the prison's line.

Clockwise from top left: *Erected after 1867 when the enlarged bounds were marked by 'DCP' stones. This inscription stands for Directors of Convict Prisons.*

On the ground at the entrance to the roadway to North Hessary Tor. (Could not be seen October 2001 - roadway resurfaced.) Note arrow above 'DCP'.

Prison 'DCP' stone at SX 5960 7425 bearing an O.S. brass bolt in its flat top. These bolts are 60mm in width and bear the letters 'OSBM' and an arrow on the circumference.

North-east corner of Churchyard where it abuts on to the old Chaplain's House, is a buttress with the plinth inscribed 'D.C.P.'.

10
RABBIT WARRENS

Warrening, that is the breeding of rabbits for both meat and pelt on a commercial scale, was an important part of the Dartmoor economy for several centuries. It was not until after the Second World War, and the introduction of myxomatosis, that the Ministry of Agriculture banned the trade.

Rabbits were once thought not to be indigenous to this country, but some bones have been found in prehistoric sites. The Normans, however, certainly re-introduced them both for food and sport, when they multiplied prodigiously, but Dartmoor is not an ideal habitat for them as it is too wet and badly drained.

Thus they were 'farmed' in warrens in a similar fashion to those on many smaller lowland estates. The most enduring remains on the moor are the many specially built rabbit 'buries', (called 'Pillow Mounds' on the Ordnance Survey maps); artificial mounds of stone set on a slope across the contour of the land with a drainage ditch around them and covered in turf, thus encouraging them to breed in the drier conditions.

The Plym valley was the most extensive area of Dartmoor devoted to the breeding of rabbits in this way, in fact the cradle, for it is known that a 'de Traylesworthy' was granted land on which to establish a warren at Trowlesworthy as early as 1272. Other warrens in the Plym valley were those at Hentor, Legis Tor, Ditsworthy and Willings Walls. Elsewhere we find them at Headland on the West Webburn and Soussons and New House to its west, at Huntingdon between the West Wallabrook and the Avon, Vag Hill Warren on Dartmeet Hill, and several other smaller ones, some purely sporting in character such as that formerly at Wistmans Wood.

Ditsworthy Warren House still exists but is now only used as a training centre for the forces. At Trowlesworthy the warren house is now a riding establishment, former warren lands extending from Spanish lake, a left bank tributary of the the Plym which acts as the northern boundary line to the Blackabrook on the southern bound, the eastern side being open moorland without a physical boundary and the western side of the river Plym itself, approximately 500 acres in extent and now National Trust Property.

Ditsworthy, which latterly took over both the Hentor and Legis Tor warrens, was almost 1000 acres in extent, and was the last to function, closing only with the myxomatosis outbreak and the Ministry ban. The bounds went as far as Eylesbarrow and Evil Combe, Legis Tor Warren being also known as 'New Warren'. On each of these old warrens there are the remains of medieval settlements, some incorporating hut circles of the Bronze Age. Those at Hentor, Ringmoor Down, Willings Walls, Spanish Lake Head and Legis Tor are all marked on the 1:25 000 Ordnance Survey map – but need a magnifying glass to distinguish them! Legis Tor Warren was provided with rabbit-proof walls on its northern and western sides, and Willings Walls, before incorporation into Hentor, was bounded by the Plym, the Hentor Brook and Spanish Lake.

R.G. Haynes, in his paper 'Vermin Traps and Rabbit Warrens on Dartmoor' (Post-Medieval Archaeological Journal), refers to a copy of an 1807 lease granted to one Peter Nicholls for Hentor Warren which reads thus:

Rabbit Warrens: Boundary Rock, HW/B1, near Spanish Lake. SX 583 643

> The Right Honble John, Lord Borringdon,
> to Peter Nicholls of Sheepstor, Warrener,
> 29th Sept 1807.

> Lease of some waste on Lee Moore and an agreement abt a Warren on Hentor etc during the life of Mrs Mary Frances Penson.

> Lord Borringdon granted – upon lease All that part parcel and portion of a certain common called or known by the name of the Lee Moor Situate and lying in the Parish of Shaugh in the said County of Devon according as the same is now meted and bounded out from the said Common of Lee Moore in manner following (that is to say) from a certain row or heap of stones joining Trowlesworthy Warren and Spanish Lake Head … about Forty land yards above the same to a large Rock marked with the initials H.W.B. No 1 from thence straight on East to another stone marked No. 2 Eighty yards above the said row or Heap of stones from thence in a straight line to another bound Stone marked No 3 Which is Forty Yards South of the

large upright rock in Hentor from thence to the Head of Shabbacombe Lake … to another bound Stone marked No 4 from thence in a straight line to Colesmills (formerly a Stamping Mill) adjoining the River Plym to another bound Stone marked No 5 … and which said Stones are in all other respects bounded by the Tenements called Willings Walls and Hentor in the said Parish of Shaugh, etc.

This lease was for a period of fifty years. To take the boundstones one at a time:

No.1: The 'certain row or heap of stones' is, in fact, the Willings Wall reave at approximately the 1100ft contour level. The 'Rock' in question bears the inscription in two lines – 'HW/B1' – and is approximately 250 yards from the reave at SX 583 643, a 'land yard' being $5\frac{1}{2}$ yards. Though an earthfast boulder, it is not marked on the old six inch Ordnance Survey map.

No.2: This is a 'set' boundstone of some 4ft in height, lettered 'H/W/B2' at SX 585 645, not due east of No.1 by any means. Again it does not appear on the old six inch Ordnance Survey map. In Devon & Cornwall Notes and Queries Haynes has recorded that he found this stone recumbent in the 1970s – it is now upright.

No.3: This was also found to be prostrate by Haynes in the 1970s, and like No.2 has been re-erected since. It is shorter that No.2, about 3ft in height and lettered 'H/W/B3'. This is marked on the six inch Ordnance Survey map, and unusually for them is not simply marked 'stone' as is their custom but gives the actual inscription.

Fig. 91 Hentor Warren boundstones

No.4: This stone was not apparently found by Haynes in the 1970s – but was rediscovered in a recumbent position in 1987 with the inscription face downwards. It was turned over to reveal 'H/W/B4' and is at SX 603 653. It is marked on the six inch O.S. map where the inscription is given as 'H.W.B.L.' which is not really surprising when one looks at the very rudimentary figure '4'. It does, however, suggest

that its purpose was unknown. In the dry summer of 1989 the stone was re-erected by the Park Ranger, but fell again shortly afterwards. *(It was standing in 1998)*

No.5: This is not shown on the six inch O.S. map and thus its original position is not precisely known. In 1987 a stone was observed lying in the water at Shavercombe Foot, without any apparent inscription. Whether it has been checked since is unknown.

Of the other warrens, Headland Warren provides us with the best marked bounds of all. Dating from 1780 or thereabouts (the date 1890 in the first edition of *Boundary Markers* was an unfortunate error resulting from my typing!), this warren embraces an area of approximately 600 acres or a square mile, with the warren house itself on the left bank of the West Webburn near its head. The warren land extends from the West Webburn/East Bovey Head divide on the east, to the Wallabrook on the Forest bounds to the west. The six inch O.S. map shows no less than 13 boundstones associated with this warren; a contemporary map of c.1785 shows only 11 plus Bennett's Cross. However, neither figure is a correct tally, for the author has found no less than 15, including Bennett's Cross, which was inscribed 'WB' as were the bound stones. This map does not show the only two stones shown on the O.S. 1.25000 maps, those parallel to the Moreton/North Bovey road and on the North Bovey/Chagford boundary, but it does confirm that the stone marked 'possible fallen stone' on Fig.92 is a recumbent one lying face downwards. The stone on the bank of the Widecombe/Moreton/Chagford road at SX 696 816 is an exception, being inscribed 'Warren Bounds' in full. Besides the 15 stones

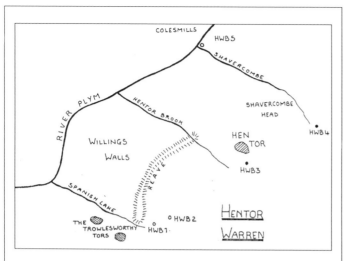

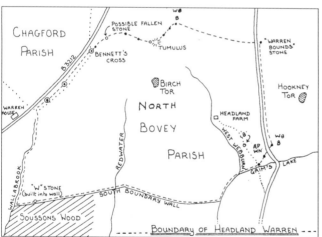

Fig. 92 Sketch maps of Hentor and Headland Warrens B.S.s.

that can definitely be ascribed to Headland Warren there is another simply inscribed 'W' built into, and possibly predating the Headland rabbit-proof south boundary wall about two hundred yards east of the Wallabrook at SX 675 803, and also a further example unsecured nearer the Wallabrook. These could relate to Soussons Warren. Of those marked 'WB' two bear an additional letter 'B', both on the side facing east and possibly indicating the bounds of East Birch Tor Tin Mine, for they are certainly not on the North Bovey parish boundary. Another stone, an orthostat forming part of an ancient wall on the drive into the farmhouse, also bears a similar letter 'B', not on the warren boundary, as do the North Bovey boundstones on the Grim's Lake. Another 'WB' boundstone near the lay-by for Grimspound bears the additional letters 'AP' and 'WN', thought to be the initials of former warreners. The warren is bounded on its northern and eastern sides by 14 of the boundstones. On the southern side is a well preserved rabbit-proof wall in which there are set two old vermin traps, on the line of medieval lynchets which the 'vermin', stoats and weasels, used as runs. These two traps are approximately 75 and 100 yards above the Challacombe track. One is complete except for its slate shutters which trapped the animal alive, the other lacking its cover stone but one, maybe not the original, was seen there at a later date. Part of a third is also on the boundary wall, a complete side piece having been used to repair the wall just to the west of the track down to the Redwater valley, clearly showing the two grooves for the shutters four feet apart. Other parts of a trap or traps are to be found in another repair on the corner of one of the fields known as the 'Four Aces', which are supposed to have been so called when, according to folklore, the wicked Jan Reynolds dropped them after having been found playing cards in Widecombe

The only stone with Warren Bounds inscribed in full.

Fig. 93

Bennett's Cross with WB.

Stone inscribed 'W' near the Wallabrook.

Inscribed 'WB' with additional 'AP' and 'WN' which may be the initials of past warreners. SX 6975 8090

Stone inscribed "W" found in the base of the wall about 200 yards from where it touches on the Wallabrook. (Photo c.1985)

B/WB stone on the Eastern slopes of Birch Tor bearing the additional 'B', possibly defining the bounds of East Birch Tor Mine.

Same stone later placed in the wall.

Church. Another in-situ trap also exists near the in-bye fields which are raised near the farmhouse, somewhat overgrown now but interesting in that it is one of the few that retains a stone at its side which supported part of the stick and wire mechanism used to release the shutters. The farmhouse has in the past served as an inn for the miners, when it was known as the Birch Tor Inn, and also as a tea house. 'Pillow Mounds' on this warren are few and far between but there are two to the west of the Redwater and a few on the eastern side near the head of the West Webburn, one of which is, unusually, circular in shape.

Vag Hill Warren, situated on Dartmeet Hill, pre-dates Headland, and has many pillow mounds, about 30 in all. A boundstone has been reported bearing the letter 'B' downstream from Dartmeet 'in trees on the edge of Vag Hill' but the author has been unable to find it amongst all the rocks in that area. The line of the boundary is known since it is described in a lease dated 23 April 1613 in the Exeter Library. The lease was granted by William, Earl of Bath, to Richard Reynell and Walter Fursland of Bickington, and reads as follows:

> waste ground called Spitchwick common lying between the river Darte on the west and south east and from thence to Heartor (*Yar Tor*) to Cornetor (*Corndon*) on the north and east to the west of Rowbrook hedge and so to Logator (*Looka Tor* or *Lucky Tor*) on the east and so to the river of Darte with free liberty to make a warren there for the keeping and breeding and killing of rabbits. And also if any rabbits go over the Darte to the Common there called Holne Commons alias Holne Cleyves between Comson (*Combestone*) hedge and Whortaparke corner or to any place in

the said Common of Spitchwicke the said Richard and Walter may kill them. Rent 10/-.

At first sight it seems strange that no mention is made of the 'B' boundstone in the lease, but this is, in all probability, accounted for by the later use of the warren in the nineteenth century when Vag Hill Warren was run in conjunction with Headland by John Hannaford, indicating the point at which the boundary left the river Dart below Dartmeet, which was not pinpointed in the original description of the bounds.

Another warren was that at Skaigh near Sticklepath and Belstone, formerly situated on both sides of the river Taw. On its boundary on the south side of the river, on a modern reave or earthen bank, is Stumpy Post, a boundstone erected by the Duchy of Cornwall to mark the point on the lower slopes of Cosdon up to which, by agreement with the Duchy, the commoners of South Zeal were allowed to enclose. This is inscribed 'DC1/SZ1'. Hemery (*High Dartmoor*) states that in 1876 the Duchy wished to rescind the licence for the warren. The first O.S. six inch to the mile map, surveyed in 1886, shows what appear to be pens at SX 634 936 marked 'Pheasantry'.

Ringmoor Down, where there are several medieval remains of farms, has three sites around the head of the Legis Lake where the outline of longhouses can still be traced at SX 567 658, 570 664 and 570 658. All are associated with reaves and cornditch walls, and in the centre of them around the head of the stream are four plain boundstones of unknown purpose to the author. All appear to be relatively modern, one is a former gatepost but it is quite possible that the settlements had connections with warrening originally.

11
STANNARY AND TINNERS' BOUNDS

Other than farming in its varying aspects, the oldest industry pertaining to Dartmoor must be that of the tinners. Tin 'streaming', that is to say the collection of alluvial tin from the river beds, is evident by the merest glance at the waste still present in the upper and middle reaches of most river valleys. This was the earliest type of working and most certainly dates from at least the twelfth century, but may, indeed, date from the Bronze/Iron Age periods, though proof is lacking. What is known, however, is that tin was worked in Cornwall at that time and there seems to have been some additional inducement to the Bronze Age people to settle in those villages where there was a concentration of cassiterite pebbles beyond that of just farming, especially on the south-west quarter of the moor, such as the Plym valley.

From early times, the tinners had their own Stannary Great Court or Parliament, and their own Stannary Laws, the Charter of Edward I defining the privileges they enjoyed, and granting them immunity from the jurisdiction of all manorial and royal courts whilst working for tin. Originally the Stannaries of Devon and Cornwall were as one, but in 1305 the counties were treated separately; in Devon the towns of Ashburton, Chagford and Tavistock being declared Stannary Towns, where it was permissable to coin the tin, i.e. to have it assayed for quality and pay the royal tax levied upon it; Plympton being added in 1328.

Our first written record of a Stannary Great Court being held is dated 1494, held at Crockern Tor, where 24 'jurats' from each of the four Stannaries attended as required, presided over by the Lord Warden of the Stannaries, appointed by the Duchy. Several later dates are known, the last meeting being held at the White Hart Hotel, Moretonhampstead, on 11 December 1786.

In 1510 a Stannary Great Court met to clarify existing laws, and whilst initially continuing to meet at Crockern Tor, a central point from a geographical viewpoint, many later courts or parliaments adjourned to Tavistock to conduct their business. The last meeting of 1786 made reference to the bounds of each of the four Stannary districts of Devon as described in records dating from 1613, 'the limits and bounds of the Jurisdiction of these Courts', which were then in some doubt, and to the customs of earlier times, but of the 24 jurors summoned to attend from each of the four Stannaries, only 5 attended from Ashburton, 6 from Chagford, 4 from Tavistock and 1 only from Plympton, all of which showed the state of the industry at that time, very much in decline and long overtaken in importance by the Cornish mines.

The copy of the 'Presentiments of the Bounds of the several Stannary Courts of Devon' dated 1613, contained in a manuscript book of 1762, described the bounds of the 4 respective Stannaries as follows:

Chagford Stannary: The limits and bounds of the Stannary Court of Chagford and the bounds and limits which divide the Two Stannaries Courts of Chagford and Ashburton are as followeth beginning from Crockerentor to Broken Borough from thence to Lower Cater, part of Lower Cater in the jurisdiction of Chagford, and the other in Ashburton, from Lower Cater to a village called Dunstone, part in Chagford and part in Ashburton and from thence to the Village called Blackslade part in Chagford and part in Ashburton and from thence to a village or Tin Work called Crownellhead and so to Swine Path Cross and from thence to Stowford Bridge and so to Teignbridge and from thence to Teignmouth the water dividing...

The Bounds between Chagford and Tavistock are these from Crockerntor North by Tavey Head and Broom Lake to the Head of a River called Ockment or Okement and from thence to the west Bridge in the town of Okehampton and from thence North to Monkokehampton and from Monkokehampton North East into a parish called Highbickington and to the River Taw and from thence as the same River runneth to Barnstaple and from thence unto the North sea as the Watter runneth – And further they present That all Devon lying within the Circuit and Compass of those Limits are within the Jurisdiction of the Stannary Court of Chagford and all Tin works lying within the said Bounds are within the Stannary Court of Chagford and all tinners inhabiting in the Towns and Parishes contained within these Bounds are and always

have been reputed Tinners dwelling within the Jurisdiction of the Stannary Court of Chagford and ought to be Contributary to all Rates and Musters as Tinners Inhabiting in that Court...

Ashburton Stannary: The Limits and Bounds of the Stannary Court of Ashburton on the North and East Parts are from Crockerentor eastwards to Riddon in Withecombe parish and from Riddon to Lower Cater from thence to Rowdon, from Rowdon to Dunstone to Chittleford from Chittleford to Blackslade from Blackslade to Crownley head in Ilsington parish, from Crownley head to Swine Path Cross thence to Lownston as the way leads from thence to Levaton and from thence as the way leadeth unto Stowford Bridge otherwise called Stowford Stone*, between Highweek and Teinggraze, and from thence to the Middle Pier of Teignbridge and from thence to the Mean Sea as the river of Teing Runneth and on the West and South parts distinguishing Ashburton Stannary from Tavistock and Plympton Stannaries – From the said Crockerentor Southward to Broken Burough and from thence to Cranelaketor from thence to Dunagoat, and from thence to Peters Cross and from thence to threeberry, and from thence to a Stone called Hobba Jame's Cross and from thence to the Range of Stones untill you come to Butterdon Burough and from thence to Broadaford, and from thence to the Seven Stones which part several parishes and from thence to Michael Burough adjoining the Sea, and all Tinworks lying within these Bounds are reputed to be within the Stannary Court of Ashburton and all Tinners inhabiting in the Towns and parishes within these Bounds are reputed as Tinners dwelling within the Stannary Court of Ashburton and are contributary to all Rates and Contributions as Tinners within the said Stannary and are Trained and Mustered among the Tinners of that Court on Contributary to the same...

*since this account dates from 1786 may the Stowford Stone be the James Templer stone inscribed with his name and date on the bridge, dated 1773, be the stone referred to, or was there an earlier marker? James had bought the derilict Stofford Esate in 1765.

Plympton Stannary: The Limits and Bounds of the Stannary Court of Plympton beginning at the full sea mark at Plymouth to the Easter End of the old Quay and from thence up the Street called St Andrews Street, and another Street there called the Old Town leaving all the Dwelling Houses over the west side and North in Tavistock Court, and so the Highway from Plymouth Northward to Uddlestor Rock (upon Roborough Downe) and from thence North Eastward to Horraplud from thence East the Way to Yannadon Cross from thence South East by Woodland Hedge dividing the parishes of Meavy and Walkhampton to Crecobye foot falling into the River of Meavy East and ascending the River of Meavy North East to Reddapit lake, and so ascending that lake Eastward to Blew Stone from thence to Horradill head, from thence South East to Broken Burough, from thence South to Market place lodge, from thence to Crannaberr and so Southward to Dunnagoat Stone in Wellake Lawe, from thence

to Saint Peters Cross, and so water Shutt the same Hill to Piggow Beacon, from thence to Modbury Steeple, and from thence to St Michael's Burrow, all Tinworks whose heads and head Wiers lie within these Bounds are reputed taken and known to be within the Stannary Court of Plympton aforesaid, and all Tinners inhabiting in the Towns and Parishes within these bounds are reputed and taken as Tinners dwelling within the said Stannary Court of Plympton, and are contributary to Rates, contributions, Trainings Musters and all other Suits and Impositions imposed upon the said Stannary Court of Plympton as it hath in time past been used beyond the Memory of Man...

Tavistock Stannary: The Limits and Bounds of the Stannary Court of Tavistock beginning at the Old Quay in Plymouth and from thence up to the Street called St Andrews Street Westward, and from thence to a Street called the Old Town westward and then from Old Town by the Highway Northward upon the North West side to Uddleston Rock (upon Roborough Downe) from the Rock called Uddlestor Rock North East into Horraplud, the North West side of the way to Yannadon Cross from thence North East by Woodland Hedge dividing the Parishes to Crecaby, from thence to the River of Meavy, and from thence to Reddapit lake Eastward and from thence to a place called Blewstone and from thence North East by Horradill Head, and from thence to Crockerntor And from Crockerntor North to Tavy head from Tavy to Bromelake, and from Bromelake to the West Bridge in Okehampton, and from thence North to

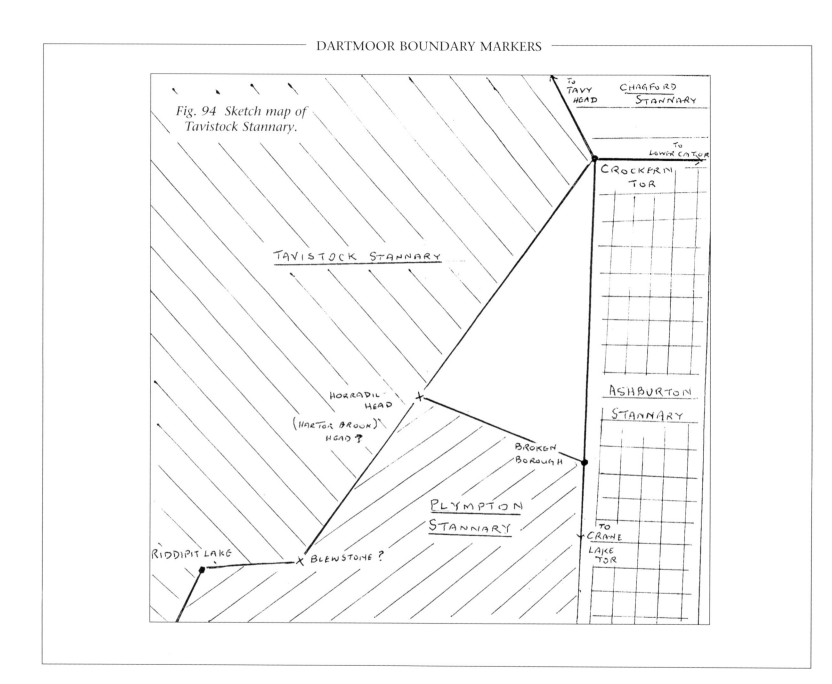

Fig. 94 Sketch map of Tavistock Stannary.

Monkokehampton and from Monkokehampton North East into a Parish called Highbickington, and from thence to Tawton and so to Barnstaple and from thence unto the North Sea and such Tinworks as lye within these bounds extending on the west to the bounds that divide Devonshire and Cornwall are within the Stannary Court of Tavistock and all Tinners which dwell within these bounds ought to be Contributors and to be rated within the Stannary of Tavistock Court.

Whilst Crockern Tor was the 'seat' of the Devon Stannary Parliament from 1305, the eighteenth-century copy of the bounds of the individual Stannaries only records the bounds of the three original Stannaries, namely Chagford, Ashburton and Tavistock, as touching upon this point. The fourth Stannary, Plympton, formed in 1328 from a part of Ashburton, did not extend thus far north, either in the recorded bounds of 1613 or 1786, but did use the cairn, Broken Borough, which is situated within the Tor Royal enclosures. Documents such as records of ancient boundaries were, of course, often copied several times, and in the manuscript copying errors sometimes occurred, besides the intentional changes. And here we have not one but two errors in the 1786 copy, the assertion by both Chagford and Ashburton that their bounds touched upon both Crokern Tor and Broken Borough, which is not possible, and the omission of a phrase in the bounds of Tavistock Stannary, the earlier records of 1613 clearly stating that they 'joynes with every Bound of Plympton Court soe far as Brokenborrow from thence to Crockeren torr' the later 1786 records making no reference to Broken Borough, and going straight from

Horradill Head to Crockern Tor, thus creating an apparent no-man's-land, in addition to other intentional changes.

It is clear that before the formation of Plympton Stannary in 1328 that Ashburton Stannary extended as far west as the River Meavy, for in 1303 tin was being coined at Ashburton from the upper reaches of that river by Richard de Stenylake and also by a Richard de Middelworthi in the Deancombe valley. It is interesting, too, to note that these Stannary Bounds extended not just over the granite country but to the Devon coast in all directions.

If we look at the boundaries of the four Stannaries as described earlier, we see that that dividing Chagford from Ashburton was designated as running from:

Crockern Tor (SX 615 757), to Riddon (SX 675 764), to Lower Cator (SX 688 763), to Dunstone (SX 715 758), to Chittleford (SX 722 757), to Blackslade (SX 728 756), to Crownellhead or Crownley head, a tin works or village (Bagtor) (SX 762 761) in Ilsington parish, to Swine Path Cross, now known as Swallerton Gate (SX 739 792), more probably referring to the cross roads but the remains of a cross still remains, to Lownston (SX 785 758), to Liverton (SX 805 792), to Stowford Bridge or Stover Bridge (SX 835 745), to Teign Bridge (SX 859 735) where there has been a bridge perhaps since Roman times at what was once just about the tidal reach, and so out to sea via the river Teign.

That between the Stannaries of Ashburton and Plympton and Tavistock ran from:

Crockern Tor to Broken Borough, the cairn in Tor Royal newtake (SX 619 722), to 'Cranelaketor', probably Great Gnats Head cairn (SX 617 679), to 'Dunagoat' (SX ???), to Peter's or Petre's Cross (SX 654 654), to 'threeberry' or Three Barrows (SX 653 626), to Hobba Jame's Cross, Hobajon's (SX 655 605), to the Butterdon Stone Row southwards to Butterdon cairn or barrow (SX 655 586), to Broadaford and 'the Seven Stones', a crossroads in the South Hams (SX 658 492) to 'Michael burrow', St Michael's Chapel on Burgh Island (SX 647 439) and thence out to sea.

The 1786 Plympton Stannary bounds give some differences in points of reference, however, on the boundary common to Ashburton, and an earlier seventeenth-century record gives us further variations. From Uddlestor Rock on Roborough Down (SX 515 672) the Plympton Stannary bounds went to 'Horraplud', perhaps in the region of Dousland, and thence along the road (B3213) to Yennadon Cross (SX 554 695), and down Woodland hedge, still on the Meavy/Walkhampton parish bounds, and down the Crecoby stream to its foot (SX 554 687), now under the Burrator reservoir. We now ascend the Meavy to Riddipit Foot (SX 570 702), and thence up that stream to the 'Blewstone' site unknown, and Horradill Head, perhaps the head of the Hartor Brook or South Hessary Tor which overlooks it, approaching Broken Borough, the ruined cairn in Tor Royal Newtake, from the west (SX 619723). We now proceed to Market Place Lodge, a most unlikely name to be associated with the Dartmoor wilderness, which in the seventeenth-century record is given as 'plain lodge', thought to be possibly a garbled reference to ruins near Sam Parr's

House near Whiteworks, and referred to in 1354 when the Black Prince said that Foresters in calving time should make lodges to tend the young deer. We again go south to 'Crannaberr' (Plympton) or 'Cranelaketor' (Ashburton), the possibilities here being either the top of Crane Hill (SX 622 690) or Great Gnats Head (SX 617 679), the latter being marked as Crane Hill on a nineteenth-century Eylesbarrow Mine map. The next point of reference is the 'Dunnagoat Stone' somewhere near the head of the Wollake, which is referred to in the seventeenth-century record as 'Turnagott Stone in Woollake Haw'. Is the word 'goad' or 'gote' significant here? The term 'Gote' has been used to describe an artificial water course and where water was bridged over, but not apparently in Devon (*English Dialect Dictionary*, J.Wright 1898), but no doubt there were also other meanings. May this be a reference to the stone at Duck's Pool (SX 625 679), from which the Wollake tinners drained the water through their workings? From the Dunnagoat Stone we go south-east to 'St Peter's Cross', in other words 'Petre's Cross' (SX 654 654) on Western Whittabarrow. Our next point of reference in the Plympton seventeenth-century record is given as 'and soe watershut the top of the Hill towards Pyles Beacon' which in 1786 becomes 'and so water Shutt the same Hill to Piggow Beacon', whilst the conterminous boundary of Ashburton Stannary gives the line of their bounds here as 'to threeberry and from thence to a Stone called Hobba Jame's Cross and from thence to the Range of Stones untill you come to Butterdon Borough'.

This Ashburton line is clear enough – Three Barrows, Hobajohn's Cross and the tumulus on Butterdon Hill – with no mention of the 'water shut', Piggon Beacon or Pyles Beacon, so what line was Plympton pursuing?

Somers Cocks suggests Main Head, the head of the Lud Brook as being the spring but this is far from the original Pyles or Piles, Beacon and Piggon Beacon is usually associated with Ugborough or eastern Beacon. Might the Water Shut be the head of the Scad near Spurrells Cross? Finally we again have a difference in points of reference between Ashburton and Plympton, the former using 'Seven Stones Cross' and the latter Modbury Steeple, before proceeding to the sea via St Michael's Burgh, Burgh Island.

Stannary Law required that tinners' bounds, that is the bounding of their sett, be marked. The charter dated 1201 gave tinners the right to 'mine for tin and dig turves for smelting tin everywhere in the moor and fiefs of Bishops, abbots and Counts as they have been accustomed to do', but by 1574 they were restricted from entering meadows, gardens, etc. where they had formerly been able to search for their tin. In 1752 a Convocation provided that 'by the common usage and custom of the Stannaries, any tinner may bound with tin bounds any wastrel lands within the County – that are unbounded or void of lawful bounds; and also any several and enclosed lands that have been anciently bounded and assured for wastrel by payment of the toll tin before that the hedges were made upon the same: and also may cut bounds in the Prince's several and inclosed ancient assessionable Duchy manors according to the ancient custom and usage within the said several Duchy Manors'. They were still virtually a law unto themselves.

The earliest type of tin bounding is described in the second half of the sixteenth century as follows:

The manner of bounding is most commonly to make four corner bounds, two at the head of the work and two more at the tail, cutting up three turves in every corner, and so consequently their side and head bounds with three turves in every place, one directly against the other.

Another somewhat later quote from the eighteenth century says:

they (the tin bounds) are limited by holes cut in the turf, and the soil turned back upon the turf which is cut in the form of a mole hill, and directly facing containing sometimes an acre – sometimes the bounds are marked with stones, and not turves, in order to preserve evidence of the limits of the bounds.

The cutting of turves is somewhat similar to the cutting of the parishes' initials that we have already seen employed in Lydford parish in the eighteenth century, and at 'Two Crosses' on manorial bounds in Widecombe parish. The more permanent small groups of six stones may also be found if a diligent search is made. Some of these are called Stannaburrows, i.e. relating to the Stannary. Crossing refers to seeing several on Down Ridge where tinning has taken place over several centuries; some years ago the author saw a very fine example above the left bank of Middle Brook (Bala country near Shipley). The tinners have left us with many indications of their former endeavours, not only the spoil heaps which are to be found in almost every moorland valley, but also numerous knacking mills, blowing houses, mortar and mould stones, etc., all part and parcel of the processes involved in the crushing and smelting of the tin ore. However 'set' boundstones relating to tinning are comparatively few and far between, and of eighteenth and nineteenth-century origins, when the setts became considerably larger than those of earlier times, many using natural features, etc.

Dockwell Mine, in the Manor of Jordan, was described by the late Hermon French (T.D.A. 1962) under the title 'A Forgotten Manor in Widecombe in the Moor', when an application to have proclaimed a pair of tin bounds dates from 1759, encompassing much of Jordan bordering on the West Webburn and held in the names of Roger Hannaford and Robert Mann. The bounds cut and pitched on 17th April 1759 were:

The Head Weare of which is on Hambledon Hill a little under Stoneslade Tor; the first side bound east by Bluestone near Kingshead Corner; the second side bound east on Wind Tor by a stone; the third side bound east near Watergate; the fourth side bound east in a field on Quannon [Corndon] a little distance from Jordan Mill; the first side bound west near Clay Park Corner [on Hatchwell]; the second side bound west in a field of Blackaton called Middle Park; the third side bound west in Broadaford Hill a little above the house; and the river leat and tail bound in a field of Quarronford called Bridge Park, a little below the steps.

The reservoir is still identifiable, and on the east side of the Wind Tor there is a rock bearing the letters 'M' and 'R' side by side which may possibly refer to these bounds.

At the head of the West Webburn there is a plain set stone which may mark the extent of East Birch Tor

Stannaries: East Birch Tor boundary stone. SX 6887 8086

Mine at SX 691 814. East Birch Tor Mine, called 'Headland' by Crossing, and extending eastwards from the middle of Chaw Gully, a deep surface working, to the West Webburn valley, also has the only known tinners' boundstone bearing the full name of the mine. It is at the western extremity of their sett, where it adjoins the old Vitifer Mine and works the same lode. The boundstone, a rectangular slab; bears the legend 'East Birch Tor' at SX 6887 8086. This mine is first recorded as such in 1836, in 1848 known as the East Birch Tor Tin Mining Co., and in 1852 became the New Birch Tor and Vitifer Consols Tin Mining Co.

Another inscribed tinners' boundstone is a natural one at Knack Mine on the upper reaches of the river Taw near Steeperton Hill at SX 614 885. In its early years the mine was known as Wheal Virgin, and the stone in question bears the letters 'WV'. It was recorded by

Tom Greeves as the result of papers found which give much insight into the working of this predominantly nineteenth-century mine, variously known as Knack Mine, Wheal Virgin and Steeperton Tor Tin Mine. Wheal Virgin is first recorded in 1799, and in 1836 a licence was granted for twelve months by the Duchy to a mine agent and two traders, all from Tavistock, to search for minerals. The bounds were:

> from a certain rock on Stone marked WV on the eastern side of the shaft known by the name Wheal Virgin to the length of three hundred fathoms Westward, being together seven hundred fathoms on the course of the lode on which the said shaft is now sinking, and one hundred and fifty fathoms north and south thereof.

The bounds here stated are very restricted compared with many other licences granted at this period of time for, as the working of the tin became a more and more expensive operation, sinking shafts as opposed to seeking alluvial deposits and the later openwork 'beam' surface workings, the setts tended to be larger and larger, with adventurers and companies working them, rather than individuals as had been the case in the time of the 'old men'.

The buildings of Wheal Virgin are on the west side of the river, as is the lode and shaft, whilst on the eastern side there is a fine tinners' reservoir and the site of the wheelpit, etc. In October, 1854 another licence was granted for working this mine, when the bounds were much more extensive covering an area of some six square kilometres, under the title 'Stepelton or Steeperton Tor', these bounds being described thus:

bounded on the south by a straight line drawn from the centre of Wild Tor to the centre of Dinger Tor; on the east by the river which flows along the Eastern side of Steeperton Tor; on the north by a straight line drawn from the confluence of the last mentioned river with the

Fig. 95 Wheal Virgin stone.

river Taw – to the centre of East Mill Tor, and on the West of a straight line drawn due south from the centre of the said East Mill Tor.

Through these papers it was possible to refer to many invoices and other documents concerning costs, employees, etc. In 1877 various pieces of machinery were purchased from Gobbet Mine (Swincombe) and for the sum of £65 they acquired 'Stamps Waterwheel, large Spun Wheel Shaft Bearings, Stamps Axle with frames and 12 Heads complete, Buddle Waterwheel, Round and Square Buddles and all gear belonging to the above and the Tin Chest Mine Bell and Windlass, all now at Gobbet Mine'. Imagine transporting all that gear up to such an isolated place as Knack Mine!

We also have evidence of other inscribed stones being used to mark the bounds of Whiteworks tin mine but in spite of having a detailed description of their sites, no-one has yet been able to find any of them. Their situations were set out in a description of the then bounds granted to William Thomas and Hugh White in 1836 by the Duchy, which were:

from Torr Royal Castle Eastward following the line of the Southern wall of Torr Royal Estate to a stone on the said wall marked 'WI' from thence in a straight line due south to the southern side of the Swincombe River,* from thence along the southern side of the said River to a Rock in the said river marked 'W11' where the Swincombe and Countycombe Rivers* meet, from thence South West by West in a direct line to intersect the old leat going to White Works on the North side of Fox Torr Hill, and so along West and Northward by the South side of the

said leat to a Rock in Sunny Corner marked 'W111' and from thence in a direct line northward to Torr Royal Castle, being a cottage in ruin at the Southern entrance to Torr Royal estate.

*(See Sketch for today's interpretation of the names of the various rivers and streams.)

The southern wall of Tor Royal newtake between the river Strane and the Swincombe was rebuilt a number of years ago, and whilst the repair was being carried

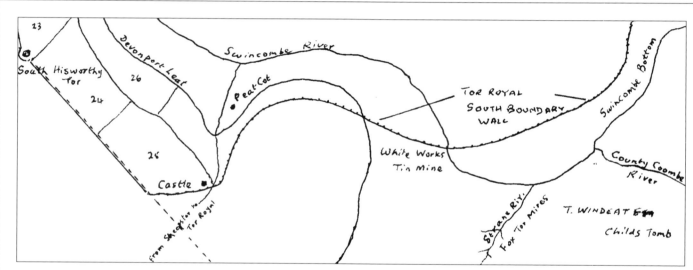

Fig. 96 Whiteworks Tin Mine Bounds of 1836.

The then Swincombe River equates with today's Strane as far as County Combe.
County Combe equates with today's upper Swincombe.
Strane Riv. equates with today's Nuns Cross Brook.
Plot 23 is named as Tor Park, Plot 24 South Park, Plot 25 Castle Park and Plot 26 as Summer Hill.

out a stone was noticed with an inscription, but put back into the rebuilt wall so that the inscribed face was no longer visible. This would have been 'W1'.

A reference to the Whiteworks boundstones also appears to have been made in papers relating to the proposed Swincombe reservoir project mooted in the late 1930s onwards, which is thought to have been the natural stone in the river bed marked 'W11', but most rocks are so encrusted with lichen that an identification has not been possible. The same applies to the one in 'Sunny Corner'.

Whilst the Whiteworks Mine workings are on the north side of Fox Tor Mire, there were at least two other mining ventures on the southern side. One of these was called Wheal Ann or Whealam, sited at the foot of a gully on Crane Hill and on a small stream of that name, the Whealam Stream. Associated with this mine is what is known as 'The Headless Cross', a granite pillar standing some 5ft in height, and having a small incised cross on its north-facing side, at SX 6130 6947. There are now no signs of the head or arms but in 1900, reported in the T.D.A. of 1901, a Dr Prowse found a stone that appeared to be at least part of the cross head, which whilst being of a very rough outline, had part of a cross in relief upon it. However, it did not fit directly onto the broken shaft that remained, other portions appearing to be missing. It is said that it was last seen in the 1950s. Prowse did not record the small incised cross now to be seen on the north side of the 'shaft'. Whether it was an original cross on an alternative route from the Plym to Tavistock via Walkhampton Common is open to doubt – sited as it is on a reave it may have been employed as a boundary marker, who knows? It is just

possible that it may be the original cross that used to occupy the boulder 'socket stone' where we now find the modern commemorative cross dedicated to Mrs S.L. Hutchison in 1966.

The River Walkham was worked for tin for much of its length, from medieval times up until the nineteenth century. The 'Staple Tor Sett' was one of three names applied to enterprises in the Merrivale area between the years 1806 and 1887. First known as 'Merryfield Bridge Mine', it later became 'Wheal Fortune' and finally 'Staple Tor Sett. Once again we are indebted to Tom Greeves for a description of the bounds, published in the *Plymouth Mineral and Mining Journal* (Vol.6, No.3), as follows:

> on the south by the road leading from Merrivale Bridge to Tavistock. On the west by the Western limits of the Commons of Devon from the said road to the corner of the hedge nearest the farm buildings at White Lake or Wedlake. On the north side by a straight line drawn eastwards from the said corner of the hedge to a place called Hanging Rock near King's Ford where the Forest Boundary intersects the Wallcombe or Walkham River – on the east by the said river to Merrivale Bridge.

Here we have apparent confusion once again, for some place the Hanging Rock in the region of Dead Lake Foot. However, in the nineteenth century, the Duchy claimed a line from Great Mistor north-westwards to Hanging Rock as their bounds, not that of the 1240 and 1608 perambulations. The main workings of this mine on the Walkham, including wheelpits, also embraced the upper part of the Beckamoor valley. By

1806, when the sett was first worked, the present road from Tavistock to Two Bridges had been completed for some years, part of the Tavistock Turnpike Trust system, having had the Turnpike Act passed in 1772 and the road completed in about 1776. The mine's lease specifically stated that it was not to interfere with the flow of water in the Grimstone and Sortridge leat, which, coming from the Walkham upstream, flowed across the sett, and above which the mine had their leat, possibly re-using an older disused channel of the Brook Mill or original Grimstone leat. This higher, now dry, channel of whatever origin once supplying the mine cuts downhill in a gully except where it crosses the present Grimstone leat, where there is a gully, showing that they must have laundered their leat over the G. & S. leat. This mine leat was, however, possibly extended after the mine closed to join the G. & S. leat below Merrivale Quarry as a temporary measure whilst the quarry, opened in 1876, re-routed that part of the G. & S. leat between the quarry and Windy Post, the cross on Beckamoor Combe, at a time when the mining ventures were at a standstill.

In recent years the site of a very productive and ancient tinners' mill was excavated at Little Horrabridge, prior to a garage being built on the site of an old stone shed. It had tinners' mortar stones built into its fabric which had been known to R. Hansford Worth. Excavation of the site was carried out by an archaeological group and produced a host of mortar stones in various types of rock, a broken mould stone and other interesting items. Many of these now make a feature to the entrance to the property, 'The Tinners Mill', others remaining within the garden. The stones in the gateway include two that are neither mortar nor mould stones, but are inscribed fragments. One bears the letters 'IB', which may possibly be a former tinners' boundstone, the other is simply inscribed with a Roman 'X', possibly the number ascribed to this mill as a registration number, in a similar fashion to the 'X111' inscribed on the door lintel of the left bank blowing house at Black Tor Falls on the Mewy.

Eylesbarrow Mine, spelt 'Ellisborough' in the earlier nineteenth-century records, was largely in the parish of Sheepstor, a sett being granted by the Lord of the Manor of Walkhampton, Sir Massey Lopes, in 1814. Extensions were later made to include Ringmoor Down and West and South Ellisborough in 1823. It was in this period, it is thought, that the whole complex, the finest on Dartmoor, was planned, using water from the Plym and its immediate tributaries to drive a series of water wheels as stamping mills running down the valley. By 1792 Crane Lake Mine, to the east of the main Eylesbarrow sett and within the Forest of Dartmoor, was in operation and in 1817 a grant was made for this mine under the title Wheal Katherine. Along the boundary of the Forest, between Eylesbarrow cairns and Crane Lake Foot, there are, on the mine maps, five 'Tin Bound' stones marked which appear to have been rough set stones, the lowest shown to be, or have been, on the left bank of the Plym opposite Crane Lake Foot. However the author has seen one, not in any of the five positions shown, and which appears to be in line between Eylesbarrow and Crane Lake Head, south of the miners' track into Princetown and of a shaft which is associated with post 1847 working, when a 50ft water wheel was installed at Deep Adit and had a flat rod system extending thus far to unwater it. So perhaps this stone defined a later grant, for in 1843, Deacon, the principal mover at Eylesbarrow went to law with Sir Ralph

Lopes over 'certain boundaries', and in 1845 a new lease was granted. By 1851 Wheal Katherine was 'in private hands', described then as 'the eastern-most sett' and in December 1851, a licence was granted to Henry Deacon by the Duchy of Cornwall.

The first grant made for 'Ellisborough' Mine, dated 1814, was shown on a 'Plan of Ellisborough Tin Mine in the Parish of Sheepstor Devon Land of Sir M. Lopes Bart' and described as:

Ellisborough Tin set together with the Original and late Grant … containing 653 acres. 1 rod. 31p. From Outham Gate in a straight line to Ellisborough abutting North on Walkhampton Common from Ellisborough in a straight line to the River Plym, abutting Northeast on the Forest of Dartmoor then down by the River Plym to Longstone Leat Head Weir, abutting Southeast on the said River Plym from Longstone Leat Head Weir along by the said leat to Thrussel Coombe abutting South on part of Sheepstor Common, from Thrussel Coombe in a straight line to Outham Gate abutting South West and west on another Part of Sheepstor Common.

The head weir of Longstone Leat was situated just below the confluence of Calveslake with the Plym, coming off the Plym's right bank. This sett was 653 acres in extent, over a square mile.

We are indebted to Dr Tom Greeves once again for a reference to six boundstones said to have been erected on 1837 to define a sett granted by the Duchy in the Erme Pits area measuring 400x150 fathoms; these boundstones said to have been inscribed with the letters 'EP' and a number. Nothing appears to be known about this sett, or its precise location, and whether they were referring to a site on the right bank of the infant Erme, above the left bank on what is now known as Erme Pitts Hill, or further afield on the Redlake where early workings have been referred to as 'Armed Pit'. The letters 'EP' did not, as might be expected, stand for Erme Pitts, but to the name of the mine, East Polgooth, in an attempt to persuade adventurers to invest in it by suggesting a linkage with the prosperous Cornish mine of that name.

The valley of the Wallabrook has also been extensively worked for tin, and at Riddon Farm, on the right bank and just within the Forest under Riddon Ridge, there is a most interesting tinners' mould stone built into the base of the wall facing on to the river at SX 6745 7656, (permission must be obtained from the farm). It has a sample mould of an eliptical shape rather than the more usual rectangular form. There is also a hardly-used mortar stone built into the same wall a few yards away. However, there is no sign left to say exactly where this blowing house was once situated but traces of tin slag were found upstream from the farmhouse several years ago. The eastern side of Riddon Ridge also bears the scars of more recent searches for tin in the shape of a couple of gullies running up to the crest. In the area there are a number of boundstones inscribed with a variety of initials, only one of which appears on any Ordnance Survey map. This is on the right bank of the Wallabrook and thus on the Forest boundary below Pizwell Bridge at SX 6713 7722 (Fig.97) opposite the point where a reave approaches the stream from the north-east. It has been referred to elsewhere as a tinners' stone but on the O.S. is simply marked 'B.S.' in their usual fashion

– it is inscribed with what appears to be FS/H, though other inscribed stones suggest that it should be read TS/H. Other inscribed boundstones have recently been rediscovered, and one of these resides in the grounds of the late Lady Sayer's property at Cator, having been used as a well cover, lettered 'RHR'. In a letter to the author she told him that, on being shown it, Hansford Worth said it was probably a tinners' stone too. This led me to assume that that was so but the pattern of the several other inscribed stones now known, and in situ, on the eastern flank of Riddon Ridge suggests that this is not the case and that they represent the bounds of properties. Within the cairn circle at SX 6680 7626 a recumbent stone bears the letters 'TS/H' on one side and 'RHR' on the other, the mason having used the second downstroke of the 'H' as the downstroke of the second 'R', as are the others so inscribed. To the west-north-west at SX 6665 7635 another 'RHR' stone stands near what appears to be tinners' trial pits. Yet another 'RHR' stone, with a crudely inscribed 'K' on the reverse side, lies near Fenny Ford at SX 7628 7600. At SX 6652 7645 a further inscribed stone is set on the line of an ancient boundary lettered 'TS' on its northern side. North-east of this another lettered 'TS/H' stands near a fine large hut circle at SX 6658 7665. Yet another, not in situ, is to be found leaning against a building associated with Whiteslade, otherwise known as Snaily House, lettered 'SL'.

Not connected with these boundstones, but in a rough line with the hut circle and the stone on the Wallabrook, there is one with an inscribed cross, apparently ancient but of unknown origin.

From her recent book, an in depth study of certain deserted Duchy farms (*Dartmoor Forest Farms*, Devon Books), Elisabeth Stanbrook has established that the boundstones inscribed 'TS' and 'TSH' were erected circa 1754 by a Thomas Smerdon, and that those inscribed 'RHR' refer to a Robert Henry Rogers, of unknown date. We can now be certain that they do not refer to tinners' setts; what other purpose could there be, for the higher part of Riddon Ridge was never enclosed? It has been suggested to the author that they may refer to rights to cut vags by the Duchy to tenants of Whiteslade, going one step further than the Manor of Dunstone, where the tenants were obliged to cut their initials in the turf to show the Reeve who had been cutting the vags. We do not know the original site of 'SL' but the initials stand for the Reverend Samuel Lane, and the letter 'K' for Kivill, both of whom had tenements in Babeny.

In the *Dartmoor Magazine* of Autumn 1999, mention was made of two more stones which had been found, and re-erected by the National Park Authority; and in the Autumn 2000 edition, yet another had come to light.

In an identical fashion to the way the letters 'H' and 'R' are linked on some Riddon stones, we also have others in the Mary Tavy area which relate to a mining sett. The two examples known to the author are numbered '1' and '5' so must be two of a series of at least five; here the letters linked together using a common limb are 'HB', one, the No.1, being shown as a 'Stone' on the old six inch Ordnance Survey map. It is now situated on the grass verge outside a house called 'Hilnor' on the Mary Tavy/Brentor road, near where the O.S. map marks 'Wheal Hope Shaft'. The other, No.5, is now acting as a step across a gateway to Downland Farm and has obviously been moved. Wheal Hope, with others, was incorporated into Wheal Friendship

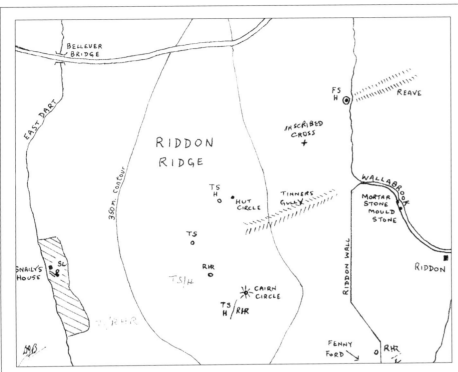

Riddon Ridge: RHR. SX 6665 7635

Fig. 97 *Sketch map of Riddon Ridge showing B.S.s/Rock with TS/H.*

Situated between the walls of Babeny and Riddon as they approach Fenny Ford, a RHR stone leans against a K stone. SX 7628 7600

283

in 1796. Another, number unknown, was put down a mine shaft in a clearing-up operation.

Bennett's Cross on the Moretonhampstead/Two Bridges road is most likely to have originally been erected as a Guide Stone, but it now serves as a bound-stone on the Chagford/North Bovey parish bounds, and as a boundary marker for Headland Warren. In addition it is near or on the famous bounds of Vitifer Mine. Crossing in *Ancient Crosses* says that 'a few loose stones will be observed near Bennett's Cross, the marks which are set up when the tin-bounds are renewed once a year. These stones are then placed as the the country people have it "brandis-wise"; that is in the form of a brandis, the name given to the triangular stands on which kettles are set on the hearth'. These are no longer to be seen!

There have been several tin mines within the Forest where their bounds touch upon Holne, and one of these was, from the mid-1800s called Hens Roost Mine or, at times known as Hexworthy Mine. As with a few other nineteenth-century mines, there were boundaries erected to define the bounds of this sett, though they do not appear extant. These bounds were described as follows:

On the east by the Boundary of the Forest from the South Eastern corner of Hexworthy Inclosures on the West bank of the Woobrook Southward to a Stone post marked H.M.1 on the said Forest boundary placed 440 fathoms South of the junction of Dry Lake Brook with Woobrook on the North by a straight line drawn true West from the South Eastern corner of Hexworthy Inclosures to a stone post marked H.M.2 erected at a distance from it of one mile and a quarter. On the South by a straight line parallel to the said Northern Boundary and drawn from the said Post marked H.M.1 Westward one mile and a quarter to a Post marked H.M.3 And on the West side by a straight line drawn from the said Post marked H.M.2 to the said Post marked H.M.3.

This description of the bounds dates from 1896 when a lease of one year was granted to Edward Mogeridge of Hexworthy and Edward Herbert Bayldon of Dawlish, one of a succession of leases granted to the latter, but the stone posts may date from 1852 when the name Hens Roost first appears.

12
WATER UNDERTAKINGS

The rainfall over Dartmoor is prodigious, and many of Devon's rivers have their source in the blanket bogs of this upland region. Their waters have been utilised by all manner of industry through the centuries; in the early days of 'tin streaming' in medieval times, the rivers were even diverted so that they washed through the workings to remove impurities. Later the water-wheel was introduced to provide power from the thirteenth century, a 'stream' of water being conducted to these by artificial open channels known as 'leats', sometimes over distances of several miles. The tinners used water-wheels in their 'blowing houses' or 'tinners mills' to propel the stamps that crushed the ore, and to work the bellows necessary to fan the charcoal in the furnace to a sufficiently high temperature to smelt the ore and obtain white tin. Later with the introduction of shaft mining the water-wheel provided the power needed to pump out unwanted water from these shafts.

Many other industries, principally the host of corn and woollen mills situated in the in-country, also relied on water for their power. Leats were dug to all these installations to provide a 'head' of water to propel the wheels, and rights to water were jealously guarded, some having to seek an untapped source well into the heart of the moor. Farm pot-water leats were often, where it was a communal supply, restricted in the amount permitted to be drawn off; regulated by means of what are called 'Bull's Eyes' or Inch Holes.

These are stones placed across the bank of the leat having a drilled hole of a specified diameter, usually an inch, sometimes 1½ inches, so that those furthest from the source are not denied a supply. There are several examples of these on the Grimstone and Sortridge Leat taking its supply from the right bank of the River Walkham some distance above Merrivale Bridge, which besides supplying Grimstone and Sortridge also supplies various cottages and farmsteads at Moortown, Oakley, Reddicliffe and the Dartmoor Inn. Holne Moor leat is another which, taken off the O'Brook, supplies Middle Stoke and Seale's Stoke farms by concrete bull's eye 'stones'; whilst the nearby West Stoke Farm obtains its supply from the Holne Town Gutter, a leat providing the village with a supply from the Ringleshutes Stream, where an old granite 'bull's eye' is in use today, replacing an even older one which still lies discarded on the bank. The number and complexity of these leats is a subject on its own and provides a fascinating facet of Dartmoor's past and present.

The first major leat taking water for mass human consumption was, of course, Drake's Leat, built in the late sixteenth century. This took water from the Meavy or Mewy under Sheepstor, at a point now inundated by Burrator Reservoir known as 'Head Weir', and supplied the town of Plymouth and the ships being victualled there. A dry granite lined section, this granite lining of a much later date, may still be seen running from the foot of the dam. Other sections can be found on Roborough Down, and tunnelled sections have also been exposed within Plymouth when foundations for new buildings have been excavated. Constructed between December 1590 and April 1591, it was some 18 miles long and six to seven feet in width, originally with just an earthen bank. When the Burrator dam was being constructed in 1893 the leat was laundered through an apperture left in the base of the dam and during the summer of that year, when there was a drought, it took the whole of the water of the Mewy. That was one of the troubles with the open leat system, insufficient water in times of drought, and the fact that it froze in the depths of winter so that no water got through to the town, but the old leat had, nevertheless, served Plymouth for three hundred years before pressures of rising population and necessary improved sanitary conditions made it imperative to construct a dam to form a reservoir.

It would seem that the Plymouth Water Authority got up to various ruses to increase their supply of water in times of shortage, and letters in the Maristow papers include allusions to at least one such case. In March 1853 a letter to the Maristow Estate solicitors, Messrs Whiteford & Co., of Plymouth, instructed them to seek payment of the sum of £5 from the Corporation 'as compromise of the trespass on Sir Ralph's property in the summer of 1844 by the tapping of Claceywell Pool'. A later letter suggests that he had been offered the same at an earlier date but had refused to accept it. In a third letter he is again pressing his claim, but no record of the outcome was found. It would have been simplicity itself to breach the wall of the pool and allow the water thus

Pictured clockwise from top:

Found recumbent at SX 578 741, south west of the North Hessary Mast.

One of the 1932 stones erected at Meavy Head.

PCWW 1917 on the road near the head of the Meavy. The stones at Sheepstor are dated 1919.

Water Works: A cast iron marker for Plymouth Corporation Water Works near the remains of Burrator Halt. Possibly on the line of extraction pipes.

released to flow down into the Newlicombe lake and thence into the Mewy, where it would have been diverted into the leat at Head Weir.

When it was obvious that a reservoir would have to be constructed in the 1880s, the original proposal was that one should be built at the site of Head Weir, and an Act of Parliament was passed to this effect in 1885. It proposed to build a dam to hold back 350 million gallons of water, but this scheme was abandoned when it was found that the rock structure thereabouts was unsuitable as a foundation due to faulting. Next in 1889 came the proposal to build the dam above the junction of the Mewy and the Hartor Brook, but this went against local opinion. The trial drill holes across the line of the site can still be seen, capped off where the sample cores were taken. Land had been purchased at the time of the original intention to build at Head Weir but it was not until 1898 that Burrator was completed, having a watershed of some 5360 acres and a capacity to hold 657 million gallons of water over an area of 117 acres. During the period 1923–28 the dam was heightened by a further 10 feet so that the capacity was increased to over 1000 million gallons.

The catchment area impounds the waters of the Mewy, Hartor Brook, Newlicombe Lake, Narrator Brook and Denecombe Brook. The boundary including extra land acquired in 1916 by Plymouth Corporation was not marked with boundstones until 1917, when a number were erected, approximately five to six feet in height, square of section and with a peaked top, bearing the inscription 'P C W W' and date. These were placed at points on the divide between Yennadon Down and the valley of the Yes Tor Brook, passing near Goadstone Pool thence to a point under Leedon Tor to North Hessary Tor between Yestor and Mewy country; from North Hessary Tor along the line of the Forest boundary crossing the Plymouth road to South Hessary Tor and Nun's Cross and thence to Eylesbarrow, between Mewy and Swincombe country; from Eylesbarrow westward to Yellowmead Farm. Over Sheepstor itself the stones are dated 1919. A boundstone was not erected at North Hessary Tor. There the tor itself was incribed with similar lettering and date on its western side. This boundary line had, however, whilst keeping to the Forest bounds where these were involved, excluded the actual source of the Mewy which is within the Forest, and in that small area of bog there are four more bound-stones of smaller stature than the earlier ones dated 1932 when this land must have been purchased from the Duchy. Between South Hessary and Eylesbarrow the Corporation's stones are intermingled with those plain ones of the Duchy set up in the latter part of the nineteenth century.

Besides the water obtained from the sources named, Burrator also receives a certain amount from the Devonport leat, constructed in 1797; the whole water system having been amalgamated when the dam was built. The Devonport leat had been constructed to supply Plymouth Dock, which expanded so rapidly in the first quarter of the nineteenth century that by 1824 it changed its name to Devonport. The original course of this leat was about 30 miles in length, but now only the upper part, the moorland section, remains functional, taking water from the West Dart, the Blackabrook and the Cowsic as far as Burrator, augmenting the Plymouth supply via a spectacular cascade.

Venford Reservoir on Holne Moor was opened on 26 June 1907, to augment more local supplies for the Torbay town of Paignton which at that time had an independent Urban District Council. Paignton had been out-growing its earlier supply for many years as the population expanded rapidly in the latter part of the nineteenth century, and in 1898 Mr Vanstone, the Paignton Water Engineer, suggested that Holne Moor might be a suitable site for a reservoir to the council, trapping the waters of the Venford Brook. Negotiations with the then Lord of the Manor of Holne, the Hon. Richard Dawson, were successfully concluded whereby Paignton acquired an area of some 700 acres of land for the sum of £11 per acre, with the Holne Commoners being compensated for the loss of grazing rights in the sum of £422, to be divided between them in due proportion. In August 1901 a tender of £27 583 was accepted for the building of the dam and ancillary work, but as at Burrator there were problems with finding a solid base on which to build the foundations so that the final cost to Paignton was no less than £119 000 plus. However that figure included the additional cost of raising the height of the dam from the originally proposed 51ft to 54ft, which in the calculations of Mr Vanstone doubled the capacity of the reservoir. In one month in 1910, 13 581 000 gallons of water were extracted, intially by way of a single 9in pipe but by 1911 another similar pipe had been installed.

With the building of the dam, the original course of the road from Holne to Hexworthy was amended, so that now we can still trace the sunken approaches to the old crossing of the Venford Brook over a single arch bridge. This never appears in times of drought as do others (as at Fernworthy) as, since 1934,

Venford Brook water is supplemented by a piped supply from the Swincombe, pumped for a distance of over five miles.

Granite boundstones were erected around the perimeter of the land purchased by Paignton and are set at fairly regular intervals of about 200 yards. Each is inscribed 'RD/H' (Richard Dawson, Holne) on that side of the stone that is still Holne land, and on the reverse side 'PUDC'. The area so marked extends as far as the Sandy Way and Holne Ridge, almost to the foot of Ryder's Hill, and on the west side along the Venford Brook/O'Brook divide.

Above left: *Holne Reservoir. B.S. inscribed RD/H - Richard Dawson of Holne (PUDC - Paignton Urban District Council - on rear). Near Sandy Way.*

Above right: *B.S. on the Venford Brook/O Brook divide, showing PUDC inscription.*

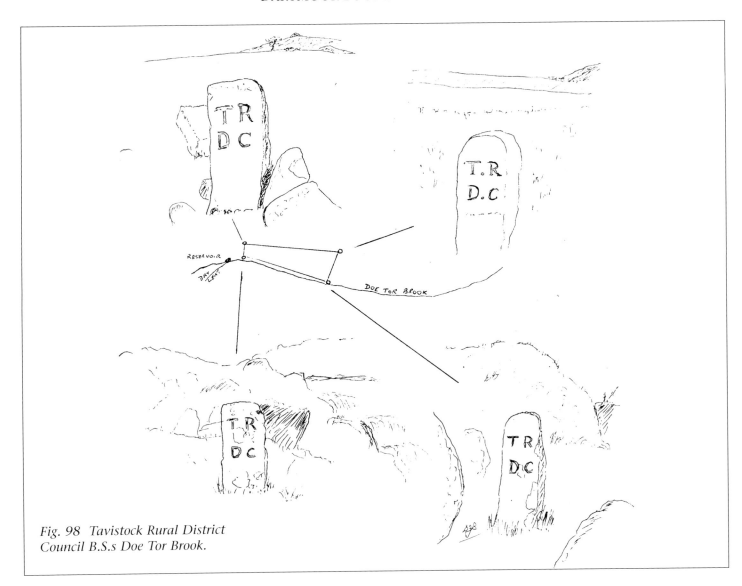

Fig. 98 Tavistock Rural District Council B.S.s Doe Tor Brook.

On the western side of the moor, Meldon reservoir is a much more recent and more controversial construction, but the waters of the West Ockment have been used by the North Devon Water Board since 1945. Above Vellake Corner there is a walled enclosure around a section of the river, and at a short distance from this wall, and around it, is a series of 11 small boundstones of concrete construction bearing the letters 'N/D/W/B'.

Further south on the western fringe of the moor another very small scheme supplied water to Lydford under the auspices of the Tavistock Rural District Council. This supply came from the Doe Tor Brook; there was no reservoir as such, just a fenced-off rectangle around the extraction point, from which there was an open leat channel. On the four corners of the rectangular enclosure there are granite boundstones bearing the initials of the Tavistock Rural District Council 'TRDC' at SX 541 852. Close by the left bank of the brook is the No.15 stone of the Willsworthy War Department markers.

Hardly a moorland stream has escaped being utilised in one way or another, and electricity has been produced for many years from water power at Chagford, Mary Tavy and Morwellham. We now see Meldon producing hydro-electric power at certain times of the year. What next?

North Devon Water Board: One of the 11 boundary markers inscribed 'N/D/W/B' around the West Ockment enclosure. SX 5601 8990

Tavistock RDC: One of four boundstones inscribed T.R.D.C. On the Doe Tor Brook.

13
THE HANGING STONES ON THE RIVER WALKHAM

There are many instances of Dartmoor place-names being repeated on different parts of the moor, and this is quite understandable when descriptive of that place, but when we find the same name applied to what appears to be a specific object at differing locations then we have troubles. It is like trying to solve a 'who done it' with red herrings and contrary opinions included. The Walkham Hanging Stones or Rocks are one such example.

Two of the more widely read earlier books on Dartmoor must be Samuel Rowe's original *Perambulation of Dartmoor*, published in 1848 from notes made in 1827-28, and William Crossing's *Guide to Dartmoor* of 1912, the latter by a man who had walked the moor for decades and talked to locals and obtained his information first hand.

Of the Walkham area of the Forest Bounds Rowe comments (p.217):

The Forest Boundary, which we last marked at Mis Tor Pan, from thence it crosses the Walkham at the Hanging Rock, to Deadlake Head,

Crossing saying (p.127):

Then descending the steep slope (from Great Mis Tor) we reach Walkham at what is known as the Hanging Rock, immediately opposite to a combe down which flows a little stream called Dead Lake. To the Hanging Rock, which marks the extreme northern part of the Walkhampton Common, the river forming its western boundary, the oft repeated story of the sheep-stealer attaches. In the attempt to climb over it with a sheep on his neck, he was strangled.

Both of these comments unequivocally place the Hanging Rock on the left bank of the Walkham, directly opposite Dead Lake Foot on the ancient Forest boundary, though Dead Lake was not mentioned in 1240 when the perambulators recorded the line hereabouts as 'et inde per mediam Mystor usque ad Mewyburghe et inde ad Lullingesfote'. (Rowe p.290.) However in 1608-09 it became:

through the midst of Mistorr moore to a rock called Mistorpann, and from thence linyallie to Deadlakeheadd wch. they thinke to be the next bound wch is called in the old records Meuborough. (Rowe p.314.)

Though this Hanging Rock ('A' on Fig 100) is not

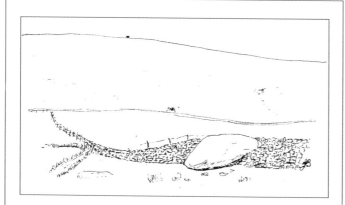

Fig. 99 Hanging Rocks at Shillapark and near Kings Ford: Shillapark ('B' on Fig 100) SX 5513 3760; Kings Ford ('C' on Fig 100) SX 5550 7774.

now identifiable, it would indeed be on the Forest boundary as we know it, and a far more plausible explanation of the name attached to it is made by Mrs Elizabeth Bidder, daughter of William and Johanna Lillicrap of Cot House on Ringmoor Down in her narrative dating from the 1830s, where she says:

> at the drift driving in the fall of the year, when cattle were gathered off the moor, and farm 'prentice lads at their first drift, they were suspended by their necks to the Hanging Stone by way of 'footing' or initiation into the rights of the moor-men.
> (T.D.A. 1893, Arts and Crafts on Dartmoor, etc. by J. Phillips)

This Theo Brown enlarges upon, (T.D.A. 1961), saying:

> during the round-up he would be taken to the Hanging Stone, an ancient forest boundary mark deep in the northern sector of the moor, mentioned in 1280. Here a halter of steel cable would be put around his neck and attached to a projecting rock, so that the boy was suspended with his feet just touching the grassy slope. Then his sponsors left him and got on with the drift. They did not return to release him for about 24 hours... A few years ago not believing this, I made enquiries and was immediately told of two Postbridge men then living who had undergone this ordeal. It is not recorded that anyone had died from it.

'Deep in the northern sector of the moor' could well apply to opposite Dead Lake Foot, more so than to other Hanging Stones to be mentioned later, and this explanation of the name more likely than Crossing's. However, if we now turn to the early nineteenth-century descriptions of the bounds of Whitchurch parish (1801 and 1832 are identical and both before the Tithe Commutation) (D.R.O. 1508/M), we see that they placed a Hanging Stone much further down-stream, thus:

> From thence to Roolstor, from thence by the remains of a Stone Wall or Fence to Hanging Stone, from thence to Walkham River

This Hanging Stone ('B' on Fig 100) is still on the Whitchurch/Peter Tavy parish bounds, the stone being the massive rounded boulder on the line of the Roos Tor Reave, and which has been incorporated into the outer wall of the Shillapark enclosures at SX 5513 7630. The much later but complementary Peter Tavy account of their bounds as recorded in 1923 and since, approaching the stone from the opposite direction, (*Tavistock Times* report, 22 June 1923), says:

> from Whitebarrow, over Cock's Hill, through Didlake Wells to Didlake Foot, down River Walkham by the right hand side, on to Hanging Stone, where we claim half of the river. Up the hill by the right hand side of Park's Hedge, out-side boundary of Shilla Parks...'

This is the lowest of the three positions given for a Hanging Stone or Rock on the Walkham, and it is interesting to note that a small tin mine, active between the years 1806 and 1887, going by the names Merryfield Bridge, Wheal Fortune and Staple Tor Sett mines successively, had bounds in this area. In May 1840 a licence was granted 'to work for minerals on a mine called Wheal Fortune in the Parish of Whitchurch within the following limits and allowing the miners to search for tin within enclosed land, i.e. Shillaparks (T.A.P. Greeves, *Plymouth Mineral & Mining Journal* Vol.6, No.3, 1976), as follows:

> so far north as the enclosures of a tenement called Shell Park, so far east as the River Walkham, so far south as the Turnpike road leading from Tavistock to Merrivale Bridge and so far west as seven hundred fathoms from the aforesaid River Walkham.

There is at that time no mention of a Hanging Rock, but in a later licence granted in 1859 to the Staple Tor Sett, the wording is amended to:

> On the South by the road leading from Merrivale Bridge to Tavistock. On the West by the Western limits of the Common of Devon from the said road to the corner of the hedge nearest to the farm buildings at White Lake or Wedlake. On the North by a straight line drawn Eastward from the said corner of the hedge to a place called Hanging Rock near Kings Ford where the Forest boundary intersects the Wallcombe or Walkham River. On the East by the said River to Merrivale Bridge aforesaid.
> (same P.M.M.J. reference as above.)

Is this in fact just a rewording of the same bounds as those granted in 1840? Neither bounds are entirely within Whitchurch parish, but the distance of 700 fathoms west from the Walkham corresponds to the distance to the Wedlake enclosures at SX 5400 7730, so are we here concerned with the 'B' Hanging Stone or is it our third candidate, 'C', that is being referred to, situated between 'A' and 'B'?

At about the same time as this reference to a Hanging Stone was made, it was also mentioned in a licence to remove granite from the commons north and south of the Tavistock road, extending north to include Roos Tor and the Staple Tors, the northern boundary being defined as:

> a straight line from a post marked P.T.G.1 placed by the boundary of the Commons at or near Wedlake (Peter Tavy) to a stone post marked P.T.G.2 on the west bank of the River Walkham at or near Hanging Rock.
> (T.D.A. 1981, p.33 Granite Working on Pew Tor, etc. by Helen Harris)

It seems most probable that this Hanging Rock is the same as that referred to in the Staple Tor Sett quote, and is situated at SX 5550 7774, marked 'C' on sketch, a fractured boulder lying in the right side of the river near the point where the dry Wheal Fortune tinners leat is taken off. What is clear is that the granite sett used the upper corner of the Wedlake enclosures, for in 1987 the author and his wife found the original P.T.G.1 stone about ten yards from the corner of the wall at SX 5475 7805, lying recumbent and covered in moss. It is an unshaped piece of stone, only about 2ft 6in in length, now approximately 2ft above ground, inscribed in two lines 'PT/G1'. Unfortunately, the 'stone post marked P.T.G.2' could not be found, though a natural rock in the right position near the dry leat channel bears the letters 'PT' and 'TO'. It was this middle 'C' Hanging Stone or Rock that the Duchy of Cornwall claimed to be on the Forest Bounds, taking a line in a north-westerly direction from Great Mistor, and show it thus on their 'Historical' map, though this is but of nineteenth-century origin when there was so much doubt about several points on this boundary. One suspects that there was some confusion between Rowe's Hanging Rock opposite Dead Lake Foot and this our 'C' stone. The doubt and uncertainty is borne out by the fact that the Walkhampton Tithe map which also shows the 'C' stone marked as Hanging Rock and Whitchurch parish extending thus far northwards, possibly attempting to meet the requirements of the wording of the Whitchurch bounds, who did not, in fact, claim to go further north than Shillaparks.

The Charter of Isabella de Fortibus, dated 1278, affirmed the granting of the Manors of Bickleigh, Buckland Monachorum and Walkhampton to the formation of Buckland Abbey, the description of the bounds of Walkhampton in the area in which we are interested reading 'and from Walkhampton to the boundaries of Dartmoor, on the northern part of Mistor, and thence towards the south by the boundaries of the Verderers of Dartmoor, that is to say, by Mistorhead and Hysforchres' (T.D.A. Vol.7, The Cistercian Houses of Devon by Robert Dymond, p.355), i.e. Dead Lake Foot. The Rev. James Holman Mason, Master Forester and Deputy Rider of the Forest was so uncertain of himself in trying to define this part of the Forest bounds, and others, that in a letter to the Rev. J.P. Jones, Vicar of North Bovey, dated 5 October 1844, he says:

> I have referred to the Charta Isabellae de Fortibus of Buckland Abbey... In the description of the charter which you have lately obtained is

there a different wording as to the part I have referred to? There is a great rock in the north side of the Walkham river named Hanging Stone, close to which is Kingford; viz the bound between the Forest (Lydford) and Walkhampton; but the lord of that manor would go higher up the stream before he turns south...

The Walkham here virtually runs north to south, our 'C' stone being if anything on the northern side. Sir Ralph Lopes, then Lord of the Manor of Walkhampton, whilst not naming the Hanging Rock or Stone, was obviously trying to get his bounds restored to their original course, his steward writing to him on 30 March 1852 saying:

I enclose sketches of the boundaries between your commons and the Forest which I hope will give you an idea of the points in dispute ... our contention is for Deadlake Foot from Mistor...
(W.D.R.O. Maristow Papers.)

It was not until 10 August, 1867 that a Deed of Agreement was drawn up between the Duchy and the Manor of Walkhampton restoring the ancient boundary line from Great Mis Tor to Dead Lake Foot.

That there was a specific term, namely 'Footing', applied to the initiation ceremony that had to be undergone by boys before they were allowed to become fully fledged members of the drifts, leads one to think that it was a practice that had taken place over a considerable period of time. The Hanging Stone, or Leaning Rock near Hexton Tor in Shaugh Prior parish, an ancient menhir marked 'Standing Stone' on the O.S. maps, may also be where this practice took place in that southern quarter of the moor. However the probability of there having been more than one such site on a short stretch of the river Walkham seems most unlikely, and what we see in all the foregoing is error piled upon error.

Theo Brown, in giving the date of 1280 for Site 'A' is obviously referring to the Foundation Charter of Buckland Abbey, the gift of lands including the Manor of Walkhampton, whose bounds in that area went up the river Walkham as far as the ancient Forest bounds, thence turning south to Mistor. However no mention is made of a hanging rock and this place-name probably has a much later origin, perhap the eighteenth century. This 'A' site is the only one on the Walkham to which demise of a sheep stealer is associated, and is one of those listed by Leslie Grinsell in Folklore (Vol.96, 11, 1985), under the title 'Hangman's Stones and their Traditions'. However, in quoting Crossing as his source, he proceeds to list it under 'Lydford, Peter Tavy', thus placing it on the right bank of the river opposite to where Crossing put it. Grinsell gives several other examples widely spread over the country, generally sited on parish bounds. The name is also associated with sites of gibbets, which were also usually on parish boundaries, but in less isolated places than Dartmoor.

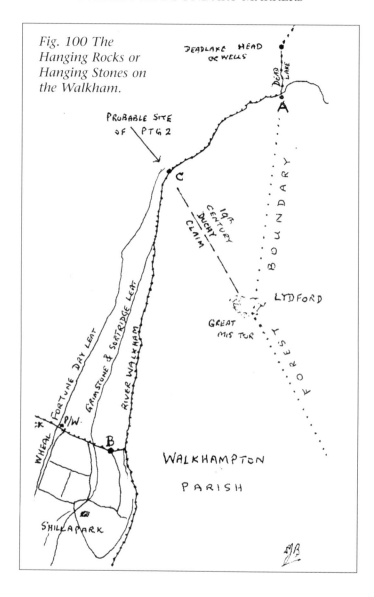

Fig. 100 The Hanging Rocks or Hanging Stones on the Walkham.

13
SOUTH HAMS SAXON CHARTERS

In the introduction brief mention has been made to two Saxon South Hams Charters dating from the ninth and tenth centuries, concerning boundaries of estates once thought to extend as far north as Dartmoor and the Forest bounds (Rose Troup T.D.A. 1929), but which have since been shown to encompass a far smaller area in the coastal region of the South Hams between the mouth of the river Erme and the Kingsbridge estuary by Finberg and others in more recent years*. The earlier of these is known as the 'om Homme' charter of 846AD, when Aethelwulf, King of the West Saxons 'grants to himself land om Homme'; and the later one, the Sorley charter of Eadgar, King of the Angles dating from 862AD. This latter was only discovered in Petre documents in the twentieth century, possibly retained by Sir William Petre following his purchase of various manors formerly owned by Buckfast Abbey prior to its dissolution in 1539.

*(Studies on Devon Charter Boundaries by Della Hooke – T.D.A. Vol.122, 1990.)

The bounds of the Sorley Charter certainly start 'from Kingsbridge out to Avon', but Troup takes us much too far north, interpreting 'West on the way to the Grey Stone' as being a reference to 'where Spurrell's Cross now is'. The term 'Grey Stone' is regularly used in relation to prominent stones marking a boundary, as on Hameldon and elsewhere, but here erroneously interpreted. She then takes us to 'the wyrttrum where the brook flows together', taking this to mean Glazemeet, where the West and East Glaze brooks converge. The 1557 Inquisition concerning the bounds of Brent Moor refer to a point 'pyrttrum', which might lead one to think her assertion is correct, but Finberg places the charter 'Wyrttrum' at the junction of minor brooks west of Kingsbridge on the boundaries of West Alvington and Churchstow parishes. The term appears to describe a certain type of location, a clearing in a wood, tree roots or the foot of a hill.

On the sixteenth-century map of Dartmoor the small portion of land bounded by the East and West Glaze brooks, and by a wall shown on the map to the north indicates an early settlement here, and the object depicted below this wall, 'a remarkable stone with 3 faces – like a pyramid – apparently so placed by men's hands to serve as a landmark for the three estates whose bounds meet at this point' is a typical description of a 'piked' stone, and the 1250 Torre Abbey Charter gives this northern point as 'Nywapitte'.

Troup takes us thence down the Glaze Brook to the Avon.

The earlier 'om Homme' estate described in the charter of 846AD includes some points common to the 962 Charter, and it is in the interpretation of this that Troup takes us to Redlake, far from the now accepted boundary. From Redlake she takes us to 'the tor at Mercecumbe Spring' which she suggests is Penn Beacon, far from the coastal site now attributed to this point of reference, and thence to 'Denewaldes Stone'. This she places, positively, 'in the northern section of Dendles Wood'. A 'Stone' is shown on the old 1890 six inch Ordnance Survey map at SX 6150 6526, but this is almost certainly the site of a Blachford Manor 'B/B' one. The later explanation of Denewald's Stone puts it at a point near Seven Stones Cross (SX 659 493), thought to have been a Longstone, which name, Langstone, is retained in the name of a local farm.

Troup also refers to the 'Old Way with the White Stones' as being the lengthy Butterdon Hill stone row on the Harford/Ugborough parish bounds but this, too, is far from where modern thinking puts the 'Old Way' and outside our limits, though a later reference to the 'Hoar Stone', another expression for a boundary marker, might have suggested Prowse's Rock under Western Beacon. 'Hoar', 'Hor', 'Har' or 'Hare' in connection with a boundary has already been mentioned in relation to Horrabridge, etc. Another probable instance of the use of this word is to be found at Chagford where, on the route out to Padley Common from New Street, the hill is called 'O'er Hill', a corruption of what was 'Hore Hill' on the 1841 Tithe map, and a considerable stretch of the old Exeter/ Okehampton road was known as the Harepath where it is on parish boundaries.

'Mere' is another word with a boundary connotation, one meaning being derived from the Anglo-Saxon 'Mearc', *Chambers Dictionary* defining it thus: 'Mere – a boundary; merestone, a stone which marks a boundary.' Thus a meresman was a person appointed to look after and affirm a particular boundary. Meacombe farm at the junction of the boundaries of the parishes of Chagford, North Bovey and Moretonhampstead may well have been so named for this reason, the Bronze Age burial chamber being very near to the point where they meet.

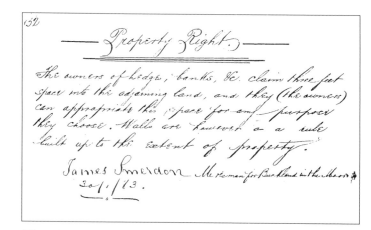

Fig. 101 *O.S. Boundary Report Book, Property Rights, 1883.*

15

PEADINGTON LANDSCORE

(endorsed 'Peding tunes land boundaries by Dart')

The Peadington landscore was first recognised for what it was by J.B. Davidson, who wrote of it more than a century ago in the T.D.A. of 1876. He had been examining various old documents formerly in the archives of the Dean and Chapter of Exeter, but at the time deposited in the Royal Albert Memorial Museum. It is a description of the bounds of a large Saxon estate, then unidentifiable, but which, later, the Rev. O. Reichell believed to belong to an episcopal charter relating to an unknown ecclesiastic estate.

Davidson described the document as late Anglo-Saxon, a strip of parchment measuring 13in x 3¼in, written in a style indicating that it dated from circa the mid-eleventh century, about the time of Edward the Confessor. However this document is almost certainly a copy, the original landscore formerly having been attached to or inserted into the charter itself, which would have been worded in general terms only. The original grant could possibly date from the eighth/tenth centuries; a Crediton charter dating from 739 granting land to the monastery there with extant documents dating from the tenth century, describing the bounds only as Peadington; another from the eleventh century including the wording of the whole charter, and a much later fifteenth-century copy of the bounds. Crediton was of monastic foundation until, in 909, it became the See, which was later transferred to Exeter in 1050 as the Saxon settlement of the country extended further westward.

Devon, west of the river Exe, was settled by the Saxons from about 750, with several settlements being made on or near the coast, other early charters relating to the South Hams dating from 846 (om Homme) and 962, the Sorley charter of Eadgar, king of the Angles, together with one covering Ipplepen and Abbotskerswell granted by Eadwig in 957.

Along, or near to, the South Devon coastline, there are several ancient settlements with names ending in 'ington', signifying their Saxon origins, and in Torbay we have no less than three; Goodrington later a sub-manor of Paignton, Cockington on the outskirts of Torquay and Paignton itself. Paignton is not a modern seaside resort as might be imagined at first glance, but has very early beginnings, though unfortunately we have no positive documentary record of the Saxon spelling of the name. It has been recorded that an Abbot Paega attended a Council of Clofesho in 803, and the *Place Names of Devon* suggest that Paignton's early name was 'Paegington', or Paega's Farm – can this be an earlier form of 'Peadington', especially if one considers that the Peadington landscore itself might well be a copy executed a century or so after the original land grant was made? At Domesday it was spelt 'Peintona' and has had many variations of spelling since, including Peintone (1237), Pynetun (1237), Peingtone (1260s), Paynton and Peynton (sixteenth/seventeenth centuries), 'Paington', otherwise 'Painton' (1654), Payington and Peyington (1567), etc., right through to the nineteenth-century Paington and Paignton.

The Manor of Paignton was certainly in the possession of the Bishops of Exeter at and before Domesday, the Exon Domesday Book entry reading:

> Peintona: Bishop Osbern has a manor called Peintona which Bishop Leofric held on the day in which King Edward was alive and dead, and it rendered geld for twenty hides. These can be ploughed by sixty ploughs. Of them the bishop has in demesne six hides and eight ploughs and the villeins have fourteen hides and forty-two ploughs. There the bishop has fifty-two villeins, and forty bordars, and thirty-six serfs, and five swineherds who render fifty swine, and four packhorses, and a salt work which renders ten pence and twenty head of cattle, and sixteen swine, three hundred and fifty sheep, and forty-one acres of wood, and eighteen acres of meadow, and forty of pasture; and it is worth yearly £50, and when he received it, it was worth £13.

Here we see no mention of a Dartmoor estate attached to the manor of Paignton, but by 1086 most of the large tracts of land, originally held under charter from the king from early times, had been broken down into Hundreds, and newly formed manors established on what had formerly been waste, followed in turn by the grouping of these manors into parishes. Nevertheless, Paignton Manor was very wealthy and prosperous, having increased in worth from £13 in 1072 to £50 in 1086. The Bishop's fat manors of Paignton, where a Bishop's Palace was built circa 1100, Bishop's Tawton and Crediton were each worth more than the whole endowment of many Devon monastic houses, besides owning the manors and Boroughs of Ashburton and Chudleigh, all of which remained in the hands of the See until the Dissolution in 1549.

It is a known fact that the Bishops of Crediton, and later Exeter, held the manor of Ashburton in Saxon times, whose bounds, as we shall see, are within the bounds defined in the Peadington landscore. The will of Bishop Aelfweald of Crediton, thought to date from circa 1008 to 1012, bequeathed, amongst other things:

> Tham aethelinge XL mansa goldes & thaera wildra aet Aeschburnan lande
> (to the nobelman 40 mancuses of gold & the wild beasts on Ashburton land)
> (A 'mansa' is the Saxon equivalent of the Norman hide.)

The Manor of Paignton had a common boundary, on its eastern side, with one of the other Torbay Saxon manors, that of Cockington, held by William at Domesday, and since this smaller manor also had a holding on Dartmoor at and after that time, one wonders whether Paignton might not have done so at least in Saxon times, especially since the bounds of Peadington and Cockington's holding also have a common boundary. One wonders how many other lowland Saxon manors might have had rights too, such as Ralph de Pomeroy who held Dunstone with Blackslade at Domesday.

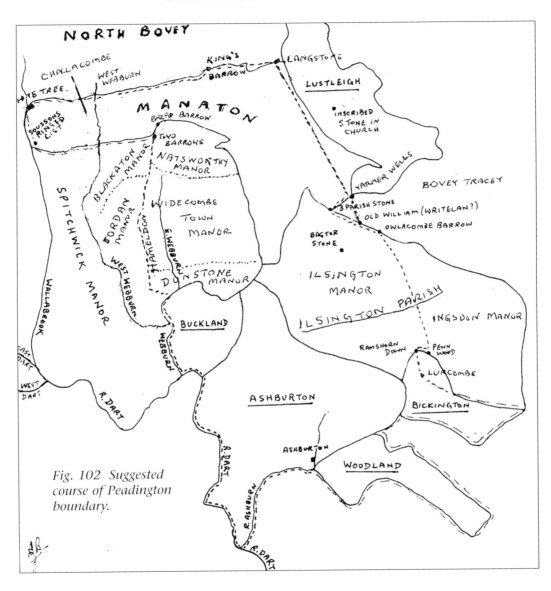

Fig. 102 Suggested course of Peadington boundary.

As we shall see, the boundary described in the Peadington landscore takes us in a clockwise direction, as do most other perambulations, similar to the thirteenth-century perambulation of the Forest of Dartmoor, generally using natural lasting features as points of reference, together with some Bronze Age remains, usually those of a funereal nature which, although elsewhere described as 'heathen' burials, were nevertheless considered to be sacrosanct. Their graves and barrows are sometimes referred to as 'Seven Stones'. Some of these ancient boundary markers are still quite easily identified, others far more puzzling, but more are either on, or close to, later parish bounds or the manors contained within them. It is generally found that old boundaries never disappear, but are amalgamated into later ones.

We commence our perambulation as follows:

1 'Peading tunes landscro thaer Aescburne ut scyt' –Peadington's land boundary at the Ashburn outfall:

The Ashburn, sometimes referred to as the Yeo in the past, gave its name to, and passes through, the ancient Stannary town of Ashburton, and enters the River Dart just below Dart Bridge, Buckfast. This is the 'outfall', still on the bounds of Ashburton and Buckfastleigh parishes, and where we start. As stated earlier the Bishops of Crediton and Exeter are known to have held both the Manor and Borough of Ashburton from early times.

2 'On Dertan stream od Wedeburne ut scyt' – along the Dart to Webburn outfall:

We now proceed upstream up the Dart to the point where the River Webburn enters the Dart at Buckland Bridge – plain sailing so far, but then we meet with difficulties in interpretation. With these difficulties in mind, it is preferable to take the next four lines of Peadington together, following the possible options open to us, thus:

3 'Up an Wedeburnan oth Widemor' – up along the Webburn as far as Widemor.

4 'Of Widemore on Cealfa dune middlewarde' – from Widemoor to the middle of the cold down.

5 'Of Cealfa dune on Sufon stanas' – from the cold down to the Seven Stones.

6 'Of Sufon stanum on Hyfan treow' – from Seven Stones to the Hive tree.

The first ambiguity is which Webburn are we intended to follow upsteam of Lizwell Meet, for there the river divides, its two sources being the East and West Webburn, the question arising being when was the East Webburn first regularly called by that name. At least from 1526 it has been referred to as the Neperell or Niprell, that name surviving in the Dunstone Manor bounds as late as the third quarter of the nineteenth century, and is the stream that, rising on Hameldon, flows down its eastern flank skirting Widecombe village. Davidson followed this branch of the Webburn in preference to the West Webburn as far as Dunstone, where he turned northwards to climb the southern end of Hameldon, which he considered to be Cealfa or the cold down, and who can dispute that the exposed whale back of Hameldon is not just that. To back up this route it has been suggested that the Saxon letter for 'th' by the omission of a single stroke becomes a 'd', thus transforming Withimoor into 'Widimor' as shown in Peadington. To support this possibility, at Dunstone there are four ancient fields retaining the name 'Willow Piece' and referred to in the mid-eighteenth century as 'Willagieres', the Saxon for willow being 'welige', i.e. withy, hence Withecombe and Widecombe. If we can satisfy ourselves on this point, and continue our course northwards along the spine of Hameldon, we now follow a line defining a part of all six Widecombe Manors with Jordan and Blackaton to the west and Dunstone with Blackslade, Widecombe Town and Natsworthy to the east. Neither Widecombe Town nor the parish had been formed at 1086, the area later named Widecombe Town being recorded as 'Wodiacoma', being held by Walscinus, today's Wooda.

By 1301 Widecombe Town was in the hands of Roger de Rus of North Hall, who, in that year, sold one acre of that land to the Dean and Chapter of Exeter, with the advowson appropriating the rights to appoint the vicar of their choosing and collect the Rectoral tithe, at the first Widecombe church, which may well have been a wooden one, the present church not being constructed until the sixteenth century. It may not be out of place to mention here the fact that whilst Domesday makes no reference to Paignton having any rights on Dartmoor, Cockington Manor (the other Torbay Saxon Manor) having a boundary in common with Paignton, was held by the King and had had 'Dewdon' added to it by 1086. Today's Jordan in Widecombe Parish, which Cockington continued to hold through several centuries whilst held in the hands of the de Cockingtons, the Mallocks and

Careys, leads one to the conclusion that it was always outside the bounds of the Peadington Charter also.

To return to following the Peadington line, we now come to a point designated in Saxon 'Seven Stones'. This is a term used by the Saxons to indicate a pre-Christian burial place, in this instance the fine ringed cist just outside Soussons Wood. Other examples of the name are at Kit Hill just over the border in Cornwall and a crossroads in the South Hams where there used to be Bronze Age remains.

This cairn circle was once on the bounds of Spitchwick Manor, within the Parish of Widecombe, and called the Ring-o-Stones by them in the sixteenth century. From there the old boundary crossed the road to an ancient Bronze Age reave which runs down to the left bank of the Wallabrook. Here we now have a broken gatepost acting as a boundstone, standing at the junction of Widecombe parish of which Spitchwick is part, Lydford (the Forest of Dartmoor) and the parish of Manaton. The author believes that this was the spot called 'hyfan treow', the hive tree in Peadington, and where there is still a clump of bushes. The ancient Saxon manorial boundaries seldom get lost, just amalgamated into the later Parish ones.

The line of Peadington follows the Wallabrook for a very short distance upstream and then turns eastward along what is now the southern wall of Headland Warren, built on another reave, thus encircling both Soussons and Challacombe. The latter settlement, whilst within the parish of Manaton, did not form part of that manor. Its early ownership seems to be obscure but at least from the late fifteenth century it formed a detached part of Kenton Manor on the Exe, and is very well documented by the Courtenays during the seventeenth and eighteenth centuries. Before 1066 Kenton was held by Queen Edith, and by the king himself at Domesday, when it paid geld for three hides and one furlong. This word 'furlong' or 'ferling' is sometimes used to describe underwood or an additional resource, so is it possibly referring to Challacombe?

We now follow our other option up to the West Webburn, which forms the boundary of the eastern side of Spitchwick Manor, and thus includes Depdona (Jordan Manor) within its bounds. We follow the West Webburn as far as the point where a right bank tributary joins it in a rather boggy place under the southern end of Challacombe, known as the Widecombe Lake, again a reference to withies. According to *Place Names of Devon*, Cealfa Down is 'near' Challacombe, but what do we make of 'middlewarde'? If we follow the Widecombe Lake westwards to its source under Ephraim's Pinch, as do the Spitchwick Manor bounds, we again reach the ringed cist, the Seven Stones. We might well assume this to be our correct course, Domesday recording 'Espicewita' as then being held by Baldwin of the King, by Edward prior to 1066.

7 'On Hyfan treowe on Hord burh' – From the Hive Tree to the treasure barrow:

From either of the two suggested sites for the hive tree, we ascend the Grim's Lake to King's Barrow, sitting prominently above the Heathercombe valley, and still virtually on the parish bounds.

In the case of our second option from Runnage, we would take the line of the Headland Warren wall, built

on a reave, eastwards, which skirts the northern ends of the considerable and ancient Challacombe strip-field system of lynchets. It may seem strange that Grimspound, the Bronze Age village, does not warrant a mention, perhaps this arises due to the Saxon's reverence to their funereal remains not extending to their village. That there are still swarms of wild bees in the area was brought home to us a few years ago when we had a rest at King's Barrow and became the centre of a swarm which obviously had a hive in the rocks.

8 'Of Hordburg on Deorford' – From the treasure barrow to the deer ford:

Following the Grim's Lake we have been following the parish bounds of Manaton and North Bovey, and we continue to do so eastwards to a spring and follow the resulting streamlet down to near Heathercombe, where it flows into a feeder of the river Bovey, and where field patterns on the far side of the feeder might well indicate a former fording place near Vogwell.

9 'Of Deorforda on Langestan' – From the Deer ford to the Longstone:

Both Davidson and Somers Cocks agree that 'Longstone' refers to a longstone from which Longstone Farm took its name, and which Somers Cocks says formerly stood at or very close to Langstone Cross on the Manaton/Chagford road.

10 'Of Langa stane on Eofede tor' – From the longstone to the Ivy Tor:

'Eofede Tor' is identified with Water, a corruption of which is thought to be have been the origin of the

Hundred of Heytor. In the eighteenth century Somers Cocks says that Water bore the alias 'Odeton', and field names perpetuate the association of water with the name 'Ivy Tor'. There are still fields called Higher and Lower Ivy Tor and the name Ivy Tor is identified with a large outcrop on Greator Farm. Other fields to the north of the tor are called Lower, Middle and Top Water Tor, in keeping with the corruption of 'Odetor' from the original 'Oefede'.

Peadington landscore: Writelan or Three Parish Stone. SX 7635 7827

11 'Of Eofede torre on Hean dune forewearde' – From the ivy tor to the fore part of the high down:

Davidson interprets 'Hean' as hayne and goes to Hayne Down, but the more probable meaning is High Down, in other words the higher part of Heytor Down on Black Hill.

12 'Of Hean dune on thone blindan wille' – From the high down to the blind well or spring:

Somers Cocks identifies the blind well as being Yarner Wells, a spring still on the Manaton/Bovey parish boundary. The term was commonly used to describe springs in old documents. Torre Abbey charters mention at least two, one within Torquay and another to define a boundary point on land bequeathed to the abbey in the Manor and Parish of Buckland-in-the-Moor.

13 'Of dam wille in Writelan stan' – Fom the spring to the inscribed or pointed stone:

Davidson says that this stone may well have already been a boundstone when the Saxon landscape was written, but does not attempt to identify it. Our general direction to Yarner Wells has been south-easterly but Somers Cocks takes us south-west, suggesting that the Writelan stone was where we now see the Three Parish Stone, a boundstone at the eastern end of an east/west reave, at the junction of the bounds of Manaton, Bovey Tracey and Ilsington parishes. It may well be ancient, but pointed it certainly is not, being quite squat and three sided. It is inscribed with the initial letters of the three parishes concerned, but these cannot be dated to Saxon times.

However continuing our south-easterly course from Yarner Wells would take us to another ancient boundstone on the Ilsington/Bovey Tracey boundary, and which may once have been such that it could be described as pointed. This is a natural but set stone at SX 7710 7792. On the earlier Ordnance Survey six inch maps it is called 'Old William', elsewhere 'William Stone'. In 1853 the then Lord of the Manor of Ilsington, the Duke of Somerset, set about strengthening the definition of his bounds and erected a number of identically shaped boundary stones bearing its name, his initials and the date, but he also inscribed the far older parish stone, Old William. The inscription now visible on this stone reads 'Wm/Stone' on the south side and '1853' on the northern side. On all other stones that he either erected or inscribed the letters 'DS' appear above the date, but here they are lacking, and the '1853' is sufficiently near the top of the stone as we now see it to suggest that it may have been broken at some time, possibly even when it was inscribed.

14 'Of tham stane on Ruwa beorh' – From the stone to the rough barrow:

This is a natural outcrop, but has the appearance of a possible barrow when viewed from the north-west. In 1851 it was recorded as Owlicombe, and other sources record Ullacombe and Owlacombe, the latter being the present spelling. In 1853 the then Duke of Somerset erected one of his boundstones on the summit, inscribed 'Owlacombe Burrow'. Grid reference SX 7765 7765.

15 'Of Ruwan beorge on Fyrspenn' – From the rough barrow to the furze pen:

From Owlacombe Barrow we continue to follow the Ilsington parish boundary and go down Green Lane for a short distance to Tipley Hill Lane, thence southeast to Penn Wood. 'Furspen', the hill covered with furze or gorse, in other words Penn Hill Wood is now covered with oak, a not unusual planting on land anciently waste, so it seems.

16 &17 'Of Fyrspenne on Wyrt cumes headod. Of Wyrtcumes heafde on Rammeshorn' –

From Penn Wood Hill to the head of the valley of herbs, from Wortcombes head to Ramshorn:

Ramshorn is another place name that has not changed through the centuries, and still on the Ilsington/Bickington bounds. From this point onwards the Saxon text reads as follows:

Of Rammeshorne on Lulca stile.
Of Lulca stile on Wice cumes heafod.
On Lymenstream oth Woggawill lacy utscyt.
On tha lace od Wocawilles hafod.
Of Wocggawilles heafde on thone weg od tha greatan dic.
Of thaere dic on thone wille on thaes mores heafod.
On tha lace to thaere sweliende.
Of Daere speliende on Yederes beorh
Of Jederes beorge on Standune (nithe) wearde oth tha gretan linde.
Of thaere linde on Dyra snaed midde wearne.
Of Dyra snaede on Hwita ford.
Of Fulan forda on Hildes ford.
Of Hildes forda on Hildeslege nordwearde oth Sole get.
Of Sole gete to Brynes cnolle sude weardum on Puneces wurdi.
Of Puneces wurthige on Hremnes cumes od Aescburnan.
Thanone on stream to Dertan

which has been interpreted as:

From Ramshorn to Lulca's Stile.

From Lulca's stile to the head of the rowan tree valley.

Along the Lemon as far as the outfall of Ogwell Lake.

Along the stream to Ogwell lake head.

From the head of Ogwell lake along the way as far as the great ditch (or dyke).

From the ditch to the spring at the moor's head.

Along the stream to the washing pool to Jedere's barrow.

From the barrow along the stony down downwards as far as the great lime tree.

From the lime tree to the middle of the deer's wood (or park).

From the deerpark to whiteford.

From the muddy ford to Hilde's ford.

From Hilde's ford along the northside of Hilde's ley (clearing) as far as 'muddy gate'.

From muddy gate along the south (north?) side of Bryne's hill (knoll) to Pimece's worthy.

From Pimk's worthy to Raven's combe's head.

From Raven's combe along the streamlet as far as the Ashburn.

Then along the stream to the Dart.

The author has not attempted to follow this section of the bounds but it embraces parts of the boundaries of the parishes of Bickington, Ogwell and Woodland, eventually taking us to Ashburton once again near Chuley Bridge where there is a modern boundstone defining the limits of Ashburton and Staverton parishes, and so down the Ashburn to our starting point at Dart Bridge. Thus in attempting to follow this Saxon boundary we have, in part, incorporated parts of the bounds of the present-day parishes of Ashburton, Widecombe, Manaton, North Bovey, Ilsington, Bovey Tracey, Bickington, Ogwell and Woodland, a vast estate.

The late author holding court from the site of the Judge's Chair, on Crockern Tor.

R.I.P.

BIBLIOGRAPHY

Albert, Wm: *Turnpike Road System in England.* Cambridge University Press. 1972.

Andriette, Eugene A.: *Devon and Exeter in the Civil War.* David & Charles, 1971.

Archaeology of the Devon Landscape. Devon County Council. 1980.

Barber, Tony: *Aspects of Ivybridge.* B.M.E. Print, 1988.

Barton, R.M.: *A History of the Cornish China-Clay Industry.* Bradford Barton. 1966.

Bray, Mrs: *The Borders of Tamar and Tavy.* W. Kent, 1879.

Breton, The Rev. H. Hugh: *The Forest of Dartmoor.* Hoyten & Cole, 1932.

Bridges, W.B.: *Some Accounts of the Barony and Town of Okehampton.* 1889 Edition, W. Masland.

Buckingham, W.: *A Turnpike Key or an Account of the proceedings of the Exeter Turnpike Trustees from 12 June 1753 to 1 November 1884.* James Townsend. 1885.

Buckland in the Moor Parish Check List. P. Belsey, D.A.S. 1987.

Burnard, Robert: *Dartmoor Pictorial Records.* Devon Books. 1986.

Butler, Jeremy: *Atlas of Dartmoor Antiquities.* Devon Books. 1991 to 1997.

Carrington, N.T.: *Dartmoor, A Descriptive Poem.* Preface by Wm Burt. Hatchard and Son, 1826.

Chambers, E.L.: *Arthur of Britain.* Sidwick and Jackson, 1927

Crossing, Wm:
   Guide to Dartmoor. 1965, David and Charles.
   Ancient Stone Crosses of Dartmoor. James G. Commin, 1887.
   Folk Rhymes of Devon. James G. Commin, 1911.
   One Hundred Years on Dartmoor. Western Morning News. 1901.
   Dartmoor's Early History and Medieval Remains. Quay Publications, 1987.

Donne, B.: *Map of Devonshire* 1765 Reprint. Percy Lund, Humphries and Co.

Duchy of Cornwall: *Future Management of the Dartmoor Estates.* Tanhoit Ltd., 1983.

Dymond, R.: *Widecombe in the Moor.* Torquay Directory, 1876

Manor of Cockington. Paper read at Exeter, 1882.

Ewens, M.C.: *The Haytor Granite Tramway and Stover Canal.* David and Charles, 1977.

Fleming, A.: *The Dartmoor Reaves.* B.T. Batsford Ltd., 1988.

Gill, C.: *Dartmoor, A New Study.* David and Charles, 1970.

Gordon, D. St Leger: *Dartmoor In All Its Moods.* John Murray, 1933.

Gover, Mawer and Stenton. *Place-Names of Devon.* Cambridge University Press, 1932.

Govier, L.: *Walkhampton, the Story of a Parish.* Church Restoration Fund. 1984.

Greeves, Dr T.A.P.: *The Devon Tin Industry 1450-1750.* Part of an Unpublished Thesis.

Grinsell, L.V.: *Hangman's Stones and their Traditions.* Folklore, Vol. 96, 11. 1985

Harris, H: *Industrial Archaeology of Dartmoor.* David and Charles, 1972

Haynes R.G.:
  Vermin Traps and Rabbit Warrens on Dartmoor. 1970.
  Post Medieval Archaeology 4. 1970.

Hemery. E.: *High Dartmoor.* Robert Hale, 1983.

Walking the Dartmoor Railroads. David and Charles, 1983.

Henderson and Jervoise: *Old Devon Bridges.* Wheaton, 1938.

Holne, the Villagers of: *A History of Holne.* 1977.

Hooke, Della: *Pre-Conquest Charter Bounds of Devon and Cornwall.* The Boydell Press, 1994.

Hoskins, W.G.: *Devon.* David & Charles, 1978.
Old Devon. David & Charles, 1966.

Jenkin, A.K. Hamilton: *The Cornish Miner.* David & Charles, 1972.

King, R.J.: *The Forest of Dartmoor.* Drayton, 1856.

Lang, Joan: *Old Cockington.* Western Litho Co., 1971.

Mobbs, A.M.: *Horrabridge & District.* 1980-82, Caradon Printers.

Page, J.L.W.: *An Exploration of Dartmoor.* Seeley & Co, 1895.

Pennington, R.R.: *Stannary Law.* David & Charles, 1973.

Pilkington, F.: *Ashburton, the Dartmoor Town.* Devon Books. 1978.

Roberts, Stephen K.: *Recovery & Restoration in an English County 1646-70.* University of Exeter. 1985.

Rowe, Samuel: *Perambulation of Dartmoor.* James Commin, 1902.

Ryan, Louise: *An Obscure Place.* Underhill, 1973.

Sellick, A.D.: *The Sellicks & Lee Moor.* Devon Family History Journal No. 36, October 1985.

Seymour, Deryck: *Torre Abbey.* James Townsend & Son, 1977.

Stanbrook, Elisabeth: *Dartmoor Forest Farms.* Devon Books. 1994.

Stephan, Dom John,: *A History of Buckfast Abbey.* The Burleigh Press, 1970.

Thomas, D.B.L.: *Archaeology of the Landscape.* Devon County Planning Department. 1980.

Thorn, C. & F: *Domesday Book, Part I & II.* Phillimore, 1985.

Torr, Cecil: *Small Talk at Wreyland.* Adams & Dart, 1970.

Tyrwhitt, Sir Thomas: *Formation of a Rail Road from the Forest of Dartmoor to the Plymouth Lime-Quarries.* Statement made at The Chamber of Commerce, Plymouth, 3 November 1818

Varwell, E.: *Throwleigh, A Dartmoor Village.* Sydney Lee, 1938

Worth, R. Hansford: *Dartmoor.* Published by the Executors of his Will, 1953

Wright, J.: *English Dialect Dictionary.* Henry Froude. 1898

Devonshire Association: *Parochial Histories of Devon, No. 1*, Dr Edward H. Young. Okehampton. 1931

Transactions of the Devonshire Association:
1871 Dymond, R.: *Historical Documents relating to Dartmoor.*
1872 Bate, C. Spence: *The Original Map of the Royal Forest of Dartmoor.*
1875 Rowe, J. Brooking: *The Cistercian Houses of Devon.*
1876 Davidson, J.B.: *Some Anglo-Saxon Boundaries now deposited at the Albert Memorial Museum, Exeter.* (Now at D.R.O.).
1878 Dymond R.: *Ancient Documents.*
1892 Prowse, Arthur B.: *The Bounds of the Forest of Dartmoor.*
1893 Phillips J.: *Arts & Crafts on Dartmoor.*
1901 Whale, Rev. T.W.: *Extracts from the Red Book & Notes on the Pipe Rolls of Henry II.*
1905 Rowe, J. Brooking: *Sir Thomas Tyrwhitt and Princetown.*
1911 Chope, R. Pearce: *Lord Dynham's Lands.*
1913 Chanter, Rev. F.J.: *Extracts from the Leger Book and other Ancient Documents of the Abbey of Buckfast.*
1920 Reichel, Rev. O.J.: *The Origin and Upgrowth of the English Parish.*
1924 Amery, J.S.: *Ashburton.* Presidential Address.
1929 Troupe, Mrs Rose: *The New Edgar Charter & the South Hams.*
1931 Worth, R.H.: *Blowing Houses in the Walkham Valley.*
1936 Bird, E.P.: *Okehampton Turnpikes.*
1936 Brown, Theo: *Folklore. Bridestowe Bounds.*
1941 Worth, R. Hansford: *Dartmoor 1788-1808.*
1943 Phillips, E. Masson: *Notes on some Old Roadside Stones in South West Devon.*
1944 Worth, R. Hansford: *The Tenants & Commoners of Dartmoor.*
1961 Brown, Theo: *Tales of a Dartmoor Village*

1962 French, H. & Linehan, Mrs C.D.: *A Forgotten Manor in Widecombe in the Moor.*
1967 Kew, J.E.: *Mortgages in Mid Tudor Devonshire.*
1968 Gawne, E. & Somers Cocks, J.: *Parallel Reaves on Dartmoor.*
1978 Price, D.G.: *Settlement on Wigford Down.*
1981 Harris, Helen: *Granite Workings on Pew Tor and Staple Tor.*
1985 Greeves, Dr T.A.P.: *Steeperton Tor Tin Mine, Dartmoor.*
1987 Phillips, E. Masson: *Ancient Stone Crosses of Devon.*
1990 Hooke, Della: *Studies on Devon Charter Boundaries.*

Dartmoor Magazine: 56, Autumn 1999; 59 Summer 2000; 60 Autumn 2000. Riddon Stones in Back Chat.

Dartmoor Preservation Association, December 1988. p.11.

Devon & Cornwall Notes & Queries:
    Somers Cocks, J.: *A Widecombe in the Moor Land Boundary.* 30, 180-3, 1967
    Dartmoor & Domesday. 30, 290-3. 1967
    Stannary Bounds of Plympton & Tavistock. 32, 26-9, 124. 1973

Haynes, *An Unusual Vermin Trap on Dartmoor.* 32, 216. 1973
    The Boundaries of Hentor Warren. 34, 97-8. 1981

Plymouth Mineral & Mining Club:
    Greeves, Dr T.A.P.: *Merrivale Bridge Mine, Wheal Fortune and Staple Tor Sett 1806-87.*
        Vol. 6, No. 3. 1976
    Robinson, Rosemary: *The Early China Clay Industry on Brent Moor.* Vol. 11, No. 1. 1980

Newspapers:
    Devon & Exeter Gazette, 25 October 1897
    Herald Express, July 1985
    Tavistock Times, 22 June 1923
    Totnes Times, 19 July 1902
    Western Gazette, 7 August 1919
    Western Morning News, 7 December 1985
    Western Times, October 1884

Tavy and Tamar, July/August 1990

West Devon Record Office – various, including Buckland in the Moor 74/578; Various Maristow papers, including 1232/2041: Petre papers: Strode Documents 73/7/2/1 & 2: Bounds of Whitchurch 1801 & 1832, 1508/M.

Maps:
John Chudleigh map of Ilsington, 1884
Bartholomew Gidley map of Gidleigh, c.1630-90
Eylesbarrow Mine Map
Swincombe area
William Woods map, 1850

INDEX